SINGAPORE AT WAR

SINGAPORE AT WAR

SECRETS FROM THE FALL, LIBERATION & AFTERMATH OF WWII

ROMEN BOSE

Published by Marshall Cavendish Editions
An imprint of Marshall Cavendish International
1 New Industrial Road, Singapore 536196

Secrets of the Battlebox first published in 2005 by Marshall Cavendish Editions
The End of the War first published in 2005 by Marshall Cavendish Editions
Kranji first published in 2006 by Marshall Cavendish Editions

Other Marshall Cavendish Offices
Marshall Cavendish Ltd. PO Box 65829, London EC1P 1NY, UK • Marshall Cavendish Corporation. 99 White Plains Road, Tarrytown NY 10591-9001, USA • Marshall Cavendish International (Thailand) Co Ltd. 253 Asoke, 12th Flr, Sukhumvit 21 Road, Klongtoey Nua, Wattana, Bangkok 10110, Thailand • Marshall Cavendish (Malaysia) Sdn Bhd, Times Subang, Lot 46, Subang Hi-Tech Industrial Park, Batu Tiga, 40000 Shah Alam, Selangor Darul Ehsan, Malaysia

National Library Board Singapore Cataloguing-in-Publication Data:

Bose, Romen.
Singapore at war : secrets from the fall, liberation & aftermath of WWII / Romen Bose. – Singapore : Marshall Cavendish Editions, c2012.
p. cm.
Includes bibliographical references and index.

ISBN : 978-981-4382-00-7 (pbk.)

1. World War, 1939-1945 – Campaigns – Malaysia – Malaya.
2. Great Britain – Armed Forces – Singapore – History. 3. World War, 1939-1945 – Singapore. 4. World War, 1939-1945 – Campaigns – Singapore. 5. Singapore – History – Japanese occupation, 1942-1945. 6. Cemeteries – Singapore. 7. World War, 1939-1945 – Monuments – Singapore. I. Title.

D767.55
940.5425 – dc22 OCN767534925

Cover photographs: Imperial War Museum; Dimitris Kritsotakis (krits/SXC.hu); Ben Johnson (Benjipie/SXC.hu)
Cover design: Darren Tan

Printed in Singapore by Fabulous Printers

Contents

Foreword vii

Preface ix

SECRETS OF THE BATTLEBOX: The History and Role of Britain's Command HQ During the Malayan Campaign 1

THE END OF THE WAR: Singapore's Liberation and the Aftermath of the Second World War 123

KRANJI: The Commonwealth War Cemetery and the Politics of the Dead 337

Index 463

Foreword

When I first came to Singapore in 1993, one of the first books I read was a small guidebook I thought would help me start to get to know the Second World War battlefields I now had the chance to explore to my heart's content. The book was new then, and aimed expressly at the history tourist market. One of the authors of *Fortress Singapore: The Battlefield Guide* was a journalist named Romen Bose. By good fortune fate brought Romen and me together, first as friendly acquaintances, before too long as the very good friends we remain today. As I came to know Romen, and to follow his energetic production of thoughtful and discriminating historical studies of aspects of the Second World War in Malaya and Singapore – all while working at a full-time job and becoming a father – it did not surprise me in the least to see what topics he chose to pursue. Romen not only had a good journalist's eye for what parts of this very human story needed further attention, he also gave us all a good indication of his interests as far back as that first battlefield guide.

The three books collected here – *Secrets of the Battlebox*, *The End of the War*, and *Kranji* – all addressed events and questions that received the kind of attention in the old guidebook any reader would recognize: 'We really do need to take another look at this point...' Romen did so, to the benefit of anyone with any level of interest in the twists, turns, ups and downs of the Malaya/Singapore experience of global total war. I have considerable experience in enduring warnings that there is no point researching this topic or that question because after all 'they have been done to death,' especially when it comes to Southeast Asia and the Second World War. I rarely took heed; neither, fortunately, did Romen. This compilation now allows both the serious reader and those with more general interest to reflect, in one volume, on Romen's insightful, tightly focused and fresh analysis of three quite significant problems in our military history. The first is how a military headquarters tried to do three things at once, and just why it could not in the end manage any: coordinate and organize the defence of an entire region, run a network of fixed defences, and fight a campaign then a battle. The second is just how hostilities actually came to an end in our region, and specifically on our island, in a delicate situation – wherein the surrendering enemy remained for quite a while far stronger militarily, on the spot, than the incoming victors. And the third is how and why Kranji became the central site of Allied historical remembrance and commemoration for Singapore. For that topic, Romen really now has made sure it is 'done to death.' Romen does not fail in all three cases to explore the crucial dimension: So what, and to what end for all concerned? That, indeed, is what makes this collection of what he once called 'bits and pieces' a work of wider importance. Drawn with discrimination and experience from extensive work in primary sources, this new omnibus from Romen Bose should find a place on the bookshelf of anyone with any reason to read about Singapore and the Second World War.

I conclude by making perhaps the strongest point I can make. I teach the military history of Singapore for a living, at the university level. Romen's books are always on my reading list, and when I take my students out into the field we take them with us.

Brian P. Farrell
Department of History
National University of Singapore

Preface

When war came to the shores of Malaya and Singapore in the early hours of 8 December 1941, little did anyone realise how ill-prepared the British and Commonwealth forces were for a fight, nor how quickly the Malayan Campaign would end, leading to a brutal occupation that would last the next three and a half years.

Nor did anyone imagine how suddenly the war would end in this part of the world, leaving a power vacuum that would be filled by nationalists, communists and even opportunists – who would eventually end up doing what the Japanese were unable to: drive out the colonial powers.

Much has been written about these aspects of war in Singapore and Malaya. Those works produced while the wounds of battle were still raw, though largely accurate, tended to bury any inconvenient truths in favour of a narrative of the victors, one that was acceptable to the returning colonial powers. In the subsequent years, attempts were made to revise and broaden these perspectives and to provide alternative histories. However, many of the secrets of the war – from catastrophic foul-ups to shining acts of heroism – remained highly classified, only timed for release long after the main actors would have taken their final curtain call.

This was the challenge I took up when I decided to write on crucial parts of the war in the region, to remove parts of the veil of secrecy on individuals, events and issues still sealed in the most secure of archives in the first decade of the new millennium. The result was three books: *Secrets of the Battlebox*, *The End of the War* and *Kranji*. All of them were aimed at helping a younger generation of researchers and readers better understand what transpired here at crucial periods during the Second World War and the implications for local populations in their ensuing bid for independence in the following years. What you hold in your hands is the result of several decades of research into archives and libraries in the UK and Asia, first-hand interviews with participants who have now mostly passed on, and unpublished manuscripts and letters, all of which reveal a wealth of little-known facts and facets of the war, and help clear up some of the mysteries that have long surrounded the fall and the eventual liberation of Singapore and Malaya.

I was very pleased when Melvin Neo at Marshall Cavendish approached me with the idea of this omnibus of sorts to mark the 70th anniversary of the fall of Singapore as it brings together for the first time three facets of the war in Singapore and Malaya which together provide a bigger picture of the monumental events that shaped these countries. The three books have also been updated throughout with additional details, latest research findings, and testimonies of several more key participants.

I have long felt that the understanding of history is formed on the basis of a disparate collection of facts and details, from differing viewpoints and periods, that when brought together help add to our jigsaw of the past. And so it is with the Second World War. The various aspects, angles, periods and people constitute pieces of the jigsaw puzzle of what happened. No book can really cover the war in totality, as the numerous perspectives thrown up would preclude the author from being able to come up with a necessarily coherent narrative, unless bits and pieces are left out, for others to comment or write on.

As such, this volume does not pretend to cover the entire war and its impact on the region; rather, it provides a better understanding into various key aspects of the Second World War whose impact are still felt today, more than seven decades after the outbreak of this global conflict.

I would like to dedicate this compilation to the memory of my father Tapas Kumar Bose, who in his own way helped shape me as an individual and as a searcher of the truth, and whose expectations I hope I met in his living years. I also dedicate this tome to the latest addition to the Bose family, Cilla Ruma Bose, and I hope that she will read this book one day, and find in it the excitement, wonder and satisfaction with which it was written. I must also thank my mother Anupama Bose, for her continual support, my brother Ajoy, sister Anita and their families. More importantly, I owe it all to my very patient and understanding wife Brigid for all that she puts up with daily, and to Lara and Olive, who are now viewing with interest what their father writes.

Romen Bose
Kuala Lumpur
21 January 2012

SECRETS OF THE BATTLEBOX

THE HISTORY AND ROLE OF BRITAIN'S COMMAND HQ DURING THE MALAYAN CAMPAIGN

Contents

	Preface to the First Edition	5
Chapter 1	Introduction	9
Chapter 2	The Discovery	18
Chapter 3	The Underground Command Centre	29
Chapter 4	The Battlebox and the Combined Operations Headquarters	58
Chapter 5	The Battlebox and the Malayan Campaign	69
Chapter 6	Occupation and Post War	102
Appendix A	Last Cable from Singapore 15 February 1942	113
Appendix B	Chronology of Events	114
Appendix C	Dramatis Personae	117
	Bibliography	119

Preface to the First Edition

This book that you hold in your hands would never have been possible had it not been for the long-suffering and continuing support of my wife Brigid, my daughters Lara and Olive as well as constant encouragement from my mum and dad.

The contents of this book are the result of 17 years of research into an area of Singapore's wartime history that has still not been investigated fully. With the death of so many of its participants and with most documents on the subject highly-classified and only recently open for research, there has been no opportunity till now to put forward the story of the Battlebox.

This book attempts to provide a very rough understanding to what the Battlebox was all about, its history, uses and final role in the Malayan Campaign. It attempts to address the gap in knowledge on one of the most crucial aspects of the Second World War in Malaya and Singapore, namely the role of the command headquarters in the campaign.

There is very little in this book that is based on secondary sources as I took the decision from early on that this work would reflect the views and opinions of the participants in the events. As a result, it has a journalistic feel to it, where the main sources of reference and facts come from the participants as opposed to official histories and later interpretations of events.

I have also taken the liberty of dramatising the first chapter based on actual facts and recollections of the various actors and I hope this makes for easier reading and provides a better understanding of the material presented.

This book is aimed at those who want to know about the Battlebox and understand what actually happened there during the Malayan Campaign. On another level, it also provides references and sources of information for those who want to do further research into the subject and will hopefully provide a good jumping-off point for more work on this topic.

Although there are limited primary and secondary sources, there is still much to write on the command and communications structures of Malaya Command with repositories like the National Archives in London and Singapore holding a wealth of documents relating to it.

I believe that history constantly evolves and a history that was written 10 years after an event will never be the same as that written 20, 30 or even 50 years later. With new documents released and different perspectives reflected, the revision of history provides us with a crucial understanding of how events are re-defined and viewed from even more differing perspectives, as more time passes. Although initial histories appear more visceral, later evaluations tend to provide a more considered perspective. However, both histories are essential if we are to understand what actually happened. With the death of the key participants, many of whom do not record their experiences, we are left only with secondary sources. For many areas of research, however, primary sources still do exist, in the form of memoirs, correspondence and reports, much of which have been filed away in the backrooms of archives waiting again to see the light of day.

I hope that I have provided many of these documents and, in particular, introduced this subject to a new audience who will hopefully become more interested in the Second World War in Singapore.

Getting to the point of a final manuscript is never easy and I have to thank numerous individuals, who through their work and friendship have contributed to this final version. I would like to single out Jeyathurai Ayadurai, managing director of the Singapore History Consultancy/ Journeys Pte Ltd, a very dear friend and military history buff, who has for long been encouraging me to get on with writing this book. Jeya, who lectured in Military History at the Singapore Command and Staff College for many years, before setting up his own company researching Singapore's history and carrying out tours based on it, has along with his right-hand woman Savita Kashyap, developed an amazing walking tour of Fort Canning as part of the company's Battlefield Tour, which takes students and tourists alike on a dramatic adventure through the Battlebox and its surroundings. Jeya, along with his wife Jennifer, amazing administrator Ms Jeya and Savita, have for long been a bouncing board for my ideas and concepts regarding this period.

I must also thank Kwa Chong Guan, former director of the National Museum and presently Head of External Programs, Institute of Defence and Strategic Studies, Nanyang Technological University. His insights into the Battlebox have proven very useful and much credit must go to him and G. Uma Devi for their initial research on the Battlebox.

I have also benefited tremendously from the Reading Room at the Imperial War Museum, London, where staff at the Department of Records and Photographs have been of tremendous help. The National Army Museum in Chelsea was also of great help in providing personal diaries of soldiers who worked in the Battlebox prior to the fall. The National Archives (formerly the Public Records Office) in Kew was literally a treasure trove of documents and maps on the command headquarters, filling in large gaps in the puzzle that is the Battlebox.

This book would never have been possible had Faridah not brought me that first clipping in 1988 and much thanks go to Felix Soh, Iris, the late Teo Lian Huay, Glen, How San, the late R. Chandran, Alphonso Chan,

G. Chandradas and Lee Ming Yen as well as the rest of the outstanding team at *The Straits Times*.

In conclusion, let me say that writing this book has been a labour of love and I remain solely responsible for any errors or mistakes within. Should you have comments on this book or if you have more information or leads for a future edition, please send me an email at romen@hotmail.com.

Romen Bose
Summer 2005
London

Chapter 1

Introduction

Sunday, 15 February 1942.

The skies over the island of Singapore were overcast, filled with black smoke and fires, smoldering throughout the island. The constant sounds of explosions and air raid sirens filled the air.

The sun could not be seen for the large plumes of smoke from burning oil tanks, destroyed by the retreating military, obscuring most of the island's skyline.

On the streets, large numbers of exhausted and battle-weary troops filled the city, their faces covered in mud, soot and grime, their bodies unwashed for weeks, their will to fight completely destroyed. Many of their comrades had been killed in the preceding 70 days with even more captured as prisoners of the Imperial Japanese Army.

These men, who were resigned to the fate that awaited them, roamed the bombed-out streets that had already become the graveyard of numerous luxury cars and sedans, abandoned in the middle of roads and in alleyways by their fleeing European owners, many with keys still in their ignition. The cars and men were the only occupants of the streets as shops and offices were boarded up and shut without any sign of the local populace about. Everyone was in hiding as if in preparation for an impending storm or typhoon.

No one believed it would come to this. The proud subjects of a mighty British colony now hiding in terror as wave after wave of bombings scarred the city and where the smoke-laden air became too heavy even to breathe.

Singapore island had been shelled for the better part of a week with constant air raids over the city, decimating what remained of the civil services, with thousands of refugees fleeing from upcountry, filling burnt-out buildings and huddled in slums throughout the city.

As the dull rays of the sun began to light the dawn, a tall, lanky figure in a sweat-drenched senior commander's khaki uniform stood on the balcony of his office on Fort Canning Hill, overlooking the burnt-out city and the chaos below.

There had been no sleep for a long, long time and there was to be no rest. He was tired, oh so very tired. All he wanted was sleep, but sleep would not come. As his blood-shot eyes roamed the city, he took a slow drag from his umpteenth cigarette this hour, his thoughts wandering to England where his daughter, Dorinda, would be getting up in a few hours, celebrating her twelfth birthday with presents and cakes and parties.

There would be no presents and cakes and parties for him. He would not be there to share her joy or to help cut the cake, to lead the festivities. He knew now he might never ever see her again, as he and more than 100,000 men stood on the verge of destruction by a superior enemy.

"How had it all ended like this?" he wondered yet again as he walked into his office filled with the stale smell of too many cigarettes and sweat from too many huddled meetings.

It was barely six in the morning when he called his assistant from the outside office, telling him to arrange for a final meeting with everyone by nine in the morning. A decision would have to be made.

He washed his grimy and stubble-filled face in the bowl of brackish water, his only concession to his appearance. The taps had long since stopped working and all that was left was the water he had washed up in for the last four days. It didn't matter. None of this mattered any more. The battles had been lost one after the other and so many, many men had given their lives.

All that he had left now was his faith. But would that save him and his men? As he knelt down at the early morning communion service, Lieutenant General Arthur Ernest Percival, General Officer Commanding, Headquarters Malaya Command, prayed that his men and the civilians caught in this bloody nightmare would survive the final onslaught of the Japanese Army that was sure to come in the next day or so.

The man who finally remained in charge of this shell-shocked and pockmarked island, Percival had withstood all that had been hurled at him and persevered, despite the massive blunders by senior and junior commanders and the lack of permission to carry out a real defence of the Malayan peninsula.

Here amidst the green and lush vegetation, which had been ripped up by heavy bombs and shelled with mortars, men from the headquarters, part of the remnants of the 100,000 strong British and Commonwealth military forces who had fought on the peninsula and had now retreated onto the island, gathered for prayers to sustain themselves for another day against an enemy that was about to overrun them.

Thanking Padre Hughes for the service held in Percival's own office, a colonial-styled building sitting on Fort Canning Hill, he was barely aware of his surroundings. Located on Dobbie Rise, it was the nerve centre of Headquarters Malaya Command, where the military defence for Malaya and Singapore had been planned, executed and ultimately lost. Built in 1926, when British supremacy in the Far East was assured, the building had become, just like these final defenders of Singapore, an anachronism in the face of the new Japanese order in Malaya.

As Percival looked out across the balcony again, Ivan Simson, Chief Engineer and the Director General of Civil Defence walked in. The news overnight had been terrible. The water supply, Simson said, would not last another 24 hours. The food supplies, he was told, were expected to last another few days while ammunition was running very low and the only petrol left was that in the fuel tanks of vehicles. All this Percival noted studiously in his Hong Kong and Shanghai Bank bill folder; the final reports of a dead city. This bill folder would last the war and Percival's captivity, finally ending up in a box of personal papers at the Imperial War Museum in London, a long-forgotten testament to one of the lowest points in British military history.

Percival knew the time had come. The decision had to be made and made quickly. He picked up the telephone and waited to be connected. The military telephone exchange finally managed to get through on an external line. Most of the extensive telephone networks throughout Singapore and Malaya had been destroyed by the enemy. What remained barely worked. It was strange, Percival thought, that in order to make such a momentous decision, he would have to use a public telephone line to get hold of the one man who had the political power to make that decision.

Lieutenant General A.E. Percival, General Officer Commanding, Headquarters Malaya Command

That man was the Governor of the Straits Settlements, Sir Shenton Whitlegge Thomas. Thomas was responsible for Singapore and the Federated Malay States but it was the immense bureaucracy and red tape of the civil administration and their lack of willingness to prepare fully for war that led to the huge suffering of the local population and the total unpreparedness for the Japanese bombings and attacks.

Days before, the Governor had abandoned his residence at Government House and was squatting at the Singapore Club in the burnt-out city. He had refused to make the decision when Percival and his senior Generals approached him in his new abode. He refused to meet with the Japanese nor would he respect their rule. He was the Governor, not a stooge of the Japanese. No, he would not surrender and he would not meet with them until they came and dragged him away.

On that fateful Sunday morning, the final logs from the switchboard at Fort Canning recorded that they were unable to raise the Governor. So it was that soon after the morning services and a short briefing by his chief engineer, Percival headed for a conference of his commanders, deep under the offices of Fort Canning, for another assessment of the situation.

Leaving his office, Percival made his way to the back of the command building. Under heavy camouflage lay a small flight of stairs leading further up Fort Canning Hill. Percival, who was accompanied by Simson and his Administrative Adjutant Brigadier Lucas, walked up the short flight of stairs that led to an opening on the side of the hill.

Flanked by two huge metal doors and with a resonance of a deep rumbling coming from inside, Percival and his two senior officers walked in slowly. Where only days ago Sikh and Gurkha guards manned the entrance to this Top Secret inner sanctum of Malaya Command, with passwords and Secret clearances demanded of all who sought entrance, the doorway now lay empty with flickering lightbulbs illuminating the path into the warren of tunnels and rooms underneath.

The lack of guards showed the desperate plight of these last defenders of Singapore. All available troops had been drafted in the last line of defence against the enemy, a line that crumbled even before it was engaged by the enemy. Now there were no guards left to man the posts and it did not matter who sought entry. All was lost.

This was the fate of the Battlebox, Headquarters Malaya Command's state-of-the-art Underground Communications Centre. Based on British Prime Minister Winston Churchill's own Cabinet War Rooms, from where the Battle of Britain and the battles of World War II were planned and fought, the Battlebox was supposed to provide British and Allied forces in Malaya and Singapore a unified command centre from which to defend and strike against the invading Japanese army. Instead, it would now mark the end of British dominance in Southeast Asia.

Percival entered a blistering inferno of heat, as the ventilation system had broken down with the cut in power supply. The back-up generators were insufficient to the task and so the entrances to the bunkers were left open at all times and could not be closed even during bombing raids as the air would then be unbreathable.

With more than 500 officers and men working feverishly in the 30-room Battlebox, the rooms were filled with the all-too-familiar sour smell of sweat and stale cigarette smoke. A constant stench also permeated the rooms as the latrines had broken down from being overloaded and there were no troops around who could fix them.

Percival walked by the chaos in the Gun Operations Room. Sector after sector had been conceded to the enemy even as late as 14 February, with most remaining battalions in tatters and communications cut off to most major units on the island. The faces of exhausted and demoralised staff officers greeted Percival as he looked at the plotting table.

As he looked over the final dispositions of troops, Percival received an urgent communiqué from the Signals Control Room. The highly secret teletyped sheet was final permission from General Sir Archibald Wavell, Supreme Commander of the American, British, Dutch and Australian Command to capitulate the Allied forces in the worst case.

The Most Secret message read:

> So long as you are in a position to inflict losses and damage to the enemy and your troops are physically able to do so you must fight on. Time gained and damage to enemy are of vital importance at this crisis. When you are fully satisfied that this is no longer possible I give you discretion to cease resistance. Before doing so all arms, equipment and transport of value to enemy must of course be rendered useless. Also just before final cessation of fighting opportunities should be given to any determined bodies of men or individuals to try and effect escape by any means possible. They must be armed. Inform me of intentions. Whatever happens I thank you and all troops for your gallant efforts of last few days.[1]

He read it carefully, then folded the sheet and put it in his pocket. He would now have to make the decision. He was finally given the permission to surrender all British and Allied forces as well as the civilian government.

If only they had given him and earlier General Officers Commanding in Malaya similar permission years before, to fight the enemy with the various services and the civilian government under his authority, things might have been very different. At the start of the War, he only had control over the army, while the air force and navy were instructed by their own service chiefs. He had no control over the bureaucratic red tape in the civil administration or even, at times, what the Australian and Indian troops were doing under their various commanders.

By 9:30am, most of the senior commanders had gathered in the room of the Commander, Anti-Aircraft Defences, Brigadier A.W.G. Wildey. Wildey had been made responsible for up-to-the-minute movements of the Japanese forces, which were being plotted out of the Gun Operations Room next door.

It was a very small and stuffy room, filled with pipes from the emergency generators set up once the power supply to the Battlebox had been cut. The atmosphere in the room was tense and the smell of defeat permeated the air as further reports of casualties and retreats trickled in.

Percival walked in with Simson and Wildey, who took their seats next to him. Seated already were Lieutenant General Sir Lewis Heath, General Officer Commanding the III Indian Corps, Major-General Gordon Bennett, Commander of the 8th Australian Division, Brigadier T.K. Newbigging, Brigadier K.S. Torrance and several other senior officers.

The only junior officer present was Major C.H.D. Wild, a staff officer from the III Indian Corps and one of the few officers remaining who was fluent in Japanese.

Major Wild, who came to play a key role in prosecuting the Japanese for war crimes after the war, described what happened in that small, stiflingly hot room.

> ... Between 0900 and 0930hrs on 15 Feb '42 I accompanied the Corps Commander in my capacity as his GSO2(O) to the final conference in the underground "Battlebox" at Fort Canning. Lt.Gen. A.E. Percival invited a review of the situation from the senior officers present. I recall in particular that the C.E. (Chief Engineer) Brigadier Simson said that no more water would be available in Singapore from some time during the next day (16 Feb): also that the C.R.A. (Chief of Royal Artillery, Brigadier E.W. Goodman, 9th Indian Division) said that Bofors ammunition would be exhausted by that afternoon (15 Feb), and that another class of ammunition, either 18pdr or 25pdr, was likewise practically exhausted. The decision to ask for terms was taken without a dissentient voice. Some minutes later, when details of the surrender were being discussed, Major General Gordon Bennett, GOC 8th Aust Div, remarked "How about a combined counter-attack to recapture Bukit Timah?" This remark came so late, as was by then so irrelevant, that I formed the impression at the time that it was made not as a serious contribution to the discussion but as something to quote afterwards. It was received in silence and the discussion proceeded.[2]

It is interesting that in the official minutes of this meeting, written in captivity and which survived the war, it was noted that Percival asked about a combined counter-attack. There was no mention of Bennett's comment. It was clear that the various commanders were all in favour of surrender but that it was Percival who would have to make the final decision.

When he asked General Heath for his opinion on the best course to adopt, the commander of the III Indian Corps, was acerbic. "In my opinion there is only one possible course to adopt and that is to do what you ought to have done two days ago, namely to surrender immediately"[3]

In the final stage of the meeting, there could have been no doubt as to what the decision would be.

Based on the water shortage, the demoralised troops, his commanders' unanimous decision to surrender and with the final permission from Wavell in his pocket, Percival could now capitulate without the loss of more troops and the death of huge numbers of civilians should the Japanese attack Singapore town. For being forced to make the decision to surrender, the blame of the fall of Singapore would forever more fall upon his shoulders, whether it was deserved or not.

The official minutes recorded dryly,

> The G.O.C., in view of the critical water situation and the unsatisfactory administrative situation generally, thereupon reluctantly decided to accept the advice of the senior officers present and to capitulate.[4]

Hostilities would cease at 1630hrs GMT with a deputation sent to meet the Japanese as outlined in flyers dropped by the Japanese air force all over Singapore days before.

Once the conference terminated at 11:15am, Percival headed to the Signals Control Room, where he drafted his last message to Wavell:

> Owing to losses from enemy action water petrol food and ammunition practically finished. Unable therefore continue the fight any longer. All ranks have done their best and grateful for your help.[5]

Throughout the rest of the day, Percival was listless. Once the decision had been made, orders had been given to destroy everything. With the last message sent to Wavell, instructions were given to destroy all the cipher and code books. Brigadier Lucas also ordered all signal equipment to be smashed up.

As this began, calls continued to come in from units all over the island for instructions. The officers at the Battlebox had none. In the afternoon and evening, there were bonfires outside the Battlebox as secret documents and files were burnt in order to prevent them from falling into enemy hands. However, much of the equipment and infrastructure in the Battlebox was left intact.

What transpired later that afternoon is well documented in history books as Percival signed the surrender document handing over the British and Commonwealth forces under his command to Lieutenant General Tomoyuki Yamashita, Commander of the Japanese 25th Army, ending 70 days of fighting down the Malayan peninsula, leading to the inglorious surrender at the Ford Motor Factory in Bukit Timah.

Much has been written on the fall of Singapore and the last hours and days of the British command as they agonised over the final surrender to the Japanese but very little has been recorded of what went on within the walls of the Battlebox and Percival's war rooms as well as the conditions that the officers and men of the Battlebox worked under. Many of these officers and men are now long gone, more than 60 years after the end of the Second World War.

What remains, however, are the rooms where these most difficult of decisions were made.

The history of the Battlebox and its surroundings as well as of the combined headquarters of the British and Commonwealth forces during the War in Malaya still remains shrouded in mystery. They were kept very secret to prevent the enemy from destroying these complex nerve centres of military operations. Even before surrender, many of the records detailing the goings-on in the Battlebox were destroyed with no traces left.

Many who died in Japanese prisoner of war camps took the remaining secrets of these facilities with them to the grave, and those who survived have passed on in recent years, making it difficult to piece together the full use and historical events that these bunkers saw. Thus, some of the events above and in this book have been extrapolated and re-created through extensive research and analysis, in order to link the various pieces of the secret puzzle and form part of the real story of what took place at the Battlebox.

In the chapters ahead, from recently declassified documents, numerous interviews, secret sources and over 17 years of in-depth investigations, you will read about the building of this long-forgotten underground communications centre, its nooks and crannies, how it was utilised in the Malayan campaign and its role in the final days of the battle for Singapore.

For the first time ever, the secrets of the Battlebox will be revealed, like the location of the Allied combined headquarters of the army and air force in Sime Road and the post-war history of these complexes that remain a historical legacy of the last world war.

Secrets of the Battlebox will shed much more light on what happened in the Malayan Campaign and in the deep dark rooms under Fort Canning Hill, rooms in which the future of Singapore and Malaysia were decided – rooms that, even today, have an uncomfortable resonance of a not-too-distant past.

Endnotes

1 Churchill, W.S. *The Second World War: The Hinge of Fate.* Houghton Mifflin Company, Boston, USA, 1950. p. 104.

2 Wild, C.H.D. *Note on the Capitulation of Singapore.* Unpublished typescript. New Delhi, India, 30 November 1945. p. 2.

3 *Proceedings of the Conference held at Headquarters Malaya Command (Fort Canning) at 0930Hrs. Sun. 15 February 1942, Papers of A.E. Percival, P16-27.* The Imperial War Museum, London, p. 2.

4 Ibid, p. 3.

5 Churchill, W.S. *The Second World War: The Hinge of Fate.* Houghton Mifflin Company, Boston, USA, 1950. p. 105.

Chapter 2

The Discovery

It was the middle of July 1988 when I walked into the newsroom at *The Straits Times*, Singapore's oldest daily, then located at Kim Seng Road.

Two weeks into a summer internship working on the General Desk at the renowned newspaper, I was relishing the fact that although only eighteen and in university, I was able to rub shoulders with some of the best veteran journalists in the trade.

So a few weeks into my internship, when I was approached by Faridah, assistant to then General Desk Editor Felix Soh, I thought I was going to get a big break.

To my disappointment, she presented me with a Forum page letter printed in the newspaper days earlier and told me that Felix wanted me to follow it up.

The letter, by Doraisingam Samuel, a former president of the Singapore History Association, claimed the existence of an underground bunker complex under Fort Canning Park in downtown Singapore. The bunker, he said, had been used by the British in 1942 during the Second World War and Samuel wanted the Parks and Recreation Department to open it and turn it into a museum.

"Oh boy," I thought to myself. Just another weak lead to follow up on, one which would most probably not pan out as there was obviously no such thing as a bunker under Fort Canning. If there was, surely we would all have known about it by now.

Yet another historical mystery that would never be solved just like the rumours of "hidden Japanese gold" claimed to have been secretly buried by Japanese soldiers in the Philippines and Thailand at the end of the War.

I made the requisite calls to get hold of Mr. Samuel but was unable to reach him. I went down to the newspaper library and searched through all the files we had on the Malayan Campaign and Fort Canning but there was no mention of any bunker or underground complex.

It seemed a hopeless task to be able to dig any deeper and even my letter to the British High Commission's Defence Advisor turned up nothing. I was later to learn that even the High Commission had no clue as to the existence of the Battlebox.

Just when I was about to give up on it all, Felix called me over to his desk.

A veteran newspaperman, Felix had worked with many newspapers in his career before joining *The Straits Times* as the very dynamic editor of the General Desk. His inspiration and energy carried most of us on, even when we didn't want to go on. He did not suffer fools gladly and many were the days when I would get an earful for submitting substandard copy or committing some grammatical or stylistic faux pas. The other interns and I were terrified of him and with good reason.

On that day, Felix was in his element. There had been several major scoops the day before and many compliments on how well the General Desk was performing. When I gave him my report, he looked thoughtful and then gave me the lead that would break open the story.

It was a picture of the outside of the alleged "tunnel complex" at Fort Canning that was opened by Civil Defence officers just months before, in February 1988, and was only briefly examined before being sealed up by the Parks and Recreation Department.

The picture had been published in the Chinese-language papers and promptly forgotten. No mention of it had been made in *The Straits Times* or anywhere else.

I was intrigued. So was there really an underground bunker like the one Churchill used, a cabinet war rooms of sorts in Singapore? I had to find out more and I called up Mr. Kwa Chong Guan, then director of the Singapore Oral History Department, who was named in the photo caption as one of the key persons involved in the February opening.

A distinguished scholar, who had researched Singapore's early history and that of Fort Canning, Kwa would later head the National Museum. He and his team were in the midst of trying to discover the secret history of this underground complex which I had yet to see for myself. Kwa along with John Miksic, an archeologist and lecturer at the National University of Singapore, had instigated the February opening of the bunker.

Kwa and Miksic said at that point only a handful of people had made it briefly into the complex and a full investigation had yet to take place.

But it was clear from Kwa's initial research that this was where General

Percival held his last meeting with senior commanders before surrendering Singapore and 100,000 British and Commonwealth troops to the Japanese.

My first question to Kwa was who was this Percival? And what was so significant about this underground tunnel?

Up until the early 1990s, secondary school students in Singapore who did not take history up to Secondary Four level were only exposed to two years of history lessons, which covered ancient history in the near and far east but nothing about the 20th century in Southeast Asia. I had known from elderly relatives that Singapore had suffered during the War but not much more. Kwa and his senior researcher G. Uma Devi gave me a quick history lesson on the Second World War in Singapore.

At the end of it, Kwa said it was unclear when exactly the bunkers were built but confirmed that there definitely were bunkers, a huge complex of rooms that were sealed up since the late 1960s.

The initial opening of the bunker on 22 February 1988, with Kwa Chong Guan and John Miksic standing to the extreme right of the picture. Singapore Civil Defence officers can be seen ventilating the complex. The bunker was only cursorily examined before being "sealed up" again.

Although information on the Battlebox was scarce, Kwa was able to locate a blueprint of the bunker complex in the Land Office at Singapore's Law Ministry. He had made enquiries in London and at the National Archives in Singapore but to no avail. It was the Law Ministry that finally located a copy of the blueprint, which was handed over to the Oral History Department.

In addition, he showed me numerous maps of Fort Canning from the turn of the century when an actual fort was located on the hill, with gun redoubts and a moat!

From the minutes of meetings among papers donated by Percival to the Imperial War Museum in London and documents from the historian Louis Allen, a rough picture began to emerge of the use of the Battlebox and the last days of Headquarters Malaya Command.

Kwa and his team had done an enormous amount of research in the hopes that the information would convince the authorities to preserve the Battlebox for future generations.

Could it be that such an interesting campaign and the building of such a highly sensitive structure occurred in this country less than 50 years ago? That night I got hold of a copy of Noel Barber's classic work on the fall of Singapore, *Sinister Twilight*, and began boning up on the Malayan Campaign.

The next day, I told Felix that we were on to one of the most exciting historical sites in the history of the Malayan Campaign. I was thrilled to finally sink my teeth into what was becoming a very exciting story indeed.

"This is the kind of excitement I like to see in a journalist", he said grinning. "But, you must make sure that you have the full story, from all angles. I want quotes from the authorities and the historians and an explanation of what actually happened 46 years ago. And I want it quick before anyone else gets this story."

I was impressed that Felix let me run with the story instead of putting a seasoned journalist on it. He knew it was my scoop and made sure I would break it when the time came.

But what I needed to do next was to see the bunkers for myself. That would be the most exciting part of this assignment.

From a copy of the blueprint that Kwa lent me, it was obvious that the bunker was large and that without actually walking through the complex, it would be impossible to write about it.

So I called up the National Parks Department, which was in charge of the Fort Canning Park and the bunkers within it, to get permission to go into the Battlebox. But the officials there refused to let me view the complex as it was "dirty and hot and was not safe for entry. Moreover, the entrance had been sealed!"

I was thoroughly disappointed. For days, I tried to get permission to go in and for days the department had been indecisive on what to do and had referred my request to higher authorities.

Finally, in frustration, I decided to take things into my own hands and go down to Fort Canning to see what was actually there.

I needed a photographer and as luck would have it, the Photo Desk was keen to send out a rookie photographer who had joined the paper after serving in the military. The photographer, whom I shall call Al, to protect his identity, was young, idealistic and very, very gung-ho.

I decided that if the entrance had been sealed and we couldn't get in through the doors, what about trying to sneak in through vents on the blueprint that appeared to lead directly into the complex? This would mean I would get an exclusive scoop on the bunker which was now being talked about in historical circles around town.

Al was quick to agree when he heard my plans as it clearly sounded like the beginnings of an exciting adventure.

So the next day, we took a quick cab ride from Times House to Fort Canning and stood at the foot of the bunker on Cox Terrace as a thick canopy of trees covered the entire area in a surreal greenish light, with the chirping of cicadas our only company in the jungle-like surroundings.

We looked all round for the vents on the side of the hill where the bunker was supposed to be located but all we could find was a disused children's playground on the top of the hill and these odd-looking mushroom shaped concrete structures. I then realised that the mushroom structures were the roofs of the vents which had been sealed on all sides to prevent nosy people like me from gaining access.

I sat next to the playground located directly above the bunker and was pondering how to proceed with my story without having any chance to see the inside.

Al then called me over to the other side of the bunker on the Dobbie Rise side of the hill. He pointed out a door in a wall that jutted out slightly and looked like a storage shed from the outside. Al asked whether this might be the entrance but I told him that the Parks Department said the entrance had been sealed so the door most probably led to a storage shed.

From his experience in the military, Al did not look convinced. "It's a strange looking storage shed which has a ventilation shaft right on top of it," he said. How could it be that a storage room would have a ventilation shaft right on top unless it led to something? But the Parks and Recreation Department said they had sealed the entrance so how come there was a door here? Could they have overlooked this door? It had been padlocked but the lock used was very flimsy.

As Al and I were tugging to see whether the lock would budge, it suddenly broke. I was now in a quandary. Should I open the door and go in and find out what was in the room? If my hunch was right, it would lead to the huge bunker complex which would earn me my first-ever scoop. Should I stay outside and not enter a place that was clearly sealed off and not meant for trespass? Going in could also mean that we would get lost or even prosecuted for entering a restricted facility!

It was a very long 10 seconds as my journalistic instincts got into gear and I dived in with Al in tow into a musty-smelling chamber. On entering, the darkness enveloped me and the musty air made me cough. We walked

The only identifiable signs of the Battlebox from the top of Fort Canning Hill, the concrete mushroom-like structures formed the top of the ventilation systems operating in the complex below. The mushrooms still remain in the park, in addition to a new structure above the emergency rooftop exit. In the background is the former barracks on Cox Terrace. It has now been converted into an arts centre and a culinary institute.

The locked door on the Dobbie Rise side of the bunker, before the lock accidentally fell apart. It could easily be mistaken for a storage shed. Note how close it is to the main road on Dobbie Rise and the drainage ditch dug in front of the doorway.

in further and a short staircase led up and down again until we were in a long corridor which was only brightened by the flashlights we had brought along.

I recorded the adventure in a notebook I had brought along.

Inside it was extremely humid and very hot even though the complex was located so deep under the hill.

The bunker was totally dilapidated with wires hanging from the walls and the rooms were flooded with two to three inches of water.

Just below the entrance, we spotted a wrecked scooter. Discoloured and rusty, it was a relic from the 40s or 50s. Ironically, wordings were penned on the bike which said, "Do Not Remove", and there it remained, for the last thirty to forty years, lying in situ until we happened upon it. I wonder whatever happened to that relic of the bunker?

Further down the passage, we spotted a doorway labeled, "Air Filtration Plant". Inside, what remained was just a shell of the machine, with its ducts all rusty and stained.

The metal doors throughout the complex were all rusted and several were falling off their hinges. Surprisingly, we found ceramic washbasins with taps intact inside some of the rooms. Most of the metal pieces and wiring had been stripped clean by looters, including light switches and furniture. All the rooms were completely stripped of any moveable objects.

In the "G" Clerks room, we found an empty stretcher that had been abandoned on the floor and decomposing in the heat and humidity of the place. It looked bloodstained but it was hard to tell 40 years on. It was eerie to see a stretcher lying in the middle of a dark empty room and I felt a cold chill run down the back of my neck. We decided not to tarry any longer and quickened our pace.

There were also toilets in the bunker. The urinals were yellowed with age and we found a light bulb at the bottom of one. The toilet bowls were no better for we found a door stuck into one and the toilet seats and walls filled with fungus growth.

Power and light sockets were also stripped and rotten planks were strewn all over the place. The clay floor tiles had begun to dissolve in the various flooded rooms, which appeared to have been waterlogged for decades. This meant that we ended up getting stuck in the wet muck every time we took a step forward. It was hard moving and we realised that it would be easier to walk on any dry spots where the tiles had not dissolved. We found lots of tiles stacked in corners and when I lifted one, it crumbled in my hands.

We also found the remains of a dog, most probably lost in the maze of rooms in the bunker. It had died of starvation or sickness, its bones a reminder not to stray too far away from the entrance.

The rusted motorcycle in the bunker. Just above the rear tyre, the words "Do Not Remove" were scribbled on. No one had moved it for more than 20 years by the time we found it in 1988.

One of the few items left intact in the Battlebox, this washbasin was located in the Fortress Plotting Room.

The toilet bowl seats showed signs of decay with fungus growth; the bowls were badly discoloured.

The room labeled "Fortress Plotting Room" had large parts of its floor dug out and a huge pile of dirt lay exposed on the side. The walls were covered with cork boards, obviously used for hanging maps and charts on the walls.

We also found several artifacts including a penknife, a spanner and a pair of pliers in the bunker and in the process, located another two sealed entrances into the bunker (Cox Terrace side and roof entrance).

There was also a metal plank standing vertically, with what seemed like red stains on it, and the walls which were covered with dangling wires were also dirtied, stained and marked with unidentifiable graffiti.

That was enough adventure and mustiness for one day as Al shot at least ten rolls of film in the bunker complex itself.

We were hot, sticky and our shoes filled with soft muddy clay from the terracotta tiles that lined the floors in the bunker. The water was believed to have been rain which came in from the vents and rooftop entrances in the decade that it was abandoned before the complex was finally sealed off.

Weary after our afternoon's adventure, I was now terrified. How was I going to explain to Felix what I had done in order to get the pictures for the story and to view the complex for myself?

It took a lot of nerve to walk up to him that afternoon and tell him what I had just done.

Felix hit the roof!

After an hour of being bawled out for such unprofessional behaviour and for jeopardising our lives, he calmed down. On the inside, he was thrilled that we had the pictures and the potential for a big scoop. On the outside, he had to set rules for these journalists who had flouted the law.

I was slightly ashamed but knew that we had a good story. However, as a result of the risk we took, I could have done much damage to the reputation of the paper and to myself. After the scolding and my promise not to do something like that again, Felix let us off, saying, "When I say take the initiative, I don't mean breaking and entering! You two are the craziest reporters I know and I must make sure not to send the two of you out together on any other assignments."

For the next few months, almost every assignment I covered was with Al!

But we still had a dilemma. In order to use the pictures, we had to get permission to go into the bunker officially and do it by the book this time. Otherwise, it would be impossible to publish the story or the pictures we had in our hands.

Again, I called the Parks Department and again they demurred. When I spoke to the senior official in charge and told him there was a door to the bunker and that it was not sealed up, he was very surprised.

If we hadn't been down to the bunker we would not have known of the existence of the door. The presence of a door meant we could go in as there was no resealed wall that would have to be broken.

It transpired that the Public Works Department (PWD), who had been involved in the February opening, felt that it would be better to put a door to the entrance rather than seal it off again for easy re-entry so they had installed a door just days after the initial reopening of the bunker by the Parks Department.

Although we even managed to get the Singapore Civil Defence Force (SCDF) from Nee Soon Camp to agree to come down and ventilate the bunkers before we went it, permission was still not forthcoming until Felix got on the line with the officials.

It seemed that they were planning a big launch of the Bunker's discovery and *The Straits Times* story would steal the thunder from their press conference in a few months' time.

Felix told them that the cat was already out of the bag and it was better to cooperate on this story so that we could publish the full picture which would then benefit everyone.

After much cajoling, the Parks Department became one of our biggest champions in making sure the story was told. Permission was quickly granted and on 23 July, together with the SCDF and S.C. Wong, a technical officer from the Public Works Department, we "officially" went into the bunker.

On arrival at the bunker, officials from the PWD were curious as to why the door was unlocked but assumed that the flimsy lock must have been removed by vandals.

Al and I didn't say a word. A few days later a new lock similar to the old one, anonymously donated, appeared next to the entrance.

Once inside the Battlebox, we documented the place thoroughly, and today the large number of photographs as to what the complex looked like when it was reopened remains in the *Straits Times* photo library for use by historians and researchers.

My exclusive story on the bunker and its history appeared in *The Straits Times* on 26 July 1988, a scoop that was the talk of the town for the next few days.

But for me, the story didn't just end there. The introduction to the history of Singapore and the secrets of the Battlebox lit a flame within me.

It inspired me to finally do a honours degree in modern Southeast Asian history in addition to a finance degree as well as making numerous trips in the intervening years to the Imperial War Museum, National Army Museum and the Public Records Office in the UK.

The past 17 years have been spent in researching and understanding the history of the Battlebox and the role it had played in the War

PAGE 14 THE STRAITS TIMES, TUESDAY, JULY 26, 1988

HOME

General Officer Commanding, Headquarters Malaya Command, Lieutenant General Arthur E. Percival, who held his last meeting at the operations bunker before he surrendered Singapore to the Japanese on Feb 15, 1942.

Percival's last stand

Singapore's fate decided in this forgotten World War II bunker

By ROMEN BOSE

LIKE a sleeping giant, deep beneath Fort Canning Park, lies a lodestone rich with the sense of urgency just before the surrender of Singapore in 1942.

It was here in this underground fortress, then known as the Headquarters Malaya Command Operations Bunker, that the decision was made for the 85,000-strong British forces to lay down their arms to the 30,000-man Japanese invasion force.

Ironically, the bomb-proof labyrinth was meant to be the "brain centre" in a battle with the Japanese. It was never used as such, for British commander Lt-General Arthur E. Percival surrendered Singapore to the Japanese, under General Tomoyuki Yamashita, on Feb 15, 1942.

Just hours before the surrender, Gen Percival and his senior officers held one last meeting in the Fort Canning bunker before going to the Ford Motor Company in Bukit Timah to meet Gen Yamashita.

Surrender was deemed inevitable because of the acute water shortage perceived by the British on Singapore island.

The giant is being stirred again, some 46 years later.

Mr D.S. Samuel, the ex-president of the Singapore History Association, wrote two recent letters to The Straits Times Forum page, urging that the bunker be reopened and turned into a history museum.

The Parks and Recreation Department, which has charge of the Fort Canning Park area, said the bunker has been earmarked for preservation.

And while it has no definite plans yet on what to do with the bunker, it welcomes suggestions from the public.

Miss G. Uma Devi, a researcher at the Oral History Department, said: "There are many plans to consider. We are hoping to turn the bunker into what it was like at Percival's time with all the maps and charts as well as the tables and the technical equipment used."

But she said this was only a suggestion.

The Oral History Department is, meanwhile, researching the history of the installations but has not been very successful in gleaning more details. "We would appreciate all the help we can get from the public," said Mr Kwa Chong Guan, the department's director.

Dr John Miksic, a senior history lecturer at the National University of Singapore, is helping the Oral History Department with the project.

After the war, the British occupied Fort Canning once again, making it the Singapore Base District Headquarters.

When Singapore gained independence, the Singapore Armed Forces used the main above-ground building as the Singapore Command and Staff College, leaving the underground bunker empty.

The nine-metre deep bunker, with more than 30 rooms, was inspected by members of the Singapore Civil Defence Force (SCDF) on Feb 22 this year.

Last weekend, a Straits Times team accompanied officers from the SCDF camp at Nee Soon as well as Mr S.C. Wong, a technical officer from the Public Works Department, into the bunker for an inspection.

The bunker, extremely humid and hot inside, was totally dilapidated with wires hanging from the walls.

Members of the public who can contribute information, documents or artifacts used in the bunker or in the Fort Canning military installations, can contact Mr Kwa Chong Guan on [illegible].

One of the rooms in the operations centre inside the bunker.

The article which appeared in The Straits Times on 26 July 1988 highlighting the discovery of the long forgotten Battlebox.

in Malaya. I co-authored a book on World War II battlefield sites in Singapore and wrote another on the Indian Independence Movement in Singapore during the Second World War. As a former Bureau Chief and correspondent, I also produced historical documentaries on the Second World War and news reports on events marking the period.

As a result of my ongoing in-depth research into the Battlebox and Singapore's World War II history, I had accumulated so much material on the Battlebox that I decided to put it all in a book. So, more than 17 years after I first set foot in the Battlebox, I have finally managed to pen down a history of this amazing complex.

Today, the Battlebox has been converted into a first-rate museum with interesting displays and animatronics to highlight what happened in Singapore and Malaya during and after the campaign. The complex has been converted to educating the young on the mistakes of the past and the opportunities for the future. A trip to the Battlebox is a must for anyone who wants a quick lesson on Singapore's wartime history.

In the next chapter, you will read about how the Battlebox came about and what its various rooms were used for and, more importantly, how it faced up to the challenge of the War in Malaya.

Chapter 3

The Underground Command Centre

The Underground Command Centre, or Battlebox, lies under one of the first hills occupied by the British East India Company after Sir Stamford Raffles landed at the tiny fishing village of Singapore in 1819.

Known as Bukit Larangan or Forbidden Hill to the Malay, Chinese and Indian villagers who lived on the island, the hill was the sacred burial ground of past Malay kings and rulers. People were forbidden from going up the hill, which may have also served as private residences for earlier Sultans and Kings. Today, the Keramat of Sultan Iskandar Shah remains one of the only visible marks of ancient burials, the site reputed to be the resting place of the last ruler of 14th-century Singapore and the founder of the Malacca Sultanate.

According to Colonel L.T. Firbank in his *History of Fort Canning*:

> By... 1 April 1819... Already a settlement was spreading over the Plain – lines for the troops at the foot of the hill, bazaar and followers quarters. The hill at the back, Bukit Larangan, now Fort Canning, had been cleared of trees, and Lieutenant Ralfe of the H.E.I. Company's Artillery, who had been appointed the first Executive Engineer, had laid a road around it (the beginnings of what is now Canning Rise, leading from Coleman Street).[1]

The earliest known sketch of Singapore town, which dates from 1823, showed the town southeast of Bukit Larangan and northeast of the Singapore River.

In sketches of the town from that period the central background shows

Bukit Larangan, which was also known as Government Hill from 1822 to 1859 before it was renamed Fort Canning Hill. The house near the summit, close to the flagstaff, was the bungalow built for Raffles during his third visit to Singapore, which he mentions in a letter to his friend William Marsden:

> We have lately built a small bungalow on Singapore Hill where though the height is inconsiderable, we find a great difference in climate. Nothing can be more interesting and beautiful than the view from this spot... The tombs of the Malay Kings are close at hand, and I have settled that if it is my fate to die here I shall take my place amongst them: this will at any rate be better than leaving my bones at Bencoolen...[2]

The house was subsequently purchased by the British government and in 1826 its cost stood on the books as $916. In 1823, the second Resident of Singapore, John Crawford, expanded and improved the house at his own expense although he did receive $150 monthly as a housing allowance.

Raffles' house remained on Fort Canning as the residence of the Resident Councillor and eventually the newly appointed Governor until it was taken over by the military in 1858.

At that point, the Governor was provided with a rented residence at the Pavilion, a house formerly occupying the top of Oxley Hill, for six months while the owner was on leave in Europe.

From 1859 to 1869, Colonel Orfeur Cavenagh (Governor 1861-67) and then Colonel Harry St George Ord (Governor 1867-73) lived in the old Leonie Hill House, off Grange Road, until Government House (the Istana) was ready for occupation.

By May 1859, Government Hill had been converted into a new strongly defended position called Fort Canning, named after Lord Canning the Governor General and first Viceroy of India. Seven acres at the top of the hill were levelled and seven 68-pounder guns were mounted in the field redoubts on the southern end, facing the Straits.

Eventually, more that 17 pieces of artillery were mounted. However, by 1892, the Fort was no longer considered effective and remained as a barracks for the garrison artillery and as the general signal station for the town. It fired salutes and time guns at 5am, noon and 9pm but no longer had any value as a defensive position with many other new forts and batteries set up to defend the Straits and Singapore town.[3]

The history of Fort Canning moving into the 20th century remains sketchy at best but we do know that the Fort finally made way for Singapore's first underground reservoir located on the top of the hill.

By this time, the military forces on the island had been reinforced with the decision to build a great naval base in Singapore.

It was seen in reports as "the most secure base south of Hong Kong" and its hinterland was more firmly under British control than Hong Kong's. More importantly, this port stood at the western gateway of the Pacific, and occupied "to the British Empire in the East a corresponding position to Gibraltar in the West"

The sum of £63 million would finally be spent in a stop-start building programme that eventually saw the huge naval base in Sembawang completed by February 1938.

But by then the prospect of war with Japan became a reality with the Japanese invasion of Manchuria and with a large amount of espionage being carried out by a network of Japanese spies throughout the Malayan peninsula.

The British strategy to defend Singapore meant that there was a need for a significant number of soldiers, airmen and sailors to fully defend the newly built base and numbers were gradually increased in the 1930s. What was also crucial was the setting up of a proper headquarters for all British and Commonwealth forces, with the main headquarters of Malaya Command being Singapore.

However, as all three services operated under separate instructions from London, three independent service headquarters were set up. The navy would operate from the brand new naval base while the air force was located at Seletar, and the army was by now based at Fort Canning.

Although the army and air force finally did set up a combined operations room at Sime Road before the war began, it proved to be very problematic. More on this in Chapter 5.

But in 1936, General Percival, General Officer Commanding, Malaya Command, noted that:

> ... the idea of the operational staffs of the fighting services working together had begun to take shape in the plans for the bomb-proof headquarters at Fort Canning.[4]

The underground command centre was thus built to house not only the operational staff of the services but also allied representatives of the French, Dutch and the Americans. Rooms were allocated to these forces in the initial blueprints for the Battlebox.

The 29 rooms built into the hill just next to the covered reservoir measured 44 metres by 48.6 metres and were located 9.1 metres below the tennis courts and club house nearby.

The whole area remained camouflaged so that from the air, the top of the hill appeared to be just an area of green surrounded by the command buildings on Dobbie Rise and barracks blocks on Cox Terrace.

Before proceeding, there are a few things that need to be explained.

Much of the information and detail on the Battlebox that you will read from here on has never been made public. Culled from top secret and highly sensitive war-time documents that have only recently been declassified by the British government and from numerous sources, who even today, wish to remain anonymous, the picture that emerges of the rooms and chambers that make up the Battlebox is quite amazing. Some of the descriptions you will read also come from a bound set of anonymous research clippings and interviews compiled by the Singapore Oral History Department and Parks and Recreation Department.

However, even with these clippings and over 17 years of continuous in-depth research into numerous archives in Singapore and the UK as well as several exploratory trips to the underground complex, the Battlebox has yet to reveal all of its secrets and there is much of the puzzle that has yet to be solved.

However, the details that have emerged provide a vivid picture of the role played by the various elements of Headquarters Malaya Command, housed in the rooms of the Battlebox, as the British military fought the advancing Japanese forces from northern Malaya all the way to the docks of Singapore harbour, in less than 70 days.

I have also modified the original blueprint to reflect the various doorways and wall positions in the rooms as they were when the Battlebox was unsealed in 1988. Thus, the blueprint shows the most accurate layout of the bunkers as they were in February 1942 as opposed to the modified rooms and layout of the Battlebox Museum today.

From the blueprint, it can be seen that there are two main entrances and an emergency roof exit, whose existence was a closely guarded secret.

I have followed the number sequence as originally listed above the doorways of the rooms, many of which are still visible today. For those rooms that are not numbered and for which we have no information, I have left blank in the hopes that sometime in the future information may emerge to help us fill in these gaps.

The Rooms

Only the most vetted and cleared individuals knew of the existence and were allowed access into the inner sanctum of the British military's nerve centre in Malaya. Even the staircase leading from the main above-ground buildings were camouflaged to prevent detection from the air. The Battlebox was so secret that most of the local staff at Fort Canning

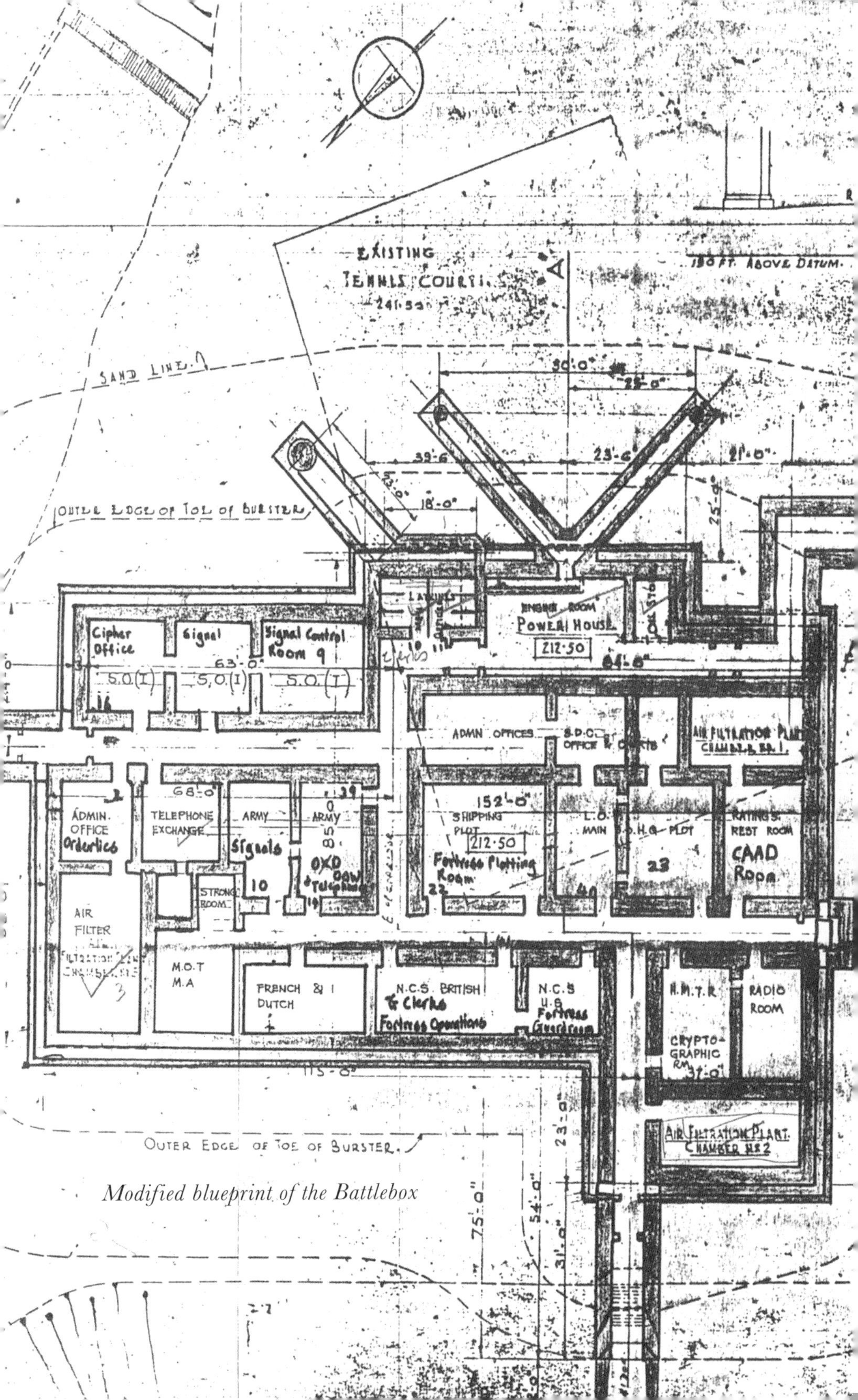

Modified blueprint of the Battlebox

and many of the British officers there did not know of the inner workings of the Battlebox and what happened within its depths. Of course there were rumours about the goings-on in the bunkers. However, all staff at Fort Canning was sworn to strict secrecy and even today, several former clerks and officers who worked in the complex still refuse to talk about their experience, after keeping mum about it for more than 60 years.

Only officers and men with proper authorisation and an official need to access the Battlebox were provided with passes and the appropriate code words in order to gain entry to the underground bunkers. Code words were changed frequently and passes closely scrutinized, in order to ensure that there was no unauthorised access. As a matter of policy, the majority of officers and men allowed into the Battlebox were "White" as very few of the local "Asiatic clerks" would have been trusted enough to be given access to the most sensitive secrets of Malaya Command. The only large group of non-Caucasians allowed access were the British Indian Army sentries and guards who manned the entrances to the bunker.

Upon entering the bunker from the Cox Terrace side, one would encounter sentries almost immediately.

According to Ray Stubbs, a Royal Navy Coder who worked in the Battlebox:

> We turned down the steps to the battlebox, tunnelled into the hillside. We descended about ten steps, then up about five or six; this was apparently some kind of defence against blast and also flooding. It also provided a convenient position for the Sikh sentry to mount his guard. As our heads appeared over the peak of the barrier I could see a turbanned figure laid against the incline, rifle and bayonet straight out in front. There was a curt challenge...Once the sentry was satisfied, we passed through the concreted passageway and came eventually to our duty station.[5]

Because of the highly sensitive work being carried out in the bunkers, the Indian Army sentries were reinforced by men from the Malacca volunteers, who were also stationed at the entrances. Later, when the War reached Singapore's doorstep, most of these sentries were removed to serve at other more vital positions in defending the island.

As you came through the main solid-iron double doors, installed in case of a gas attack, there was a long hallway which was well-lit and filled with a low-level buzz of the ventilation system and wall-mounted lights that illuminated the chambers.

The door to each room remained locked at all times with access to each of these chambers restricted to essential personnel only. Signs stating "No

Smoking", "No Eating" and "No Talking" were put up to ensure minimal disruption to operations. There were also posters warning of "loose lips" and the need for operational secrecy.

Although officers in the various rooms could communicate with one another, most rarely saw their colleagues in the other rooms. They used telephones routed through the telephone exchange and vacuum suction message tubes that lined the complex. Using a small container wrapped in rubber, an officer would put a document in the capsule; insert it in the tube which would then be sucked to the other end of the pipe, the destination of the document. These pipes linked several key rooms like the Signal Control and Gun Operations Room as well as the XDO to the Fortress Plotting Room. Many remember the "thud" when the containers reached their destination.

Orderlies and Air Filtration Plant No 3 (Room 2)

This is where the other ranks would rest when taking breaks from their shift and also where the dispatch clerks (DRLS) would send incoming and outgoing packages and mail. This facility was eventually shifted to the signal office on the opposite side of the hallway.

A doorway inside the orderlies' room led into Air Filtration Plant No 3. Inside the Battlebox were three air filtration plants that were built to provide breathable air even during a gas attack. Because the equipment was large and generated a lot of heat, the underground complex was never very cool and when more people began to fill the corridors in the final stages of the battle for Singapore, it was absolutely boiling.

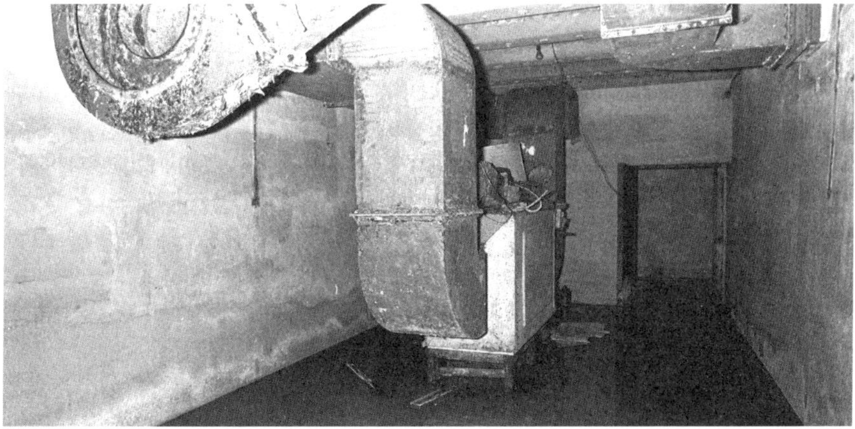

Air Filtration Plant 3. Note the size of the filtration machine and flooded interior of the room. The machine was removed and this room has now been converted into a gift shop in the Battlebox Museum.

Telephone Exchange

When the Battlebox was unsealed in 1988, the telephone exchange rooms were found with huge gaping holes in the ground, created most probably by the huge telephone exchange machines used in connecting external calls through to the various rooms in the complex and internal communications within the Battlebox.

The exchange was connected to all military and most civilian switchboards throughout Malaya as well as the military scrambler phone lines to the various units and forward positions, including most of the operational headquarters of the divisions.

As the War progressed, the signals traffic increased dramatically but the signals office in Kuala Lumpur, headquarters of Heath's III Indian Corps and the front-line headquarters for the battles raging in northern Malaya was only connected to Fort Canning through the ordinary civilian telephone exchange.

What this meant was that it was impossible to get immediate battlefield reports and updates from northern Malaya. As the main military communications system was based on civilian phone lines, various units and divisions jammed up the available lines with urgent reports and calls for instruction, rather than relying on their antiquated and very often broken-down signals communications system. As the remaining telephone lines were also choked with civilian calls upcountry, it proved to be an untenable situation.

Routing calls through the public phone exchange meant there was a 45-minute delay even in connecting Percival to Heath in Kuala Lumpur. As quite a lot of battlefield reports and tactical discussions were conducted over the telephone system, this meant that by the time the senior officers were able to get in touch with one another, events had already overtaken the decisions that needed to be made.

Eventually, the telephone exchange at Fort Canning set up a priority list with first priority going to calls by Percival, next the scrambler phone calls to Fort Canning and then the others. With the Malayan Civil Service swamped by the onset of the war, it was impossible to get more dedicated phone lines added. It was only after Percival personally made representations to the telegraph company that it finally gave the Signals office in Kuala Lumpur a direct line to Fort Canning. However, by this point, it proved useless as the British had lost most of northern Malaya in a matter of weeks and the war had shifted to southern Malaya. The dedicated line was used only for a week before the British evacuated Kuala Lumpur.

The top photo shows what the telephone exchange looked like when it was unsealed in 1988. The hole in the floor is where the phone exchange machine was located. The present mock-up, though not the same sophisticated equipment as the original, is an example of the type of equipment used.

The Signals Section (Rooms 16, 9, unknown)

The three rooms containing the Cipher Office, Signal and Signal Control Room received most of the coded transmissions coming initially from the other two services and later from the Commander-in-Chief, American-

British-Dutch-Australian (ABDA) Command, General Sir Archibald Wavell's office in Java. This is where outgoing messages were also sent to be transmitted to the various sub-headquarters and units in the Malayan theatre and remained the only outgoing wireless circuit to London in operation after Singapore fell.

There were two types of messages that were received, Most Important and Secret. The important messages were marked Urgent while the highly sensitive and secret messages were marked ICW, or In Cipher Wireless. This meant they were sent coded (in cipher) and paraphrased via Morse code and would require decoding on receipt before the message could be read.

Many signals from the field were sent to Fort Canning via wireless transmitting stations throughout Malaya attached to divisional headquarters. Units were also able to raise Fort Canning using portable wireless sets and during the last days of the battle for Singapore, Fort Canning signals would receive distraught pleas for help via these wireless sets throughout the island.

All radio networks used the code and link system, which was designed to deny information to enemy intercept and intelligence services. This was done by issuing daily, secret groups of three letters (code signs) to HQs of all formations and units down to company/squadron HQs. These code signs would authenticate the signals being received and would prevent the enemy from being able to send fake messages on captured wireless equipment. The codes were changed daily at 0001 Z hours (Theatre Operations time). Sub-units merely added a figure to the code sign of the parent station and sub-sub-units a letter.[6]

Simple codes were also used to disguise map references and orders and it wasn't until 1943 that complex encoding systems like SLIDEX cards were introduced. In Malaya, pre-war codes were used but there has been no evidence so far to suggest that these early codes had been broken.

The main line of military communication on Singapore Island was through buried fixed cables which linked Fort Canning and other headquarters with all the coastal artillery sites, air strips and divisional headquarters. During the war, Command Signals was responsible for communications coming in and out of Singapore while Fortress Signals was responsible for internal communications.

Signal Room

The Signal Room was what many referred to as the 'post office'. This was where messages were picked up or sent off. It was occupied by about seven men per shift, three signal men, two orderlies and two clerks.

The shifts were arranged by Signal headquarters but the room was not locked up like most because the ventilation was very poor.[7]

A normal day would start with the signal operators receiving a situation report from the field sent via wireless or from the cables and once decoded, it would then be handed over to the signal officer, who would then forward the report to the various commands and operations rooms, and should it warrant it, finally ending up on Percival's desk.

The main types of signals received usually concerned troop movements and new dispositions on the ground. These details would be forwarded to the fortress plotting and gun operations room as well as the relevant commanders who were in need of the detailed positions.

Cipher Room

The Cipher Room was where all these messages were decoded and encoded using the various military code books and enciphering equipment. The messages sent or received were supposed to be destroyed after three days, for which a large shredder was set up.

However, when Fort Canning was bombed heavily in January 1942 and the power supply cut, the emergency generators provided an incompatible voltage for the shredder, which then had to be abandoned following which all documents had to be burned.

By late January 1942 as the Japanese advanced across southern Malaya, the cipher office was shifted out of the Battlebox and the room was left empty and non-commissioned officers began using it as a place to sleep.

Signal Control Room

The Signal Control Room was reported to have two local communication links or circuits and overseas circuits with Hong Kong, India, Ceylon and the Dutch East Indies (Indonesia), which would then relay messages to London.

Complete silence was essential in this room in order to take down the Morse code being received from the various links. A duty signal officer would be stationed here to verify and authenticate the messages received which would then be sent to the Cipher Room for decoding before being handed over for dispatch to the Signal Room. Large signal equipment lined the walls as operators with headsets manned the receiving and transmitting units. The men were divided into three shifts a day but by January 1942, it was impossible for the operators to keep up with the huge flow of traffic. More men were drafted in from signal units that had evacuated from upcountry in order to cope.

One interesting aspect of this room is the Japanese graffiti found on its walls which indicate that it was used during the Japanese Occupation. Mainly a list of Japanese soldiers and their units, one of the more curious ones is the name Percival written in Hiragana script followed by the name Yamashita (the Commander of the Japanese forces in the Malayan Campaign), underlined by the phrase, Yamashita Shogun, giving the reader no doubt as to who was the victor in this place.

The graffiti show that at least these few signal rooms were occupied by the Japanese, most probably because of their communications links and as a shelter for soldiers who were guarding the Japanese Defence Headquarters which used the external buildings during the Occupation.

Jim Howard, an Australian military photographer during the war, parachuted into Singapore on 28 August 1945, days before the official Japanese surrender, and entered the bunker complex, where he saw Japanese soldiers occupying these rooms and using the communications facilities. Obviously, the equipment was not sufficiently destroyed by the surrendering British as the Japanese were still able to use the signals equipment. Howard noted the rooms nearby were barely furnished and the Orderlies Room had bunks and were occupied by Japanese guards who also cooked there, with the stench of ammonia in the air, the result of someone using the inner recesses of the bunker as a public latrine.[8]

XDO, OOW & Telephones and XDO & Signals Room (Rooms 39, 14, 10)

OOW stands for Officer of the Watch, while XDO is an abbreviation for the Extended Defence Office, which was a crucial element in defending the Singapore Fortress. The XDO was in command of all the local naval defence elements, including local patrol vessels as well as the navy signal stations and boom defence vessels. This was the naval liaison office with the Army, in order to better coordinate with the coastal and fixed artillery commanded by Brigadier Arthur Drury Curtis, Commander of Singapore's Fixed Defences.

Lieutenant Commander David Copley, who served as secretary to the Extended Defence Officer, described the inner workings of this almost aquamarine blue room:

> This was a medium sized room, in which were a number of wireless transmitters and receivers and benches with telephones. The walls were covered with all kinds of charts (maps of the local area), a large notice board and various of the current war time posters, warning of secrecy such as 'walls have ears'. Off this room were several doors to

those parts reserved for the officer of the watch, and certainly others of a higher station. There was a slight hum from the air conditioning, supplemented by a whirring fan.

My job there was to code and decode wireless messages, and to receive, and make telephone calls (all scrambled for security purposes). The messages by transmitter would have been to and from ships of the Royal Navy, escorting convoys in and out of Singapore, or on patrol in nearby waters. Telegraphic communication was with other military and naval establishments, such as the naval base and gunnery commands.[9]

Original signs over the XDO Room gave the author and researchers clues as to the function of the various rooms and helped identify the room where Percival and his commanders made the decision to surrender. Parts of the XDO Room's aquamarine blue walls can be seen.

The urinals were in better condition and looked useable except that the water supply had not functioned since the early 1940s. Amazingly, the toilets were one of the few rooms that were actually dry.

Latrines (Rooms 10, 11)

There were latrines provided in the underground bunker, one for the use of officers and the others for non-commissioned officers and men. There were no facilities for women as the majority of bunker's personnel were male and there were no female clerks working in the Battlebox. Because they were heavily used and constantly clogging up, by the time of the Battle for

Singapore in February 1942, the facilities were no longer useable and the stench from the toilets was making it hard to work in the Battlebox. Much of the toilet remains intact with the toilet bowls and urinals still standing.

At the junction in front of the latrines is a concrete pedestal. What this was used for is still unknown.

Power House and Oil Store

This was the location of the emergency power generators that were to keep the Battlebox fully operational in case the power supply was cut. Vents from the engine room lead all the way to the surface on the top of the hill, where the oddly shaped mushroom structures are actually the sealed-up vents. These structures still exist today and are an interesting curiosity in the park above the bunkers.

When Fort Canning became the target of heavy bombing and the external power lines were cut, these emergency generators were brought on-line to supply the electricity needed.

However, the small amount of power it generated was not enough to keep the ventilation system going at full speed so it became stiflingly hot and unbreathable in the rooms. The huge and oily concrete stumps, on which the massive generators were located, still exist today but the oil drums and most of the machinery were looted long ago. When the bunker was unsealed in 1988, the area was flooded but has since been pumped dry.

If you continue past the engine room, you come up to a passageway which turns left and then right again before it leads to a metal staircase.

This was the beginnings of the emergency exit built into the underground bunker for use in escape. The emergency exit was kept a secret from most of the bunker's inhabitants as it was only to be used by the senior commanders in case of a full-scale attack on the Battlebox. Most did not know of the emergency escape hatch and staircase which remained hidden beyond the power house.

Fortress Command

Occupied by the Fortress Commander, Major General Keith Simmons, this room at present has been recreated using one of two rare pictures of this complex obtained from the Imperial War Museum, showing how the General used it as his wartime office.

The Battlebox was actually more Simmons' headquarters than Percival's. From here, Simmons would be able to command any battle or skirmish fought on the island. Under his command came the Fixed Defences

The engines and electrical equipment in the power house had been stripped and all that remained was the concrete blocks and a few remnants of the machinery. It was flooded and the water was more than 5 inches deep at certain parts. There was also an oil slick from the excess oil abandoned in the bunkers. The square windows in the back were ventilation shafts. We found old t-shirts stuffed in them. An abandoned oil drum can be seen in on the left background.

The emergency rooftop exit was located behind the power house. The area was flooded with up to a foot of water when first opened. Today, a new rooftop structure has been installed so that visitors can get a better view of the passageway.

commanded by Curtis and the Anti Aircraft Defences, commanded by Brigadier A.W.G. Wildey.

As Percival noted in his book, *The War In Malaya*:

> The Commander of the Singapore Fortress was responsible for the defence of Singapore and adjoining islands and of the eastern area of Johore. He had under his command all the fixed defences, i.e. coast defence guns and searchlights, the anti-aircraft defences, the beach defence troops, the Straits Settlements Volunteer Force (except for the battalion at Penang), and the various fortress and administrative units. It was a pretty important command, especially as he also became heavily involved with civil problems connected with the defence of Singapore. In addition to this he had the responsibility for the defence of the east coast of Johore where the small port of Mersing, connected to Singapore by a good motor road, had always been thought to be a likely landing place for an invading force. For the defence of this area he had to rely on what field troops could be made available from Singapore – not a very satisfactory state of affairs and one about which I never felt very happy.[10]

Simmons faced an enormous challenge in commanding the final stages of the battle for Singapore. The War had already been lost and the delaying actions he was forced to take clearly took a toll. Simmons had earlier been in command of the British forces in Shanghai when he was forced to evacuate as the Japanese Army advanced. Yet again, he was faced with a similar situation. This time, Simmons refused to leave. He was interned as a POW along with Percival and the other senior commanders after the fall of Singapore. The smaller room is believed to have served as Simmons' bedroom during the last days of the campaign.

"G" Clerks Fortress Operations (Room 19, 41)

The "G" Operations room was the main centre where field reports and dispatches would come in from the signals and various other offices to be compiled into a situation report and submitted to Percival and his commanders. The clerks in this room were also responsible for handling all staff papers and communications for Percival and Simmons.

As part of the general staff, these men would co-ordinate all the instructions issued and distribute the various issued orders while compiling that day's summary reports and documents for the Fortress Commander. Percival's last communiqué to the troops after the surrender was issued from "G" Ops.

It was in this room, in 1988, that a decomposing stretcher was found which has now been removed. When it was used, what it was used for and what became of its occupant is still a mystery.

However, since the last edition, new evidence has come to light as to who could have been the likely occupant of the stretcher.

Captain V.L.F. Davin (later Major) was an officer with the 5/14th Punjab Regiment and had been injured in a vehicle accident in Northern Malaya on 14th December and having been injured was unfit for combat but was still able to contribute and so was made a staff officer at Fort Canning just weeks before the fall.

The "G" Clerks were responsible for dispatching and receiving all staff and administrative paper for Percival and Simmons. It was at "G" Clerks that Percival drafted his final note to British and Allied troops on the island. Note the water-logged floor.

I had given Davin a tour of the Battlebox in late 2005, and despite the fact that he had forgotten much of what had transpired so many decades ago, he still recalled the stretcher:

> If it came from 1942, it would have been the stretcher of Major (Charles Erling Bernard) Catt, of my Battalion – 5/14th Punjab Regiment – who was also on the staff of Malaya Command. He used to go out on patrol on the island to bring in direct reports to General Percival or Brigadier Torrance. He did not have to do this, it was a purely personal action by him. On 15th February he went out, as usual, just before the surrender and was shot in the stomach during this last patrol, before the surrender. I heard about him being a casualty and went and saw him being carried in to the Battlebox on a stretcher. He had insisted on making his report before going to hospital. In my opinion, it is the stretcher he was carried in on as, to the best of my knowledge, there were no other casualties amongst the Battlebox staff that day or before (except for my being blown backwards by a shell as I was coming off duty some days earlier, which did not involve any loss of blood or the use of a stretcher).[11]

Fortress Plotting Room

Although details are sketchy, the rotting cork boards on the wall clearly indicate that the plotting room was filled with maps of the various areas of operations, from the initial Japanese invasion on 8 December 1941 to the last lines of defence around the burnt-out town of Singapore on the morning of 15 February 1942.

The Plotting Room is believed to have been linked to the signals section and the Gun Operations room with all details of the Japanese advance and Allied troop dispositions plotted meticulously on a huge table in the centre of the room, manned by clerks and plotters who would receive decoded field movement reports on numerous telephones in the room and plot the various air and defence positions along the peninsula and finally on Singapore island itself.

The room was initially built as a shipping plot to identify where the various Royal Navy elements were located and explains why it is so close to the XDO rooms. The XDO would have provided naval plotting data and intelligence would have been received to show the various positions of the enemy and Allied positions, with additional details coming from the Operations Room at the naval base.

After the first few days of the campaign, with the loss of the two capital ships, HMS *Prince of Wales* and HMS *Repulse*, the plotting room lost most of its purpose as there was no longer a need to plot the naval movements without any big ships.

It was used for the smaller evacuation operations and troop transfers but no longer served a very significant purpose until it was converted in the last few days for the battle of Singapore Island, when the combined operations headquarters moved back to Fort Canning.

It is believed that this is the room where the last naval and troop movements were plotted before the surrender.

Gun Operations Room

The Gun Operations Room is where the air attacks and details were plotted from data provided by signals and via telephone links.

The Royal Air Force's first lines of warning were highly secret radar units that provided advanced warning of Japanese air attacks over Malaya and Singapore.

Radio Detection Finding units or Radar units, and the Radar Installations and Maintenance Units based throughout Malaya and Singapore were linked by trunk lines to Filter Rooms, which would plot the various aircraft formation information, known as "tracks" and would forward it to the Fighter Operations Rooms at the various air bases and by

This was the vertical plank, embedded in a concrete base block and discoloured, with red stains on it. Note the floor next to it has been dug up and is filled with brackish water. The wires hanging were loose pieces that were not stripped by looters. It is believed that the holes were dug by treasure hunters in the hopes of discovering hidden treasure buried in the bunker.

signal circuits from Kuala Lumpur (co-ordinating all northern radar units) to the RAF Headquarters in Sime Road and to the Gun Operations Room at Fort Canning.[12]

It was in this way that the radar units spotted the first wave of Japanese bombers that were going to attack Singapore in the early hours of 8 December 1941. It was picked up by radar more than 75 miles away from the target, which meant that it was spotted more than an hour before the actual bombings took place. Although the Filter Room had given Malaya Command and the Governor immediate warning of the Japanese air attack, it took the Governor more than 35 minutes to respond as he was unable to be located. Also, as he had given strict instructions that only he could authorise the use of the air raid sirens, the Governor's approval was crucial. In any event, though the approval was finally received, the civil authorities were still unable to locate the air raid warden responsible and so the sirens only came on after the first bombs hit Singapore at 4:15am. Although this advanced early warning system might have given the residents of Singapore precious time to prepare for the attack, the lack of appreciation for the advanced warning system meant that the initial use of radar was an exercise in futility.[13]

As the war progressed, radar units began withdrawing from upcountry and destroying their equipment before they fell into enemy hands. Most of the RDF units were withdrawn to Singapore with the various radar units linked by radio telephony sets to the Cathay Building, now a central coordinating point, from where tracks were relayed via tielines to the RAF Filter Room in Katong, which would subsequently forward the details to the Fighter Operations Room at Air Headquarters in Sime Road and to the Gun Operations Room at Fort Canning.[14]

When the forward headquarters moved back to Fort Canning on 11 February 1942, the filter room in Katong was sending the tracks directly to the Gun Operations Room at Fort Canning as contact with Air headquarters had been lost.

In the last days, the whole radar outfit was disbanded as there was nowhere left to set up radar positions and the staff of these units were offered to Malaya Command to help supplement the weary men at the Gun Operations Room.[15]

For Major Hugh Lindley-Jones, who worked in this room, it was a very trying time:

> We Gun Control Officer's job was to plot the progress of the enemy air attacks on a large table map using information received from Radar stations and visual observers, to check that the evidence was credible and then pass it on to the various anti-aircraft gun sites around the island. They were then prepared to try to shoot down the planes and knew the general direction, numbers and heights of the formations.
>
> The map on the table covered all Malaya, all the way up the Isthmus of Kra, in order to cover one of the air bases in Alor Star. The raids were plotted by little wooden markers with room for three lots of figures, the raid number, the number of planes, and the height in thousands of feet. These wooden markers showed direction and would have been three to four inches high.
>
> For this, there were at least two duty officers who were responsible that all ran smoothly and who had to intervene if they thought that anything was going astray. We also had some 10 to 15 on duty that received the information and plotted it on the map and others who relayed the news to the gun sites, generally by land telephone lines.[16]

A mock-up of the Gun Operations Room in the present museum reflects part of the original condition but with a plotting table and counters more reminiscent of the Cabinet War Rooms in London.

Commander Fixed Defences

Brigadier Curtis was responsible for the fixed defences of the island. His room has also been recreated in the present museum using another rare photograph from the Imperial War Museum.

The Fixed Defences of Singapore were divided into two fire commands, i.e. the Changi Fire Command which covered the approaches to the Naval Base and the Faber Fire Command which covered the approaches to Keppel Harbour and the western channel of the Johore Straits. Each Fire Command had one 15-inch gun, one 9.2-inch gun and a number of 6-inch guns as well as searchlights and other equipment.

Brigadier Curtis' role was to make use of the Fortress Plotting and Gun Operations Room to ensure that accurate information was being relayed to the coastal artillery and additional fixed positions on the island to ensure that any intruders from the sea were destroyed.

Even before the enemy launched its assault from the Skudai and Melayu rivers on the opposite bank of Singapore island on the night of 7 February 1942, Curtis had already ordered the big guns on the island to traverse round and provide supporting and harassing fire on the Johore Straits. It was a myth that the guns of Singapore could not be traversed 180 degrees and the heavy fire on the northwestern shores during the battle for Singapore clearly proves this.

However, of greater significance was the fact that these guns, which

A mock-up of the Commander Fixed Defences Room, showing Brigadier A.C. Curtis at his desk. The mock-up is based on a rare photograph taken within the bunker complex.

were meant to fire on ships, were armed with mainly armour piercing (AP) shells. AP shells had only a small charge in its head which would explode upon hitting the ship's hull causing much damage.

On land, however, most of the shells would hit the ground with a loud thud and not cause much damage. As the guns were meant to target ships, there were very few High Explosive or HE shells in their magazines. The HE shells which were needed to cause significant damage to troops and armour were in very short supply. So, while the guns were able to provide artillery support, they proved ineffective because of the wrong type of ammunition (see *Table of Ammunition*).

Lieutenant-Colonel C.C.M. Macleod-Carey, who was at the Faber Fire Command, recounts the communication with the Fixed Defence HQ at the Fort Canning Battlebox in those last few days[17]:

> It was Friday, 13 February 1942 and I was watching the sun rise from my command post on top of Mount Faber, Singapore. The rays from the red orb of the sun radiated in ever widening shafts of red; just like the old 'Rising Sun' flag of Japan used to be.
>
> I remember that I was feeling pretty gloomy at the time but this evil omen gave me an uncomfortable sense of impending doom.

Singapore at that time was obviously in its death throes and there seemed very little future in it…

…About midnight the following night, a signal came from HQ at Fort Canning saying an unidentified ship had been located just outside the minefield covering the entrances to Keppel Harbour and that no British ship was in the area. I was at that time second in command of the 7th Coast Artillery Regiment covering Keppel Harbour with its powerful armament of 15-in, 9.2 in, 6-in and a host of other smaller weapons. There was another similarly equipped regiment defending the Naval Base at Changi. I rang up the port War Signal Station, our line with the Navy, which was manned by sailors. There was no reply and we discovered later that it had been evacuated but for some reason no one had informed us. I then ordered the 6-in batteries at Serapong, Siloso and Labrador to sweep the area with their searchlights. Almost immediately a ship which seemed to be of 8,000 tons was illuminated at a range of 7,000 yards just outside the minefield. We challenged the ship by Aldis lamp but the reply, also by lamp, was incorrect.

TABLE OF AMMUNITION[16]

Commander Fixed Defences		**Brig. A. D. Curtiss**		
7th Coast Artillery Regiment		**Faber Fire Command**		
	Guns	Max Range (yards)		Ammunition (rpg)
Buona Vista Bty	2 x 15in	36,900	250AP	no HE
Connaught Bty	3 x 9.2in	31,600	250AP	30 HE
Pasir Laba Bty	2 x 6in	17,000	500AP	50 HE
Siloso Bty	2 x 6in	17,000	500AP	50 HE
Labrador Bty	2 x 6in	17,000	500AP	50 HE
Serapong Bty	2 x 6in	17,000	500AP	50 HE
Silingsing Bty	2 x 6in	17,000	500AP	50 HE
9th Coast Artillery Regiment		**Changi Fire Command**		
Johore Bty	3 x 15in	36,900	250AP	no HE
Tekong Bty	3 x 9.2in	31,600	250AP	30 HE
Sphinx Bty	2 x 6in	21,700	600AP	50 HE
Pengerang Bty	2 x 6in	21,700	600AP	50 HE
Beting Kusah Bty	2 x 6in	21,700	600AP	50 HE
Changi Bty	2 x 6in	21,700	600AP	50 HE

15in and 9.2in guns were manned by British gunners. All 6in guns were manned by Hong Kong and Singapore gunners, all Punjabis from India. There were also 11 minor associated batteries with a total of seven 12pdr and 20pdr quick-firers.

> Fortunately, in order to assist in this sort of situation, the Navy had posted an excellent rating who was standing by my side. We had a copy of 'Jane's Fighting Ships' and the rating pointed to a photograph of a Japanese landing craft carrier and said, 'I reckon that's it, sir'. I gave the order to 'shoot' and within seconds all 6-in guns opened up with a roar. The guns had been permanently sited and even without radar, which had not been installed, their instruments and range finding gear were so accurate that preliminary ranging was unnecessary. Direct hits were scored at once. Flames, sparks and debris started flying in all directions. The crew could be seen frantically trying to lower boats but it was all over in a matter of minutes, after which the ship just disappeared to sea.
>
> This action was reported to Fort Canning but it is strange that it has never, so far as I know, been mentioned in an official account. Most likely the record was lost together with a good many other documents in the subsequent events after the surrender of Singapore.
>
> Next morning, we were ordered to fire the guns at the very large number of oil tanks situated on the islands around Pulau Bukum about three miles from Keppel. Something like 200,000 tons of oil were set on fire.

Commander Anti-Aircraft Defence Room (Room 27)

Of all the rooms, this would probably be the one of greatest historical significance as it was in this room that the decision to surrender Singapore to the Japanese was taken on the morning of 15 February 1942.

The CAAD Room was initially occupied by Brigadier Wildey of the Royal Artillery.

As Percival noted, Wildey was responsible for the defence of selected targets in the Singapore area against hostile air attack. He had under his command four heavy anti-aircraft regiments, one light anti-aircraft regiment less one battery which was under the III Indian Corps, and one searchlight regiment. During an attack, Percival noted that the RAF's Group Captain Rice, the coordinator of the air defence of the Singapore area, was authorised to issue orders to him direct. Most of the guns were static and the range of the 3.7's was "very limited by modern standards"[18].

While in captivity, Wildey along with several other senior officers prepared reports of their various commands and in the documents now with the Imperial War Museum, he outlined the preparation for the anti-aircraft defence[19]:

> In the three years before Dec 1941, the A.A. defences had been fortunate in having had excellent co-operation by the R.A.F. not only in day-to-day routine flying, but in connection with some fifteen combined exercises spread over this period each lasting three days. These exercises were in the nature of "Silent Practice" for both guns and aircraft and results in every case were closely analysed and compared with those previous exercises. They were of the utmost value in training of Gun Control Room (Gun Operations Room in Fort Canning), Fighter Control Room, Observer Units and Bty. Command Posts, and in developing a sound technique.
>
> ...Static gun positions for the defences of Singapore had been developed in accordance with the W.O. (War Office) plan of 1936, as amended and extended by the plan approved by the C. of S. (Chiefs of Staff) Sub-committee in 1940. Construction of new positions was proceeding with the estimated dates of arrival of new equipments and of recruits, on arrival of new units. It was up to date, though far from complete, in Dec. 1941...
>
> ...Communications between Gun Control Room and such positions as had been completed were functioning fully, and communication between the G.C.R. and Fighter Operations Room was entirely satisfactory. In addition, an observer tower, manned by a special team of observers and look out men had been established in the Naval Base, to give warning of the approach of low flying attacks on installations in the Naval Base. This tower was connected tele-phonically to Bofors troop and gun stations, G.C.R., and Naval Operations and A.R.P. (Air Raid Precaution) HQs. A function of the tower, which had a very wide range of visibility, was to provide the Gun Control Officer with a running commentary on the progress of enemy raids...
>
> ...The total number of hostile aircraft destroyed during the campaign was 130, verified by independent observation. This figure is up to approximately 8 Feb., after which no accurate returns could be obtained, though a number are known to have shot down after that date. Including them and probables it is safe to say that some 200 Japanese aircraft were put out of action permanently by A. A. D.

Although the report outlines the actions taken by the anti-aircraft units with direction from Fort Canning, Wildey, however, was upset over the lack of mobility among his troops and more importantly, effective control of the defences:

> … the static equipment were at a great disadvantage compared with the mobile ones, especially after the Japanese had reached the North Shore of the JOHORE STRAITS. For lack of transporters and transport, guns had to be abandoned as the enemy advanced into the island.
>
> … The second lesson is this: that in a fortress such as Singapore an air defence commander (as distinct from an A.A. Defence Commander) should be appointed. Only when all the means of air defence, including fighter aircraft are under one commander, can the best air defence be achieved. The appointment of an A.D. Commander was repeatedly pressed in the month before December 1941, but the only concession was the appointment of an Air Defence Co-ordinator, who had no command over available fighter aircraft, and who functioned largely through an Air Defence Committee, whose recommendation had first to be notified by the chiefs of the three services before they became operative. A very great deal of useful work was done by this committee, and during operations the liaison between the A.A.D. Commander and the co-ordinator and their staff was always cordial and satisfactory, but it is certain that had there been a Commander, Air defence, with fighter aircraft actually under his command, a better air defence of Singapore could have been achieved with the means available.[20]

Brigadier Wildey's report summed up the air defence situation in the closing days of the battle. Once the RAF had pulled out its remaining aircraft, by the middle of January 1942, the anti-aircraft guns were no longer needed to defend the air fields and aerodromes, thus many were disbanded to form infantry units. This meant the skies over Singapore were clear for Japanese aircraft to bomb the town at will, with Fort Canning receiving a major brunt of the bombing and artillery shelling.[21]

The situation got so bad that the above-ground buildings were continually being hit and smouldering fires could be seen all over the hill command. It was because of the impunity with which the Japanese were bombing the British command that Percival decided to hold his final conference in the bomb-proof Battlebox.

It is curious that when the Battlebox was opened in 1988, a huge rectangular tank was found occupying much of this room. It was later discovered to be an oil storage tank and pipes in the room suggested it was used as a supply for the diesel generators which powered the ventilation system in the complex. As more than a third of the small room was occupied by the tank, there was obviously a very limited amount of space. Moreover,

A mock-up of what the CAAD Room looked like on 15 February 1942, as Percival and his senior commanders met in the room to decide the fate of 100,000 British and Commonwealth troops in Malaya. A large oil tank that occupied a quarter of the room has now been removed in order to accommodate audio visual equipment.

the noise and smell from the tank would have made it impossible to work in for any prolonged period of time.

Although it was Wildey's room, it is believed that he would have barely used it in the lead-up to and then the final battle for Singapore. As such it must have been one of the only vacant rooms in the bunker and one of the closest rooms to the Gun Operations and Plotting Room where details were coming in on the last movements of troops and air defences before the final surrender. It must have been very uncomfortable for close to ten persons to squeeze into the CAAD Room and even harder to concentrate given the unbreathable air and stiflingly hot conditions in the bunker. Nonetheless, this is where the final decision was taken to surrender Singapore.

Although the role of each room in the underground complex has been explained, there is still much to be said on how the Battlebox came to be the final location set for the decision of the final surrender, especially since Percival had moved his headquarters to Sime Road just two days before the Japanese invasion on Malaya.

What now unfolds is the story of the relocation of Malaya Command's nerve centre and how, despite the creation of a new combined headquarters, it finally ended up in a retreat to the Battlebox in less than two months.

Endnotes

1 Firbank, L.T. *A History of Fort Canning.* unpublished typescript, Singapore, c.1960s. p. 2.

2 Ibid, p. 3.

3 Ibid, p. 8.

4 Percival, A.E. *The War in Malaya.* Eyre & Spottiswoode, London, 1949.

5 *Stubbs, Ray, Personal Account, The Battlebox : Research Clippings* (date unknown), Oral History Department, Singapore.

6 Forty, George. *British Army Handbook 1939-1945.* Sutton Publishing, Gloucestershire, 1998. p. 90.

7 *The Battlebox: Research Clippings* (date unknown), Oral History Department, Singapore.

8 *Howard, Jim, Personal Account, The Battlebox : Research Clippings* (date unknown), Oral History Department, Singapore.

9 *Copley, David. Personal Account, The Battlebox : Research Clippings* (date unknown), Oral History Department, Singapore.

10 Percival, A.E. *The War in Malaya.* Eyre & Spottiswoode, London, 1949. p. 49-50.

11 Davin, V.L.F. "Secrets of the battlebox", email to author, 20 November 2005. Catt is listed as having died on 16 February 1942. Commonwealth War Graves Commission website, http://www.cwgc.org/search/casualty_details.aspx?casualty=2822162, accessed 13 October 2011.

12 *History of the RDF organisation in the Far East 1941-2, Papers of Wing Commander T.C. Carter P180.* The Imperial War Museum, London.

13 Ibid, p.5.

14 Ibid, p. 6.

15 Ibid, p.10.

16 *Lindley-Jones, Hugh. Personal Account, The Battlebox : Research Clippings,* Oral History Department, Singapore.

17 Macleod-Carey,CCM. *Singapore Guns, War Monthly,* Issue 34, p.34-39.

18 Percival, A.E. *The War in Malaya.* Eyre & Spottiswoode, London, 1949.

19 *Report on A.A. Defences Malaya, Dec.1941–Feb 1942, Papers of A.E. Percival,* P16-27. The Imperial War Museum, London, p. 4.

20 Ibid p. 5.

21 *Papers of Brigadier AWG Wildey, 98/16/1.* The Imperial War Museum, London.

Chapter 4

The Battlebox and the Combined Operations Headquarters

Although the Battlebox remained a crucial piece in the command and control of Malaya Command, it was, by 1941, too small to house all the operational staff Percival required for a unified headquarters:

> In order to ensure co-operation in war a bomb-proof battle headquarters was constructed at Fort Canning, where it was intended that the Combined Operations Staff of the three services should work. This headquarters, however, was already too small by the time it was completed and, although it was occupied during the operations, it was never actually used for the purpose intended.[1]

Despite this, the Battlebox played a crucial role as a result of the lack of a real combined operations headquarters but more on this later.

Percival, who had taken over as General Officer Commanding, Malaya Command in July 1941, decided to create a new Combined Operations Headquarters in Singapore.

He was now tasked to prepare Malaya for a possible attack by Japan and was under enormous pressure to ensure the three services were working towards this. Percival became very good friends with the RAF's Air Officer Commanding, Air Vice-Marshal C.W.H. Pulford:

> There was some consolation, however, and that was in the person of the Air Officer Commanding Far East, Air Vice-Marshall C.W.H. Pulford, who had a short time before arrived to take over command. An ex-naval officer and a keen exponent of the torpedo-bomber in

> naval warfare, he was a man of my own way of thinking in most matters military or non-military. We immediately struck up a close friendship which was to endure until we parted on the eve of the fall of Singapore, he to meet his death with the rear-admiral (Admiral Spooner) and I to spend long years in captivity. As my family was not with me, he lived with me at Flagstaff House, and I believe that our close comradeship was not an unimportant factor in fostering the spirit of co-operation which, from the time of our arrival, developed between our respective Services both on the headquarters staffs and in the field units.[2]

Flagstaff House was located on Sime Road, a huge double-storey bungalow, just before the Singapore Golf Club, sharing the same road.

Percival's home was just next door to the brand-new RAF headquarters, which had been completed in 1940. The RAF had been looking for a suitable headquarters for several years and numerous locations at Oxley Rise and Institution Hill had been considered before the Air Ministry agreed to the large site on Sime Road. The Headquarters would also be home to the Air Officer Commanding and provide administrative and operations rooms for the RAF. Initial costs for the new headquarters rose to £218,700 and were eventually approved with construction completed in two years.[3]

As the AOC's residence was enormous and RAF Headquarters was already short of space, Pulford decided to move in with Percival while his residence was then used as part of the headquarters office space.

As Pulford was one of the few who actually supported Percival in the internal politics of Malaya Command, it seemed logical for Percival to co-locate his new combined operations headquarters with the RAF, which would not only be next door to his residence but he would also be able to count on the support and help from his friend who would be working just next door.

However, the other Chiefs in Singapore did not feel the need to relocate. As a result, the navy only provided liaison officers at the combined headquarters but decisions could never be made by these low-level representatives:

Air Vice Marshal C.W.H. Pulford, Air Officer Commanding, RAF Malaya

> In 1936 the headquarters of the Naval Commander were in Singapore City. The Army headquarters were at Fort Canning, also in Singapore City, but those of the Royal Air Force were at Seletar on the north side of the island. In order to improve cooperation, the then AOC moved his headquarters into Singapore City, but about the same time the Naval headquarters were moved to the Naval Base on the north side of the island, to enable the commander to supervise better the rapid developments which were taking place there…
>
> … When the Commander-in-Chief, Far East (Air Chief Marshal Sir Robert Brooke-Popham) was appointed (1941), the problem of the location of headquarters again came to the front. If his headquarters had been located in the Singapore city area they would have been closer to those of the Army and Air Force and of the Civil Government, but would have been separated from those of the Commander-in-Chief China Station with whom much preliminary planning had to be done. Also the Far East Combined Bureau (Intelligence) which had come under the Commander-in-Chief China Station was located at the Naval Base. The Commander-In-Chief Far East was largely dependent on this bureau for his intelligence. He therefore decided to establish his headquarters at the Naval Base with the intention of moving to the Sime Road area should operations develop in Malaya. This is what actually happened.[4]

Brooke-Popham gave Percival immediate permission to build the new combined operations headquarters at Sime Road and work began without prior funding allocated from Whitehall. This upset the administrative mandarins at the War Office and Air Ministry as no funding approval or tender had been sought for the building of the new headquarters.

The Chief Engineer, Far East, had appointed the construction firm of Tan Eng Wah (the lowest of seven bids) in August 1940 to build the RAF's hutted office accommodation. Later, temporary accommodation was needed and Tan Eng Wah was paid a further £20,000 to carry it out. However, by mid 1941, there was no time left to call for quotes and tenders so the Chief Engineer gave the £120,000 combined headquarters project to Tan Eng Wah. After strong objection, Whitehall finally gave approval for a waiver of tender for the project on 17 January 1942, a month after the complex had already been built and three weeks before the Sime Road headquarters was abandoned to the advancing Japanese. However, it is not clear whether Tan Eng Wah was ever paid the full £120,000 as Singapore fell very shortly after the headquarters was completed.[5]

The new requirements for the combined headquarters were big. Office accommodation was built for 100 officers, 230 other ranks and 35 "Asiatic clerks", and housing for 42 officers, 5 warrant officers, 50 sergeants, 150 other ranks and 25 clerks, comprising "hutted accommodation for officers, officers mess and single officers' quarters, sergeants mess and quarters, huts for rank and file with dining halls, cookhouses, institutes, bath houses and latrines, large combined operations room, signal offices, guard room, mechanical and electrical services and all external services, with camouflage". The buildings would be dispersed in a rubber plantation and this would involve the extension of roads, lighting, water and drainage.[6]

By September 1941, the War Office informed Malaya Command that the Treasury's Inter-Service Committee had finally agreed to spend the £120,000, as an "operational necessity"[7] for "the extension of the accommodation to house, in temporary construction, the headquarters of the Army Command, Malaya, together with some additional Royal Air Force personnel, and to the erection of a combined operations room...."[8]

The new facilities at Sime Road consisted of several rows of hutted offices. On one side was RAF headquarters and on the other Army headquarters. The GOC and AOC, as well as senior officers, had offices located about a hundred yards from the Combined Operations Room.

Adjoining these offices was the Combined Operations Room, where the staff officers and clerks of the two services could work and plot the progress of operations. The room was filled with large plotting tables and charts, and manned round the clock. The room had direct phone lines to the Battlebox and the war room at the Naval Base, as well as secure links to the III Indian Corps in Kuala Lumpur via the telephone exchange at Fort Canning. The RAF had also built an independent wireless transmitting station at Sime Road and this would be used for all signals traffic generated by the Combined Headquarters.

The Battlebox at Fort Canning, however, would still remain crucial in operations. The Anti-Aircraft Gun Operations Room, which plotted air movements and was in control of all AA positions (which were mainly near airbases) in Malaya, was still located at the underground communications centre. The Naval Extended Defence Office, which controlled the sea-lanes off Singapore, would also remain at the Battlebox. Simmons, the Fortress Commander, took charge of the Battlebox, in order to coordinate the defence of Singapore.

On 6 December, 1941, barely two days before the Japanese invasion, the new combined headquarters at Sime Road was finally completed.

> ...It will thus be seen when hostilities started the headquarters of the Army, the Royal Air Force and of the Civil Government were grouped in one area (Sime Road and Government House), while

> those of the Commanders-In-Chief and of the Rear-Admiral Malaya were grouped in another (Naval Base), some 10 miles or more apart. This was far from an ideal solution, but possibly the best under the circumstances... This problem of the location of headquarters has been discussed at some length as showing the difficulties of reconciling the requirements of independent Services. Had there at that time been a Supreme Commander with an integrated staff probably many of these difficulties would have disappeared... The location of headquarters of the two Commanders-in-Chief and of the Fighting Services was a problem which received a great amount of attention but which was never satisfactorily settled. Probably there was no satisfactory solution.[9]

The new headquarters would prove to be a real challenge due to the poor construction of the buildings, the lack of space and the fact that most of the time the entire staff and commanders of the two headquarters would be in the combined operations room as their offices were too far away from the room.

However, even before the war started, Headquarters Malaya Command was faced with a more pressing problem – manpower:

> ... With the increase in the garrison as the defences developed and the relations with Japan became more strained, so there was an increase in the strength of Headquarters Malaya Command. The senior General Staff Officer, who had been a 2nd Grade Staff Officer in 1935, became a Brigadier in 1940. The senior Administrative Staff Officer was a Brigadier i/c Administration who, as is customary, was responsible to the War Office for control of expenditure on the administrative side. With the expansion of the command in 1941, the "A" and "Q" Branches were separated, a Deputy Adjutant General being appointed as Head of the "A" Branch while the Brigadier i/c Administration remained responsible for the "Q" Branch...
>
> ... After the outbreak of war with Germany the filling of vacancies on the staff became more and more difficult as the supply of trained staff officers in the Far East became exhausted. Regular units serving in Malaya were called upon to supply officers with qualifications until it became dangerous to weaken them any further and selected officers were sent for a short course of training at Quetta. The supply of trained officers from Home was naturally limited by the non-availability and by the difficulties of transportation...

> ... In 1941, sea voyages from the United Kingdom were taking 2 to 3 months so that there was a long delay in filling staff vacancies from Home even after approval had been given. In consequence, the strength of Headquarters Malaya Command was usually much below establishment. When war with Japan broke out there were less than 70 officers on Headquarters Malaya Command, including the Headquarters of the Services. This is about the war-time establishment of the Headquarters of a Corps. Our resources were thus strained to the limit...
>
> ... At the same time even before war broke out with Japan, the work at Headquarters Malaya Command was particularly heavy, including as it did war plans and the preparation of a country for war in addition to the training and administration of a rapidly increasing garrison. In addition, the Command was responsible for placing orders to bring up to the approved scale the reserves of all supplies and stores except as regards weapons and ammunition. In fact, Headquarters Malaya Command combined the functions of a local War Office and those of a Headquarters of a Field Force.[10]

Despite these challenges, the Combined Operations Room and the new headquarters at Sime Road were up and running on the morning of 6th December 1941. However, Percival would not be there to inaugurate the opening of the new complex. He was in Kuala Lumpur meeting with Brooke-Popham and Heath, discussing whether to implement Operation MATADOR, an offensive plan to capture parts of Siam (Thailand) and prevent a Japanese bridgehead, based on reports that Japanese troops would shortly be landing in Malaya.

The Location

There has been much controversy in recent years as to the location of the Combined Operations Headquarters at Sime Road.

A plaque was set up by the National Heritage Board next to a pill box on Sime Road to mark the site and it reads as follows, "The gun shelter, built sometime before 1941, defended Flagstaff House, the operational Headquarters of the British Army and Air Force during the Malayan Campaign".

Many have criticised the authorities for putting up the plaque, firstly because they say Flagstaff House was never in Sime Road and as such the pill box could not have been built some time before 1941 to defend the Combined Headquarters which was only set up in early December 1941.

The criticisms have been leveled because the history and location of the Combined Operations Headquarters were shrouded in secrecy in 1941 and with most of its occupants dead during the war; a proper account of its use has never been given.

The mystery still continues to haunt researchers as a majority of documents relating to the combined headquarters were destroyed in the fall of Singapore.

However, recently declassified files at the National Archives in London have provided a map of the area where the Combined Operations Headquarters was located, which shows the above-ground buildings that were constructed from the late 1930s to 1941.

There are two maps, which were declassified in the early 1970s and show the Sime Road area.

The first is a blueprint showing the layout of RAF Headquarters Far East in Sime Road in 1939, before the decision to set up a combined headquarters and combined operations room. It shows clearly a huge compound that was built by the RAF to house its headquarters, when it was shifted from Seletar by Pulford.

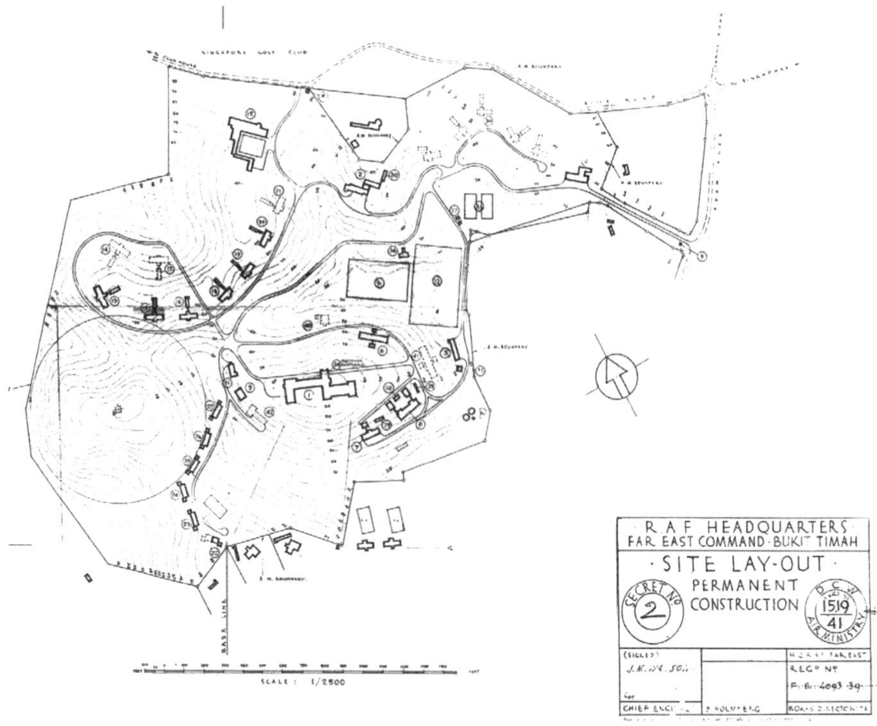

Blueprint from 1939 showing the layout of RAF Headquarters Far East in Sime Road.

The new compound, with the AOC's house, was next to Flagstaff House, Percival's official residence, on Sime Road. On the blueprint, Flagstaff House is not listed but the building has been drawn in. As it is adjacent to the AOC's House, the residence next door was clearly Flagstaff House.

Therefore, the pill box located on Sime Road was built to guard the RAF Headquarters and the AOC's Residence, work on which had begun in 1939. Flagstaff House and the RAF Headquaters and can be seen on the map but Flagstaff House was never the operational headquarters of the Army and Air Force. The AOC's house, however, was used as offices by RAF Headquarters. Therefore, the pill box did end up being used to guard Flagstaff House, the AOC's residence and the combined operations headquarters.

The newer map, an extracted photocopy of a larger map dating from the early 1950s, shows the two houses but the AOC's residence had changed in shape and structure and was now labeled, Commander-in-Chief's Residence (C-in-C, Far East Air Force), while the pre-war GOC's residence (Flagstaff House) was labeled as private property.

The post-war map also showed the hutted structures built in 1941 to accommodate the new army headquarters and the combined operations room. The long lines of hutted offices on the map were part of where the Army and RAF headquarters were located.

The 1950s map also shows a plotting shed in the Commander-in-Chief's compound and ancillary facilities that are labeled as part of the HQ Malaya area. The RAF Headquarters was shifted to Changi and renamed HQ FEAF (HQ Far East Air Force). The offices in Sime Road were taken over by the Air Ministry's Department of General Works (AMDGW) as well as by the MPBW HQ (Ministry of Public Buildings and Works). As there was obviously no need for a plotting shed for the works departments, the shed and the office buildings nearby must have been part of the earlier Combined Operations Headquarters. Just opposite the AMDGW offices are the outlines of a building, which are believed to be some of the hutted offices of the Army. Together, this whole area would have been the nerve centre of the British and Commonwealth land and air forces as the Malayan Campaign began.

Many of the bungalows and residences listed in the 1939 blueprint do not exist on the 1950s map as many were not built due to financial constraints while other structures were added as part of the new complex. The RAF Headquarters building as listed in the 1939 blueprint also does not exist, giving more support to the fact that the AOC's residence was used as offices for RAF Headquarters.

The map of the post-war RAF compound shows the residence of the Far East Air Force's Commander-in-Chief, which had come to be known as Air House or the Air Marshal's House. Admiralty records from the post-war period show that the Air Officer Commanding, RAF, no longer shared accommodation with the GOC at Flagstaff House but now resided at Cluny Road. The Commander-in-Chief, Far East Land Forces, who was based in Singapore, now took over Flagstaff House while the General Officer Commanding, Malaya Command (and subsequently Singapore Base District), moved into Draycott House along Stevens Road.[11]

Another residence on Kheam Hock Road, Command House, was temporarily occupied by the GOC before he moved to Draycott House and

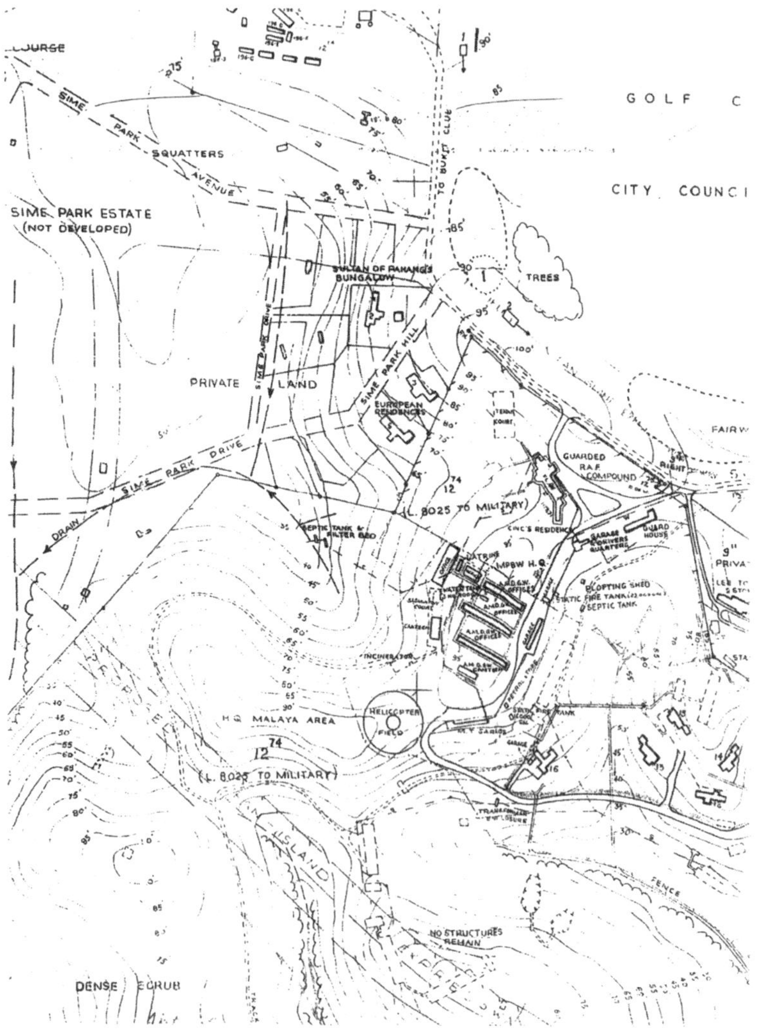

Post-World War II map from the 1950s showing the layout of military buildings at the Sime Road Complex.

Command House then became the residence of the Chief Justice.

In Colonial Office correspondence from the late 1950s, Command House, Air House and Flagstaff House were named as choices for the new residence of the UK Commissioner-General for Southeast Asia.[12] With Yusof Ishak appointed as the Yang Di-Pertuan Negara (Head of State) of Singapore, there was no longer a British Governor of Singapore and the Commissioner General, Lord Selkirk, based in Singapore, would then be the most senior UK representative on the island and would have to have a residence befitting that stature. The Commissioner General eventually became the British High Commissioner to Singapore when the Republic gained independence in 1965. In the end, the Colonial Office decided not to take any of the three options but rather to keep Eden Hall, the earlier residence of the Commissioner General.

Command, Air and Flagstaff House were handed over to the Singapore Government sometime in 1971 as part of the disposal of British military real estate, when the British forces finally pulled out of the island. Treasury minutes valued Flagstaff House at £414,650, Air House and the surrounding land at £1,025,521 and Command House at £239,312. The files, declassified in 2004, indicate that the Singapore Government received these residences and numerous other military facilities and moveable assets as gifts worth about £135 million (S$405 Million) when the British pulled out.[13] This was in addition to the £50 Million committed by the British Government in 1968, over a five-year period, to mitigate the economic effects of the planned withdrawal of British forces in the area. However, the £135 million figure was revised down to £109 million as the British government decided to hold on to the MPBW HQ and the compound surrounding Air House at Sime Road as well as several other facilities in Singapore for a while longer. Most of these facilities are believed to have been eventually handed over to the Singapore Government.[14]

Command House was then occupied by independent Singapore's first Chief Justice and later became the official residence of the Speaker of Parliament but remained unused by him. It was then refurbished in the 1990s and used temporarily as the residence of the President of Singapore while the Istana (Government House) was being restored.

At present Command House lies vacant. There is no information on what happened to Air House and Flagstaff House, or who are their present occupants, after the buildings were handed back to the Singapore government. Today, the combined headquarters area at Sime Road has been redeveloped but some of the bungalows attached to the compound have been preserved and are at present being rented out to expatriates who enjoy living in one of the few "black and white" colonial homes on the island.

Endnotes

1 Percival, A.E. *The War in Malaya*. Eyre & Spottiswoode, London, 1949.

2 Ibid

3 *0.5., Command Headquarters, 26 October 1938, Air Ministry File No: S35559/Pt II, AIR2/1603.* The National Archives, London.

4 Percival, A.E. *The War in Malaya*. Eyre & Spottiswoode, London, 1949.

5 *275, D.U.S.,15 January, 1942, Air Ministry File No: S35559/Pt II, AIR2/1603.* The National Archives, London.

6 *Accomodation for Army Headquarters, Malaya, at Bukit Timah, Treasury Inter-Service Committee, August, 1941, AIR2/1603.* The National Archives, London

7 Ibid

8 *118/MALAYA/207(F.W.1b), 29 September, 1941, AIR2/1603.* The National Archives, London.

9 *Percival, A.E. Draft of Despatches, P16-27.* The Imperial War Museum, London.

10 Ibid

11 *Land Occupied by the United Kingdom Services in Singapore, undated, ADM1/28453.* The National Archives, London.

12 *Extract from note about accommodation for the U.K. Commission in Singapore, c1959, CO1030/873.* The National Archives, London.

13 *Undated Treasury Minute, 1971 concerning the gift of fixed assets and equipment to the Government of Malaysia (Singapore portion), WO32/21583.* The National Archives, London.

14 *Undated Treasury Minute, 1971 concerning the gift of fixed assets and equipment to the Government of Singapore, WO32/21684.* The National Archives, London.

Chapter 5

The Battlebox and the Malayan Campaign

As the battle for Malaya began on 8 December 1941 and the losses on the British side began to mount, the mood in the Combined Operations headquarters became sombre indeed. As state after Malayan state fell to the oncoming Japanese while the Allies retreated, there was a sense of gloom in Sime Road that the end was nearing.

> The new combined headquarters for the army and RAF had only opened in Sime Road just two days before hostilities began. Although the main operations and war room were now located at the combined headquarters, the Navy still operated its own operations room at the Naval Base and stationed liaison officers at the Sime Road headquarters. Moreover, the Battlebox at Fort Canning would still be occupied by Simmons, along with the anti-aircraft Gun Operations Room and the Naval extended defences offices. This meant that the battle for Malaya would be fought from the new Sime Road headquarters while the Singapore defences and operations would be carried out of the Battlebox, with the exception of anti-aircraft gun defences for Malaya which would still be run out of the Battlebox.[1]

In theory, there was a very clear separation of duties and lines of communication. In practice, however, the lack of skilled manpower to run two almost identical war rooms and insufficient clarity among field commanders and officers in Malaya meant that many operational calls and signals were still being routed to Fort Canning which then had to be re-routed to Sime Road. As a result, the decentralised war rooms created greater confusion and down time as it took ages for ground intelligence and reports to filter up and be represented on duplicate situation charts and plots so that planners at Sime Road could work on an attack strategy while plotters at the Battlebox could advise anti-aircraft batteries throughout the peninsula to open fire on targets.

Headquarters Malaya Command took its signals situation seriously. Command Signals was responsible for communication sent outside the island while Fortress Signals was responsible for signals within the island. However, this distinction became blurred with the quick losses faced up-country and Fortress Signals ended up with the role of keeping the battlebox and combined headquarters operational. It was critical that the command headquarters and formations remain in communication and Fortress Signals worked continuously in the days leading up to hostilities, preparing the various trunk and cable lines for use by field and rear headquarters.

On the first of December, Fortress Signal's War Diary showed that at 1100hrs, the codeword "SEAVIEW" had been issued, the command for troops to move forward into prepared positions throughout Malaya. An hour later, the codeword "OILCAN" was issued, ordering the mobilisation of the Federated Malay States Volunteer Force.[2]

By 6 December 1941, it was clear that the Japanese were going to attack and after meetings with Heath in Kuala Lumpur, Brooke-Popham, in consultation with Percival, ordered Fortress Signals to issue the codeword "RAFFLES", the order to bring all troops to the first degree of readiness.[3]

The amount of intelligence predicting a Japanese attack was overwhelming. Air reconnaissance and intercepted signals traffic had indicated an impending Japanese fleet headed towards Malaya. Prior to the outbreak of War, signals intelligence became crucial in determining the state of readiness of the Japanese forces and their exact plans in attacking Malaya.

A "Y" SIGINT (Signal Intelligence) Unit had been set up at the RAF wireless transmitting station in Kranji (No. 52 W.U.), picking up information on the strengths of the Japanese naval air arm from air to ground and ground to air traffic.[4]

The "Y" unit was part of the Far East Combined Bureau, set up in Hong Kong in 1934 and charged with the interception and decoding of Japanese signal intelligence. The FECB was officially known as the Centre for Operational Intelligence and Signals (COIS), which provided the most sensitive and secret operational information for British commanders in the field.

The FECB was based at the headquarters of and reported to the Commander-in-Chief, China Fleet, Vice Admiral Sir Geoffrey Layton at the Naval Base in northern Singapore. As this was a major source of intelligence, Brooke-Popham also needed to be close to this facility and so did not locate himself at the Battlebox at Fort Canning or in the Combined Headquarters at Sime Road. What this meant was that the Commander-in-Chief, Far East and the Naval Commander for Malaya were based at the Naval Base while the Army and Air Commanders were based at Sime Road. Thus the defences of Malaya were split between the Naval Base and Sime Road, with the Battlebox becoming a third command centre to take charge of the Singapore aspect of operations.

As a result, all intelligence information received and decoded had to be routed by the FECB to the two other service chiefs at Sime Road with a copy to the Battlebox as needed:

> In Hong Kong days the office of the Captain of the Staff China Station, in practice, formed the intelligence Section of the Sigint Organisation which predominated over it in numbers but was itself administratively under the COIS. At Hong Kong and later Singapore where it was known as the FECB, the COIS organisation was an inter-service one and equipped to handle collation and dissemination of Naval, Military, Air and Political Intelligence.[5]

The dissemination of intelligence was sent by 'Most Secret' signals originated by FECB. In their offices at the naval base and Fort Canning, a card index of naval and naval air intelligence was started and although some reference to back material was possible, a lack of manpower meant that there was no production of regular summaries.

Although the FECB suffered from insufficient manpower, the receiving stations picked up very useful intelligence that was becoming more worrisome by the day. Signs of Japanese intentions for an attack were obvious in the intercepted Japanese diplomatic traffic. However, the military commanders in Southeast Asia had little faith in these new forms of intelligence gathering and disregarded much of the contents of the daily situation reports.

Despite FECB intercepts on an imminent Japanese invasion, Brooke-Popham announced that Japan could not go to War before February 1942.

In general, Malaya Command's intelligence unit relied on the local intelligence branches of the civilian police and its remit was only to cover what was happening within the country. As such the General Staff Officer (Intelligence) for Malaya Command produced an appreciation of situation arguing that Japanese forces could not land on the east coast of the Malay Peninsula in the monsoon then prevailing and that there was only one road down the peninsula, which could be held by two battalions. More importantly, it noted that tanks could not be used in the country.

Brooke-Popham, Percival and his fellow generals, who had access to the "Y" and intelligence intercepts from the FECB, clearly failed to grasp the importance of the information they were provided with. Even if they did, their actions showed that the information they had received was obviously rejected in the decisions they made.

The FECB had found a Japanese spy holed up in Singapore. Through intercepts, it had determined that a Japanese Major General was concealed in the Japanese Consul's office in Singapore as a "language officer who reported closely upon the numbers and efficiency of the British forces there. Apparently also the correspondence with him included an outline of the plans forecast and estimates of the length of time and strength necessary to knock out certain defensive positions"[6].

The intercepts, which had been translated verbatim and were filled with flowery Japanese speech, were sent to Malaya Command. Instead of acting on the report, the officer in charge poked fun at the flowery speech and refused to take the report seriously.

Again from diplomatic sources (intercepted diplomatic telegrams from Tokyo) the FECB informed Malaya Command of the Japanese arrangements for notifying their decision to commence hostilities. The words "East Wind" and "West Wind" appearing at the end of certain broadcasts meant that it had been decided to break off relations with the US (East), USSR (North), UK (West).[7]

FECB urgently alerted Hong Kong and the Americans at Corregidor to this message but it was Hong Kong who first heard the fateful message on 7 December 1941. On that day, as Japan geared up for its attack on the American Fleet in Pearl Harbor and British forces in Malaya, the Japanese diplomatic and consular messages between Tokyo, the Philippines, Malaya and the Netherlands East Indies, which had formed the bulk of diplomatic special intelligence for the FECB, suddenly ceased.

A few months earlier, the Japanese had also changed its JN25 code, the main code used by the Japanese military in communicating with its units. Through a lack of staff and machinery, the JN25 code was left to Bletchley Park and Washington. Days before the Japanese invasion, they changed their fleet code. So by the evening of the 7th, FECB was unable to read the Japanese air, army and fleet signals, and all diplomatic signals, which they had previously been intercepting, had also stopped.

This in itself, however, should have been a big enough warning for the generals at Malaya Command that the Japanese attack was imminent.

Just before Pearl Harbor in Hawaii was attacked at 3:25am on 8 December 1941 (Tokyo time), the Japanese 25th Army's 18th Division had already landed at Kota Bahru in Northern Malaya at 2:15am. Another

Japanese Division, the 5th, landed in Singora and Pattani in Southern Thailand at 4am.

The Japanese landings at Kota Bahru were met with stiff resistance. These landings marked the start of the Malayan Campaign, the Japanese planned conquest of Malaya.

The Japanese plan was to capture Singapore, where the British naval base and the headquarters of the British Army were located. On the same day, 17 Japanese navy bombers flying from Saigon (now Ho Chi Minh City), attacked the Keppel Harbour docks, the Naval Base in Sembawang as well as the Seletar and Tengah air bases in Singapore. The "Y" station, which had been keeping a 24-hour watch, gave the warning at 0345 hours of the pending air attack over Singapore. The top-secret radar facilities had also been tracking the large number of Japanese aircraft and provided a warning of a large convoy of unidentified planes headed for Singapore. However, Governor Shenton Thomas' decision to disallow sounding the air raid sirens without his explicit permission meant that the sirens came on only after some of the first bombs had hit Singapore. The lights of the city were ablaze as the official responsible had taken home the keys to the light switch boxes.

Following the outbreak of hostilities, it was recommended that the commanders at Singapore should receive all the aid they needed for the defence of Singapore and the army and RAF had enough "Y" operators in Singapore to receive and translate the necessary Japanese army and air traffic.

However, the lack of cooperation from the navy, the naval Extended Defence Office at the Battlebox and the new combined air and army Headquarters at Sime Road meant that a naval disaster that could have been prevented was about to occur.

At dusk on 8 December, the *Prince of Wales* and the *Repulse*, two capital ships and Singapore's main naval strength, also known as Force Z, left for their ill-fated journey to intercept the Japanese landings in Malaya – a trip which left more than 800 Allied sailors dead and the two ships sunk when Japanese aircraft intercepted and dive-bombed the two ships and their escort vessels off Kuantan on 10 December, marking the end of the naval war in the campaign just two days after hostilities began.

The two ships were alongside the main wharf and could be seen from the FECB's offices at the Naval Base on 8 December. However, the two ships disappeared on the 9 December and that visual disappearance was the last bit of information the FECB had on the two ships. The FECB had earlier given notice of a Japanese fleet off the South China Sea and this was what the ships had gone to investigate. However, no one at the

Battlebox or combined headquarters had told the FECB that Force Z had been scrambled to meet this threat. Not keeping the FECB informed about ongoing operations meant that the signal intelligence officers were not overly concerned about a Japanese report in P/L (plain language) on 10 December, which said British capital ships were sighted at a specific position off Kuantan. Although Malaya Command and the Admiralty were informed immediately, no one at these headquarters had pieced the two together and realised that Japanese fighters had obviously spotted Force Z and were now planning to destroy it. Had the FECB been kept in the loop, it is highly likely that defensive air cover would have been sent sooner to aid the capital ships, rather than only after receiving distress calls from the floundering vessels.

The Japanese decision to use plain language for operational purposes in emergencies was also surprising as it was expected that they would always communicate in code. As a result, a linguist was continually on duty at the "Y" station in Kranji to deal immediately with such intercepts. This was good news.

> They reported that three new uncyphered codes, apparently naval, air division and air to ground, were being used extensively by the Japanese during operations and they thought it was very promising and they also noted that Jap. P/L (plain language) sighting reports of our forces were invaluable – Interpreters were continually on duty at the W/T station and passed information by telephone to the War Room (at the Combined Headquarters at Sime Road).[8]

However, the intelligence gained was sent to COIS, which felt it was of a low grade and did not need to be distributed to the Commanders-in-Chief. This meant that the Commanders-in-Chief were kept out of the loop on many of the signals coups achieved by "Y" station.

Moreover, with the failure to activate Operation MATADOR early enough to forestall the Japanese in Thai territory, the British high command gave the enemy enough time to build a beach head and land an attacking force that pushed hard against the British defenders.

The confusion in the first few days, which led to many retreats, marked how the British would fight the entire campaign.

The level of confusion and the lack of information in the rear headquarters verged almost on the comical. Unclear orders and diversions of troops meant that military communications in Malaya were affected. There were insufficient secure telephone lines from III Indian Corps in Kuala Lumpur to the combined headquarters at Sime Road and Headquarters Malaya Command at Fort Canning. As a result, it was impossible to get updated reports on what was happening in northern Malaya. Some of the forward field headquarters of the various fighting divisions which relayed reports to their corps headquarters in Kuala Lumpur were unable to get a response on further directions from Heath as Heath was unable to get in touch with Percival in Singapore in order for strategic decisions to be made:

> ...We turned up at the signal office (Kuala Lumpur) and found a situation of almost panic. All the lights on the sixty line switchboard were lit and waiting to be put through and the only direct line to Singapore was not being used. A call from General Percival to be put through on the scrambler phone to HQ Far East had been kept waiting as the new man did not know how to initiate such a call.[9]

As a result, the new combined headquarters, with limited communication lines and working with inexperienced staff up-country posed a serious problem from the start. Thus, this lack of a proper command, control and communications setup contributed in part to the daily losses faced by the British.

The situation at the Battlebox had also become more complicated with new anti-aircraft gun positions being set up as old ones were captured by the enemy. By the middle of December, Fortress Signals had to install a fourth multiphone at the Gun Operations Room to accommodate three new gun positions.[10]

As the overall operational headquarters in Malaya, the combined headquarters at Sime Road should have been at the centre of command, control and communications. Instead, the commanders had huge difficulty even determining what was happening on the ground and then even more problems in issuing orders. Often, Percival would have to drive all the way up to Kuala Lumpur in order to consult with Heath and shape the direction of the battles. With overloaded communications facilities, it was not until the end of December that Fortress Signals set up three new 7-pair cables from Sime Road to the Bukit Timah exchange[11] in order to ease the signals traffic situation and provide enough signal lines for combined headquarters to communicate directly with other divisional and corps headquarters in the field rather than through the Fort Canning exchange.

The idea of a combined headquarters, which Percival had pushed through, was, in theory, sound:

> A large room where the army and air force staffs could work at Sime Road adjoining R.A.F. Headquarters. On the other side of it were built offices for the Army operational staff. The idea was that the staff officers of the two services and their clerks should all work in the

> Combined Operations Room, though they had their own rooms to which they could go if they wanted to. This was excellent in theory. In practice, it had many faults. It meant that our staff officers were permanently in that room because they could not in fact work in two places. That in turn meant that their clerks were permanently there too and – worse than that – it meant that the commanders had to spend much of their time there, so as to be close to their staff officers. Had we worked entirely in our own offices, either we or our staff officers would have been faced with a journey of a hundred yards or so every time we wanted to talk to each other – and that during the black-out was not too pleasant.[12]

More importantly, the newly built huts and facilities for the combined headquarters suffered from shoddy workmanship and poor planning. There was a lack of desk and planning areas as well as effective ventilation and cooling machines:

> The conditions in the Combined Operations Room were not conducive to good work or clear thinking. They were too cramped and there was too much noise. The problem may not arise again in these days of integrated staffs, but I am sure the right solution in those conditions is for staffs to work in their own offices and to have a common room where everything of interest to all Services, i.e. situation maps, intelligence reports, messages, etc., can be seen, and where conferences can be held. It may seem a small point to some, but I feel sure that all who have had experience of the working of headquarter staffs will agree with me that the conditions under which they work have a very great influence on their efficiency and, in consequence, on the efficiency of the fighting formations which they direct.[13]

The stresses of an inadequate headquarters and war operations room clearly handicapped British decision making and the large time lags in giving instructions would have in part led to early retreats by inexperienced troops, who could not wait for instructions that may or may not have even been received by their commanders in the rear.

By Christmas Day 1941, Hong Kong had fallen and the Japanese had seized all Malayan territory lying north and west of the Perak River. This included Penang Island, the states of Perlis, Kedah, Kelantan and a greater part of Perak.

They had also destroyed the backbone of the RAF squadrons and seized all its northern airstrips, thanks in no small measure to a British traitor based at the Alor Star airfield who conveyed flight and attack plans to the Japanese via a secret wireless transmitter. By the time he was caught, Captain P.S.V. Heenan had contributed significantly to the huge loss of RAF aircraft and northern airfields in the theatre. The airfields would never be recaptured.[14]

It was a losing battle all the way down the peninsula and by 30 January, the retreat of the British and Commonwealth troops was almost complete with the loss of the whole of Malaya. Piped across by Highland bagpipers, the Argyll and Sutherland Higlanders' slow march across the causeway linking the Malayan mainland to the island of Singapore marked the end of the battle for Malaya and the start of the battle for Singapore.

By January, the FECB had also packed up most of its kit and were preparing to sail off for Colombo, in anticipation of the fall of Singapore. Major John Westall, a Royal Marine Staff Officer (Intelligence) at the signals office in the Naval Base noted that Japanese "naval intelligence was unobtainable by the end of Jan 1942. All reporting officers had fled or been captured... FECB had left for Colombo and Staff Officer (Intelligence) Singapore was mainly engaged on liaison with the civil authorities"[15].

In defence of the intelligence officers, he pointed out that the giving out of a general and effective warning of impeding Japanese attack was the responsibility of the FECB and this is what they did. They also warned about the departure of a big Japanese convoy which Admiral Tom Phillips and Force Z (HMS *Prince of Wales* and HMS *Repulse*) had attempted to intercept before they met their end on 10 December:

> Further action would have been taken on these reports had it not been for the fact that up-to-date information from these – 'particularly sources' was treated as being so secret that no action could be taken.[16]

> The FECB had left two interpreters, Colgrave and Cooper, along with minimal equipment, to provide air intelligence while the rest of the team evacuated. Cooper started to work on Japanese naval air R/T (radio transmissions).

> He proved that it could be taken and used and was drafted into carrying out watches with Colgrave at the headphone. Cooper, who had lived in Japan found the work comparatively easy. Japanese security was not high and after study of bomber radio transmissions they were able to elicit that formations, recognizable by some sort of unchanging pet names, specialised upon certain targets. Thus when the unit airborne was recognised its probable target could be foretold, while from counting the number of individual calls and acknowledgements the strength of the forces airborne could

> be assessed. Results were telephoned to the local RAF defence and several successful actions were fought, when after the first two or three days the RAF learnt to rely upon the accuracy of this information. A certain small amount of low-grade cipher was taken and read but R/T were the thing.[17]

However, this intelligence information proved to be too little, too late. The RAF in Malaya had been effectively destroyed, thanks to Japanese attacks and Captain Heenan's treachery. It was now an issue of how to prevent an even greater loss of lives and destruction of military forces. The RAF finally, through the combined operations headquarters in Sime Road, began providing this signals intelligence to the various anti-aircraft batteries throughout Malaya. Although it was sporadic, the information did help to partially counter some air attacks. This, however, remained more the exception than the rule.

However, very little of this signals intelligence actually reached the Commanders-in-Chief. After the fall of Singapore, Vice Admiral Sir Geoffrey Layton, the Commander-in-Chief, China Fleet (to whom FECB reported in Singapore) had escaped to Ceylon along with the rest of the bureau. He gave the outfit a week to come up with useful information or be shut down. Layton commented that the two officers left in Singapore had come up with more results than the bureau put together. Layton had never received the extensive intelligence findings that the FECB had given to Malaya Command nor was he made aware of the bureau's warnings about the *Prince of Wales* and *Repulse*. As COIS had filtered most of the reports to Layton, it was ironic that the unit which provided so much useful intelligence was now going to be shut for not allegedly providing any information.[18]

By 31 January 1942, Johore state was in the hands of the Japanese. The retreating forces blew up the Causeway behind them, creating a 60-yard gap, but this was quickly repaired by Japanese engineers by 11 February and was used to bring tanks and mechanised vehicles onto the island.

One of the reasons for the swift descent of Japanese troops down Malaya was their ingenious use of bicycles and boats made of light steel and kapok wood, many of which were confiscated from the local population.

Moreover, the Japanese, after campaigns in China and additional training, were better suited to the climate and ate off the land as opposed to the Allied troops, many of whom had only recently been in-country and did not eat the local food which was rice-based.

The Japanese also used old roads and paths in the jungles to outflank most of the Allied troops who guarded the main north-south road and left their sides exposed. By using small boats, the Japanese were able to land behind the British troops and create confusion in rear areas causing the British to retreat further.

As the British had lost most of their naval elements and the RAF was almost non-existent after the first week of war, their positions were easily strafed and most troop movements had to be done in the cover of darkness.

The Japanese use of armour in the form of tanks allowed them to plough through the weak British defences and race down the peninsula, with the Allies in full retreat.

As lines of communications were destroyed, it was hard to determine what was happening in the front lines and junior officers made tactical and strategic withdrawal decisions without consulting senior commanders, leading to missing units and a very confused picture of the war on the plotting tables at the combined headquarters in Singapore.

Before the Japanese invasion in late 1941, Percival had ignored all proposals by Simson to shore up the northern defences of Singapore. Simson pointed out that all the fixed defences were guarding the south against an invasion from the sea. He was quite sure that the Japanese assault would come from the north, across the straits instead.

However, Percival felt that it was bad for the morale of the troops and civilians if such measures were taken. Percival also believed that the Japanese assault, if it came from the north, would come from the northeast where four batteries of 6- and 15-inch guns provided firepower. This thinking differed from his original assessment as a staff officer in Malaya Command in the 1930s when he predicted an attack from the northwest. His original assessment would prove prophetic. Thus, Singapore was deprived of solid northern defences.

Till late 1941, everyone believed that Singapore, the "Impregnable Fortress", would not be affected by the war. She was protected from the north by thick Malayan jungles and from the south by coastal guns, spotted all along the eastern and southwestern coasts of Singapore. Troop reinforcements and the arrival of the *Prince of Wales* and the *Repulse* lulled the people into feeling that the British could easily drive off the Japanese.

Percival had about 80,000 troops disposed all over peninsular Malaya in fortified positions, guarding airfields and important installations. He had no tanks (only bren carriers) and 150 obsolete planes. His navy had suffered a great loss with the sinking of the *Prince of Wales* and the *Repulse*. Britain had no ships left to send down to Singapore and the attack on the American Pacific fleet at Pearl Harbor meant that the US had no major battleships in the region that could assist the British.

The Japanese 25th Army – comprising the 5th, 18th and Imperial Guards Division – had about 67,000 men with 150 tanks and 560 first-line aircraft. Though smaller in number in terms of men, it had superior air support, naval elements and tanks.

Besides the British troops, Singapore's local units consisted of four battalions of the Straits Settlements Volunteer Corps and a small civil defence force. With the impending Japanese attack, the Chinese put aside their various differences and offered their services to the Governor, Sir Shenton Thomas. As a result, the Chinese National Council was formed on 31 December 1941 under the leadership of Tan Kah Kee, a prominent businessman.

Receiving enthusiastic support, the council, through volunteers like Lim Bo Seng, organised labour forces to maintain essential services and construct defence works. Selected members were trained for combat and guerrilla warfare in Japanese-occupied territories. Soon they became the pioneering members of the Malayan People's Anti-Japanese Army.

As the Japanese gathered on the banks of the Johore Straits before beginning their invasion of the island, Percival's plan for the defence of Singapore was to divide the country into three defence sectors. Heath was put in command of the northern sector, with the British 18th Division, the Indian 11th and what remained of the 9th Division under his command; Major General Gordon Bennett, Commander of the Australian Imperial Forces, was in charge of the western sector, with his relatively fresh Australian troops and the untrained Indian 44th Infantry Brigade under his command; Simmons took care of the southern sector, with the 1st and 2nd Malaya Infantry Regiment, the Straits Settlements Volunteer Force, fortress troops and fixed defences under his charge.

Bennett's defence of the 4.5-mile northwest coastline, stretching from Kranji River to Sarimbun River, was very weak. It was far too extended for his troops, numbering around 750 men. The mangrove swamps and the heavy jungle prohibited construction of defence obstacles. This was to prove fatal.

At Kluang, Johore, on 1 February 1942, Lieutenant General Tomoyuki Yamashita, the Commander of the Japanese forces in the Malayan Campaign, revealed his assault plans to his commanders. The initial thrust would be aimed at the northwestern shoreline. He tasked the 5th and 18th Divisions for the job. The Imperial Guards Division would create a diversion in the east (Pulau Ubin) to fool Malaya Command, and heavy artillery bombardment would be directed along the entire northern sector of Singapore to conceal the actual landing areas.

After securing a foothold in Singapore, Yamashita's first task was to capture Tengah airfield, followed by the capture of Mandai village. The next target was to be the Bukit Timah high ground and then to the Seletar, Pierce and MacRitchie reservoirs. Yamashita hoped to cut off the water supply to the island and force an early surrender of the British.

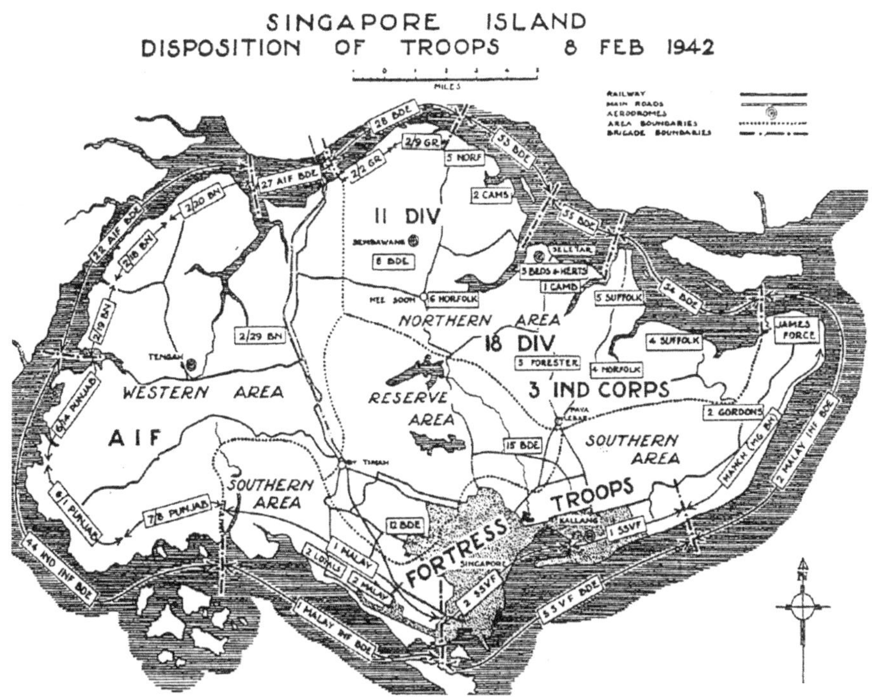

Percival's final disposition of troops before the Battle for Singapore. The Australians in the northwest would face the brunt of the enemy invasion.

Meanwhile, the Japanese air force, free to roam Singapore's skies, raided the Royal Navy's oil storage tanks at the Naval Base, sending huge columns of dense black smoke into the air. They also attacked the Tanjong Pagar railway station.

Japanese intelligence dispatched two teams of swimmers across the straits on 3 February to gather information on the Australian artillery and troop positions. They reported back after three days with very accurate sketches.

On 6 February, Yamashita shifted his headquarters to the Sultan of Johore's Palace at Bukit Serene. This provided him with a good view of the key targets, only a mile away across the Straits. The Palace was never harassed by the Australians who were guarding that sector because it was the ancestral home of their old friend Sultan Ibrahim, who was very close to Bennett. Any damage to his residence would have had extensive repercussions to these ties.

Soon after nightfall on 7 February, 400 men of the Japanese Imperial Guards Division landed and occupied Pulau Ubin in a feint attack. They encountered minimum resistance. Though large troop movements in the Johore rubber plantations across from the north western sector of Singapore had been sighted earlier, no action was taken as Percival received the intelligence report only hours before the attack.

The Japanese artillery began intensive firing and Japanese planes also began bombing the military headquarters within the western sector. Telegraph and telephone communications were destroyed in this bombardment. By nightfall, communications throughout the northwest defence areas were in shambles and communications between the front line and command headquarters were broken.

On the night of 8 February, Japanese troops of the 5th and 18th Division began to cross the straits using sea craft hidden near the water's edge. These were launched in the backwaters of the Skudai, Danga, Perpet and Melayu rivers. This first assault was repelled by Australian machine-gunners, but other sea craft were able to seek and infiltrate gaps in the defence line.

By the third wave, the Australians were outnumbered and overwhelmed as machine gunners soon ran out of ammunition and the troops were crippled by the breakdown of communications with their command headquarters. At midnight, a red star shell burst over the Straits indicating to Yamashita the 5th Division's successful landing on Singapore soil. A white star shell burst later, to confirm the 18th Division's successful infiltration.

The Australians were unable to hold back the Japanese advance towards Tengah airfield for long. The Australian commander, Brigadier H.B. Taylor, planned to counterattack the Japanese's two-pronged movement towards Lim Chu Kang Rd and Choa Chu Kang Rd, but was foiled as the frontline troops were in disarray. He endeavoured to form a defence line running down Lim Chu Kang Rd to its junction with Choa Chu Kang Rd and westwards to Choa Chu Kang village. However, heavy artillery fire and Japanese air bombardment forced him to withdraw to the Kranji-Jurong line on the afternoon of 9 February.

The Kranji-Jurong Line was an arbitrary line drawn from Kranji river to Jurong river. Loss of areas along this line meant that the Japanese would be able to advance down to the city from the west and through Bukit Timah Road.

Due to the importance of this line, Percival ordered reinforcements to the Bukit Panjang-Keat Hong Road junction to the right of the line. One Australian brigade was to remain holding the Causeway sector while another brigade would try to stabilise the Kranji-Jurong Line. The 44th Indian Brigade in the west was also withdrawn to the left of the Kranji-Jurong Line while another Indian Brigade was to move to the Bukit Timah race course to protect the island's vital food and petrol supplies located nearby.

However, Percival knew this might not be enough to hold back the Japanese and made preparations for a last desperate stand. He planned to hold a perimeter covering Kallang aerodrome, MacRitchie and Pierce reservoirs and the Bukit Timah supply depot area. He issued this instruction in secret to his three commanders. But these instructions were soon to be misunderstood by Taylor.

On 10 February, the Japanese suffered one of their major losses at the Kranji river. The Imperial Guards, while moving up the Kranji river at midnight, got bogged down in the mangrove swamps and lost in the tributaries. Many died when Australian soldiers set fire to oil from demolished fuel tanks which gushed into the waterways burning everything in sight.

General Nishimura, the commander of the Imperial Guards, in panic, wanted permission to withdraw but was reprimanded by Yamashita. However, through a misunderstanding of orders, the Australians started withdrawing from the causeway sector, giving the invaders the liberty to move further inland.

It was at this time that Yamashita first stepped onto Singapore island in the predawn darkness and set up his mobile headquarters in a rubber plantation just north of Tengah airfield.

Over at the Kranji-Jurong Line, Taylor, who received a coded signal modified by Bennett, regarding Percival's last stand plans, misread them. He took it as an instruction to head immediately to the defence perimeter positions. This set in motion a series of related withdrawals from the northern sector of the Kranji-Jurong Line which allowed the Japanese to swiftly take control of Woodlands Road.

At 1:30pm on the same day, the 44th Indian Brigade was also in full retreat from the southern extreme of the Kranji-Jurong Line following clashes with Japanese infantry units and having suffered heavy air and artillery bombardment. Through a series of miscalculations and miscommunication, the Kranji-Jurong Line was wrested away from the British by mid-afternoon.

Japanese tanks also made their first appearance on the island on 10 February. They were floated across the Straits to Lim Chu Kang Road early in the day, and joined in the battle at dusk. They made their way down Choa Chu Kang Road and stopped at the Bukit Panjang Village and Bukit Timah Road junction to wait for more ammunition supplies and support artillery. The Australian troops were no match for the tanks and fled to the hills east of Bukit Panjang Village.

11 February 1942 was Kigensetsu, the anniversary celebration of the coronation of Emperor Jimmu, who founded the Chrysanthemum Throne and began the present dynasty. This was also the day Yamashita had hoped to capture Singapore.

Ammunition supplies were running low for the Japanese forces. He had letters dropped over Headquarters Malaya Command areas urging Percival to give up his desperate fight, hoping for an early surrender.

It was also on the morning of 11 February that Percival finally moved his Combined Operations Headquarters from the compound in Sime Road back to the Battlebox at Fort Canning. With this, he abandoned his home at Flagstaff House and would, from now, be sleeping in his above-ground office at Fort Canning. Four days later, it would all be over.

> At 6am on the eleventh, after a few hours' sleep at Sime Road, I woke up to the sounds of machine-gun fire. Thinking it was probably only some anti-aircraft fire, I sent my A.D.C., Stonor of the Argylls, who had been untiring in his efforts to help me the whole campaign, out to investigate. He soon came back saying there appeared to be a battle going on beyond the end of the golf-course about a mile from where we were. I thought it was time to move. We had prepared an alternative headquarters on Thomson Road but there was no point in going there now, so I decided to join rear headquarters at Fort Canning.[19]

At the Battlebox, the situation had become confused as the whole of the Combined headquarters along with air liaison elements shifted their operations into the complex. Air Headquarters had decided to move to 300 Thomson Road but by 12 February was already overrun. With that the RAF's role came to a final halt in Singapore.

By now, there was not much of the battle left to direct out of the Battlebox. The whole of Malaya had been lost and more than half of Singapore island had already been occupied by the advancing Japanese. It was now just delaying tactics. As the staff officers and planners shifted, the joint operations room and communications facilities were blown up at Sime Road. (However, the Sime Road complex would still play a role in the lives of captured British civilians in Singapore. In the middle of the Japanese Occupation, the huts that made up the combined operations headquarters were converted into a civilian internment camp. The European civilian population, which had till then been housed at the civilian prison in Changi, were shifted to Sime Road in order to make more room for the surviving Allied POWs who had returned after building the Thai-Burma Death railway. Governor Shenton Thomas' wife, Lady Thomas, was also interned at the Sime Road camp.)

At Fort Canning's Battlebox, the Plotting Room (which had now been taken over by the General Staff) and the Gun Operations Room became the main operational rooms as the combined headquarters had now been reduced to directing the last bits of fighting on the island.

There was an excess of staff with no particular role to play.

> Accommodation there was very congested as Headquarters Southern Area and Anti-Aircraft Defences were also there. The General Staff went into the bomb-proof shelter which had been constructed before the war. It was never meant to hold as many bodies as this and the ventilating arrangements were inadequate. In consequence, the staff room became terribly hot and the staff worked under most unpleasant conditions.[20]

Although the main above-ground building was never directly hit, the shells fired by Japanese artillery came very close. Most of the officers and staff were now camped out at the headquarters with several adjoining houses requisitioned as mess halls to feed the large numbers now at Fort Canning.

Eric Lomax, a signaller, who survived the war, described the last days in the Battlebox.

> ...This was the 'Battlebox'. I went in and didn't come out for three weeks. The siege of Singapore for me was a series of clipped shouts for help over the radio and terse bulletins of disaster...
>
> ...I spent most of my time underground in the Battlebox, hearing and relaying orders, passing on information, sending out instructions for desperate recombinations of units to try to stop the collapse...
>
> ...Not that I saw daylight much: we worked eighteen hours a day, and slept on the floor of the command centre among the radios and phones. Our offices were a series of connecting rooms, so that runners and despatch riders were always coming through and stepping over tired bodies. We saw nothing until the very end, and what we heard was confused. We knew that the Japanese had taken the reservoirs and turned off the taps; we could hear their unchallenged planes bombing and strafing every day. The big ships were leaving Keppel Harbour with civilians; troops were deserting and wandering around the city. Towards the end the commanders couldn't even give sensible orders because there was so little information coming in. I saw General Percival a few times, walking in a corridor of the Fort or through our signals centre, a gaunt, tall figure looking utterly dejected and crushed; he was already a broken man. He was about to have his name attached to the worst defeat in the British Army's history.[21]

A day earlier, Wavell was in Singapore for a 24-hour visit to assess the situation. He had taken over from Brooke-Popham in early January 1942 and was now Commander-in-Chief, ABDA Command, which covered the Malayan theatre and the Dutch East Indies. He was not impressed by what he saw in Singapore. Churchill had urged that "Commanders and senior officers should die with their troops" and that "It is expected that every unit will be brought into close contact with the enemy and fight it out".[22]

However, reports of troop desertions from the front lines and of large numbers of soldiers in Singapore town had begun filtering into the Battlebox and Captain Davin was sent by Brigadier Torrance to investigate.

> I had met various groups of Australian soldiers who were wandering around Singapore town and not under any command and being generally bolshie. There was one group of three tall and very fit looking men whom I asked why they were not with their units. Their response was that they hadn't come to fight without air cover and that they were leaving.
>
> To which I replied by asking them about the Indian and British troops that had already been fighting without air cover for two months. Their response was and I quote (I have always remembered the exact words) "More fool them". They went one way and I limped away another. At least one of them had a Tommy-gun and I was in no position to do anything more.[23]

It was clear to Wavell that a large number of men from the various Commonwealth forces holding the island were demoralised and it was unlikely that Percival could produce a more "offensive spirit and optimistic outlook" among the men. Before leaving, Wavell scribbled down an Order of the Day, which was to be sent out by the signals at Sime Road. The message read:

> It is certain that our troops in Singapore Island greatly outnumber any Japanese who have crossed the straits. We must destroy them.
>
> Our fighting reputation is at stake and the honour of the British Empire. The Americans have held out in the Bataan Peninsula against far heavier odds, the Russians are turning back the packed strength of the Germans, the Chinese with an almost complete lack of modern equipment have held the Japanese for four-and-a half years. It would be disgraceful if we yield our boasted fortress of Singapore to inferior forces.

> There must be no thought of sparing the troops or the civilian population and no mercy must be shown to any weakness. Commanders and senior officers must lead their troops and if necessary, die with them. Every unit must fight it out to the end and in close contact with the enemy.
>
> Please see that the above is brought to the notice of all senior officers and by them to the troops.
>
> I look upon you and your men to fight it to the end and prove that the fighting spirit that won our Empire still exists to enable us to defend us.[24]

The Order was given to Percival just before Wavell left early in the morning of 11 February. While boarding his Sunderland seaplane in the dark, Wavell fell from the quay and broke two small bones in his back. As a result, for the next crucial four days, the most senior commander running the War in Malaya was doing it from bed.

Percival planned to transmit Wavell's Order of the Day in the morning of 11 February but because his Sime Road headquarters retreated to the Battlebox, was unable to issue his and Wavell's directive until late afternoon. By then, Percival's order to the men were no more than just words:

> ...In units the troops have not shown the fighting spirit which is expected of men of the British Empire. It will be a lasting disgrace to us if we are to be defeated by an Army of clever gangsters our inferior numbers in strength.
>
> The spirit of aggression and determination to stick it out must be inculcated to all ranks. There must be no further withdrawals without orders. There are too many fighting men roving about the back areas. Every available man who is not on essential work must be used to stop the invaders.[25]

With the collapse of the Kranji-Jurong Line, the Imperial Guards started to move down to their target, the MacRitchie and Pierce reservoirs. They had also managed to repair the causeway by now and began moving more tanks, men and equipment across.

The defending troops by this time were badly demoralised. Thousands of exhausted and frightened stragglers left the fighting to seek shelter in large commercial buildings.

On 12 February, the defenders clashed with Japanese troops at Bukit Timah Road, south of Bukit Timah Village, Nee Soon Village and Pasir Panjang.

Over at the general staff operations room in the Battlebox, Percival marked out Singapore's final protective perimeter. It was 28 miles long, enclosing Kallang airfield, Thomson village, MacRitchie reservoir, Adam Road, Farrer, Holland and Bouna Vista Roads.

By this time, Singapore was already coming under heavy air attack with almost daily bombings by Japanese aircraft. Royal Navy officer David Copley noted that when Fort Canning came under attack by aerial bombs and field artillery, the General Staff (Intelligence) clerks were made to destroy every document in the Battlebox and above-ground buildings, including archives going back a few decades. Lorry loads of documents were sent to the municipal refuse incinerator until it was overrun by the Japanese. Those that were too sensitive were fed page by page into fires in local clay cooking stoves on the balconies. Smoke from these fires could be seen drifting across Fort Canning, darkening the already smoky air. According to Copley, who was involved in the destruction of documents, navy coders also destroyed their books outside the Battlebox:

> So one day towards the end, a most urgent, most severe message came to the GOC Malaya from General Wavell just after he had visited Singapore and returned to India (*sic*). The GOC and his staff could not decipher the message because the books had been destroyed because of the nearness of the Japanese and similarly the naval authorities had no cipher or code books still undestroyed.[26]

Eventually, a code book was found to decode Wavell's order but it was clear that no one expected the defenders to hold on for much longer.

On 13 February, Yamashita moved his headquarters forward to the bomb-damaged Ford Motor factory. He feared a prolonged war once Percival had dug in at his last defensive position to wait for relief reinforcements. He had not enough men or ammunition for a long war. Thus, he tasked the 18th Division to capture Alexandra Barracks and the Imperial Guards to capture MacRitchie quickly before Percival had settled in at his last stand. The massacre at the Alexandra Military Hospital was a result of the 18th Division's attack, with innocent doctors and nurses killed as they tried to save patients on the operating table. Japanese soldiers bayoneted the staff and patients alike, killing over 200 in the hospital.[27]

Hordes of people had already begun trying to evacuate from Singapore in whatever vessels they could find. As women and children tried to board ships destined for Australia and India, unruly troops who had abandoned their units tried to get on board the ships in order to escape the island. Many of the ships which were packed to the gunnels did not make it, not because of the number of people aboard, but because they were bombed and attacked by Japanese aircraft as they tried to flee the island.

Many essential staff and personnel lost their lives during the evacuations. Top Secret documents and vast gold bullion from the Straits Settlements treasury that were being shipped off the island were also lost when the ships carrying them were sunk by the Japanese fleet off the Singapore coast.

Many fleeing vessels managed to get through the Japanese blockade to the islands off the Netherlands East Indies (present day Indonesia) and escaped but the remaining stragglers were eventually caught by the Japanese within a month of the fall of Singapore.

It was at Pasir Panjang that the 1st and 2nd Battalions, The Malay Regiment, began their epic 48-hour stand against the Japanese. They held on stubbornly while others along the lines were toppling. Only when the regiment was almost wiped out to a man was the ridge given up.

Over at the Battlebox in Fort Canning, the lack of information was deafening as the operations room did not have an accurate update of what was happening outside the war rooms. Pleas for help and reinforcements as well as blood-curdling screams were heard over the radio as the hapless residents of the bunker tried in vain to communicate with units being destroyed by enemy shelling and attacks.

In a meeting in the underground complex, Heath and Bennett urged Percival to surrender as the civilian toll was mounting while the troops were too exhausted, demoralised and disorganised to continue. Percival, however, still refused to yield. The recently decoded message from Wavell had instructed Percival to fight to the last and give no consideration to any other factors. Percival said that he had his honour to consider and the question as to what posterity would think if they surrendered the large army and fortress. To this, Heath commented dryly, "You need not bother about your honour. You lost that a long time ago up in the North." Plans were drawn up for the evacuation of key personnel but only a few would survive the tightening noose of Japanese warships in the waters surrounding Singapore.[28]

14 February dawned bitterly on the defending forces. The Japanese 18th Division continued their assault on the besieged Malay regiment and the Imperial Guards Division swarmed out of the MacRitchie area to battle the Allied forces. Water failure was imminent and epidemic threatened the overpopulated city.

Wavell, safely ensconced in his Java headquarters, sent Churchill a telegram indicating that the end for Singapore was very near:

> Have received telegram from Percival that enemy are close to town and that his troops are incapable of further counter-attack. Have ordered him to continue inflict maximum damage to enemy by house-to-house fighting if necessary. Fear however that resistance not likely to be very prolonged.[29]

Wavell wanted permission to allow Percival to surrender and Churchill gave it to him:

> You are of course sole judge of the moment when no further result can be gained at Singapore, and should instruct Percival accordingly, C.I.G.S. concurs.[30]

This signal marked the final play in Singapore's death pangs as Wavell now could give Percival the permission he so desperately sought in order to end the continuing slaughter. However, Wavell would wait till the morning of 15 February before conveying this permission

For the civilian population, it seemed to be the end of the world. The city had been devastated by bombings, the constant air raid sirens and the artillery barrages which made the town look like a scene out of Dante's *Inferno.*

For the few remaining civilians that were still manning at the various public services, it was a very trying time. Cuthbert Oswald Donough, a local Eurasian boy, was working for the Cable and Wireless office at Robinson Road. C&W was the civilian cable office, from which urgent signals, military and civilian, were still being sent to London and various other parts of Southeast Asia as the city collapsed outside its walls.

By 12 February, C&W was still able to transmit signals via its underground submarine cables to Banjoewangie, East Java, via the Cocos islands to Cottesloe, Western Australia and then to South Africa through to London. All acceptance counters for telegrams were closed to the public and the Phonogram (telephone) service was suspended. Only government, military and press messages were accepted for submission as all clerical staff except those in the operating and engineering departments were released from duty. There was so much confusion that even secret and sensitive military signals, that could not be sent through the Battlebox's signals office because of the heavily choked circuits, were sent by dispatch riders to the C&W office, where they were then sent via civilian cable lines to London. The C&W office acted as a secondary signal office for Malaya Command and a teletype between Fortress Signals and C&W was operational right to the very end.

A small unit of RAF signallers, believed to be the remnants of the radar unit, had also shifted from their base to the C&W's Robinson Road offices and had set up their own circuits there in a bid to make contact with their units in Java. Although they were unsuccessful, they remained camped in the ground floor offices of the C&W as upstairs, Donough and his colleagues were furiously dispatching the last signals out of Singapore:

> Then came that fateful Friday, 13 February. (C&W's) General Supervisor A.G. Blackwell came to the office in the early morning. He took down the names of staff working in the Instrument Room (operating staff) and Control Room (technical staff), he then sent a message himself and destroyed the punched slip. He told us he was leaving and we would close down the circuits and go home. As he left, I called out to Ronnie Barth who was standing close to the outgoing monitor, which was still switched on, to read from the outgoing slip what Blackwell had sent. Barth read out, "To MD/London, Now closing down. Goodbye. Most unlikely able evacuate please inform wives". [31]

As they had not received any instructions from Fort Canning, Donough thought it strange that the circuits should be shut down. With hundreds of urgent telegrams that had to be sent before the city fell, Donough and his colleagues decided to rebel:

> I punched an XQ (circuit route) on a KBP (keyboard perforator) and rushed it off on the Batavia (Jakarta) /Banjoewangi circuit saying, "Please keep circuit open. Staff still on duty." Ronnie Barth, Dick Lesslar, Ken De Souza, Bruce Armstrong and I decided that we would stay on till the end.
>
> That morning the ack-ack (anti-aircraft) gun positions just behind our office building was bombed in an air raid. The guns were destroyed and the gunners killed. Then came repeated raids by fighter planes, machine gunning our building. We were thankful that our window panes were made of solid steel. The noise was both deafening and terrifying. At about noon, our building was bombed. The bomb fell on the rooftop but did not penetrate the roof. The other went through the air-well. The damage was not serious – only the Battery Room and the Carpenter's Workshop were affected...
>
> ...Later that afternoon, an army major came with orders that we must destroy all the transmitting and receiving equipment in his presence. We protested but to no avail. We took heavy tools from the workshop and smashed all the transmitting and receiving automatic equipment. After the officer left, Bruce Armstrong broke down and

> cried, exclaiming, "Is this the end?" I comforted him and told him I'll find a way to resume circuit working (*sic*) using manual equipment. I spoke to senior technician Louis Le Mercier who told me he could start up and establish the ship-watch circuit but the working circuit cable terminal will have to be taken from its existing position and transferred and connected to the equipment on the ship-watch circuit. I told him I could do that and promptly did it while he was setting up the necessary equipment. Within minutes we made contact with Banjoewangi by slow speed hand sending and established a working circuit with Banjoewangi relay station, who agreed to receive our traffic for re-processing and re-transmission to destination stations. So we got cracking again, taking turns to do the hand-sending on the recorder keys which was slow and laborious. We got ourselves organised and continued to accept Government and press messages for onward transmission.
>
> That evening, the teleprinter circuit to the Military Command Centre at Fort Canning went dead. The line appeared to have been interrupted. Messages were brought to and fetched from us by drls (despatch riders).[32]

It was clear that Donough and his team were now flouting the instructions to deny the enemy access to all vital equipment. However, the need to make sure that Fort Canning still had a line out to the British forces in Java and that remaining Government signals were sent out made Donough stay at his post despite the heavy shelling and fear that Japanese soldiers would capture them at any moment.

By 15 February, the situation looked hopeless and the team at the C&W were in fear for their lives. If caught by the Japanese, they would surely be executed for assisting the enemy in sending out military signals:

> ...It became apparent that the battle for Singapore would soon end. All messages on hand were cleared. In the evening, after transmitting the last communiqué on General Percival's intended surrender to the Japanese commander on 15 February, we advised Head Office, through Banjoewangi that we were closing down. As a final gesture, we asked the members of the military forces who were taking shelter in the building to come up and write out their last messages to their loved ones and we would have them transmitted. This they did with deep emotion. We sent these messages off and closed down the circuit, leaving Mercier to dismantle the equipment. We then buzzed off before the Japanese soldier got us.[33]

For the rest of the War and for more than 50 years after its end, no one knew of these courageous few men, who risked their lives to keep open Singapore's last communication link with the free world as Japanese troops were less than a mile away.[34]

On the morning of Sunday, 15 February, Japanese troops finally broke through the north of the city as the defending troops along the south coast were retreating.

So it was at 9:30am that General Percival and his senior commanders met at a Commander's Conference in the Commander, Anti-Aircraft Defence Room, in the Battlebox, to discuss the "tactical situation and any other matters which might be raised".[35]

Present at the meeting were Heath, Bennett, Simmons, Wildey and Simson as well as Brigadier Goodman, Brigadier Royal Artillery; Brigadier Torrance, Brigadier General Staff; Brigadier Lucas, Brigadier in charge of Administration; Brigadier Newbigging, Deputy Adjutant General; Inspector General of Police Dickinson and III Indian Corps interpreter Major Wild.

Percival asked the formation commanders to report on the tactical situation in their respective areas.

All the commanders reported that there had been no major change in the situation since the previous day. There had, however, been some infiltration on the front of the 18th Division (a position west of Adam Road).

Percival then said he regretted to inform the conference that the administrative situation was less satisfactory. He also noted that although the Woodleigh and Mackenzie water pumping stations were still working, there was still very heavy wastage from broken mains and pipes. As a result, the supply in the Fort Canning Reservoir had fallen from 12 million gallons to 2 million gallons since the previous day and fall would be drained within the next hour or so.

Simson had reported that he gave the whole thing another 24 hours. In response to queries, he repeated that the water position was critical, that the rate of breakage of mains and pipes exceeded repair and that the meagre water supply still available could not now be guaranteed for more than 24 hours and that if a failure took place, it would take several days to obtain piped water again.

The commanders then began to discuss methods on how to economise water and of storing it in receptacles for the use of troops. The Japanese were now in complete control of the Pierce and MacRitchie reservoirs, although water was still flowing to the pumping stations. However, the Woodleigh Pumping Station was now within a few hundred yards of the enemy's forward troops.

Percival also noted that food reserves had now been reduced to about two days, though there were large quantities in the Bukit Timah and Race Course depots which were in enemy hands.

Touching on ammunition, Percival noted there were still adequate reserves of small arms ammunition as there were 4 million rounds in the Fort Canning magazine. However, all the available 25-pounder ammunition had already been issued and there were only 200 boxes of Bofors ammunition (Anti-Aircraft) left while mortar shells were also very short.

The commanders then gave an estimate of what ammunition was likely to be in the forward echelons and methods of economising ammunition were discussed. Only enemy forces of company strength or more would be engaged by artillery fire and only really low-flying aircraft should be engaged by the Anti-Aircraft Artillery, though it was agreed that it was difficult to restrain the gunners from firing at anything within reach.

On the petrol front, it was reported that the only petrol which remained apart from a small dump on the polo ground was what was in vehicle tanks. The commanders agreed to review the list of vehicles in use in order to keep as many off the road and so increase petrol reserves.

It was now that the meeting began to get tense as Percival asked the commanders on their views as to the best course to adopt.

Heath, who had been quiet for a while then weighed in. "In my opinion there is only one possible course to adopt and that is to do what you ought to have done two days ago, namely to surrender immediately,"[34] he said. Heath then went on to express his view on the danger of relying on the numberless pools of water where leakage had filled bomb and shell craters as the chief source of water supply for the troops and residents, saying a very serious situation would arise if his troops were left without water.

Heath noted now that there was no longer any Bofors ammunition left, the Japanese could come and bomb any target they liked with little or no opposition.

Visibly weary, Heath said there was no way to think they would be able to resist another determined Japanese attack and to sacrifice countless lives by failing to appreciate the situation would be an act of extreme folly. He ended by urging immediate surrender.

Gordon Bennett, the Australian commander, agreed with Heath.

Percival then said it was Wavell's order that they should continue to struggle at all cost and without consideration to what may happen to the civil population. "It is our duty to continue fighting as long as we can," he said.[36]

To this Heath replied, "How can General Wavell command this battle from Java?"[37]

It was then that Percival mentioned the counterattack. "I have been considering the possibility of launching a counter-attack shortly, the first object of which would be the recapture of our food depots in the Bukit Timah area. Is this not possible?"[38]

Bennett burst out, asking, "How do you think you are going to maintain the troops if you did get them there? It's quite impracticable." Heath agreed with his Australian colleague.[39]

Asked for their views, General Simmons said that though he was reluctant to surrender, he could see no alternative; most of the other participants remained silent or agreed with surrendering. "There was no dissentient voice".[40]

With Wavell's "discretion to cease resistance" signal already in his pocket, Percival then "in view of the critical water situation and the unsatisfactory administrative situation generally, thereupon reluctantly decided to accept the advice of the senior officers present and to capitulate".[41]

Heath urged that no time be wasted in putting the decision into effect as the negotiations might take some time and that they should be concluded that day.

The conference then decided to send Brigadier Newbigging and the Colonial Secretary as well as an interpreter to meet the Japanese and invite a delegation to visit to Singapore to discuss terms.

On the time of surrender, it was decided that Percival would request a cessation of hostilities from 4:30pm (GMT) and he made it clear, however, that hostilities should continue until definite orders to cease fire were issued.

Discussing what to do about weapons and ordnance, the commanders agreed that weapons would not be destroyed pending the issue of further orders but that orders should be issued for the destruction before 4:30pm of all secret and technical equipment, ciphers, codes and secret documents.

The conference ended at 11:15am (Malayan time) and with that the events of the Ford Motor Factory followed, leading to the ending of hostilities. A three-man deputation went to Bukit Timah Road at 2pm, where negotiations with Lieutenant Colonel Sugita, Yamashita's staff officer took place.

Instructed to raise a Japanese flag above the Cathay building, the tallest building then, the deputation left after agreeing to a meeting later that day at about 4pm. After the deputation had returned to Fort Canning, Percival, along with Brigadier Torrance, Brigadier Newbigging and Major Wild, made their way to the Bukit Timah Rd to be met by Sugita and were brought to the Ford Motor Factory at about 5:15pm.

It was here that Percival met Yamashita for the first time. Percival tried to stall for time but Yamashita demanded an immediate unconditional surrender or a massive assault on the city would follow. Percival caved in and signed the surrender document at about 6:10pm.

With that the Malayan Campaign came to an end in 70 days.

Percival arrives at the Ford Motor Factory in Bukit Timah in the late afternoon of 15 February 1942 to surrender Singapore. From left to right: Major C.H.D. Wild, Staff Officer III Indian Corps (interpreter), Brigadier T.K. Newbigging, Chief Administration Officer, Lieutenant Colonel Sugita, Intelligence staff officer to General Yamashita, Japanese soldier, Brigadier K.S. Torrance, Brigadier General Staff, Malaya Command and Lieutenant General Arthur E. Percival, General Officer Commanding, Malaya Command.

Percival signs the surrender document at the Ford Motor Factory in Bukit Timah. On the table is a Japanese-English dictionary brought along by Major Wild, the interpreter. General Tomoyuki Yamashita, Commander of the Japanese forces, is seated at the extreme left of the photograph.

At about 7pm, Torrance came to the Operations Room and drafted an order for the cease-fire to go out at 2000 hours. The order was issued in the name of Simmons, the Fortress Commander:

> Fire will cease at 2030hrs tonight 15/16 Feb 42. Troops will remain in present positions. No movement without permission this HQ. There will NOT repeat NOT be any destruction of arms, equipment maps or records.[42]

There was some confusion as to who was to sign this last order. Finally, it was handed to a Major Waller, who put in an additional line, "all arms and amn (*sic*) to be collected as far as possible", before he signed it. Arms were collected and piled in the entrance porch. The Japanese did not appear.

Percival, who remained listless the whole evening, then went over to the signals office and sent out the last communiqué to troops from Headquarters Malaya Command:

> "It has been necessary to give up the struggle but I want the reason explained to all ranks. The forward troops continue to hold their ground but the essentials of war have run short. In a few days we shall have neither petrol nor food. Many types of ammunition are short and the water supply, upon which the vast civil population and many of the fighting troops are dependent, threatens to fail. This situation has been brought about partly by being driven off our dumps and partly by hostile air and artillery action. Without these sinews of war we cannot fight on. I thank all ranks for their efforts throughout the campaign."[43]

Brigadier Hubert Francis Lucas, who was in charge of Malaya Command's administration, dashed off a last letter to his wife Irene as negotiations for the surrender were ongoing, and which managed to reach her despite the odds, and is now placed with Lucas' papers at the Imperial War Museum:

> My Most beloved Irene,
>
> The hunt is up at last and we have sent in a flag of truce as the water supply is running short – has failed in many places – because China town (*sic*) has been bombed & shelled that the pipes are all broken & the ruins prevent them being mended. Also the Chinese civilians have had very heavy casualties and it is just murder to go on any longer. Our poor hospitals have had an awful time too. As we closed

in more and more on the town we had to move them back & back & even then they were under fire as well as bombs. At present the front line is between Gillman and Alex., Changi & Selarang.

I had to come back quite early on. Tyersall Park was burnt out – frightful. My chaps have played up awfully well & nothing has broken down thank God. The troops are very tired but still fighting in spite of continuous dive bombing & machine gunning.

The Navy & the Air Force are all gone. They managed to take some technical experts and staff officers with them. All the heads of branches & services stayed. I sent Palmer, Cols Brown & Taylor & Major Heathcote. I hope they will arrange to rescue us soon!

I moved into the office about five days ago as I had a battery on either side of the Tanglin house & things were getting a bit noisy. I shot Whiskey who knew nothing; paid off the servants & brought in my bedding, a suitcase & later retrieved my tin uniform case. Whether the Jap will let me keep any of it I don't know... Sime Road was on fire as a result of enemy fire a few hours after the General (Percival) left. Singapore has been a bit depressing lately with fires from burning dumps & depots all over the place. The Japs, I think, intend to use Fort Canning as they haven't shelled it yet though they have been putting them past each side & over cautiously. However, I have managed to sleep very well most nights and am very well in myself. Padre Hughes gave us Holy Communion this morning in the General's office. Percy (Percival) has been very calm & cool in what must have been a frightful ordeal for him. Stringer (Brigadier CH Stringer, Deputy Director Medical Services) has been magnificent. Evelegh (Brigadier GC Evelegh, Deputy Director Ordnance Supplies) has done very well. Richards – Davis' successor has been a little weak – but the show has functioned. We have got practically all the wives away (including Mrs Stringer, Curtiss & Wildey at the very last) – also Irene Lees & a good many nurses & VADs.

Well old darling take care of yourself & the kids & don't worry about me. God has been extraordinarily kind to me & I'm sure he will go on looking after me. If this gets to you it will be a marvel and a good omen… Keep your chin up & your faith in God. Good-bye for the present my darling. God bless you and the kids.

Your ever loving Hoodie[44]

For the rest of the evening, the signal circuits continued to relay lists of names of troops who were on Singapore Island and presumed captured, before dismantling the connections to the outside world.

> ...I was told by another officer that he had heard we were about to surrender. Early that evening a dead silence enveloped the old fort. In the signals rooms, everybody went to sleep, depression and exhaustion flooding in, as we collapsed on mattresses laid on top of cables and land lines. The spring of tension that had kept us going for weeks had been broken.[45]

Endnotes

A After the War, Donough was afraid to mention their bravery as it was an act of defiance of company and military regulations, an offence for which they could be charged. In the mid 1990s, Donough and Barth finally revealed their role in keeping Singapore's communication lines open. However, most of the individuals involved were dead by then and all records of the event were destroyed when Singapore fell to the Japanese on 15 February 1945. Although many listened to Donough's story, none knew whether it was true or the figment of an old man's imagination. Donough told me his story in late 2004 and it rang a bell. When I was looking through the files at the Imperial War Museum a few years back, I came across a miscellaneous Cable and Wireless document filed in the archive, which I had copied and kept for future reference. I now went back to the document. It was dated 15 February 1942 and was on the letterhead of the South West Pacific Command Java. It was addressed to a Major Kistner at General Headquarters in Bandoeng (Wavell's Headquarters) and was titled, Last Communique from Singapore. In it, the Manager of the Eastern Wireless Service in Java had listed the details of the last messages from Cable and Wireless in Singapore. It confirmed Donough's story that C&W was still operating on 15 February and that the C&W Singapore had sent the fateful signal that Singapore had surrendered. It also listed the personal messages of the soldiers it had forwarded on that fateful day. The final message from Singapore read, "Suggest you stand by in case anything comes from G.O.C. stop Anything further definitely ignore goodbye and good luck stop". Donough had clearly been there when these last messages were sent and his story was obviously true. He and his colleagues have never been recognised for their bravery and for the decision to get the job done despite overwhelming odds. The full communiqué is in the Appendix.

1 *21404 Cipher 27/7, 31189.118/Malaya/207, 27 July 1941, AIR2/1603.* The National Archives, London.

2 *WAR DIARY, Singapore Fortress Signals, December 1941, WO172/156.* The National Archives, London.

3 Ibid

4 *ORGANISATION AND EVOLUTION OF JAPANESE NAVAL SIGINT, PART VI, HW50/59.* The National Archives, London.

5 Ibid, p. 2.

6 *TABLE TALK – ARTHUR COOPER, ORGANISATION AND EVOLUTION OF JAPANESE NAVAL SIGINT, PART VI, HW50/59.* The National Archives, London, p. 2.

7 *ORGANISATION AND EVOLUTION OF JAPANESE NAVAL SIGINT, PART VI, HW50/59.* The National Archives, London, p. 4.

8 *ORGANISATION AND EVOLUTION OF JAPANESE NAVAL SIGINT, PART VI, HW50/59.* The National Archives, London.

9 Wilson, Duncan. *Survival was for Me.* Wigtown, GC Books, 1991. p. 40.

10 *WAR DIARY, Singapore Fortress Signals, December 1941, WO172/156.* The National Archives, London.

11 Ibid

12 Percival, A.E. *The War in Malaya.* Eyre & Spottiswoode, London, 1949. p.185.

13 Ibid

14 Elphick, Peter. *Odd Man Out: The Story of the Singapore Traitor.* Hodder & Stoughton, London. 1993.

15 *ORGANISATION AND EVOLUTION OF JAPANESE NAVAL SIGINT, PART VI, HW50/59.* The National Archives, London, p. 3.

16 *Loss of Singapore Feb 1942 and its lessons for NID, ORGANISATION AND EVOLUTION OF JAPANESE NAVAL SIGINT, PART VI, HW50/59.* The National Archives, London.

17 *ORGANISATION AND EVOLUTION OF JAPANESE NAVAL SIGINT, PART VI, HW50/59.* The National Archives, London.

18 Ibid

19 Percival, A.E. *The War in Malaya.* Eyre & Spottiswoode, London, 1949. p.278.

20 Ibid

21 Lomax, Eric. *The Railway Man.* Vintage, London, 1996. p. 68.

22 Churchill, W.S. *The Second World War: The Hinge of Fate.* Houghton Mifflin Company, Boston, USA, 1950. p. 100.

23 Davin, V.L.F. "Secrets of the battlebox", email to author, 20 November 2005, a similar version also cited by Elphick, Peter. *Singapore: The Pregnable Fortress.* London: Hodder and Stoughton, 1995, p. 461.

24 *Order of the Day, 10 February 1942, Papers of A.E. Percival,* P16-27. The Imperial War Museum, London.

25 *FORTRESS COMMAND: INDIAN CORPS: A.I.F.: SOUTHERN AREA, 11 February 1942, P16-27.* The Imperial War Museum, London.

26 *Copley, David. Personal Account, The Battlebox : Research Clippings.* Oral History Department, Singapore.

27 *The Atrocity at Alexandra Hospital, Singapore 14/2/42, Papers of Lieutenant S.E. Bell, 88/63/1.* The Imperial War Museum, London.

28 *Proceedings of the Conference held at Headquarters Malaya Command (Fort Canning) at 1400Hrs. Fri. 13 February 1942, P16-27.* The Imperial War Museum, London.

29 Churchill, W.S. *The Second World War: The Hinge of Fate.* Houghton Mifflin Company, Boston, USA, 1950. p. 105.

30 Ibid

31 Donough, C.O., *Events leading to Fall of Singapore on 15 Feb 42 (9.2.42 to 14.2.42).* Copy of manuscript with Author, 1998. Interview in September 2004.

32 Ibid, p. 9.

33 Ibid, p. 9.

34 *Proceedings of the Conference held at Headquarters Malaya Command (Fort Canning) at 0930Hrs. Sun. 15 February 1942, Papers of A.E. Percival, P16-27.* The Imperial War Museum, London.

35 Ibid, p.2.

36 Ibid, p.3.

37 Ibid, p. 4.

38 Ibid, p. 4.

39 Ibid, p. 4.

40 Ibid, p. 4.

41 Ibid, p. 4.

42 *Signal, 15 February 1942, Papers of Lieutenant Colonel TH Newey, 85/50/1.* The Imperial War Museum, London.

43 *Signal, 15 February 1942, Papers of A.E. Percival, P16-27.* The Imperial War Museum, London.

44 Papers of Brigadier H.F. Lucas, 397 90/2/1. The Imperial War Museum, London.

45 Lomax, Eric. *The Railway Man.* Vintage, London, 1996. p. 69.

Chapter 6

Occupation and Post War

On the morning of Monday, 16 February 1942, Chinese New Year's Day, the victorious Japanese Army marched into Singapore town.

Pre-arranged units moved about the city and into Fort Canning where weary Allied headquarters troops awaited them.

Signal officers like Eric Lomax had slept on the floor of the bunker for more than 10 hours after the cease-fire the previous day:

> The following morning I stepped outside and saw four cars moving slowly up the hill, small rising sun pennants fluttering on their wings. Their occupants sat bolt upright, arms stiff by their sides. They drew up outside the main entrance and a group of Japanese officers got out, long swords in black scabbards hanging from their dark green uniforms. They were the first Japanese troops I had ever seen. They strode confidently into the Fort.
>
> These people now ruled Malaya, dominated the seas from India to Polynesia and had broken the power of at least three European empires in Asia. I was their prisoner.[1]

The defeated Allied forces continued to occupy Fort Canning for the next few weeks, as soldiers and officers who were being marched off to Changi and some of whom were being used for clearance works in the city continued to take supplies from the Command HQ's stores and used the above-ground barracks as shelter until all Allied troops were permanently removed to Changi.

However, by the evening of 18 February, the main buildings at Fort

Canning had been taken over as the Defence Headquarters by Major General Saburo Kawamura, the Japanese Commandant of Singapore, while General Yamashita was encamped in Bukit Timah.

Under the command of the Defence Headquarters were the Kempeitai, the Japanese military intelligence and security unit, which was believed to have used rooms in the battlebox as torture chambers before they moved to the Young Men's Christian Association (YMCA).

Ian Ward, in his book, *The Killer They Called A God*, noted that Kawamura held a meeting with his senior commanders Miyamoto and Ichikawa as well as Kempetai deputy Oishi that evening at Fort Canning, where the formal operational order for the screening and the killing of Chinese civilians was passed down.

The order, known as the Sook Ching operation, involved killing and torturing an estimated 25,000 to 50,000 Chinese as a reprisal for their alleged sympathy for the Nationalist and Communist Chinese fighting against the Japanese Army in China.

Throughout the Japanese Occupation, it is believed that most of the rooms in the underground complex were left abandoned while the above-ground facilities were used.

Although not much else is known about the Battlebox during this period, there were reports, however, of the signals rooms being used during the occupation for communications.

Jim Howard, an Australian war photographer, parachuted into Singapore, following the Japanese surrender announcement on 15 August 1945. At the time, he held three ranks, a Lieutenant-Colonel in the Army, a Wing Commander in the air force, and a Commander in the Navy. However, he entered Singapore as a "civilian" as this arrangement allowed him to move around more easily. Howard landed by parachute on 28 August 1945 and entered the Battlebox one or two days later. Here, he saw Japanese soldiers occupying the signal rooms and using the communications facilities. The rooms nearby were barely furnished and the orderlies room had bunks and were occupied by Japanese guards who also cooked there.

Liberation

Once the war ended and the British returned to Singapore, Fort Canning reverted to being the headquarters for the British military.

Although Lord Louis Mountbatten, Supreme Allied Commander, Southeast Asia, used the Cathay building as his headquarters, the Allied Land Forces Southeast Asia immediately began re-occupying Fort Canning. Eventually, it became the Headquarters of the General Officer Commanding, Singapore Base District.

The Battlebox, however, was left empty and had by this time been stripped clean by looters during the last days of the occupation.

As the British Military Administration in Singapore began rebuilding the colony and the returned services began to reorganise on the ground, the Battlebox and its operations rooms were forgotten and left abandoned.

By 1963, with Singapore and Malaysia planning to merge as part of the Federation of Malaysia, the Singapore Base District agreed to move its headquarters out of Fort Canning to the General Headquarters of the Far East Land Forces in Tanglin.[2]

With both countries now on the eve of independence, the British government had agreed to move aside its forces so that local defence units could be raised in the country.

By March 1963, it was already decided to vacate Fort Canning, which would now become home to the 4th Federal Infantry Brigade of the Federation Army in Singapore.[3]

In an exchange of letters between the Singapore and Malayan governments in London during the Malaysia talks for merger, it was determined that Fort Canning would be the base for a Federation army for three years before being released to the Singapore Government for development.

The 4th Brigade would merge with the headquarters staff of the Singapore Military Force and the first and second battalions of the Singapore Infantry Regiment.

The rapid buildup of the brigade included the setting up of an Armed Forces Maintenance Corps and the completion of a new Singapore camp at Ulu Pandan for the 2nd Singapore Infantry Regiment.

On 19 August 1963, The 4th Federal Brigade took command of Fort Canning:

> …the colourful handover ceremony was watched by officers and ranks of both armies. The salute was taken by Maj-Gen E.A.W. Williams, GOC Singapore Base District and Brigadier P.E.M. Bradley, Commanding 4th Federal Brigade.[4]

When Malaya, Singapore, Sabah and Sarawak gained independence from the UK as the Federation of Malaysia on 31 August 1963, the 4th Brigade was in command at Fort Canning, raising the Malaysian flag over the new federation.

While Singapore was part of Malaysia, there were about 4,000 Malaysian troops attached to the 4th Federal Brigade on the island. These included, at separate periods, both the 6th Royal Malay Regiment and the 9th Royal Malay Regiment.

The brigade remained in Singapore from 1963 till after the separation of Singapore and Malaysia which led to Singapore declaring its independence on 9 August 1965.

Singapore felt threatened from its inception and the need for its own defence force was clear after incidents as outlined by then Prime Minister Lee Kuan Yew in his memoirs:

> When Parliament was due to open in December 1965, four months after our separation from Malaysia, Brigadier Syed Mohamed Bin Syed Ahmad Alsagoff, who was in charge of a Malaysian brigade stationed in Singapore (4th Federal Brigade at Fort Canning), called on me and insisted that his motorcycle outriders escort me to Parliament. Alsagoff was a stout, heavy-built Arab Muslim with a moustache, a Singaporean by birth who had joined the Malayan Armed Forces. To my amazement he acted as if he was the commander-in-chief of the army in Singapore, ready at any time to take over control of the island. At that time the First and Second Singapore Infantry regiments (1 and 2 SIR) of about 1,000 men each were under Malaysian command. The Malaysian government had placed 700 Malaysians in 1 and 2 SIR, and posted out 300 Singaporean soldiers to various Malaysian units.
>
> I weighed up the situation and concluded that the Tunku (Tunku Abdul Rahman, the Malaysian Prime Minister) wanted to remind us and the foreign diplomats who would be present that Malaysia was still in charge in Singapore. If I told him off for his presumptuousness, Alsagoff would report this back to his superiors in Kuala Lumpur and they would take other steps to show me who wielded real power in Singapore. I decided it was best to acquiesce. So for the ceremonial opening of the first Parliament of the Republic of Singapore, Malaysian army outriders "escorted" me from my office in City Hall to Parliament House...
>
> ...Shortly after separation, at the request of the Malaysian government, we had sent the 2nd battalion SIR to Sabah for Confrontation duties. We wanted to demonstrate our good faith and solidarity with Malaysia even though a formal defence treaty had not been concluded. This left their barracks, Camp Temasek, vacant. We then agreed to a Malaysian proposal that one Malaysian regiment be sent down to Camp Temasek. The 2nd battalion SIR was due to return from its duties in Borneo in February 1966, and arrangements

> were made at staff level for the Malaysian regiment to withdraw. The Malaysian defence minister requested that instead of reoccupying Camp Temasek, one Singapore battalion should be sent to the Malayan mainland to enable the Malaysian regiment to remain where it was. Keng Swee (Goh Keng Swee, then Singapore Defence Minister and Deputy Prime Minister) did not agree. We wanted both our own battalions in Singapore. We believed the Malaysians had changed their minds because they wanted to keep one battalion of Malaysian forces in Singapore to control us.
>
> The Malaysians refused to move out, so the SIR advance party had to live under canvas at Farrer Park. Keng Swee saw me urgently to warn that if our troops were under canvas too long, with poor facilities for their mess and toilets, there was the risk of a riot or a mutiny. He compared himself to a British General in charge of troops the majority of whom were Italians. The Malaysians could take advantage of this and, through Brigadier Alsagoff, mount a coup. He advised me to move from my home in Oxley Road into the Istana Villa in the Istana domain and to post Gurkha police guards around just in case. For the next few weeks, my family and I stayed there with a company of Gurkhas on standby.
>
> Shortly afterwards, the British vacated a camp called Khatib in the north of Singapore, near Sembawang. We offered it to the Malaysians and they agreed in mid-March 1966 to move out of our camp to Khatib, where they remained for 18 months before withdrawing of their own accord in November 1967.[5]

It would take a few more months more before the Federal Army would vacate Fort Canning and move most of their troops off the island.

Speaking in the Singapore Parliament on 25 January 1968, Mr Lee announced the final pullout of more than 1,000 troops of the 4th Malaysian Federal Brigade.

> (Lee) told the House that all Malaysian Army units had been withdrawn from Singapore by the end of last year, following a letter from the Malaysian Deputy Prime Minister, Tun Razak, to Singapore's Minister for Defence, Mr. Lim Kim San, on Nov 14. Tun Razak had written to say that as Singapore had increased its armed forces for its own defence, it was no longer necessary to station Malaysian troops in Singapore. ...The last units to leave here were mostly infantrymen and members of the Reconnaissance Corps.[6]

By then, the Malaysian government was only maintaining the Royal Malaysian Navy Base at Woodlands, which remained the headquarters of the Malaysian Navy till the late 1980s, with the complete pullout from the Woodlands base in the early 1990s.

Things appeared bleak for Singapore as the British forces, which had promised under an earlier British Government to remain engaged in

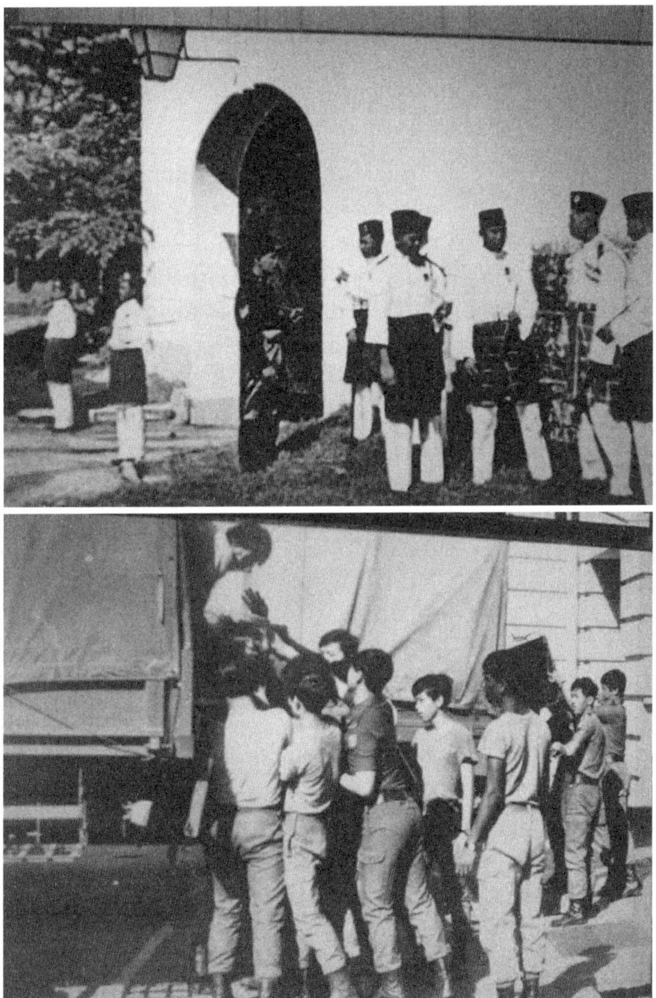

In the post-War period, Fort Canning became the headquarters of the Singapore Base District, before it was handed over to the newly independent government of Malaysia for use by Federal Troops in 1963. The top picture shows preparations for a parade by the 4th Malaysian Federal Brigade at the old fort gate, located on the ground above the Battlebox. In the 1970s, it housed the Singapore Command and Staff College, who were the last occupants of the above-ground buildings before some of the buildings were restored in the 1980s. The second photo shows SCSC officers and men packing up equipment before vacating Fort Canning in 1976.

Singapore till the end of the 1970s, had now decided to pull out of Singapore by 1970/71.

As the British began their massive pullout east of Suez, after the change in political leadership in the UK and a massive defence review, London was persuaded to hand over much of its facilities and equipment to the Singapore government.

The impact of the British move was very significant for an economy that virtually depended on the military presence on the island.

In public talks and discussions, many were concerned with the repercussions of the move.

> ...It may be that the total unemployed and underemployed in Singapore now amounts to between 50 to 80 thousand. The withdrawal of the British Forces may throw another 100,000 people on the labour market over the withdrawal period... The Finance Minister recently pointed out that in spite of tremendous efforts new jobs had been created only at the rate of 5,000 a year since 1963. The EDB (Economic Development Board) planners calculate that an investment of $25 to $30 thousand is required to create one new job. This means that Singapore will need a total investment of nearly $3,000 million to keep the unemployment rate down to its present level before the British forces withdrawal.
>
> ...Obviously the help to be given by Britain must be substantial and in hard cash. It is no use to say that investment from Britain will be encouraged to fill the gap. A businessman invests money because he thinks he will make a profit on the investment, he does not do it out of charity because a British political party (and not even his own political party) has broken promises regarding the military bases...[7]

From 1968 to 1969, the British Government handed over $135 million worth of property to the Singapore government, including the Naval Base worth about $12.7 million at the time.[8] In the end, the British Government handed over more than $400 million worth of fixed and moveable assets to the Singapore Government.[9]

Other properties included the three RAF bases at Changi, Seletar and Tengah, the Far Eastern Land Forces (FARELF) Headquarters at Tanglin as well as the Pasir Panjang complex occupied by the British Army. It also included Flagstaff House, Command House and Air House as well as several other major residences of British service chiefs in Singapore.

With Fort Canning now empty and the Singapore Armed Forces trying to build up its fledgling defence force, the above-ground buildings were handed over to the newly set up Singapore Command and Staff College.

The aims of the SCSC were to prepare senior officers for Staff and Command appointments at Battalion, Formation and Ministry levels and to provide the institutional framework for formulating operational doctrines at the highest levels.

The general education subjects were prepared by Mr Doraisingam S. Samuel, the first General Education Officer of SCSC and later Head of the Education Department at Singapore's Ministry of Defence

Mr Samuel who later became President of the Singapore History Association, was the man who had sent the first letter to the *Straits Times* in 1988, setting in motion the whole chain of events in the re-discovery of the Battlebox.

Sometime in the late 60s, it was decided to seal off the underground bunkers as it was a security risk so near the college and for fear that people might get lost in the tunnels. The Battlebox was then sealed off till its re-discovery, almost two decades later.

The SCSC remained on Fort Canning till the mid 1970s before it moved to Seletar Camp, leaving the above-ground buildings and the bunkers surrounding the former Headquarters Malaya Command empty.

In the mid 1980s, the above-ground barracks was restored and converted for use as an arts centre and for cultural events on the slopes of the hill.

In the meantime, the National Parks Department had decided to preserve the Fort Canning buildings and began searching for suitable investors to develop the Battlebox as a museum.

The main above-ground building of Headquarters Malaya Command was restored and partially re-developed in the 1990s. In 1993, the National Parks Board gave a 30-year lease of the above-ground buildings and the Battlebox to eye-care products firm Alliance Technology and Development for slightly over $51 million.[10]

Its subsidiary, the Fort Canning Country Club Investment Ltd, restored the above-ground buildings and converted it into the Fort Canning Country Club.

It spent $3 million restoring the Battlebox and creating a state-of-the-art museum within the walls of the bunker. The Battlebox museum was formally opened on 15 February 1997, fifty-five years to the day Singapore fell. The Battlebox's first curator Tan Teng Teng and military historian Dr Ong Chit Chung carried out extensive research to create a realistic atmosphere in the bunker.[11]

Using special audio and video effects, high-end animatronics and specially crafted figurines, the museum did a very credible job in bringing visitors back to the morning of 15 February 1942. With well-researched displays and interactive installations, the Battlebox was brought back to life, no longer a nerve centre of military forces but more a reminder of how crucial a good headquarters and command staff are to any military operation.

However, the severe financial crisis that hit Southeast Asia in late 1997 meant that the Country Club and museum faced very lean times. By April 2002, Alliance Technology and Development had been placed under judicial management with debts totaling almost $1 billion. In November that year, the families behind cinema operator Eng Wah Organisation and The Legends Golf and Country Resort in Johor bought the struggling club "for just over half of its $15 million asking price".[12] It purchased another 30-year lease from the National Parks Board at $85 million and with significant investments and improving economic times, run the club and museum as a more profitable venture.

The club was re-launched as The Legends Fort Canning Park in November 2002, a town club located in the middle of Fort Canning Park.

Although relatively successful, club members did not fully utilise the eight restaurants and bars, a 10,000-sq-ft gym, three swimming pools, a spa, a private members' lounge with wireless Internet, meeting and dining suites, a grand ballroom and a children's centre.

After major renovations, part of the heritage building was re-opened in November 2010 as Hotel Fort Canning – the hotel wing of The Legends

This photograph taken outside the Battlebox's Dobbie Rise entrance shows the staircase leading down to the above-ground buildings in the background. These stairs were initially camouflaged and were known only to highly cleared staff of Headquarters Malaya Command. The steps, made of rough stone, were crumbling in 1988. As part of the conservation efforts, a new staircase was installed, which is now safer and more accessible.

Fort Canning Park – with the rest of the building still housing the club. Described on its website as an "urban oasis", the 86-room hotel promises "a unique sojourn" with "all the amenities of a 5-star city resort, inclusive of outstanding food & beverage outlets."

When my wife Brigid found out about it, she booked the family in for a short stay at the hotel in December 2010. I did not know what to expect, but when we arrived was amazed at the way the building had been restored. As we made our way to our room, I told my wife that Percival's office was on the second floor of this building and his was the one with the tall windows and the balcony overlooking the city. I said, "I wonder if they have made the room into the 'Percival Suite?'" Laughing, we walked up the stairs and to Room 213, and I was stunned when I opened the door. Room 213 was not called the Percival Suite, but it is exactly where the general's office would have been, sharing the balcony with Room 215. The concrete pillars that would have separated Percival's inner and outer offices still remain from that time, as do the lovely views. It was a treat to be able to spend the night in Percival's office, just like he did 70 years ago – but in definitely much more comfort and in peaceful surroundings.

More than 60 years after the end of the Second World War, the Malayan Campaign still remains a key defining moment in the history of Malaysia and Singapore. The battles fought in Malaya and torture and deprivation imposed by Japanese troops are seared in the minds of those who lived through it. For many in my generation, who were born more than 30 years after the War, the stories of elderly relatives and old war veterans have come to shape our collective perception of what happened in those dark days back in 1942.

For many, it is not easy to remember those days much less record them down on paper. As a result, historians today face huge gaps in trying to piece together what actually happened during those 70 days when the fate of Southeast Asia was determined in the rice paddies and plains of Malaya.

Although this book has attempted to give a clearer picture of the Battlebox and the crucial role it played in those final days, it is by no means comprehensive or complete. There are many more secrets and turns to the story that have yet to be revealed. Although most of the highly sensitive files on Singapore have been opened to the public, a few are still sealed by the British Government and will not be declassified till 2045.

Many more stories and details of the Fall of Singapore have been lost with the passing of those who witnessed the final death throes of the city. Even with the release of all files on the War, we will never get the full picture of the Battlebox. It is a puzzle that brings with it more questions for every answer that it provides. It is hoped that in the coming years, many of those who are still around and who read this book will find it in themselves to come forward and give their account of what happened in the Battlebox and in the final hours before the Surrender on that fateful Sunday afternoon, six decades ago.

Endnotes

1 Lomax, Eric. *The Railway Man.* Vintage, London, 1996. p. 70.

2 Yeo, Joseph. *Defence:The big switch has begun, The Sunday Times.* 3 March 1963.

3 *Takeover without a shot at Fort Canning, The Straits Times.* 5 March 1963.

4 *Malay Mail*, 20 August 1963.

5 Lee, Kuan Yew. *From Third World to First: The Singapore Story: 1965-2000.* Times Editions, Singapore. 2000.

6 Pestana, Roderick. *Malaysia pulls last troops out of Singapore, Malay Mail.* 26 January 1968.

7 Hazell, R.C. *Economic and Social Effects of the British Withdrawal from Singapore.* A talk for Rotary West, Singapore, 5 March 1968.

8 Rozario, Francis. *Handover of $135m property, The Straits Times.* 5 February 1969.

9 *Undated Treasury Minute, 1971 concerning the gift of fixed assets and equipment to the Government of Malaysia (Singapore portion), WO32/21583.* The National Archives, London.

10 *The Straits Times*, 13 November 2002.

11 *The Straits Times*, 15 February 1997.

12 *The Straits Times*, 15 November 2002.

Appendix A: Last Cable from Singapore

SOUTH WEST PACIFIC COMMAND,
JAVA

15th FEBRUARY, 1942.

LAST COMMUNIQUE FROM SINGAPORE

For Major Kistner General Headquarters BANDOENG.

Following are details of Cable and Wireless final stand at SINGAPORE stop

1840 Japs have not got us yet, but very near stop We have phone to Fort Canning stop G.O.C. Fort Canning advises us to surrender stop We don't know exactly position stop Office roof shambles and place full dust and smoke stop

2148 We have surrendered Armistice now on stop

2156 Surrender not official and not for publication stop We have been informed fighting has ceased stop

2205 Personal messages from following members Army Signal Staff Giblin Price Flynn Benny Reeves accepted and forwarded by Cable and Wireless Staff stop

2206 Now we off goodbye for present stop

2210 Suggest you stand by in case anything comes from G.O.C. stop Anything further definitely ignore goodbye and good luck stop

Thus the final word from SINGAPORE over the Cable was at 2211/15th stop All above times S'pore times stop Please acknowledge

Manager,
EASTERN.

This is the list of last cable messages sent out of Singapore prior to its fall on 15 February 1945. This document verifies C.O. Donough's story of keeping the cable office open right till the bitter end.

Appendix B: A Brief Chronology of Events

1936	War Office approves building of underground command centre at Fort Canning as part of Headquarters Malaya Command plan for defence of Malaya; work begins
1939	Air Ministry approves plan for location of new RAF headquarters in Singapore at Sime Road; work begins
1940	Underground Command Centre at Fort Canning is operational
May 1941	Percival takes over as General Officer Commanding, Malaya Command
June	Brooke-Popham sanctions immediate work on building of new Army Headquarters and Air Force and Army Combined Operations Room at Sime Road adjacent to RAF Headquarters
1 Dec	*Prince of Wales* and *Repulse* arrive in Singapore
6 Dec	First Degree of Readiness ordered (RAFFLES), new Army headquarters and Combined Operations Room begins operations at Sime Road
7 Dec	FECB warns Brooke-Popham that Japanese invasion on Malaya imminent
8 Dec	Japan attacks Malaya, Thailand, Pearl Harbour and Hong Kong. First air raid over Singapore. Planned Operation MATADOR (pre-emptive strike into Thailand) abandoned but two small probes made, one codenamed KROHCOL, designed to capture the strategic height known as "The Ledge" in Southern Thailand
9 Dec	Kuantan airfield abandoned
10 Dec	*Prince of Wales* and *Repulse* sunk off Kuantan
11 Dec	Krohcol column fails to reach "The Ledge" and retreats
12 Dec	British forces from Kota Bahru commence retreat down rail line to Kuala Lipis
13 Dec	British forces retreat south of Jitra

15 Dec	Fighting in Gurun, followed by retreat
16 Dec	Penang under seige
17 Dec	Penang evacuated
23 Dec	British withdraw across Perak River
25 Dec	Hong Kong surrenders
30 Dec	First Japanese land attack on Kuantan
30 Dec – 2 Jan	Battle at Kampar followed by further retreat
3 Jan 1942	45th Indian Brigade arrives in Singapore
4 Jan	Allied troops take up position at Slim River
7 Jan	Slim River battle fought. Japanese spearhead attack with tanks and British forces pushed back. Central Malaya now open to Japanese. General Sir Archibald Wavell, new Supreme Allied Commander, South West Pacific, visits Malaya
11 Jan	Japanese march into Kuala Lumpur
13 Jan	53rd British Brigade of 18th Division arrive in Singapore
14 Jan	Australian 8th Division deployed in Johore attack. Successful ambush at Gemas with heavy Japanese loss
15 Jan	Battle at Muar with two battalions of the 45th Indian Brigade broken
19 – 23 Jan	Japanese forces cut off Australian and Indian troops from Bakri/Yong Peng Area
24 Jan	Australian reinforcements arrive in Singapore
27 Jan	22nd Indian Brigade cut off at Layang Layang and destroyed
30 – 31 Jan	British Forces retreat across the Causeway to Singapore island with Singapore under continuous air attack
5 Feb	Remainder of 18th Division arrives in Singapore
7 Feb	Japanese begin artillery shelling of island
8 Feb	Japanese launch amphibious attack in the evening against Australians

10 Feb	Kranji-Jurong Line lost to Japanese. Wavell makes last visit to Singapore; injures back when he falls off quay when leaving Singapore and is hospitalised and runs rest of campaign from bed.
11 Feb	Percival moves the Combined Headquarters from Sime Road to the Battlebox at Fort Canning
12 Feb	British retreat to final perimeter around Singapore town
15 Feb	Percival surrenders Singapore; Malayan Campaign ends
18 Feb	Japanese occupy Fort Canning
8 Sep 1945	British re-occupy Fort Canning, becomes Headquarters of Singapore Base District
19 Sep 1963	Malaysian Fourth Federal Infantry Brigade takes over Fort Canning as part of Malaysia merger Agreement
Mar 1966	4th Federal Infantry Brigade pulls out of Fort Canning; complex handed over to the Singapore Armed Forces
Late 1967	The SAF's Singapore Command and Staff College established at Fort Canning
Mid-1975	SCSC vacates Fort Canning for its new premises in Seletar Camp
Mid-1980	Some of the above-ground buildings re-furbished as an arts centre
Mid 1990s	Conservation and re-development by the Parks Department and National Heritage Board
15 Feb 1997	Launch of Fort Canning Country Club and the Battlebox Museum
Nov 2002	Launch of Legends Fort Canning Park and the Battlebox Museum

Appendix C: Dramatis Personae

ARMY

General Sir Archibald Wavell	Supreme Commander, South West Pacific Command/Commander, ABDA Command
Lieutenant General Arthur E. Percival	General Officer Commanding, Headquarters Malaya Command
Lieutenant General Sir Lewis Heath	General Officer Commanding, III Indian Corps
Major General Gordon Bennett	Commander, 8th Australian Division
Major General F. Keith Simmons	Commander, Singapore Fortress
Brigadier A.D. Curtis	Commander, Fixed Defences
Brigadier T K Newbigging	Chief Administration Officer
Brigader Ivan Simson	Chief Engineer, Malaya Command
Brigadier K.S. Torrance	Brigadier General Staff, Malaya Command
Brigadier A.W.G. Wildey	Commander, Anti-Aircraft Defences
Lieutenant-Col C.C.M. Macleod-Carey	Deputy Commander, 7th Coast Artillery Regiment
Major Hugh-Lindley Jones	Gun Control Officer, the Battlebox
Major C.H.D. Wild	Staff Officer, III Indian Corps
Eric Lomax	Signaller, Malaya Command

AIR FORCE

Air Marshal Sir Robert Brooke-Popham	Commander-in-Chief, Far East
Air Vice Marshal C.W.H. Pulford	Air Officer Commanding, RAF Far East

NAVY

Admiral Sir Tom Phillips	Commander, Force Z (HMS *Prince of Wales* and HMS *Repulse*)
Vice-Admiral Sir Geoffrey Layton	Commander-in-Chief, China Fleet
Lieutenant Commander David Copley	Secretary to Extended Defence Officer, the Battlebox
Ray Stubbs	Royal Navy Coder, the Battlebox

JAPANESE

Lieutenant General Tomoyuki Yamashita	Commander of Japanese forces in Malayan Campaign
Major General Takuma Nishimura	Commander, Imperial Guards Division
Major General Saburo Kawamura	Japanese Commandant of Singapore

OTHERS

Sir Shenton Whitlegge Thomas	Governor of Singapore, 1935-1942
Sir Stamford Raffles	Founder of Singapore
Cuthbert Oswald Donough	Operator, Cable & Wireless, Singapore
Lee Kuan Yew	First Prime Minister of Singapore
Goh Keng Swee	Singapore Deputy Prime Minister and Defence Minister
Doraisingam S. Samuel	President, Singapore History Association
Felix Soh	Associate News Editor, *The Straits Times* (1988)
Tunku Abdul Rahman	First Prime Minister of Malaysia
Brigadier Syed Mohamed Bin Syed Alsagoff	Commander, 4th Federal Brigade

Bibliography

Primary Sources

The National Archives (Public Records Office), London

AIR2 Air Ministry Papers, Far East, Accomodation, 1930-1942

ADM1 Admiralty: Real Estate, Far East, 1968-1972

CAB65 War Cabinet: Minutes, 1939-1945

CAB66 War Cabinet: Memoranda, WP and CP series, 1939-1945

CAB79 War Cabinet: Chiefs of Staff Committee Minutes, 1939-1945

CAB80 War Cabinet: Chiefs of Staff Committee Memoranda, 1939-1945

CAB94 War Cabinet: Overseas Defence Committee, 1939-1942

CAB100 War Cabinet: Daily Situation Reports, 1939-1942

CAB105 War Cabinet: Telegrams, 1941-1948

HW50 Far Eastern Combined Bureau, 1936-1945

OD39 Ministry of Overseas Development and Overseas Development Administration: Malaysia and Singapore Department and successors,1966 to1973

WO32 Disposal of Real Estate, 1970-1975

WO172 Malaya Command Papers, 1939-1942

WO203 Military Headquarters Papers, Far East Forces, 1941-1945

WO216 Chief of Imperial General Staff Papers, 1935-1942

Imperial War Museum, London

Carter, Wing Commander T.C., Papers

Cazalet, Vice-Admiral Sir Peter, Papers

Heath, Lt Gen Sir Lewis, Papers

Kirby, Lt Col S.W., Notes on Singapore, 1936

Percival, Lt Gen A.E., Papers

Simpson-Oliver, 2nd Lt E., Papers

Thomas, Governor Sir T.S.W., Communique, Feb 16, 1942

Wild, Lt Col C.H.D., Notes on the Malayan Campaign, Notes on the Capitulation of Singapore

National Army Museum, London

Deakin, Lt Col C.C., and Webb, Maj G.M.S., 5th Battalion/2nd Punjab Regiment Papers

Frith, Lt Col The Rev John, 2nd Baluch regiment – Malaya Campaign Notes 1939 – 15 Feb 1942

Jones, Col J.L., Papers

Kelling, G.H., British and local forces in Malaya 1786-1945, unpublished Thesis, 1981

Macleod-Carey, Lt Col C.C.M., *Singapore Guns, War Monthly*, Issue 34, pgs 34-39

Malaya Command, Tactical Notes for Malaya 1940: Issued by the General Staff, Malaya Command, reprinted by General Staff, India, 1941

Others

Author Interview with C.O. Donough, 2 September 2004

Research Clippings on the Battlebox, Oral History Department, Singapore

Secondary Sources

Despatches

Brooke-Popham, Air Chief Marshall Sir Robert, Commander-in-Chief in the Far East, Operations in the Far East from 17 October 1940 to 27 December 1941, H.M.S.O., 1948

Percival, Lt. Gen A.E., Operations of Malaya Command, from 8 December 1941 to 15 February, 1942, H.M.S.O., 1948

Wavell, General A.P., Despatch by the Supreme Commander of the A.B.D.A. area to the Combined Chiefs of Staff on the operations in the South-West Pacific from 15 January 1942 to 25 February 1942, H.M.S.O., 1948

Books

Attiwell, Kenneth, *The Singapore Story*. New York: Doubleday, 1960

Barber, Noel, *A Sinister Twilight: The Fall of Singapore 1942*. Boston: Houghton Mifflin, 1968

Bennett, H. Gordon, *Why Singapore Fell*. Sydney: Angus & Robertson, Ltd., 1944

Braddon, Russell, *The Naked Island*. London: Werner Laurie, 1952

Brown, Cecil, *Suez to Singapore*. New York: Random House, 1942

Chapman, F. Spencer, *The Jungle is Neutral*. Singapore: Times Editions-Marshall Cavendish, reprinted 2005

Chin Kee Onn, *Malaya Upside Down*. Singapore: Jitts, 1946

Churchill, Winston S., *The Second World War. Vol 4 The Hinge of Fate*. Boston: Houghton Mifflin, 1950

Cooper, A. Duff, Old Men Forget. New York: Dutton 1954

Donahue, Arthur G., *Last Flight from Singapore*. London: Macmillan, 1944

Falk, Stanley, *Seventy Days to Singapore*. New York: G.P. Putnam's Sons, 1975

Gallagher, O.D., *Action in the East*. London: George G. Harrap, 1942

Grenfell, Russell, *Main Fleet to Singapore*. London: Faber & Faber Ltd, 1951

Kirby, S.W., *Singapore: The Chain of Disaster*. New York: Macmillan, 1971

Low, N.I., *When Singapore was Syonan-To*. Singapore: Times Editions, reprinted 2004

Mant, Gilbert, *Grim Glory*. Sydney: Currawong, 1945

Morrison, Ian, *Malayan Postscript*. Faber & Faber, 1943

Owen, Frank, *The Fall of Singapore*. London: Michael Joseph, 1960

Percival, A.E. *The War in Malaya*. London: Eyre & Spottiswoode, 1949

Simson, Ivan, *Singapore: Too Little, Too Late*. London: Leo Cooper Ltd, 1970

Tsuji, Masanobu, *Singapore: The Japanese Version*. Translated by M.E. Lake. New York: St. Martin's Press, 1960

Smyth, John., *V.C. Percival and the Tragedy of Singapore*. London: Macdonald, 1971

Articles

Bose, Romen, *Percival's Last Stand. The Straits Times*, 26 July 1988

Canning as National Preserves. The Malay Mail, 20 February 1969

Farming plans for Naval Base land. The Straits Times, 1 August 1963

Malaysian Army takes over Fort Canning. The Malay Mail, 18 Sept. 1963

Pestana, Roderick, *Malaysia pulls last troops out of Singapore. The Straits Times*, 26 January 1968

Rozario, Francis, *Handover of $135m Property. The Straits Times*, 5 February 1969

Sam, Jackie, *Federation Army to use Fort Canning as Base. The Sunday Times*, 28 July 1963

See, Constance, *Historic Command House up for rent at $30,000 a month*. Home, *The Straits Times*, 4 April 1993

Takeover without a shot at Fort Canning. The Straits Times, 5 March 1963

Thousand acres of WD land for Singapore. The Straits Times, 9 July 1963

Yeo, Geraldine, *Lion City Memories. Life!, The Straits Times*, 11 March 1999

Yeo, Joseph, *Defence: The big switch has begun. The Sunday Times*, 3 March 1963

Picture Credits

Romen Bose: page 23 (top), 25 (bottom), 37 (top), 41 (both), 43 (bottom), 49, 50, 55(both), 110. The Imperial War Museum, London: page 11, 59, 96 (both), 113. By courtesy of *The Straits Times* with the permission of Singapore Press Holdings: page 20, 23 (bottom), 25 (top), 35, 43 (top), 45, 47. By courtesy of the Battlebox: Page 37 (bottom), 107 (both). Map on page 81 reproduced from *The War in Malaya*, published by Eyre and Spottiswoode. Every effort has been made to trace and credit the sources of photographs and illustrations used. Please contact us if there have been any inadvertent errors or omissions.

THE END OF THE WAR

SINGAPORE'S LIBERATION AND THE AFTERMATH OF THE SECOND WORLD WAR

Contents

	Preface to the First Edition	127
Chapter 1	Introduction	129
Chapter 2	British Pacific Policy	142
Chapter 3	Clandestine Forces	153
Chapter 4	The Early Surrenders	192
Chapter 5	Operation TIDERACE	199
Chapter 6	Reoccupation	216
Chapter 7	Operation ZIPPER	229
Chapter 8	The Final Surrender in Singapore	238
Chapter 9	Locations	257
Chapter 10	Postscript	280
Appendix A	Chronology of Events	290
Appendix B	List of Operations	292
Appendix C	Operation ZIPPER Order of Battle	294
Appendix D	Ships Anchored in Singapore Roads during the Ceremony of Surrender	295
Appendix E	List of Notable Personalities	298
Appendix F	Reproduction of Original Documents	310
	Selected Bibliography	330

Preface to the First Edition

I have always held a fascination for the last days of the war in Singapore and the eventual British reoccupation. As a child, I would spend hours at the Surrender Chamber on Sentosa Island, where wax figures of then Vice Admiral Lord Louis Mountbatten and his aides accepting the surrender from General Seishiro Itagaki on 12 September 1945 are frozen in time. Through the years, I have come across scraps of information and anecdotal evidence of the British recapture of Singapore and Malaya and I must thank my uncle, Mrinal Kanti Dutta, a history buff himself, who was always on the lookout for books on the war and would present me with very rare tomes on the fall of Singapore and the eventual liberation of the island.

However, it was not until I received the British Council's Chevening Scholarship in 2004 for a year's study in the United Kingdom that I was given the opportunity to go through the entire series of documents pertaining to the end of the war, ensconced safely at the National Archives in Kew. I would like to thank the Council's Errim Mahmoud and Sandra Bodestyne for their continued support and help.

I would also like to take the opportunity to thank the various individuals and organisations that have been crucial to the completion of this book: The President and Mrs S.R. Nathan; Lim Neo Chian; The Imperial War Museum; The National Archives, London; The Australian War Memorial; Dr Gareth Stanton and the Media and Communications Department, Goldsmiths College; The British Council; The Singapore Tourism Board; The National Library, Singapore; The National Archives, Singapore; C.O. Donough; Jeyathurai A.; Jennifer A.; and of course my Mum and Dad, Ajoy, Anuradha, Nita, Hari, Nisha and Anusha. A very special thank you to Brian Farrell for helping to spot the loopholes of logic and giving incisive comments on how to write a better book. I must also thank Benny Chung, my editor at Marshall Cavendish whose unflagging enthusiasm and patience led to the writing of several of the appendices in this book.

This book, on the end of the war, does not purport to be a comprehensive tome on the period nor does it attempt to reveal all that is known about the events then or even provide a social history of the times. This book is an attempt to help readers understand better what actually happened during those few months in 1945 when the war was at an end and it appeared, to the newly reinstated colonial masters at least, that the future of the peoples in Malaysia and Singapore would be determined by whichever power controlled Southeast Asia.

The End of the War reveals many secrets of the Second World War that have been hidden in highly sensitive files and long forgotten. It tries to better explain how Britain decided to retake its possessions in Malaya and Singapore and the various ways in which they went about doing this. It also sheds light on wartime heroes like Lim Bo Seng and the role he played in the clandestine Allied operations leading to the end of the war. It concludes by revealing the actual Japanese surrender in Singapore and how the Allied forces finally returned to Malaya and Singapore. A theme that recurs throughout this book is of how endings have led to new beginnings. The fall of Singapore in 1942 led to the formulation of a British policy to retake the area, as well as the creation of resistance groups and clandestine movements. The end of the war led to the beginnings of nationalism and the eventual demands for independence and the creation of independent countries less than two decades after the Japanese surrenders.

It is hoped that this patchwork of vignettes into the various aspects of the period will stimulate greater discussion among a younger generation of readers and encourage more research into a very chaotic but historically significant point in time.

As veterans return to these sites over the next few years to commemorate events and remember fallen comrades, I hope that many who read this book will come forward and give their perceptions and tell their stories of the end of the war.

Romen Bose
14 July 2005

Chapter 1

Introduction

4 September 1945.

It was a still morning in the seas off Singapore. There was not even a breeze about as he stood on the deck of the ship. All he could see ahead of him were the grey hulks of warships that filled his view of the harbour. Sweat dripped down his chin as the coolness of the dawn evaporated and the early rays of the rising sun foretold the sweltering day ahead.

He had waited since dawn, dressed immaculately in a white, open-collared shirt, pressed khaki field uniform and polished boots. The dress sword at his side glinted in the morning light. As the ship gently rocked in the wake of the larger vessels, he took a sip of the tepid tea that had been proffered hours earlier, idly wondering whether he would still be a free man when this day was over.

Before him lay the might of the British Royal Navy. A naval cruiser and several destroyers had converged at the agreed rendezvous point just outside Keppel Harbour, their large guns all trained at the city. The sea now glittered with the oily slicks discharged by these behemoths as they lay anchored, floating and waiting. The sound of their engines created a dull throb in the still air. There was clearly a sense of anticipation in the air. It was as if the last scene from an epic play were about to begin, the cast of characters now gathering off stage, just before everyone would be cued to their places and the curtains raised.

The British had come to Singapore to take back what, they claimed, had rightfully belonged to them. They were here in force and no one expected these victors to be magnanimous.

How the tables had turned.

Less than three years before, he had been at the forefront of a conquering army that had liberated the Asiatic peoples all the way from Burma to the islands of the South Pacific. The Imperial Japanese Army had been the vanguard of a new East Asia Co-Prosperity Sphere, welcoming an era where the peoples of Asia would rule themselves, under the guidance of the Chrysanthemum Throne, of course. The Showa era was to herald untold successes for the Japanese people and lead to a glorious reign.

Instead, the Second World War had led to huge defeats and millions killed. Defeat after defeat had demoralised the imperial army and led to starvation and abject poverty throughout the empire. No longer could Japan hold its head up high. Vast areas of the homeland had been destroyed and the enemy had succeeded in routing most of the Japanese army.

He had lost many friends and colleagues in the last three years; too many to count, too many to mourn over. Even here, where only the stories rather than actual experience of the horrors of the Burma Campaign had filtered through, there was a deep sense of foreboding that the end was near.

Southeast Asia was to be the last stand before the enemy took the fighting to the home islands. It was supposed to be the last big battle before Armageddon. But it never came.

All the suffering, the torture of the local populace for information on fifth columnists, the quelling of resistance groups and the planning for a spirited defence of Malaya had all come to naught.

Two horrific bombs dropped on Hiroshima and Nagasaki meant the end of the war had arrived and along with it the humiliating result of having to surrender to the enemy.

As he stood on board the Japanese submarine chaser flying a black and white surrender flag in Keppel Harbour, General Seishiro Itagaki was angry. Angry that an empire as great as Japan had been defeated. Angry that despite the huge numbers of lives lost, the cause he had fought for all his life was now relegated to the dustbin of history. Angry that his commander-in-chief, Field Marshal Count Hisaichi Terauchi, had refused to surrender to the Allied forces, feigning ill health. And angry that he would have the humiliating task of surrendering his country's forces at a location which had symbolised the empire's victory over its enemies only three years before.

Itagaki had served in the Kwantung army in China in 1936 and celebrated the creation of the Japanese puppet state of Manchukuo with Emperor Isenjiro Pu Yi (in *pinyin*, Aixin Jueluo Puyi) as its titular head. Itagaki became Minister of War in Prime Minister General Hideki Tojo's military cabinet of 1941 and commanded the 17th Area Army in Korea.

As Japan's fortunes began to wane, he ended up commanding the 7th Area Army in Singapore and was in charge of all Japanese forces in the area when Japan announced its unconditional surrender on 15 August 1945. Less than three years after that date, Itagaki would be hanged as a war criminal[1].

But that would be in the future. For now, Itagaki waited aboard the chaser, pacing nervously and refusing to talk to his naval counterpart who stood calmly to one side.

Vice Admiral Shigeru Fukudome, Commander of the 10th Area Fleet, was much more of a character. Described as an opportunist, Fukudome was very ambitious and always sought to further his own career and objectives at the expense of fellow officers. Even now, he was looking for ways to ingratiate himself with the new masters of Singapore in an attempt to save his skin and hopefully earn himself a position in a post-war Japanese government. He was intelligent, talked freely, and appeared to be "a markedly superior Japanese officer". Even though he understood English, he had chosen to converse through an interpreter at the upcoming meeting with the British in order to give himself time to think of appropriate responses to questioning. However, unbeknownst to him, a top-secret cable from Washington earlier in the day had revealed to British commanders that Fukudome had been director of the 1st section (Plans and Operations) of the Japanese naval staff at the time of the attack on Pearl Harbour. He was one of the officers principally responsible for planning the destruction of the American fleet and was regarded by the Americans as a war criminal[2].

In ending up at Singapore, Fukudome's track record had not been entirely spotless. In late March 1944, just before the battle in the Marianas for the islands of Saipan, Palau and Truk, Fukudome had been in a plane crash in the Philippines. He was Admiral Yamamoto's successor as Chief of Staff for the combined fleet, and had been carrying the battle plans for the Japanese fleet but lost them in the crash. The documents were retrieved from the crash site by Philippine resistance fighters and smuggled to the Americans, who then translated them with the help of two Hawaii-born Nisei soldiers – Japanese Americans who had signed up to serve in a special unit in the US army. General Douglas MacArthur later sent the translation to Hawaii where this "operational-level coup" greatly aided Admiral Raymond Spruance a few weeks later as he met the Japanese at the Battle of the Philippine Sea, a major defeat for Japanese naval aviation that saw the loss of more than 400 Japanese aircraft and the severe crippling of three Japanese aircraft carriers[3].

These two men, with two very different pasts, would now hand over the entire Japanese force in Singapore to the British.

The Allied forces had called for this hasty meeting on board a warship only five days before. The Japanese had expected the British to take over the Malayan peninsula before heading to Singapore but it was now clear that the British had made a lightning dash to Singapore to recapture the island first. Itagaki was still not sure if the meeting was to arrange for a surrender or if it would be the surrender itself. The one thing he was sure of was that, after the meeting, he would clearly be living on borrowed time.

Suddenly, the HMS *Sussex* began signalling Itagaki's vessel. The submarine chaser drew alongside the large cruiser and Itagaki and Fukudome were invited aboard[4].

In true British naval tradition, the two Japanese general officers were piped aboard the *Sussex*. The decks of the *Sussex* and the surrounding escort warships were filled with curious officers and ratings, all trying to get a good look at the historic event unfolding before their eyes.

The two men, followed closely by their staff officers, were introduced to the captain of the *Sussex* and escorted to a small cabin where they were disarmed. There, they were made to wait until the representatives of Vice Admiral Lord Louis Mountbatten, the Supreme Allied Commander, Southeast Asia (SACSEA), were ready to meet them.

The meeting was to be held in the Admiral's Dining Room. The rectangular room, normally used for meals, had been cleared of all its glass and accoutrements in order to fit a long table covered with green cloth. As a psychological ploy, the row of chairs intended for the Japanese delegates was kept some distance away from the table in order to make them feel uncomfortable and prevent them from leaning onto the table or using it effectively.

As the Japanese waited in the anteroom, Mountbatten's army representative, Lieutenant General Sir Alexander Frank Philip Christison, General Officer Commanding (GOC), 15th Indian Corps, entered the dining room. Christison, who had served in the Burma Campaign and who would end his career as a General Aide-de-Camp to King George VI, would lead the proceedings[5].

He was followed by Rear (later Vice) Admiral Cedric Swinton Holland, Mountbatten's naval representative, who had led the top secret emergency dash to recapture Singapore. By his side was Major General Eric Carden Robert Mansergh, Commander of the 5th Indian Division, who would be leading the first Allied division in the reoccupation of Singapore.

Rounding off the group was Major General Sir Herbert Ralph Hone, the civil administration officer who later would set up a post-war British military administration in Singapore.

Christison was relieved that Itagaki had turned up for the meeting. He had feared that the general would change his mind at the last minute and

The Allied generals: Posing for an official picture in the cramped Admiral's Dining Room on board HMS Sussex, *after General Itagaki signed the terms of agreement for the surrender of Singapore on 4 September 1945 are (left to right, seated) Lieutenant F.P. Donachie, Major General E.C. Mansergh, Brigadier General N.D. Wingrove, Lieutenant General Sir A.F.P. Christison, Vice-Admiral C.S. Holland, Captain C.F.J. Lloyd Davies and Major General H.R. Hone.*

put up a struggle. As the British fleet in the harbour was not loaded for an assault, Japanese resistance would have meant the wholesale destruction of the Allied forces gathered off the coast of Singapore.

At 11.00am, the Japanese officers were summoned to the Admiral's Dining Room. Itagaki and his aide led the delegation as they marched into the room and stood at attention. They saluted and bowed to the Allied generals but remained standing until instructed to sit down.

The atmosphere was very tense and the air was filled with expectation. Security was tight – a marine was posted at the doorway – and for a moment, there was pin-drop silence as each side sized up the other.

Not giving Itagaki a chance to begin, Christison cleared his throat and spoke through his interpreter. He asked the Japanese officer for his name, rank and appointment and Itagaki responded[6].

Christison: Are you entitled to speak for the Field Marshal Count Terauchi, Supreme Japanese Commander, Southern Region, on Army matters?

Itagaki: Not entirely for the whole area, but only for the landings in the Singapore area.

Christison: Do you know the Terms of Agreement signed in Rangoon?

Itagaki: I know of the Agreement signed in Rangoon and, furthermore, I have complied with what I ought to have done in Singapore with regard to this Agreement.

Christison then asked Fukudome to identify himself and asked whether he had Terauchi's authority to discuss the Japanese surrender. Fukudome, smiling and winking, responded in kind.

Christison: Do you abide by the Imperial decision to cease hostilities and are you prepared to carry out the orders of the Supreme Allied Commander, South East Asia?

Itagaki: Yes, I am quite prepared.

Although he appeared meek, Itagaki, from the start, wanted to ensure that his men would not face the wrath of the victorious Allies. When asked what his plans were, he asked for the Japanese troops to be segregated away from the Allied troops.

Itagaki: For future plans, we wish to avoid possible clashes between the Allied Army and consider our forces should be as far away as possible. I am now constructing temporary barracks in the following areas: (1) West of Island, in Jurong–Choa Chu Kang; (2) East of Island, between Singapore–Changi Roads from Ulu Bedock–Simpang Bedock (Ulu Bedok–Simpang Bedok) Bugis Estate–Honyeyang Estate (Bugis Estate–Hougang Estate); – which I should like to use. As a temporary construction is not yet completed at present, our Headquarters will be in the Raffles College.

However, for the British commanders, the bigger concern was the level of violence and lawlessness in Singapore during the phoney surrender, the three weeks between the announcement of the Japanese surrender and the British arrival in Singapore to reoccupy Malaya. Christison was worried that his troops would have to quell riots.

Christison: Is there any sabotage, looting or local civil disturbance taking place in the Singapore area?

Itagaki: With regard to the maintenance of law and order there are no riots of a serious nature but there is every sign of possible looting and some sort of violence of a small nature which is under the guard of our Forces now and we have also suspicions certain Societies are being formed but we are taking every possible step to suppress them. We are also collecting information about them.

Christison: I rely on General Itagaki to keep law and order until my Forces take over.

He then told Itagaki that Mansergh's troops would be landing in Singapore the next day at Keppel Harbour and the wharves. Rear Admiral Holland instructed Fukudome to use Japanese minesweepers to sweep the channel ahead of the Allied troops to ensure a clear path into Singapore. The waters around Singapore were still unsafe.

Fukudome: ... Inside Keppel Harbour all is safe. Boom still exists and is visible above water... Since the beginning of this year the Americans came over and dropped magnetic or other mines in the areas coloured red and blue on the chart. The channels are quite safe but outside these, everything is uncertain.

Asked about the occupants of Keppel Harbour, Fukudome said there were no warships there although there were submarines.

Fukudome: At present there are no Naval boats in Keppel Harbour. There are two German submarines in Keppel Harbour... only guarded by Japanese guards.

The British officers ordered the Japanese delegates to keep the harbour clear of all ships during the landings on 5 September. Christison gave Itagaki a copy of the *de facto* surrender agreement, the *Instructions to the Japanese Forces under Command or Control of Japanese Commanders Singapore Area* (see "Appendix F: Part 1") which he asked Itagaki to study before signing.

The Japanese were caught completely off-guard. Itagaki and Fukudome were not expecting to sign anything. Moreover, they had to translate the document and understand it fully before agreeing. For four hours, Itagaki and Fukudome were holed up in the ante-room with their staff officers

Lieutenant Colonel Itoga, Captain Onoda and their two interpreters as they went over the terms of surrender[7].

The Japanese forces on Singapore island and in Malaya were to be treated as "surrendered personnel" rather than as prisoners of war. This would mean that the Allied forces, with their limited troops and resources, would not have to set up special prisoner of war camps and guard the Japanese as prisoners. The Japanese would be disarmed but could continue to wear uniforms and badges of rank. Japanese commanders would remain responsible for the maintenance and discipline of their own troops, for public order, for the protection of banks, and for the feeding of civilians in territories that had hitherto been under their control.

Essential services such as light and water were to be maintained and guarded until Allied forces had assumed control; aircraft would be grounded and remain so. No demolitions would be permitted; and damage to bridges, waterways, railroads, telegraphs and telephones, stores of food, and cattle belonging to civilians had to be prevented. To implement these instructions, the Japanese would be allowed guards of 100 men for military stores, dumps and vehicle parks, for dock installations, for bulk holdings of cash, and for Japanese hospital patients who could not be moved.

The Japanese were to also provide the location of fortifications, camps of Allied prisoners of war (POWs) or internees, aircraft and airfields, weapons and ammunition. The status of broadcasting stations, radar and signal equipment, rolling stock, workshops, harbour facilities, war materials and food stocks were also to be reported. Charts of minefields and booby traps were also demanded. All documents, records, ciphers and codes would be handed over together with nominal rolls, orders of battle, lists of medical supplies, shops used by the Japanese and stocks of petrol and oil. A final clause insisted that all requisitioned or stolen goods and property were to be restored.

In addition, the Japanese were ordered to submit a list of all the graves of Allied troops and civilian internees. All Japanese flags, emblems and memorials other than graves were to be removed before the 5th Indian Division landed the following day.

These were unacceptable demands. Itagaki had to act to ensure that he was able to negotiate a more conditional surrender. On returning to the conference table, he was insistent that the Japanese view prevail. One of the main clauses he wanted amended was the instruction for the Japanese forces to be reduced immediately and marched to the mainland. Itagaki argued that no quarters existed there, north of Johor Baru.

Itagaki: ... The present situation is that we are just removing to the Jurong district and the temporary barracks are only

> half-finished. If we are to be ordered to the mainland, it would make a terrible mess of everything. If possible, we should like to be given a certain amount of time in which we could prepare for the secondary movement.

He said it was difficult to maintain law and order on the mainland in view of the actions of certain elements, chiefly communists, and suggested they should be concentrated on the Indonesian islands of Munda and Bintan.

However, Christison would not compromise. This was a surrender and not a treaty negotiation. He promptly told Itagaki that the Japanese 46th Division was still armed and would be able to defend itself in a move to the mainland. Mansergh noted that the 46th Division would be allowed to keep only small arms but would be disarmed once the 5th Indian Division took over responsibility for the area. Moreover, as the Indonesian islands Itagaki mentioned were part of Dutch territory, Christison said the Dutch would have had to agree to the proposal first. Until then, Japanese forces would have to move to Johor.

Itagaki also wanted to remove the clause prohibiting reprisals against anti-Japanese resistance and guerrilla forces.

> Itagaki: We do not take reprisals for anything that has happened in the past, but in the future, it will be difficult for us to distinguish if they are really guerilla (*sic*) forces or whether they are unattached and are persons who are attacking us from purely personal motives. We will have to protect ourselves and it is difficult for us to discriminate.

> Christison: These guerilla (*sic*) forces will be in uniform and will wear a uniform like this (he produced an officer wearing the uniform) and they will wear a beret with three stars like this one.

> Fukudome: We can give you an actual incident where, after the cessation of hostilities, a person wearing that cap approached Japanese Naval personnel and told them to help the Allies now (that) the war was over. He was in possession of a machine gun. He called himself a Communist. It happened in the southernmost part of the Malayan Peninsula, and he tried to get the Japanese to join his party. It is difficult for us to distinguish that sort of person.

Holland:	How can you guard against this sort of thing? Such acts were only committed by individuals and not by battalions.
Christison:	This is the general policy. Such personnel will be treated by you as though they were Allied Forces. They all know hostilities have ceased and any hostile acts by them shall be resisted by you and the individual handed over to us.
Itagaki:	It will be difficult for any Japanese Army personnel to resist a person who carries arms.
Christison:	We are leaving you the 46th Division until our arrival. You can take what action you like against hostile acts. Call on General Mansergh if you want any help.

There was no option but to accede. Itagaki and Fukudome reluctantly agreed to the terms.

The only clause where the Japanese won a reprieve was on the issue of saluting and the surrender of swords. The Japanese delegates refused to budge on the point, insisting that as these were not terms outlined in Rangoon, they needed permission first from Field Marshal Terauchi, Commander-in-Chief of the Japanese Southern Army. As such, the clause was held in abeyance but was nonetheless implemented shortly after the reoccupation.

Mansergh also issued additional orders to Itagaki to ensure that the 5th Indian Division could take over quickly[8]. Orders issued to the Japanese commander of Singapore island instructed every member of the "Japanese forces and puppet forces" that still remained on the island to wear a white armband. Mansergh also ordered all Japanese wives, families and members of the "Japanese comfort corps" to accompany their various formations during the withdrawal from the island. However, hospital staff were to remain on duty and the Japanese were instructed to leave a guard or sentry at all buildings that were vacated in order to prevent looting during the transition period.

At about 4.00pm, the two Japanese officers again left the dining room as the instrument was retyped. At 6.05pm, a little more than seven hours after the meeting first began, General Itagaki and Vice Admiral Fukudome signed the surrender agreement and handed over close to 96,000 Japanese troops in Singapore to less than 10,000 Allied troops on the seas off the island.

General Itagaki, Commander of the 7th Japanese Area Army, signing the initial surrender terms on board HMS Sussex, *4 September 1945. Itagaki is being assisted by his Chief of Staff, Lieutenant Colonel Itoga, as Staff Officer Captain Onoda looks on.*

Fukudome, who had smiled and winked at the enemy commanders during the meeting and was at pains to convey his goodwill, smiled and saluted as he left the room, continuing his efforts to ingratiate himself with the British commanders. Itagaki, however, appeared to be a broken man. He wept as he walked out of the room, no longer a general but a "surrendered enemy personnel".

And so came the actual surrender of Japanese forces in Singapore on 4 September 1945. This almost-secret surrender was never publicised. In the following days, even major British newspapers did not mention the Singapore surrender but only reported that British forces were nearing Singapore. The British Government and Allied media were more concerned with the official surrender of the Japanese in Singapore's City Hall on 12 September 1945. It did not matter that Japanese forces in Southeast Asia had already effectively signed a surrender of troops in the region on 28 August 1945 in Rangoon. The drama and pomp of the official surrender were important in order to show that the British had returned and were in full control, even if the 4 September ceremony on the *Sussex* had already signalled their return to the region in force, with the strategic and symbolic recapture of Burma and Singapore.

Mountbatten's strategy for the reoccupation of British territories in Southeast Asia was to create an impression of a takeover by superior forces.

If the Japanese were made to believe that they were outnumbered, they would be less likely to consider a counterattack. More importantly, it would help to instil order and calm among the recently liberated Asian populace, who had remained in a power vacuum for almost a month during the so-called phoney surrender period between the surrender of the Japanese and the arrival of Allied forces to enforce a reoccupation.

Singapore, being Britain's jewel in the Far East and the symbolic site of its defeat at Japanese hands in 1942, had to be retaken at speed and with as much pomp and pageantry as possible. The reoccupation of Singapore was so crucial to British strategy that it occurred four days before the recapture of the rest of Malaya. The official surrender ceremonies could be held later and it was only after the Allied troops landed on the beaches of Morib and Sepang on the mainland that Mountbatten had his moment of glory on the steps of City Hall.

The famous images of Mountbatten accepting the Japanese surrender from Itagaki in the City Hall chambers are what most people would identify with from that time. The official surrender ceremony, however, would never have taken place had the signing and agreement on board HMS *Sussex* not happened. Within a day of the *Sussex* surrender, 35,000 Japanese troops were transported off the island to be housed in prisoner camps in southern Johor.

Although the events of 12 September 1945 closed the chapter on the Japanese military domination of Asia, they also marked the beginnings of the communist insurgency in Southeast Asia. The British were not completely prepared to resume control of the region and the resulting phoney surrender period led to huge communal clashes between the Malays, Chinese and the Indians. The communist-inspired Malayan People's Anti-Japanese Army (MPAJA) killed those whom they accused of having collaborated with the Japanese forces – and later those identified as non-sympathisers – in their bid to form a communist state. Where once the races were able to live and work side-by-side under British rule, this period of lawlessness and retribution, accentuated by the years of Japanese repression, planted some of the seeds of hatred and contempt each ethnic group held towards the other, a problem that would plague the post-war road to independence.

Like many other aspects of the end of the war in Singapore and Malaya, the proceedings of the Japanese surrender on board HMS *Sussex*, although partly reported in Allied newspapers of the time, have long been forgotten and are remembered by only a select few who were intimately involved in the top-secret recapture of British possessions in Malaya and Singapore at the end of the Second World War.

The events that led to the signing on board HMS *Sussex* are also just as mysterious and intriguing and go to the heart of explaining what actually happened in the closing days of the war and how Singapore and Malaya came to be liberated in September 1945.

Using highly sensitive documents and files that have only just been opened to the public, close to 60 years after the event, this book traces some of the most secret operations and plans undertaken to liberate Singapore and Malaya, revealing the last remaining secrets of the end of the war in Singapore and Malaya.

From the top secret TIDERACE operations to retake Penang and Singapore, to the final fate of secret agents like Lim Bo Seng, the story of the liberation of Singapore and Malaya has its foundations in the fall of Singapore on 15 February 1942.

Endnotes

1 Ammentorp, Steen. "Biography of Seishiro Itagaki". *The Generals of WWII.* [Internet]. Accessed 28 January 2005. Available from: <http://www.generals.dk/general/Itagaki/Seishiro/Japan.html>.

2 *SMC 857/17, No 74490 AK3, 17 September 1945, WO203/2308.* London: The National Archives.

3 Harrington, Joseph D. *Yankee Samurai: The Secret Role of Nisei in America's Pacific Victory.* Detroit: Pettigrew Enterprises, 1979. 190–91, 195–97.

4 *Letter of Proceedings – OPERATION TIDERACE. 18 September 1945, ADM116/5562.* London: The National Archives. 3.

5 Ammentorp, Steen. "Biography of Sir Alexander Frank Philip Christison". *The Generals of WWII.* [Internet]. Accessed 28 January 2005. Available from: <http://www.generals.dk/general/Christison/Sir_Alexander_Frank_Philip/Great_Britain.html>.

6 *Verbatim Report at Meeting on board* HMS Sussex, *4 September 1945, between Representatives of the Supreme Allied Commander, Southeast Asia, and Representatives of Field Marshal Count Terauchi, Supreme Japanese Commander, Southern Region. 3408/E.I.14232/45, 27 October 1945, ADM116/5562.* London: The National Archives. 1–14.

7 *Instructions to the Japanese Forces under Command or Control of Japanese Commanders Singapore Area. 4 September 1945, ADM116/5562.* London: The National Archives. 1, Appendices A, B, C, D.

8 *Orders of the Commander Occupying Force to the Japanese Commander of Singapore. 31 August 1945, WO203/2308.* London: The National Archives. 1–2.

Chapter 2

The British Pacific Policy and the End of the War

The fall of Malaya and Singapore in 70 days with the loss of close to 125,000 British and Commonwealth troops along with a huge amount of war material was an enormous blow to the British war effort. More importantly, the loss of the major supplier of the world's rubber and tin meant that they would have to find other sources for these crucial materials of war.

Although Britain had been forcibly ejected from Southeast Asia and moved slowly in developing a Pacific strategy, one thing remained clear after the devastating defeats in late 1941 and early 1942. It did not see the discontinuation of the British presence in Southeast Asia as the end of imperial rule[1] but as a setback. Many held the view, expressed in 1945, by then British foreign secretary, Sir Anthony Robert Eden, that there was "not the slightest question of liquidating the British empire"[2].

Regardless, just as in the First World War, Britain could not hope to triumph without American assistance. However, because American pre-war foreign policy was anti-imperialist by nature, getting their help in recapturing former British colonies would be a real challenge. More importantly, the war against Germany was viewed as much more crucial with the majority of Allied forces and material headed for the European theatre. Nonetheless, the appointment of Lord Louis Mountbatten as the Supreme Allied Commander, Southeast Asia (SACSEA), at Quebec in August 1943 put Britain in a position to restore its place as a great power in Southeast Asia[3].

The biggest challenge facing British planners lay in how to deploy its meagre resources against the Japanese. With the loss of its colonies, the situation in Southeast Asia seemed bleak, with Eden noting that, "there was nothing for it but to wait and hold our end up as best we could, leaving most of the talk and proposing to others", namely the Americans[4].

However, the surrender of the Italian navy in September 1943 and the disabling of the German battleship *Tirpitz* helped free up British naval forces from home waters and the Mediterranean, allowing British military planners to take a fresh look at Southeast Asia.

British Prime Minister Winston Churchill was also keen to recapture British possessions in Southeast Asia, hoping that if the inhabitants of these territories saw the British as liberators, they could expunge the shame of defeat and rebuild the British Empire. During 1944, Churchill, supported by the Foreign Office and Southeast Asia Command (SEAC), argued with the British chiefs of staff for an attack against north Sumatra, codenamed Operation CULVERIN[5].

Lacking adequate intelligence on Japanese troop strength in Malaya and Sumatra, the chiefs strongly disagreed, with many feeling it better to send land and air forces to Australia, in support of the American flank towards the Philippines and Formosa (Taiwan). Also, American planners were concerned about CULVERIN, which some felt might undermine the position of General Douglas MacArthur, the newly appointed Supreme Allied Commander of the Southwest Pacific Area.

Throughout 1944, the differences in opinion between Churchill and his chiefs left senior British military leaders frustrated. During discussions on plans for Southeast Asia, Churchill kept insisting on operations against the tip of Sumatra and refused to look at anything else. As these meetings dragged on endlessly, Field Marshal Sir Alan Brooke, the chief of the Imperial General Staff, wrote in his diary that Churchill had

> ... lost the power of giving a decision. He finds every possible excuse to avoid giving one. His arguments are becoming puerile, for instance he upheld this evening that an attack on the tip of Sumatra would force a withdrawal of Japanese forces in northern Burma and would liquidate our commitment in this area. We have conferred for 7 hours!!! with him today to settle absolutely nothing. Nor has he produced a single argument during the whole of that period that was worth listening to. I am at my wits' end and can't go on much longer![6]

By 10 August 1944, with recent successes in Imphal and Kohima, a strategy for an amphibious landing at Rangoon, codenamed Operation DRACULA, was approved by Churchill and the chiefs of staff. The plan would require American assistance in terms of air support and assault shipping but was accepted as it avoided a prolonged campaign in northern Burma[7].

However, Churchill continued to vacillate on the issue of the kind of offensive to take in the rest of Southeast Asia. As the war dragged on in Europe, the timetable for defeating Japan was once again extended, showing clearly the need for Soviet help. The Allies had hoped to start moving resources to Southeast Asia by the end of 1944 but with the failure of Operation MARKET GARDEN in Arnhem in September, and the Ardennes offensive in December, planners predicted that Germany would not be beaten before the winter of 1945[8]. The setback at Arnhem immediately removed crucial resources from DRACULA. The US joint chiefs of staff diverted two infantry divisions, scheduled for the Pacific in May 1945, to the European theatre.

By June 1945, the bloody battle for Okinawa had increased the pressure on US military and civilian leaders to bring the war to a quick end. With intelligence reports calculating between 30,000 to 60,000 troops moved to the Japanese islands to defend the homeland, plans for the invasion of Kyushu and Honshu were developed, codenamed Operation CORONET and Operation OLYMPIC, respectively. However, before the British could commit to an all-out effort in attacking the Japanese homeland, they needed to recapture Southeast Asia.

Cut off from the rest of the Japanese empire, the strategic value of the Japanese Southern Army in Southeast Asia had been greatly reduced by December 1944, after the loss of Leyte in the Philippines. Still, even though the Japanese forces were lacking munitions and men, staff planners at SEAC and the Joint Intelligence Committee (JIC) correctly anticipated that the Japanese would attempt to delay the advance of the British for as long as possible in Burma, Malaya, Indochina and Siam[9]. In an effort to divert Allied forces away from the homeland, the Japanese ordered a division from Sumatra to reinforce Siam and a division from Celebes to reinforce Singapore. In March 1945, the Japanese also assumed military control of French Vichy Indochina and reinforced it with three divisions. The commander-in-chief of the Southern Army, Count Hisaichi Terauchi, had already based himself in Saigon in late 1944. The JIC predicted that it would take at least another 12 months to force a collapse of the Japanese position in Southeast Asia.

The British reached Rangoon in May 1945, successfully executing a scaled-down version of Operation DRACULA (Operation MODIFIED DRACULA). With the Japanese in retreat, SEAC planners began drafting an amphibious assault plan for the west coast of Malaya codenamed Operation ZIPPER, which was scheduled for September 1945. The plan called for the capture of advanced naval and air bases on Phuket island in Thailand (Operation ROGER) and Penang island in Malaya (Operation JURIST) before the activation of Operation ZIPPER. The invasion of

Singapore island, codenamed Operation MAILFIST, would then occur relatively soon after ZIPPER was launched, by which time the Allied troops who had landed on the west coast would have forced the Japanese into retreat down the Malayan peninsula.

However, SEAC Intelligence reports indicated that ZIPPER and MAILFIST would face an uphill challenge as the Japanese were already planning a strong defence of Malaya:

> With the fall of Rangoon, it has become increasingly evident that the Japanese anticipate an early assault on Malaya itself. Consequently, a considerable strengthening and allocation of troops is now taking place, including the reported arrival of up to four battalions from SIAM, although in view of the size of the garrison in SIAM, it is possible that these troops originally came from F.I.C. (French Indochina). In addition, elements of 37th Division are reported to have arrived in Bangkok from F.I.C. in early July. The possibility arises, therefore, that this division is also in transit to MALAYA... The garrison in MALAYA... will probably be further reinforced by the retention there of all troops arriving from N.E.I. (Netherland East Indies).... It is obvious that the Japanese regard SINGAPORE as our ultimate objective, but it is difficult to say which they consider the most likely area for the initial assault...[10]

Intelligence indicated the Japanese had more than 24 infantry battalions and 75 tanks in Malaya amounting to more than 59,000 troops. This, they believed, would rise to 29 infantry battalions, or about 72,000 troops, and 75 tanks by ZIPPER's D-day[11]. To counter this, ZIPPER called for the massing of the 5th, 23rd, 25th and 26th Indian Divisions, the 3rd commando brigade and one parachute brigade of the British 6th Airborne Division, amounting to more than 100,000 troops. Even so, British intelligence expected "formidable opposition to coastal landings at major bases is likely to be presented by base forces and guard forces consisting of naval shore-based troops, roughly equivalent to our marines"[12].

However, this planning went into a tailspin with the dissolution of the British coalition government on 23 May 1945 in preparation for a general election in July 1945. The first shock came with the sudden announcement by the intervening caretaker government for the quick release of personnel serving in the various theatres of war. This, compounded by the fact that the War Office planned to reduce the army's overseas tour of duty by four months, left planners frustrated. In an exchange with the chief of Imperial General Staff (CIGS), the commander-in-chief of the Allied Land Forces in Southeast Asia, Lieutenant General Sir Oliver Leese, noted that the planned tour of duty reduction, codenamed PYTHON, would reduce forces for ZIPPER and MAILFIST from seven to six divisions. In addition, heavy cross-posting of officers and men between all divisions in Burma would also be necessary to replenish the depleted ZIPPER divisions mounted from there, causing a "considerable strain on all formations since they will have to reorganise concurrently with their task of completing the annihilation of the Japs in Burma"[13]. As there was no way to repatriate officers and other ranks whose tour of duty would end just before ZIPPER, these troops would have to stay in India and Burma for several months before they could be sent home, creating morale and discipline problems. In order to defuse the situation, Mountbatten and the Commander-in-Chief, India, Field Marshal Sir Claude Auchinleck, agreed to suspend the implementation of PYTHON for troops taking part in ZIPPER.

To further ease the manpower situation, the chiefs of staff noted that only once Singapore was captured would priority be given to the creation of a Commonwealth force for the invasion of the Japanese isles[14].

As a result, British participation in the American-led CORONET and OLYMPIC was based on the premise of a quick recapture of Malaya and Singapore, with strategic planners indicating that Allied forces would have to face close to 96 Japanese divisions in the final fight for the Japanese home islands. Although Churchill gave his approval for ZIPPER and MAILFIST, the assault phase of ZIPPER and the entire MAILFIST plan was never carried out as the war ended very abruptly. By then, Churchill was also out of government, with Clement Attlee taking over as prime minister.

American President Harry Truman's decision to drop the atomic bomb on Hiroshima on 6 August 1945 and a second bomb on Nagasaki on 9 August 1945 resulted in the Japanese surrender on 15 August 1945.

The sudden surrender meant that SEAC planning for the amphibious invasion to recapture their possessions in Southeast Asia had quickly been superseded by events. They would now have to move fast in order to reclaim their territories from the surrendering Japanese before a power vacuum developed.

On 4 August 1945, Mountbatten's American deputy, Lieutenant General Raymond Wheeler, on learning from his chief that the Americans were about to end the war shortly, ordered SEAC planners in Colombo to come up with a plan to recapture Singapore ahead of a modified ZIPPER, which would now be carried out sans heavy armaments and assault troops and without the Singapore component[15]. The recapture of Rangoon in May 1945 and the decision by Mountbatten to advance directly to Malaya, instead of first seizing Phuket, made it unnecessary to implement ROGER. Singapore would have to be recaptured as the primary objective as fast as possible, as part of a separate plan. So, a top-secret plan was hatched specifically to capture Britain's most prized possessions in the Far East. The emergency reoccupation of Singapore (SHACKLE)[16] and Penang (FLASHLIGHT) would involve a large naval and air force with the 5th Indian Division and the 3rd commando brigade. Wheeler noted that this new top-secret plan, codenamed TIDERACE, should not interfere with ZIPPER but rather spearhead the recapture of Southeast Asia. He concurred with his planners that it was crucial to reoccupy Penang first before taking Singapore:

> On strong representations of Commanders-in-Chief, I agreed that the first phase of this operation was to reoccupy FLASHLIGHT... in order to provide a firm advanced naval and air base, from which to advance to SHACKLE[17].

The planners rushed out an outline plan for TIDERACE in less than four days. The 30-page document outlined the plan to "occupy SINGAPORE as soon as possible after the capitulation by the Japanese government, securing as a preliminary measure an advance anchorage and all-weather air base"[18].

It noted that once the capitulation of the Japanese in Singapore had been negotiated,

> ... it is essential that the occupying forces arrive as quickly as possible and in the maximum possible strength for the maintenance of law and order and for purposes of prestige. It follows, therefore, that the occupying forces should be at least one division in strength, with maximum show of naval and air forces. Furthermore, this division should arrive as a whole or at least be concentrated on the island by the evening of the day on which the landing takes place[19].

Planners stressed the importance of capturing Penang first as "the advanced anchorage and air base should include an airfield which can be used in all weathers as a staging base for the fly in of the 5th Division to SINGAPORE, if required. This condition is met only at PENANG where the airfield is all-weather and believed to be in good condition" [20].

X-day would mark the date on which the operation would begin. On X+12, the force, to be mounted from Ceylon and Burma, would arrive off Penang and a demonstration by Liberator aircraft from Rangoon, including leaflet-dropping, would take place. A cruiser with two destroyers would then proceed to a position approximately two miles off Fort Cornwallis. Known as Operation JURIST, the sub-plan to retake Penang would see

SACSEA's representative and the naval force commander, who would already be on board, negotiate the surrender of the Japanese forces there. On the completion of negotiations, the naval force commander would then be transferred to a destroyer, which would remain in Penang while the cruiser headed down to Singapore.

Meanwhile, a minesweeping force would start clearing a channel in the Straits of Malacca. The cruiser with SACSEA's representative would then arrive at Phillip Strait in the morning of X+14, passing through the swept channels. The Japanese garrison commanders would then be ordered out to the ships where negotiations would be carried out for the surrender of the garrisons in Singapore and Malaya[21]. Should this prove successful, the 5th Division would then land on Singapore at dawn on X+15, with the first objective being the Keppel docks and Kallang Airfield. As soon as the docks were occupied, the remaining convoy would be signalled in.

Should the Japanese put up a strong resistance, the plan called for the force to abandon the operation and await the beginning of ZIPPER, which would have a small assault force. TIDERACE was to be an occupying force and was thus not equipped to deal with any significant resistance.

Rear (later Vice) Admiral Cedric Holland was appointed the naval force commander and SACSEA's naval representative who would take the Japanese surrender in Singapore.

SACSEA's military representative was to be Major General Mansergh, general officer commanding (GOC) of the 5th Indian Division, the force that would reoccupy Singapore. The 5th Division, which had been serving in Burma, would temporarily report directly to headquarters, Allied Land Forces Southeast Asia (HQALFSEA), and later to the 15th Indian corps HQ, headed by Lieutenant General Christison.

> Thus, the reoccupation of Malaya would take place in three phases. Phase one would be the recapture of Penang island (Operation JURIST). Phase two would be the recapture of Singapore (Operation TIDERACE) by the 5th Indian Division and phase three would be the landing of the ZIPPER forces in the Port Dickson–Port Swettenham area in accordance with the original ZIPPER plan to reoccupy the rest of Malaya[22].

With the Japanese surrender on 15 August 1945, planning for TIDERACE went into overdrive.

Rear Admiral Holland held several planning meetings to work out the forces needed for TIDERACE. The first part of the operation would be to get the necessary force into Singapore at the earliest possible moment. The force, once landed, would need to complete three objectives: first, to "show the flag" and assume control from the Japanese; second, to deal with the prisoners of war (POWs) and internees; and third, to disarm and contain the Japanese forces[23].

SEAC planners were also concerned about the way Allied troops were to treat Japanese forces and outlined several broad considerations that would have to be taken into account in determining this policy[24], namely how the local population would deal with the continuation of Japanese rule after the Japanese surrender announcement but before the British resumed control; the need to impress upon the Japanese the strength of the Allies and the magnitude of the Japanese defeat as well as the need to raise the morale of the local population.

The problems of internal security would also require urgent attention, and much information would have to be gathered to obtain an adequate estimate of conditions. The immediate relief and early repatriation of Allied POWs would be the first call upon TIDERACE's resources. The treatment of Japanese prisoners were also a concern:

> A further problem is the treatment to be accorded to the surrendered Japanese and to Japanese civilians remaining in occupied territories (this will presumably have to be covered in surrender orders). Closely connected with this is the necessity to bring home both to the Japanese and to local populations the magnitude of our victory. Propaganda organisations and film and photographic units will have to cover the Japanese surrender and ensure that the maximum worldwide publicity is given both to it and to the successive acts of liberation by Allied forces[25].

Holland, however, only saw a very limited role for himself as SACSEA's naval representative and Naval Force Commander in that he "stated that his responsibilities in this operation only extended until Commander 5th Division was established ashore and was satisfied that he had secured the island of Singapore"[26]. Therefore, most of these considerations of policy towards Japanese forces and surrendered Japanese personnel were left to Major General Mansergh and the various departments at SACSEA.

Holland did not see the usefulness of clandestine resistance groups operating in Malaya like Force 136 in helping to contact the Japanese in Malaya or in helping the 5th Indian Division gain control of Singapore. With the Japanese defeat, the thinking was that the Japanese would no longer put up a resistance so there was no need for clandestine forces. However, the eventual threat that Force 136 was crucial in stemming, as will be seen later, did not originate from the Japanese. As a result of Holland's approach, Major General William RC Penney, SEAC's Intelligence

Director, instructed the head of 'P' division (Clandestine Operations) that Force 136's "... role during the occupation was to supply information and to keep the guerrillas quiet"[27].

Holland also noted that the phasing in of the 15th Indian corps HQ, which would take charge of Mansergh's 5th Indian Division, did not concern TIDERACE. This disregard for the setting up of the corps HQ to command the ground troops in Singapore meant Holland was to be surprised later when, just before the surrender proceedings, instead of Mansergh, Christison turned up to accept the Japanese surrender as Mountbatten's military representative.

Setting the date for X-Day also proved a formidable challenge as this was dependent on when General MacArthur would take the Japanese surrender in Tokyo. It was only after the Tokyo surrender that any other official surrender could take place. When it became clear that the surrender ceremony in Tokyo Bay would take place on 2 September, the go-ahead was given for TIDERACE's X-Day. The constantly changing date for the Tokyo surrender meant X-Day was postponed three times before it was finally fixed as 21 August 1945[28].

However, with X-Day set for 21 August, British convoys would only arrive in Malayan waters on 2 September at the earliest. They would not be able to take over from the Japanese in Singapore until 5 September. Worse still, ZIPPER would only be implemented on 9 September. As Emperor Hirohito announced Japan's surrender on 15 August, this meant that most of Malaya and Southeast Asia would remain in a power vacuum for close to a month – the time that it would take TIDERACE and ZIPPER to be implemented.

Appreciating the need to shorten this phoney surrender period, Mountbatten, on 20 August, a day before X-Day, sent a signal in the clear to Japanese Field Marshal Count Hisaichi Terauchi, commander-in-chief of the Southern Army, in Saigon:

> You are to send a representative or representatives with plenipotentiary powers to meet my Chief of Staff at RANGOON on Thursday, 23 August, to arrange the orderly surrender of all Japanese land, sea, air and auxiliary forces in the area of your command. Your plenipotentiaries are to bring your official seal of office and your written, signed and sealed authorisation that they are fully empowered to act on your behalf.
>
> These representatives are to travel in not more than two unarmed aircraft to be provided by you. These aircraft are to be painted all

> white and are to bear upon the side of the fuselage and top and bottom of each wing green crosses easily recognisable at 500 yards[29].

The representatives were ordered to bring details on the strengths and locations of troops and equipment, charts of all minefields and swept channels, airfields, aircraft, location and status of Allied POWs, submarines, ships, stocks of food, petrol, hospitals, rubber stocks and radio stations in the region. As instructed, the Japanese acknowledged receipt of this signal through a broadcast on Saigon Radio that was repeated every hour for six hours on 22 August 1945.

Now the stage was set for the first surrender meeting in Rangoon – but the decision to allow a phoney surrender period in Malaya would come to haunt British forces. The clandestine resistance movements built by the Special Operations Executive's Force 136 in the jungles of Malaya would now become a formidable force to be reckoned with, marking the start of insurgent problems for the returning British.

Endnotes

1 Baxter, Christopher. "In Pursuit of a Pacific Strategy: British Planning for the Defeat of Japan, 1943–45". *Diplomacy & Statecraft*, vol. 15, no. 2, June 2004. 253–277.

2 Eden, Anthony R. *Minute for Churchill, PREM 4/31/4.* London: The National Archives, 8 January 1945.

3 Baxter, 2004. 254.

4 Eden, Anthony R. *The Eden Memoirs: The Reckoning.* London: Cassell, 1965. 425–426.

5 Baxter, 2004. 256.

6 Brooke, Field Marshal Alan F. "Diary Entry for 8 August 1944". *War Diaries 1939–1945: Field Marshal Lord Alanbrooke.* London: Weidenfeld and Nicolson, 2001. 578.

7 Baxter, 2004. 258.

8 Ibid. 261.

9 *Japanese Strategy and Capacity to Resist, JIC(45)136(0)(Final), 28 April 1945, CAB 81/128.* London: The National Archives.

10 *Estimate of Enemy Situation and Reaction to Operation ZIPPER, No.35094/GSI(a)(iii), Main HQ ALFSEA, 17 July 1945, WO 203/4489.* London: The National Archives.

11 Ibid. 5.

12 Ibid. 3.

13 *Personal for CIGS from LEESE infm Supreme Allied Commander and C-in-C India, TAC 3503, 170800 June 1945, WO 203/2158*. London: The National Archives.

14 *Portal, Minute, COS(45)124. CAB 79/33*. London: The National Archives, 11 May 1945.

15 *For Mountbatten From Wheeler, KANMO 237, 110945Z August 1945, WO 203/2158.* London: The National Archives.

16 In order to preserve operational security, key locations were referred to in code in the planning and operational documents. Singapore was referred to as SHACKLE, while Penang was codenamed FLASHLIGHT.

17 Ibid.

18 *Outline Plan for Operation TIDERACE, 8 August 1945, WO 203/2157.* London: The National Archives.

19 Ibid. 1.

20 Ibid. 2.

21 Ibid. 6.

22 *ALFSEA Operational Directive No. 7, 10146/G(0)1, 12 August 45, WO 203/2308.* London: The National Archives.

23 *Aide Memoire on Japanese Capitulation, Conference Secretariat Minute 5/212, 11 August 1945, WO 203/2158*. London: The National Archives.

24 Ibid.

25 Ibid. Appendix B: 3.

26 *Minutes of a Meeting of TIDERACE Planners Held in Hut 121G HQSACSEA at 1030 Hours on Sunday 12 August 1945, TR/001/A, W0 203/3104*. London: The National Archives.

27 Ibid. 2.

28 *TIDERACE Postponed, August 251215Z, C.IN.C. E.I.F., WO 203/2307.* London: The National Archives.

29 *From Admiral Lord Louis Mountbatten SACSEA For Field Marshal Count Terauchi, Commander Japanese Southern Army, 201341Z August 1945, HS1/328.* London: The National Archives.

Chapter 3

Clandestine Forces

Much has been said about the role of the Special Operations Executive (SOE) in clandestine operations in Southeast Asia during the Japanese occupation. As the battles raged during the Malayan Campaign, SOE's Orient Mission, led by Basil Goodfellow, had trained groups that were left behind enemy lines in a bid to help build resistance and carry out sabotage missions against the Japanese.

In the last days before the fall of Singapore, the SOE also began training Chinese nationalists who would help resist the Japanese onslaught. Training was also carried out for Chinese communists, who had been released from British jails in Singapore and Malaya, forming small brigades of fighters who had initially put up token resistance against the Japanese when they invaded the island.

By late 1942, however, these Chinese nationalists and communists had taken to the jungles of Malaya and begun organising themselves as a guerrilla army. The SOE trained and put behind enemy lines a total of some 365 Chinese communists, including a Special Intelligence Service (MI6) team with a wireless set. However, the sets available in 1942 were not powerful enough to transmit to the SOE Far East Operations base in India and the groups simply disappeared into the Malayan jungle.

Although Lieutenant Colonel (later Colonel) Frederick Spencer Chapman was commander of the 11 European groups which the Orient Mission had planted in enemy-held Malaya in early 1942, nothing had been heard from them for more than a year. With the loss of Malaya, two Orient Mission officers, Captain (later Major) Richard Neville Broome and Major (later Colonel) John Davis, based themselves in Sumatra to maintain contact with clandestine groups operating in Malaya. Following the Japanese occupation of Sumatra, they sailed a native junk across the Indian Ocean to India where they joined SOE's India Mission. The India Mission, led by Colin Hercules Mackenzie and Gavin Stewart, later became known as Force 136[1].

Whitehall had two main clandestine outfits operating in the Far East at the outbreak of the war, namely the SOE Orient Mission (which then merged with the India Mission) and the Special Intelligence Service Far East, SIS(FE), the forerunner of today's MI6.

The SIS's predecessor, the Secret Service Bureau, had been created in October 1909, to control secret intelligence operations in the UK and overseas and became the Secret Intelligence Service in the inter-war years[2]. However, by the start of the Second World War, some elements of the SIS had been brought under a new organisation, the Special Operations Executive, which had been created in July 1940, to carry out guerrilla warfare activities behind enemy lines while providing assistance and training to local resistance groups[3].

Following the fall of Malaya and Singapore, SIS(FE) agents escaped to India and its headquarters was then based in New Delhi, with a forward base in Calcutta. It was at this time that SIS changed its name to the Interservice Liaison Department (ISLD), following a similar change of name to its outfit in Cairo, and it stayed in Delhi until 1944 before it moved to Ceylon. By then, the ISLD(FE) came under the direction of Mountbatten's SEAC, which had been created in 1943, and operated side-by-side with SOE's Force 136 which was also located there. Both clandestine services by December 1943 would come under SEAC's 'P' division, which coordinated their work as well as cooperation with the American Office of Strategic Services, the forerunner of the CIA[4].

ISLD groups behind enemy lines collected raw intelligence and data, forwarding it to ISLD(FE)'s own collation section in Kandy, which processed the information into source reports for SEAC and their sphere of operations included China, Burma, Indonesia, Thailand and Malaya[5].

However, ISLD operatives saw SOE operations in enemy territory as overtly offensive compared to their more discreet approach and this created a large amount of friction between the two outfits as both operated simultaneously in the occupied territory, leading to each keeping the other out of the loop on their operations and activities[6]. As such, ISLD agents often complained that they were uninformed of SOE sabotage and guerrilla activities, which heightened Japanese security and so made it very hard for them to move about or carry out their own clandestine operations[7].

In late 1942, the SOE's India Mission (which now included the Orient Mission), lacked both men and materials and was attempting to build a base of recruits and, just like the SIS(FE), it began operations in

Calcutta. However, with the creation of the Malayan Section, operations moved to Meerut. While in Calcutta, Broome and Davis spent their time unsuccessfully searching for Chinese, Indians and Malays who had escaped from Singapore. Amongst those interviewed were hundreds of Chinese seamen stranded by the war[8]. Many were illiterate and others simply unsuitable. None of the men were willing to go back into Japanese-occupied Malaya. Then, they met a young Straits-born Chinese businessman named Lim Bo Seng.

Lim Bo Seng and Operation Gustavus

Lim was born in China on 27 April 1909. He and his family migrated to Malaya when he was a boy. In 1925, when he was 16, the family moved to Singapore. There, he continued his studies at Raffles Institution and in 1928 passed his Senior Cambridge Examinations. He then furthered his studies at the University of Hong Kong.

Like many overseas Chinese of his time, Lim was a Chinese patriot. In the 1930s, when Japan's actions in China became increasingly hostile, Lim, who was now back in Singapore, became active in raising funds for anti-Japanese activities.

He was violently anti-Japanese and during the 70 days leading to the fall of Singapore he had mobilised thousands of Chinese into the Civil Defence Corps. Many of them would lose their lives once the Japanese took over, massacred by their new rulers in the infamous *Sook Ching* operation just days after the British surrender. Lim escaped and turned up in Calcutta where he joined the SOE team. Taking advantage of his top-level contacts with nationalist government officials in Chungking, Lim made two trips to China to elicit support. A number of Malaya-born Chinese University students soon began to arrive in Pune for training. This group was codenamed DRAGONS.

Lim's top-secret personnel file, held in the MI6 archives and sealed for the last 60 years, was only declassified in January 2005. Among other things, it showed the trips to Chungking were not only a recruitment exercise but also involved an undertaking of a more personal nature[9].

Lim was director of Hock Ann & Co Ltd, one of several companies forming the Brick Selling Agency. The group sold bricks and material to the British in Singapore prior to the fall of the island. The Royal Navy had placed an order with the Brick Selling Agency for material worth $40,000 (Straits Settlements Dollars) and collected it prior to Singapore's fall. As a result of the quick defeat in Malaya, no payment had been made. In Chungking, Lim approached the British embassy in an attempt to get the money due to him.

The embassy contacted the former Malayan surveyor, who confirmed the contract to the senior surveyor, Ceylon and India. However, the Malayan surveyor noted that the contract was for only $4,447 (Straits Settlements Dollars). Moreover, he "regretted that payment could NOT be made except to the duly authorised agent of the Brick Selling Agency. If Mr Lim could produce a Power of Attorney, or similar instrument, authorising him to collect credit for the Brick Selling Agency, the matter would then be given consideration"[10]. It was further noted that Lim was director of "one of several companies forming the Brick Selling Agency, but as the bricks were sold by several companies of the agency, the matter could only be settled through the agency and NOT through a separate firm"[11].

As the bricks sold were actually solely from his company but transacted through the Brick Selling Agency, Lim was obviously frustrated that the monies owed to his company would not be paid. In the meantime, he had been placed in the Malayan Country Section (MCS) of the India Mission and Major FS Crawford, an agent at the Section, informed the embassy that there would be a "reply drafted after talk with Lim". With plans for insurgent operations in Malaya, Crawford recollected that Lim agreed to drop his demand for compensation until after the war[12]. The issue was given very short shrift after the war and correspondence in the files at the National Archives in London indicate that the matter was not raised further but was instead dropped quietly, without any mention being made to Lim's family or the remaining companies of the Brick Selling Agency[13]. As a result, the compensation owed to Lim and the agency has remained outstanding for more than 60 years.

Lim was interviewed by Lieutenant Colonel Basil Gerritsen Ivory, the officer who is believed to have headed the SOE's Chungking outfit. Ivory, along with the MCS in India, determined that Lim would be recruited as a senior member of the MCS Chinese Section and employed in the field as an agent.

Lim's rate of pay was set at Rs 300 per month, increasing to Rs 1,000 per month when he was in the field. Force 136 then undertook to look after the education of Lim's brother, who was studying in Calcutta, and paid him a monthly stipend of Rs 300.

Designated agent No. BB 192, Lim went under the aliases of Tan and Tang, with the most common being that of Tan Choon Lim[14]. In signals to headquarters, however, Lim was only referred to as 192, in order to protect his identity and that of his family. Lim was married to Gan Choo Neo and had seven children as well as an extended family who were still in Japanese-occupied Singapore.

In his enlistment record, it was noted that Lim's dependants would be entitled to a Major's pension when his death was established. In a signal to

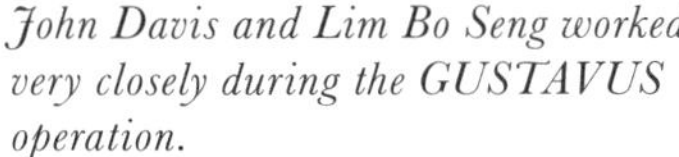

John Davis and Lim Bo Seng worked very closely during the GUSTAVUS operation.

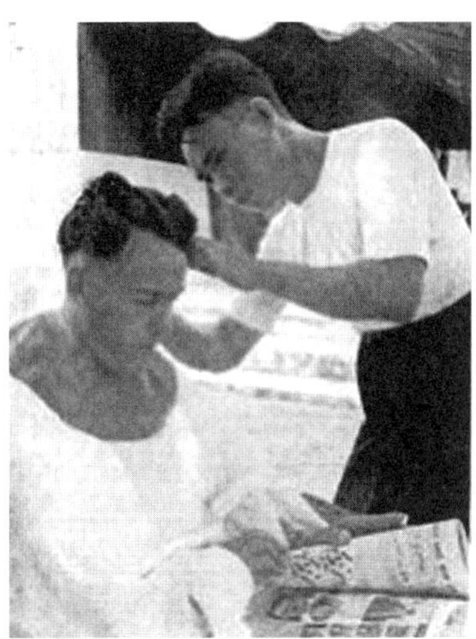

Richard Broome, after the war, having a haircut.

the Finance section after the war, the MCS noted that, "In a minute dated 20/9/43 and initialled by Col Ivory, it is stated that in the event of death, he (Lim) is entitled to Major's pension payable either as a lump sum or as an annual payment. This would be payable from the date of death, less any sums paid out thereafter"[15]. However, this simple pension would become a major issue after the war.

After being reunited with his brother in Calcutta, Lim joined forces with Davis and Broome. As soon as the nationalist Chinese Kuomintang (KMT) agents had been chosen, they had to be trained for their dangerous and specialised work. One of the agents Lim recruited was Tan Chong Tee. Tan (Ah Lim/Lim Song/Lim Soong/Lim Shu/Tan Tien Soong/Tan Thiam Seng) was born in Singapore in 1916 and had studied at the Kheng Cheng Primary School and Swatow Public Middle School in Singapore before attending the Chungking National University of Art:

> Upon the outbreak of the Second World War, I was furthering my studies in Chungking. Hearing that the Japanese had penetrated Malaya, causing untold suffering to numerous families, I decided to sacrifice my studies and respond to the call of the Central Government of China for volunteers to go to India for training in intelligence work. Accompanying me in the pioneer batch to depart from Chungking were Lim Mong Seng alias Tan Choon Lim (Lim Bo Seng)... We arrived at Calcutta by air and were received by Major Goldfarer (the liaison officer for Force 136). The next day, we departed by train for

> Poona (Pune), and from there by military transport to the Sungari Hills (Singarh Hills near Singarh Fort) for training. The training staffs were Captain Davies (*sic*), Captain Broome and many others[16].

By this time, Mackenzie, as one of the leaders of the India Mission, was also concerned about what should be done with the SOE-trained communist guerrillas that had been left behind in the Malayan jungles in January 1942. The India Mission decided to work with the guerrillas but adopted the stance that until plans were made to retake Malaya, the communists should be restricted to mounting attacks from their jungle bases, leaving the Japanese holding the towns. In the urban areas, where they had fomented industrial disputes prior to the war, they would continue to do so and carry out sabotage. This policy towards the communist guerrillas and the eventual supplying of weapons to the communist-backed Malayan People's Anti-Japanese Army (MPAJA) would, after the war, help the MCP in their armed insurgency against their wartime ally and colonial master.

The first step in rebuilding a British clandestine presence would be to insert a party of agents back into Malaya to make contact with the communists and to find out if Chapman and his stay-behind parties were still alive. The first operation launched in Malaya was codenamed GUSTAVUS I. The party, consisting of five nationalist Chinese, was led by Davis. On 24 May 1943, the first group of Force 136 landed on the beaches off Lumut. After bumping into a Malay man and woman upon stepping ashore, Davis hid in a rubber estate and sent out the Chinese agents to make contact one at a time. An ethnic Hokkien Chinese man named Wu Chye Sin (Goh Meng Chye/Ah Ng) was chosen to go first not only because he was very keen and resourceful but because his dialect was commonly spoken in the area. He was dressed as a destitute and his cover story was left to his discretion.

Wu found a rubber-tapper overseer named Tan Kong Cheng (Kong Ching) and his wife, "to whom he had spun his hard-luck story, only to be told uncompromisingly that he did not speak or look the part. He changed his ground accordingly and, after 24 hours of almost non-stop talk, these people became his staunchest friends and agreed to go to all lengths to help him once they were assured he was not a guerrilla – of whose extortions they appeared to be very much afraid"[17].

Another of one Davis' agents, Lung Chiu Ying (Ah Loong/Ah Long/Ah Ying/Ah Eng), had chosen to get work at a coffeeshop in order to gather information and meet the other agents. He found himself at a shop in Segari market near the bus station. Very understaffed, the owner offered him $10 (Straits Settlements Dollars) a month as "under-coolie"[18]. In half an hour, he was at work, with the proprietor having promised to obtain the necessary paperwork. One of his first customers was Wu, who was surprised to see Lung established so quickly. Lung was happy with the arrangement and the owner of the shop also turned out to be a good friend of Tan Kong Cheng.

In the meantime, Li Han Kwang (Lee Han Kwong/Lee Tsing/Lee Ah Cheng), Davis' third agent, crossed by boat to Pangkor island to start making arrangements for a boat to take Davis out to the submarine rendezvous (RV) point:

> He crossed over without difficulty, but once there, his apparent aimlessness was noted by a Malay policeman, who questioned him. Being unable to give any satisfactory answers, Tsing (Li Han Kwang) blustered indignantly and insisted on being searched. Fortunately, though dressed in his oldest clothes, he had $60 in his pocket, and this re-assured the policeman, as the poorer a Chinese was in Malaya at that time, the more suspect he was. Nevertheless, Tsing was arrested and taken to the police station, where he insisted he was able to obtain a guarantor. He was allowed to go unescorted to find one. He went straight to the shop of a Toochew (*sic*) he had met on the boat. With some hesitation, the man sent a coolie to the police station to vouch for Tsing. The Malay corporal would not accept the guarantee, but let Tsing go, saying that he would make a very thorough investigation the next day. The Toochew then introduced Tsing to the only person who could really help him – the unofficial headman of the village, Choy (Chua Koon Eng)[19].

Once Chua was persuaded to help, he set about creating a proper cover for Li. He introduced Li as the son of an old acquaintance and set him up as a fishmonger. The next day, Li returned to report to Davis with a present of fresh fish. Within a week, he had gotten so effective that his new firm had already sent two consignments of fish down the coast. It would obviously be much easier to keep RVs if it could be combined with legitimate trading. However, to do this, it was necessary to borrow a boat from Chua and to get his help in arranging the trading voyage. It was impossible not to tell Chua the real reasons for the trip and, on being told, he agreed to take responsibility for all shipping arrangements. Chua also told Li he was in touch with 800 guerrillas in Setiawan. Li then arranged to meet Davis and sail from Pangkor on 25 June 1943 in order to make GUSTAVUS' first RV.

With GUSTAVUS I landed and operational, GUSTAVUS II was infiltrated into Malaya. This second group consisted of Broome and three other Chinese agents: wireless operator Liang Yuan Ming (Lee Choon/

Lee Chuen), agent Yi Tian Song (Chan Siak Foo/Tan Shi Fu/Tan Sek Fu) and Tan Chong Tee. Although GUSTAVUS II reached Malaya, "Davis considered the presence of more than one European an embarrassment at that stage, (so) it was decided that he alone, with Lee Chuen, Ah Lim and Sek Fu should go in on the next sortie"[20]. Davis returned to Colombo with GUSTAVUS II and returned to Malaya on 27 July 1943 on GUSTAVUS III. On 12 September, Broome arrived in Malaya on GUSTAVUS IV.

By this time, the network in Malaya had expanded considerably, noted Broome:

> The initial success of our organisation in Perak was entirely due to Ah Ng (Wu Chye Sin), whose outstanding ability, good sense, courage and initiative made him the key man from the beginning. In a way, this was unfortunate, in that the other men relied on him and visited him far too much. After launching himself as a relative of Tom (Tan Kong Cheng) at Segari, he quickly gained a great deal of influence both there and in Lumut, and before long had started a business in Ipoh. This business was a shady concern of mushroom growth similar to many that have sprung up since the occupation. It dealt in rice, lubricating oil, gold, etc., all articles which are unlawfully traded in and mostly smuggled. It brought about the most valuable contacts, including Japs, who like making money on the side. Many people with a certain amount of 'pull' were thus compromised and available to us. The locally recruited newspaper man, Lee (Moh Wing Pun), was installed as Ng's (Wu) manager in the Ipoh office and Ah Lim (Tan) became the Lumut representative[21].

Davis was more blunt about Wu's business venture, where the "(e)mphasis was on a 'get rich quick and no questions asked' basis"[22]. Broome noted that:

> ...the extent of Ah Ng's (Wu) achievement before the collapse may be judged by the fact that he was chief owner of a motorboat operating between Singapore and North Malaya and also had a lorry and private car. He was on good terms with several high-ranking Chinese detectives, some of whom were satisfactorily compromised and who expected to warn him of any impending action by the Japs. Ng himself was well aware of his danger through the connection with Bill (Chua Koon Eng) and was always trying to clear himself of this embarrassment, but the fact that we had had to rely on Bill in the initial stages put a burden on the whole of our organisation which could never be shaken off[23].

The field operatives were always short of funds and in March 1944, Lim Bo Seng would finally leave his hideout in the jungle to help sort out this problem[24]. However in October 1943, Lim Bo Seng was still safely ensconced in Colombo, training more field agents and operators for future operations in Malaya. On 1 November 1943, the *O24*, a Dutch submarine commandeered for use by Force 136, surfaced off Sembilan island in the Straits of Malacca to land the GUSTAVUS V party led by Lim. In-country, Lim was to be known as Tan Choon Lim. Many of the SOE's wireless sets were too heavy (450lbs) to be carried into the jungle camps and had to be buried. So, when Lim arrived with two 30lb sets, they were prized assets. Much of the supplies Lim brought along were lost as they were transported ashore. As the guerrillas needed arms, medicine, vitamins and money, these items were to be included in the next shipment. However, after the January 1944 RV, most of the following ones would be missed, leading to a huge shortage of funds and supplies.

Davis noted that Lim arrived in camp at the end of November, having travelled by car. His stores were all left at Jenderata to be brought up when possible as the Japanese were very active throughout the Bidor and Telok Anson areas at the time[25].

By January, a representative from the headquarters of the communist Anti-Japanese Union/Force (AJUF) turned up to negotiate a working agreement. A two-day conference was held with Chang Hong, an elected representative of the MCP on the one side and Davis, Broome and Lim as the "military representatives of the Allied C-in-C (commander-in-chief) Southeast Asia (who were) fully empowered to cooperate with any anti-Japanese party in Malaya"[26]. Chang Hong was in reality an alias for Lai Teck, the Secretary General of the Malayan Communist Party (MCP), who had come in disguise to negotiate the agreement with the British. Lai Teck was accompanied by the MCP's Perak State Commissar, Chin Peng (also known as Chen Ping or CTP), who would succeed Lai Teck as Secretary General of the MCP and launch the Communist Insurgency five years later[27].

By this time, Davis and Broome had managed to contact Chapman, who walked into their camp with members of the communist guerrillas in tow on Christmas Day 1943. Now all three, along with Lim, would plan the next moves.

With the agreement of the MCP, Force 136 concentrated their efforts on getting their wireless transmitters up to camp and operational, raising finance and "strengthening our organisation on the plains"[28].

However, due to heavy Japanese air activity and the proximity of the SOE's Belantan camp to the plains of Tapah and Bidor, it was decided to move into a *Sakai* (an aboriginal tribe) camp, on the lower slopes of

Gunung Batu Puteh. They finally located the camp at the house of the village headman, Pa Kasut (literally 'Father Shoe'), with the camp then known as Pa Kasut.

By January 1944, Davis noted the network in the plains had been well laid-out and established:

> Tsing Li was installed in a small fish business at Pangkor with several partners and was helped by Bill (Chua), who was friendly and fatherly towards him. His job was to maintain our sea RVs by junk. Unfortunately, he proved quite unfitted for this job and Ng (Wu) had to involve himself with Bill a great deal in getting right his mistake. It was this that led to Bill's knowing far too much about our whole organisation. After I arrived, Tsing was left merely vegetating in Pangkor with nothing to do... Ah Tsing did very well at the beginning and was responsible for the organisation of the successful junk service for RVs. Later, however, owing to his bull-headedness and lack of common sense, he became dangerous and had to be taken off this work, so that he was doing nothing for us till the collapse. His escape was a fine piece of work and saved Ying's (Lung Chiu Ying) life. Unfortunately, he blotted this record by intrigue and general bad behaviour in camp, which can be only partly excused by the very trying circumstances we lived in...
>
> ...Ying, after starting as a coffeeshop boy in Segari... later became our chief RV keeper and did the job – despite the failures – with very great courage and resource. His cover was always bad, because, although he had all the necessary papers, he had no specific employment; at the end Ng (Wu) was negotiating to set him up in a wine shop in Ipoh.
>
> Sek Fu, who was the last out before Tan (Lim), was installed as owner of a sundry shop in Tapah, and had a manager who was not employed by us or in our secrets. He was nervous at first but carried on very well. Previously he had spent some time tucked away in a rubber estate near Ipoh with Lee's (Moh Wing Pun) father, but it had not proved possible to launch him at that time and he had returned to camp[29].

Broome noted that Tan Chong Tee, "did very well when set up as Ng's (Wu) agent in Lumut but had little opportunity to show his ability, since he was engaged in settling down and had little else to do until the collapse. Was loyal and cheerful throughout"[30].

The network, according to Tan, consisted of an interior and exterior section. The interior was headed by Davis at Pa Kasut's camp and the exterior consisted of field agents stationed in Ipoh, Lumut and Pangkor[31]. Everything began to fall in place with the arrival of Lim Bo Seng, and Tan was ecstatic at the prospect of working again for Lim:

> Ultimately in the beginning of March 1944 the headquarters of the Organisation was established at Ipoh with the arrival of the Leader Tan Choon Lim (Lim), who came from India in December 1943. The principal objects of the organisation were to: 1. Unite with the Resistance Army, 2. Transfer materials and personnel into the interior, 3. Establish a wireless station and 4. Maintain sea communication...
>
> ... Maintenance of sea communication, which entails the meeting of submarines by our sailing boats to bring in materials, money, jewellery, etc., is the lifeblood of our organisation. With certain misunderstanding(s) between Lee Ah Cheng (Li Han Kwang) and Capt. Davies (*sic*), Ah Long (Lung Chiu Ying) was sent to assist the former. The main work of going out to sea was subsequently performed by Ah Long.
>
> From May 1943 all the objects originally mapped out were proceeded with successfully according to plan, and in March 1944, I was informed by our leader Tan Choon Lim that the first stage of our mission can be stated as successfully completed, and we were asked to carry out the second stage, i.e. organisation and propaganda.
>
> Owing to lack of funds, the activities were confined to Perak... Goh Meng Chye (Wu Chye Sin) was sent to Singapore by our Leader to raise a big sum in order to enable representatives to be sent to other states. The persons who were to have been approached in Singapore were Soh Hun Swee, Ong Pia Teng, Koh Chee Peng, etc[32].

From the base at Pa Kasut's camp, Broome was pleased with the progress being made but realised that something had to be done to improve their financial situation:

> When Tan (Lim) arrived, he immediately applied himself to the problem of raising money. He had three old friends in Malaya of whom he had great hopes, one being Soh Hun Swee and the others a banker and a schoolteacher whose names I forget. He described the three people to Ng (Wu) and provided him with means of recognition, and Ng then made a trip to Singapore to see them. He reported on his return that Hun Swee was non-committal and clearly frightened

> to do anything, but he had had much more success with one of the others and hoped on a subsequent visit to make an arrangement to actually get some money. Tan was greatly disappointed to hear about Hun Swee, in whom he had put great faith[33].

With finances very tight, Davis, Broome and Chapman were heavily reliant on the RV drops which would have brought in much needed funds, in the form of gold bars and coins, as well as medical supplies. However, Broome and Davis were both unable to make the February and March RVs due to enemy activity and illness. As a result, Lung was sent to make the RVs but failed to make contact.

So by March 1944, Force 136's financial situation in Perak state was very bleak. Lim, who had until then been in the jungles with Davis, Broome and Chapman, decided to go into town, according to Broome:

> The decision to let Tan (Lim) go out was taken with great reluctance but was in my opinion a correct one. There was no reason at that time to fear any danger, and things appeared to be going very well. Tan could obviously do a great deal of good by going out, whereas in the jungle he was merely wasting his time. The plan was that he should spend as short a time as possible in Ipoh and try and arrange a safe hideout whence he could direct our organisation without being two days journey away in the jungle; he had great hopes of finding a place on a rubber estate belonging to a friend of his on the Cameron Highlands road... In the middle of March Tan left camp to join Ng (Wu) in Ipoh. The reasons for this step were:
>
> a) Ng was having difficulty in getting our projected financial backing and Tan felt his personal touch was necessary.
>
> b) Tan was worried over Ng's business which was absorbing too much of Ng's time and was, Tan thought, being run on far too unstable lines despite high profits.
>
> The plan was Tan's own and we only agreed after long discussion. It seemed to us, however, an essential move if we were to make any progress at all. Tan was accordingly installed in a house (No. 12, Conoly Road) in Ipoh as Ng's uncle. Again, we were reluctantly compelled to centralise far too much on Ng. The reasons for this were as before, i.e., Ng was the only man capable of fixing the necessary passes, which had to be done by personal influence and judicious bribery. It was intended that Tan should return to camp as soon as he had put things straight below[34].

As Davis later admitted:

> We were, at this time, under the grave misapprehension that the attack on Malaya would come in summer 1944 and therefore considered our intelligence system should be speeded up even to the extent of taking risks which would not otherwise be warranted[35].

Things, however, began to go seriously wrong shortly after Lim settled in Ipoh. As a result of a counter-espionage operation in January 1944, the Japanese had captured a communist guerrilla, who revealed the existence of a clandestine Allied network operating on Pangkor island. Many post-war accounts and authors claim that Lai Teck, who was a triple agent working for the British, Japanese and the MCP, was the one who revealed Lim's identity and the existence of the Ipoh network. However, Chin Peng, Lai Teck's successor, refutes this allegation:

> It has been claimed that Lai Te (Lai Teck) had learned of Lim's identity at the Belantan meeting the previous December and, as a result, was able to identify him to the *Kempeitai* (Japanese secret police). As I alone escorted Lim, under his alias, to Belantan, attended all sessions of those negotiations and stayed with Lai Te the entire time he spent at the camp, I know this particular conjecture to be baseless. I personally did not learn of Lim's true identity until immediately after the war. Even then, I did not consider the information important enough to pass on to anybody. Lai Te, therefore, could never have been able to identify Lim for the *Kempeitai*. The reality is, Lim Bo Seng was betrayed by one of his own men[36].

By mid March 1944, the Japanese had begun a full-scale counter-espionage operation on Pangkor island and were searching all sea-going vessels. Although Li Han Kwang was on the island, the Japanese missed him and were unable to locate the RV boat as it had sailed out with Lung to make the March RV in order to collect more funds and supplies. Lung, however, returned empty-handed and went to see Lim before he headed to the Pa Kasut camp to report to Davis and Broome. Tan, who was based at Lumut, also went to see Lim with the same information. The missed rendezvous meant no new funds would be forthcoming for at least another month. So, Lim sent Wu back to Singapore once again in the hopes of getting more funds.

However, in late March, the *Kempeitai* placed a detachment of more than 200 Japanese soldiers on Pangkor. The *Kempeitai* were also involved in anti-espionage activities and on the afternoon of 21 March, *Kempeitai* counter-espionage teams began searching all the islands around Pangkor. The next day, Pangkor was surrounded, but Li managed to escape.

By 23 March, unable to trace Li or Chua on Pangkor, Tan left Lumut and contacted Lim, who told him that Lung had already visited him and that Pangkor was surrounded by Japanese. Tan recalls the circumstances:

> Ah Long (Lung) also stated that while he was at Pangkor, a demand was made by someone for $25,000 (Straits Settlements Dollars), which was promised by our organisation to the Resistance Army (AJUF) but the demand for the money was not carried out in the manner arranged by us. Chua Koon Eng, our Pangkor representative, was stated to have asked the man to come the next day, on which day (23 Mar) Koon Eng went away from Pangkor. In view of the circumstances, I advised our Leader to leave Ipoh, but he considered it advisable to remain until he heard from Goh Meng Chye (Wu), whom he said he (had) sent to Singapore to raise funds. I was instructed to go to our firm, Kian Yick Chan (Chop Kian Yick Chan, 77, Market Street, Ipoh), to await news of Goh Meng Chye[37].

By 24 March, the *Kempeitai* had tracked Chua down and arrested him at Teluk Murrek. This was the beginning of the end. Chua confessed and implicated Li in the spy ring. The Japanese laid a trap for Li (who had already escaped from Pangkor by then) and, using Chua as bait, captured him shortly after. Under duress, Li was forced to confirm Chua's story but managed to avoid adding anything to what the Japanese already knew.

Then, using Li as bait, the *Kempeitai* held back further arrests of the other Chinese members in the hopes of getting at the British masterminds. Li had been taken to Ipoh and detained at the *Kempeitai* headquarters, where some Japanese soldiers, Chinese detectives and a few 'comfort' girls lived in a large house. Li was treated very well. The Japanese were hoping to get more details through kindness and perhaps turn him. He was not locked up – although he was kept under constant guard. On 26 March, Li made a daring escape:

> He was being looked after by two women when one of the Japanese wandered into the room stark naked – a Japanese habit. This outraged the natural Chinese modesty of the girls to such an extent that they walked out of the room, thus giving Tsing (Li) his chance. He got up, too, as if it had been already agreed, and said he was going to have a bath and got away through the bathroom window, climbing from the second storey to the street. He then ran wildly down the street and jumped into a taxi, telling the driver to go towards the main road. As

> soon as he could, he told the driver he was an escaping guerrilla. The driver responded magnificently and shouting *"Tai ka ting pau"* (We're all of us of one blood) proceeded at full speed to Bidor, where Tsing immediately entered the jungle, first borrowing his fare from the local AJUF guides. Tsing knew nothing of the fate of the others, beyond hearing one of the detectives say he had to go to Tapah, which may have meant he was after Sek Fu (Yi Tian Song)[38].

However, the next to be captured would be Tan:

> A few hours after the disappearance of Ah Cheng (Li Han Kwang), the Japanese found out about his abscondment and searched all rendezvous. They arrived at Kian Yick Chan to find (*sic*) Goh Meng Chye (Wu), but unfortunately they found me there. I suspected that something was wrong and planned to escape. I reached the Teng Ah Hotel at 10.00pm but was immediately followed by armed guards. Being unarmed I was unable to offer a fight. Determined to sacrifice myself, I sent word through the waiter to Mok Kee (Moh Wing Pun), a member of the Organisation, of my arrest. Within five minutes of my arrest, Mok Kee and Sek Fu (Yi), who happened to be in Ipoh, were accordingly informed, and they in turn immediately informed our leader[39].

Yi, who happened to be in Ipoh, was then alerted by Moh, who told him of Tan's arrest:

> Moh Wing Pun (in charge of the liaison post at No. 4, Clare Street, Ipoh) received information from Ah Seng, a waitor (*sic*) employed in the Oriental Hotel, Ipoh at about 10.30pm on the same night, that Lim Soong (Tan) was being arrested. He immediately conveyed the message to Chan Siak Foo (Yi Tian Song) (in charge of the liaison post, Chop Yee Kee Chan, No. 65 Main Road, Tapah), who at the time (was) staying at Yan Woh Lodging House, Hale Street, Ipoh. He (Moh) also called on Chan Choon Lim (Lim Bo Seng), our officer-in-charge, at his residence, No. 12 Conoly Road, Ipoh, to make the same report and ask for his instructions.
>
> By this time, the reason of Lim Soong's arrest was not known yet. So Chan Choon Lim instructed him (Moh) to go into this matter, find out what had really happened and make an effort to save Lim Soong. Moh was also instructed to tell Chan Siak Foo to report the matter to the headquarters at the mountain of Bidor as quickly as possible

> and to inform Ah Loong (Lung Chiu Ying) not to come down from the mountain...
>
> Moh Wing Pun had lost no time to carry out the above instructions. On the morning of March 27, the next day, he found out that Chop Kian Yik Chan, our organising centre, No. 77 Market Street, Ipoh, had been raided and closely watched by the enemy. Upon receiving Moh's report on the above and after some considerations, Chan Choon Lim decided to escape by car with Moh Wing Pun as driver. They were unfortunately stopped and arrested at a junction near the 7th milestone of Jalan Gopeng.
>
> Siak Foo (who was returning to Tapah before heading to Bidor) was arrested at his post... on the early morning of 28 March 1944. Wong Kwong Fai (Wu Chye Sin) was arrested at Kuala Lumpur while on his way back to Ipoh from Singapore on 31 March 1944. He determined to end his own life by crashing his head against the wall in the lock-up at the Kuala Lumpur Police Station. His attempt, however, was unsuccessful though he collapsed with a fractured wound on the head bleeding profusely[40]...

Davis, Broome and Chapman meanwhile remained unaware of what was happening in Ipoh:

> About 20 March Ying (Lung) brought us a letter from Tan (Lim) saying that Ng (Wu) had left for Singapore to continue his financial discussions. He also told us that Bill (Chua), the night before, had had a mysterious visit from two men claiming to be AJUF representatives and demanding money with menaces. Bill was said to have kept his head and not disclosed his relations with AJUF. This visit was mysterious and alarming, because Bill had been for a long time our chief agent in Pangkor for financing the guerrillas. It seems clear now that his two visitors were working for the Japs[41].

It was now time for the April RV but, as the two previous ones had failed and Japanese patrols had been stepped up, it seemed unwise for Broome, Davis or Chapman to go[42]. Thus, Lung left on 29 March to keep the rendezvous. That same evening, he was back in camp with Li, whom he had met on the way. Obviously, there had been a disaster:

> On hearing Tsing's (Li) story we immediately, with C.T.P.'s (Chin Peng) help, sent out messengers to warn Tan (Lim) and Sek Fu (Yi).

> We could do nothing for Ng (Wu) in Singapore or for Lim in Lumut, the only hope for them was a warning via Tan, if we could reach him in time. The messengers went out repeatedly but were unable to find either Tan or Sek Fu at the addresses given or to hear any word of them. Clearly we were much too late[43].

Chua, who had cooperated fully with the Japanese, was released shortly after, noted Broome:

> Bill (Chua) was released and is now back in his business in Pangkor under strict Jap control. All the junks in Pangkor are now owned by a firm under Bill's direction.
>
> In assessing Bill's culpability in this matter, it should be borne in mind that he helped us loyally and enthusiastically from the beginning. He was not chosen by us as the result of careful consideration, but came into our orbit entirely fortuitously. Had he chosen, he could have ruined our whole venture at the start; instead he decided to help and did so. We always took it for granted that he would break down if arrested[44].

Even if Broome could forgive Chua's actions, it was his confession that had led to the destruction of Force 136's network in Perak and Lim Bo Seng's capture and eventual death. In captivity, Tan Chong Tee revealed the privations they faced:

> In spite of terrible torture, we refused to speak for the time we were arrested, but after three days we were shown the evidence of Lee Ah Cheng (Li). We then realised that the organisation was smashed. We decided therefore that we should not sacrifice needlessly, and we hoped that one of us might live through the torture to clear our names[45].

Tan could hear Lim being interrogated. He noted that "the Japanese tried to force Lim to cooperate with them but he refused. They even got his friends in Singapore to come over to persuade him, but he was not moved.... Instead, he reminded the rest of us to remain firm and not to surrender to the Japanese"[46].

On 24 April, Lim Bo Seng, Yi Tian Song, Moh Wing Pun and Tan Chong Tee were transferred to the Batu Gajah Jail and placed in cells on the second floor. Lim protested against the ill-treatment of POWs by refusing food. He asked that his portion of sweet potatoes be distributed to the rest of his comrades[47]. After 20 days, Lim, Moh and Tan were struck by dysentery.

Tan Chong Tee (left) and his leader, Lim Bo Seng (right): Tan heard Lim being tortured in Batu Gajah Prison and subsequently confirmed Lim's death on 29 June 1944.

"Through the ill treatment of the Indian Dresser and the casualness of the Indian Doctor..."[48], Lim was bundled up in an old blanket and left without food and water in an empty room meant for dying prisoners. For the next three nights, Lim held on, dying in the early hours of 29 June 1944. His remains were buried in a pauper's grave on the outskirts of the jail.

In 1995, Tan Chong Tee penned his memoirs on Force 136. Written 50 years on, Tan described vividly his role at Lumut and the death of Lim[49]. However, Tan confessed that in his post-war report to Davis and Broome, he had covered up details on Wu Chye Sin's womanising and several other indiscretions prior to the destruction of the network and did not report Moh Wing Pun's 'traitorous' confessions to the Japanese. Although Tan did finally tell Davis about Moh's breakdown under interrogation and Tan's belief that Moh had collaborated with the enemy, Davis did not act on it.

Clearly, there are discrepancies in Tan's initial statement in 1945 and in his memory of those events 50 years later. Now, 60 years on, it is not easy to tell which version is more closely related to fact or who the actual traitors were. Wu was very highly regarded by Davis and Broome, as was Moh. Regardless, all these members of Force 136, with the exception of Chua Koon Eng, will always be viewed as heroes.

By January 1945, Davis, from the jungles of Perak, was forced to signal Colombo (Force 136 headquarters) that the network had been destroyed[50].

Lim Bo Seng's funeral in Singapore, December 1945. It would take more than 3 years before Mrs Lim would receive the pension promised to her husband.

Although Davis, Broome and Chapman claimed no knowledge of what happened to Lim, Davis' signal on 4 February 1945 left no doubt as to the reason for the collapse:

> From DEE (Davis): 192, NG, TSING, SEK FU, LIM arrested late March, owing collapse of BILL (Chua) under arrest[51].

No trace was left of Lim and his network of agents in Perak and it would be more than a year later, after the Japanese surrender, that much of what happened would come to light.

With the end of the war, Force 136 was keen to find out the fate of its ill-fated GUSTAVUS mission members in Perak. Frantic signals were sent from Colombo to field operatives in Malaya to track down Lim Bo Seng and his agents.

By 28 August 1945, Tan Chong Tee, Wu Chye Sin and Yi Tian Song were released by the Japanese. Tan rushed to Penang and got in touch with Force 136 elements there who flew him to Singapore. After some confusion, Tan met with the SOE Singapore head, Derek Gill Davies, who was then able to ascertain what actually happened.

Signals in Lim Bo Seng's file show that by 30 August 1945, Force 136's Perak outfit was busy looking for traces of Lim. By 6 September, brief reports were filtering in from Perak and it seemed very likely that Lim was still very much alive and Tan might have been wrong:

> Report on my demand to KEMPEI chief for return of our agents captured PERAK March 44. Members of KEMPEI say that the men were captured at Gopeng. LIM BO SENG entered BATU GAJAH Prison 29th July '44. Released 25th August 45[52].

However, the next day, it was all too clear that Tan was right:

> AH HAN back from IPOH. Jap story mainly true. LIM BO SENG died of dysentery in hospital[53].

Force 136's MCS was in shock. One of their key operatives was now confirmed dead. They needed more details and had to locate Lim's remains before relaying any message to his family:

> Try locate LIM BO SENG's grave. Record statements witnesses his fate. Do not inform his wife yet[54].

Tan along with Gill Davies and an Anglican priest, the headmaster of St. Andrew's School where Lim's sons were studying, called on Mrs Lim. It was a devastating blow for a family that had survived the hardships of war and occupation, only to be confronted with the worst news of all.

In a signal to Force 136 HQ, Gill Davies outlined the deprivations the Lim family were facing and the need to provide urgent closure:

> Have had most distressing meeting with Mrs Lim Bo Seng. Complete family have suffered terribly at hands of Japanese.
>
> Eight male members missing. All property ruined and very large financial loss.
>
> Have given Mrs Lim 5000 rpt 5000 dollars. I must have some guidance what compensation I can pay as the people cannot be left to starve. Lims estimate their losses at 1,000,000 rpt 1,000,000 dollars.
>
> Am putting pressure on Japanese through Army to find out exact fate of Lim Bo Seng. Would stress importance of quick and generous settlement.

> Emphasise fully-recognised valuable service rendered by Lim Bo Seng to British prior to fall Singapore and afterwards with this force. Also, he had outstanding claim on British naval contract[55].

Lim's family was not the only one affected. On returning home, Tan discovered that his mother had died. His elder brother had also been killed in February 1942, leaving behind his sister-in-law and four children who were living in abject poverty. Tan asked Davies for money to feed his family and for housing for the children but there was not much that Davies could do[56].

Compensation for Lim Bo Seng's family would not be straightforward. Lim's brother, who was still studying in Calcutta, found that his stipend had been stopped, leaving him no money to live on. An urgent signal from the MCS to Force 136's finance section called for the immediate resumption of the payments.

Force 136's finance section did not appreciate the nature of the compensation or why Lim was to be treated so specially:

> Fixed procedure in all cases is to cease payment salary and allotments six months after person reported missing on present information. Regret unable authorise any further payment to nominee (Lim's brother).
>
> Who authorised Gill Davies pay Mrs Lim Bo Seng 5000 dollars. Realise that in hardship cases small immediate payments necessary pending final decision liquidation committee but this is equivalent of nearly pounds 600 rpt pounds 600 sterling at present rate.
>
> Loss sustained by Lim family is not SOE responsibility. HQ are only responsible compensations in respect of death Lim Bo Seng when this has been confirmed[57].

In several more signals, SOE's Group B finance section dressed down Gill Davies for making the $5,000 payment and noted that, "In view Gill Davies payment to wife of nearly 600 pounds sterling, no further payments can be made until full facts known and award determined by liquidation committee"[58].

Gill Davies and the MCS were incensed at the rulebook attitude taken by their financial section. Over the next few months there were more signals to Colombo and more refusals.

Although the finance section did not appear to appreciate Lim's contribution, the Chinese nationalist government did. By December 1945, they had voted an *ex-gratia* payment of $400,000 (Chinese nationalist dollars) to Mrs Lim for services rendered by her husband. More importantly, memorial services for Lim, attended by thousands, had been held in Ipoh and Kuala Lumpur and would now be held in Singapore, sponsored by the British Military Administration. Yet, payments of a military Major's pension, promised to Lim when he signed on, had not been paid to Mrs Lim.

Under pressure, the finance section agreed that they would only pay Mrs Lim $4,632 extra as full and final compensation, after deducting the amount paid by Gill Davies earlier. No mention was made of a pension or compensation for the Brick Selling Agency contract[59].

By 11 December 1945, the Chinese nationalist government in Chungking had issued a citation appointing Lim Bo Seng posthumously to the rank of Major General, asking the British legation to hand the citation to Lim's family in Singapore. This was a further embarrassment to Force 136, who still could not iron out Lim's compensation. The MCS finally hit out in a signal to the finance section, referring to the agreement signed by Ivory in 1942:

> Contract initialled by Col Ivory rpt Ivory calls for compensation either in form Majors pension to widow or at discretion force 136 lump sum equivalent to such pension
>
> Majors pension pounds 170 rpt 170 plus pounds 36 for each child total for wife and seven children pounds 422 rpt pounds 422 per annum... Equivalent is over pounds 6200 rpt 6200...
>
> ... Surely record sheet not rpt not necessary for decision in view of tariff fully documented...
>
> ... This is not a case of compensation to an agent, fulfilment of a contract in which one party has come to be recognised as the Chinese foundation of Sino-British resistance in Malaya and the other party has become identified with British rule in Malaya. Request urgent re-consideration. The imagination boggles at the nature of the uncommon enthusiasms of Lim rpt Lim Family, Chinese and British Community if your proposed settlements is even mentioned in such circles[60].

This stiff opposition from the MCS prompted the finance section to cable London for support, claiming that the payment had been "ridiculed" by the country section. As there was no progress, Davis intervened and convinced the finance section that an annuity should be purchased for the duration of Mrs Lim's life and for 15 years more in the event of her death. Although Mrs Lim should have rightfully received £422 a year, the finance section finally agreed to recommend a pension of only £400[61]. The section then submitted this revised proposal to London on 10 January 1945 with the suggestion that payment of the pension begin on 1 January 1946. None of this was made known to Mrs Lim, who would eventually end up with a pension of only £400 a year.

However, the actual determination of how the pension should be paid and the logistics of it was not easily settled. It would take special intervention by the successors to the SOE to ensure that Mrs Lim received the £400 annually. In the end, the pension payment was only approved in January 1947, with the British government providing compensation almost three years after Lim had died and long after everyone else had recognised his contributions[62]. Compensation for the $40,000 Brick Selling Agency contract remains outstanding.

Today, Lim Bo Seng is viewed not only as a nationalist Chinese hero but a Singaporean hero as well. His sacrifice for Singapore is mentioned in modern-day secondary school history textbooks and he is treated as a national hero by Singaporeans despite Lim having really fought for Britain and the nationalist government in Chungking. Yet 60 years on, although he is valorised by a country that did not even exist at the time of his death and is remembered by the nationalist government in Taiwan, Lim Bo Seng has been forgotten by the organisation and the empire for which he gave his life.

Force 136 Operations

Many other SOE operations, including sabotage missions, were more successful. The SOE carried out numerous operations, landing agents in Malaya with teams operating in every state by the end of 1944 (see map). Down under, their Australian counterparts, with former Orient Mission member Lieutenant Colonel Ivan Lyon at the helm, carried out one of the most successful sabotage raids against Japanese shipping in Singapore in 1943. Operation JAYWICK has become legendary in special operations circles, where Force 'Z', under Lyon's command, sailed from Darwin to Singapore in a fishing boat, and then using specially designed fol-boats, sneaked into Singapore's Keppel Harbour and stuck limpet mines on the hulls of numerous ships. This resulted in the destruction of more than 50,000 tonnes of enemy shipping.

However, the following year, in an attempt to carry out a similar operation in Singapore Harbour, Lyon and his men were killed while fleeing through the Indonesian islands. Although Operation RIMAU succeeded, Lyon's Force 'Z' was effectively destroyed.

Nonetheless, the build-up of agents and supplies in the Malayan jungles continued. Through numerous night-time airdrops and operations like

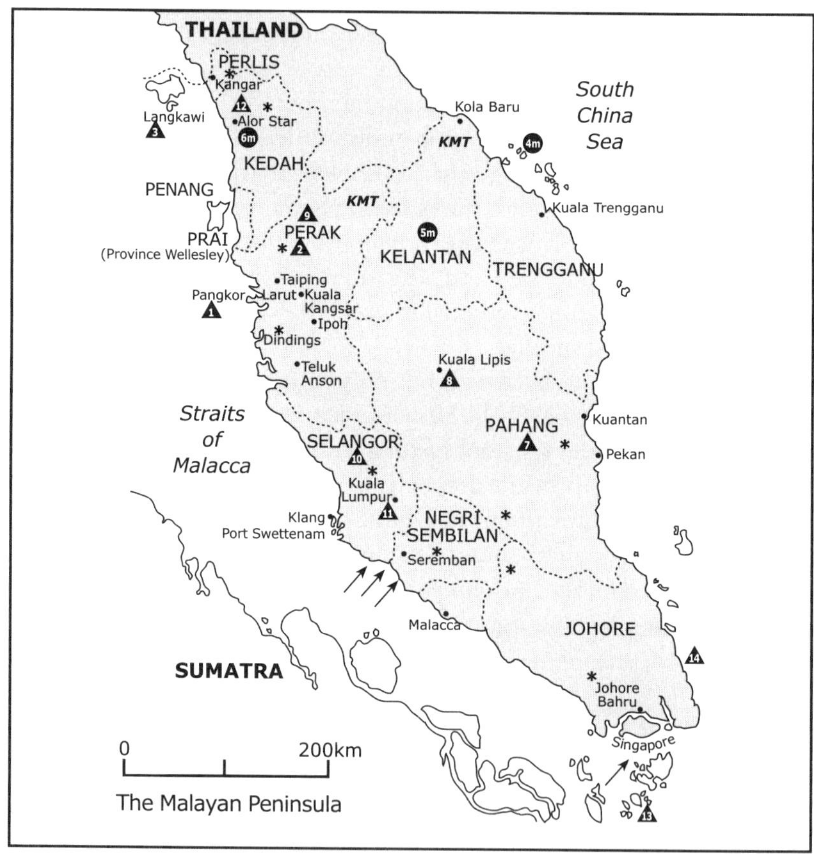

1 GUSTAVUS/REMARKABLE
2 John Davis's camp & radio
3 MULLET
4 OATMEAL
5 HEBRIDES
6 FUNNEL
7 PONTOON
8 BEACON
9 EVIDENCE
10 GALVANIC
11 Major Ian MacDonald's party
12 Major Pierre Chassé's party
13 RIMAU
14 CARPENTER/MINT
* MPAJA
KMT Kuomintag
m Indicates a Malay based party
↗ Operation ZIPPER

Force 136's drop zones and infiltration points for its various operations in Malaya.
(Based on a map reproduced with permission from Gough, Richard. *The Jungle was Red.* Singapore: SNP Panpac, 2003)

CARPENTER and FUNNEL, Force 136 grew considerably in size. By 1945, Force 136 was involved in the planning for ZIPPER and felt the clandestine units in Malaya could play a key role in the reoccupation.

In his signals to Colombo, Davis emphasised the urgency for a quick decision on the role of Force 136 in ZIPPER. Mountbatten had raised the issue in Whitehall as early as July 1944 and his views were put to the War Cabinet in a secret memorandum on 9 December 1944. Mountbatten pointed out that the cooperation of any local resistance in Malaya would depend on Britain's post-war plans for that country and these should be explained to the population beforehand.

His view was that a favourable atmosphere needed to be created to assist the setting-up of a future post-war administration and "our agents" would need general guidance on the subject. However, despite pressure from Mountbatten, the British Government was not prepared to commit itself publicly to any post-war solution. As far as Force 136 was concerned, it simply had a military, not political, objective to fulfil.

From March 1945, there was a great effort to build up the necessary guerrilla forces for ZIPPER but this was not a priority until the success of Operation MODIFIED DRACULA in May. Although the plan was to divide Malaya into eight sections, roughly corresponding with MPAJA's eight regiments, there was also a need to coordinate the Malay guerrillas and Chinese nationalist resistance forces as well.

It was estimated that 300 men of all ranks would need to be infiltrated, together with arms, supplies and wireless sets. In addition, due to the questionable loyalty of the MPAJA, gurkha support units would also be needed to protect the agents and their Drop Zones (DZs). All this created not only a huge demand on resources but also the need to find a solution to the problems of resupplying the agents on the ground during the monsoon and obtaining enough aircraft to fly the sorties needed[63].

Eventually, SACSEA provided a general outline of the part the MPAJA would be expected to play in ZIPPER, now pencilled-in for the first week in September. Apart from ambushing Japanese columns, the resistance should seize all bridges, railway stations and power stations to prevent them from being destroyed by the Japanese.

The plan for ZIPPER, when it finally emerged, consisted of three main operational areas, namely the Malayan states of Johor, Perak (where Davis was based) and Selangor, the last of which would cover the city of Kuala Lumpur and the proposed invasion beaches of Sepang, Morib and Port Dickson. As all west coast road and rail communications ran through these states, control by the guerrillas would effectively isolate the Japanese throughout Malaya. The first Force 136 party (GALVANIC) to land in Selangor in May 1945 was led by Lieutenant Colonel Douglas Keith

Broadhurst, a pre-war police officer in Malaya[64].

However, as the end drew nearer, racial tensions began emerging. The murder of SOE's two Chinese nationalist operators by the communists highlighted the very complex political situation that laid below the surface in Malaya. In Chinese communities in Malaya, communist supporters of Mao Tse Tung (in *pinyin,* Mao Zedong) were forced to co-exist with their sworn enemies, the KMT, who were supporters of the nationalist government in China. Within this political mix, the communist MPAJA guerrillas had agreed to support the return of the British, while some more radical guerrilla leaders wanted to seize power and install a Chinese communist government[65].

Meanwhile, there was growing support amongst Malays for the new, Japanese-sponsored Malay nationalist movement. The Malays had their own views about the post-war future of Malaya and believed that they should have special rights and privileges as the original inhabitants of the country. This did not include power-sharing with the Chinese. At that point in time, very little was known in SEAC about the Malay nationalists, who, with Japanese encouragement, wanted independence from Britain and were prepared to resist the return of British troops to Malaya. With the help of the Japanese chief of staff in Singapore, several Malay leaders formed an organisation for the independence of Malaya. It was called Kesatuan Rakyat Indonesia Semenanjung (KRIS), or the Union of Peninsular Indonesians, and it sent three representatives in July 1945 to meet with Indonesian nationalist leader Sukarno.

Two months earlier, Japanese officials in Singapore had discussed the implementation of Indonesian independence. Following that meeting, the Malay Lieutenant Colonel, Ibrahim Yaacob, was urged to convene a meeting at the Station Hotel in Kuala Lumpur on 17 August 1945 to support Indonesian independence and get Malaya included in that new state. However, opposing these groups were the SOE's anti-Japanese Malay guerrillas in north Malaya. For instance, near Kuala Lipis, SOE's BEACON party had the support of the local Malay District Officer, Che Yeop Mahideen, who promised to recruit 500 volunteers. A second party, MULTIPLE, located east of Raub, had 250 armed Malays but was under threat from a hostile local MPAJA patrol. In the state of Pahang, 750 Malay guerrillas had the support of the Sultan. Ironically, the Sultan had also been nominated by the Japanese-sponsored Malay nationalist movement to head their government in a post-war independent Malaya[66].

In June 1945, the simmering racial tensions between the Malays and Chinese finally exploded, with disastrous consequences in west Johor. Although the tension between the Malays and Chinese was not new, it dramatically increased when the British-trained and mainly Chinese resistance guerrillas began demanding taxes, supplies and intelligence from Malay *kampongs* (villages) and towns. These were interspersed with reports of Malay women being kidnapped to work in guerrilla camp kitchens while others were molested or used as comfort women[67].

Although some Malays joined the MPAJA voluntarily, others were obviously conscripted. In what appeared to have been a campaign of terror throughout the countryside, the MPAJA killed any Malays and Chinese suspected of collaborating with the Japanese and destroyed their homes. Many people simply disappeared – particularly Malay policemen, government officials and district and village headmen. The bodies that were eventually found showed signs of extreme torture and mutilation[68].

Two MPAJA regiments involved in the Johor clashes were the 3rd at Segamat and the 4th covering Kota Tinggi, Johor Baru and Muar. In May 1945, a Malay headman who had refused to collect the MPAJA taxes was abducted by the Kangkar guerrillas while on his way to Yong Peng. His body was never found[69].

Retaliatory raids by gangs of Malays and Chinese against one another led to the loss of innocent lives. As clashes spread, Chinese refugees fled into adjoining areas, bringing with them stories of Malays on the march attacking Chinese communities, cutting women and children down with knives. Malays repeated stories of arrogant communist guerrillas butchering or beheading Malays. Some captured by the MPAJA were drowned, others scalded to death with hot water or given the water treatment until their stomachs distended.

The communal violence in the absence of any real and effective authority led the Malays to form *kampong* defence groups, which in June 1945, became the foundations of the Sabilillah army led by Kiyai Salleh Abdul Karim. Members of this group eventually collaborated with the Japanese in attacks against the MPAJA detachments in Asam Bubok, killing the MPAJA leader Seng Nga[70].

SACSEA's lack of understanding of the complex political situation in Malaya became apparent when, in an attempt to defuse this racial conflict, the RAF dropped leaflets on 20 July, in both Malay and English, warning that those responsible for the violence would be severely dealt with when the British returned. As there were no leaflets printed in Chinese and the British were arming the Chinese resistance groups, it was obvious the message was meant only for the Malays. The leaflets strengthened the Malay view that the Chinese and MPAJA had the support of the British, thereby encouraging those uncommitted Malays to support the Japanese-sponsored KRIS[71].

By the end of July, Mackenzie realised that an effective plan for the use of Force 136 in the reoccupation had to be drawn up. In a top-secret paper to Captain G.A. Garnons-Williams, Head of 'P' division (Clandestine Operations) at SEAC, Mackenzie noted that members of Force 136 in the field should be attached as small liaison detachments on the staff of the various formations and units involved in ZIPPER and TIDERACE. They would then be able to advise on local conditions, provide updated intelligence and most importantly, "control local guerrilla units through the British Officers in the field in accordance with the Senior British Officer's requirements"[72].

Force 136 had infiltrated 77 British officers in-country and these men had set up 40 wireless transmitting (WT) stations throughout the country. Mackenzie felt that ZIPPER and TIDERACE commanders would benefit from Force 136 help as they would be able to clear drop zones and airfields for the reception of airborne units while providing guards and patrols on vital lines of communications. Force 136 could also provide a nucleus for the creation of a disciplined police force to prevent civil disturbances and looting as well as distribution of foodstuffs and other essential commodities. The WT stations could also be used for the passing of instructions "for the Senior British Officer concerned to local authorities, including possibly enemy units and formations"[73].

However, the main contribution of these clandestine forces would be to help fill a power vacuum, should it occur – clearly a prophetic prediction of events to come:

> Whilst it is understood that every effort will be made on the part of the military authorities to ensure that there is no hiatus in the handover from the Japanese to the British, it is pointed out that if such a hiatus does occur, the above-mentioned British Officers and WT sets will be available; and that it will be possible for them to receive instructions from higher authority[74].

In meetings with Rear (later Vice) Admiral Cedric Holland, who had just started planning for TIDERACE, it was clear that Force 136 did not have a role in Singapore. SEAC planners also did not see a need to activate Force 136 as no lag time was expected between the surrender of the Japanese government and the reoccupation by British forces. Therefore, 'P' division instructed Force 136 to "stay where you are". Moreover, General Douglas MacArthur did not want the British to appear as if they were taking the surrender of the Japanese and ordered Mountbatten not to accept the surrender of any Japanese forces before MacArthur himself did so on 2 September 1945. Mountbatten's acceptance of this edict and the resulting power vacuum in Malaya proved a serious miscalculation on the part of the returning British forces.

By the end of the first week of August 1945, John Davis, who was still in Perak, received a signal informing him that the Japanese surrender was imminent and providing directions outlining the role Force 136 was to take in the matter:

> The general policy is to keep resistance forces concentrated in their areas and as much under the control of Allied officers with them as is possible. Every effort will be made to avoid clashes between resistance forces and Japanese forces.
>
> Personnel of clandestine organisations in the field will be prepared to carry out the following tasks when required. In order to carry out these tasks, clandestine organisations will continue to remain under cover.
>
> a) To provide local intelligence particularly with regard to action taken by the Japanese to comply (or otherwise) with surrender orders.
>
> b) To provide topographical and other local information to the Allied occupational forces when these arrive.
>
> c) To provide guides and interpreters to Allied occupational forces.
>
> d) In certain cases to establish contact with Allied POW (prisoner of war) Camps.
>
> e) In the event of continued Japanese resistance in certain areas, or failure to comply with surrender orders, to concert the action of resistance forces with the operations of Allied Forces as required by the Allied Commander concerned.
>
> As a last resort, if either means of establishing contact with Japanese commanders fail, clandestine organisations may be required to establish contact in accordance with instructions to be given at the time[75].

Clearly, Force 136 personnel were to remain where they were. Davis, like most other members of the MCS, was enraged. In a signal to Colombo, he noted it was unreasonable to:

> ... expect the guerrillas to remain half-starved in the hills while the Allies leisurely took over the administration from the Japs.... The

> MPAJA expect and await specific orders and not vague directives.... I am satisfied that 3,000 armed guerrillas with Force 136 parties would obey reasonable orders.... They must be fully-equipped, rationed and used by us... and be given the full share in the honours of victory.... The matter is very urgent and there is a serious risk of a disastrous anticlimax[76].

'P' division realised that the "stay where you are" instructions placed Force 136 in an untenable position and, appreciating that the nationalist takeover of the Netherlands East Indies could be repeated in Malaya, rescinded the order on 23 August.

SEAC signalled John Davis that while avoiding clashes with the Japanese, the MPAJA in conjunction with Force 136 officers should take over responsibility for ensuring law and order in those areas not occupied by the Japanese. They should also prevent the MPAJA from seizing power. Field officers were told to contact local Japanese commanders to reestablish a British presence but not to "receive any surrenders". Meanwhile, they were to gather intelligence about any POW camps in their area and the condition of any airfields.

When they learnt that the ban on entering towns and villages had been removed, MPAJA HQ instructed its eight regiments to move into towns evacuated by the Japanese. There, the guerrillas formed a two-tier authority. On the township level, they developed People's Committees which nominated representatives to attend State People's Congresses. These Congresses became responsible for the rescue of refugees, communications and general security. The Japanese, however, remained responsible for law and order.

However, this peaceful takeover would change quickly in Singapore as the Allied commanders had ordered all non-essential Japanese troops to gather in the southern part of the Johor state. Once the MPAJA 4th Regiment guerrillas in south Johor learnt that the Japanese were withdrawing from Singapore city, they ignored Force 136 instructions and moved across the causeway to base themselves at the Singapore Japanese Club, located on the site of present-day Selegie Complex.

As the Naval Force Commander for TIDERACE, Rear Admiral Holland did not see the need for Force 136 help in Singapore and Malaya during the operation; the gap in power was viewed as minimal. SEAC planners clearly did not expect such savage violence to break out and were taken by surprise when the communal clashes spread throughout the peninsula. As a result of Holland's decision not to use clandestine forces to control the rebel elements of the MPAJA, Force 136 officers remained where they were and were unable to act in the chaos that ensued in Singapore.

The reduction of the number of Japanese troops in the city led to outbreaks of violence and anarchy. Against a background of public jubilation that Japan had been defeated, the Malay guerrillas and MPAJA raided army depots for weapons. Collaborators were hunted down and their bodies left hanging from trees. Mistresses of the Japanese had their heads shaved, and were paraded and spat on before being beaten or stabbed to death by the crowds. Revenge, retribution, summary executions and fear swept through the city[77]. Records of the communal violence that rocked the island were not kept by the Japanese as it was not seen as an attack against them but more as clashes among locals. As such, many of the killings and disappearances went unreported and forgotten in the chaos of the last days of Japanese rule.

In desperation on 25 August, when an appeal to SEAC and Force 136 officers to cooperate in maintaining law and order failed, the Japanese commander issued a proclamation banning demonstrations and meetings of more than 500 people. This was ignored, and law and order in the city collapsed[78].

SEAC was of the view that the Japanese would be able to maintain effective control in Malaya despite Japan's surrender. However, the communal violence that was sweeping across Malaya meant that only the MPAJA was in control in many towns and villages throughout the peninsula. There was no way in which SEAC could help restore order in Malaya despite appeals from the Japanese. SEAC could only instruct the men they had in Malaya, namely, the 77 SOE operatives in-country. These operatives did not have any military force or weapons with which to maintain order. Force 136's main armed force was the MPAJA, which was effectively controlled by the MCP. Until SEAC landed its own troops, Force 136 had to rely upon the goodwill of the MPAJA under the agreement signed in December 1943. This meant that Force 136 officers in-country were powerless to stop rebel elements of the MPAJA from exacting revenge on the Malay population.

Moreover, the head of Force 136 in Malaya, Colin Mackenzie, was concerned for the safety of his men. They were based with the communist guerrillas during the vacuum between the Japanese surrender and the initial arrival of Allied forces as part of TIDERACE, planned for 3 September, which was still more than a week away. The bulk of forces would only arrive with ZIPPER, which was slotted for 9 September. Although the MCP was a banned organisation at the outbreak of the war, it was the only resistance group with sufficient size and manpower in Malaya. The MPAJA consisted mainly of Malaya-born Chinese whose status was inferior to the Malays, with very few having citizenship in the country. Obviously, the Chinese communists had increased in influence during the war years and the Chinese would expect a better deal from the returning British. Unless this were guaranteed to some extent, some local MCP leaders might rebel. In a signal to London on 24 August, Mackenzie asked for a statement that would help British liaison officers in any discussions with the communist guerrillas[79].

As the request dealt with a better deal for the Chinese in post-war Malaya, it was seen as a civil affairs matter, and the War Office's civil affairs department wanted to discuss the future with the Malay rulers first. A frustrated Mackenzie became more worried that the delay could be misunderstood by the MPAJA and that its reaction would not only place his men in serious danger but that a British military response would then damage post-war relations.

While the questions were being debated in Whitehall, the MCP leaders in Malaya took matters into their own hands, meeting and agreeing on a post-war manifesto. As the Royal Marines were coming ashore on Penang on 3 September 1945, the MCP published its manifesto for post-war Malaya with a demand for a democratic government in Malaya and Singapore with all races having the opportunity to vote and obtain the rights of citizenship. The MCP had temporarily abandoned their plans of armed insurrection and national liberation for one of self-government. However, the days of submissive colonial peoples were clearly gone. The MCP would not be happy as a subject of colonial rule, with the demand for independence from Britain, clearly the next logical step.

In the four weeks since the Emperor of Japan's surrender announcement, Japanese authority in most of the territories under SEAC had effectively slipped to local nationalist organisations. In Malaya, by agreement with SEAC, some 70% of towns and villages were controlled by the communists. The remainder was held either by the KMT, Malay Home Guard or, in some cases, the triads[80]. The Japanese had recorded 212 attacks against their military units, police or strategic installations. Apart from 63 Japanese and 31 Malay policemen killed, a further 357 Malay policemen had disappeared, their bodies never to be recovered[81].

The role given to the MPAJA following the Japanese surrender was that they should control towns and villages not occupied by the Japanese. However, some units took over towns regardless of whether the Japanese were there or not. For some 12 weeks after the surrender, Force 136 personnel were the only authority in many of these villages until the military or civil government eventually took over. There were numerous confrontations between Force 136, the MPAJA and the Japanese during this period but in general the MPAJA held to their side of the bargain.

When the 25th Indian Division eventually reached Kuala Lumpur on 13 September, they found Davis and elements of Force 136 already established in the city. Although the MPAJA had earlier signed an agreement with Davis, Broome, Chapman and Lim to assist the return of British administration and to use the MCP's peaceful popular front strategy, they were deemed as a potential threat to British colonial strategy. On 12 September 1945, while some of the leaders of the MPAJA were basking in the glory of the official Japanese surrender at the Municipal Building in Singapore, Headquarters Allied Land Forces Southeast Asia issued curt instructions to the MPAJA that their operational role had ceased and they were to hand over their weapons and disband.

Despite many people in Malaya welcoming the return of the colonial masters, it was the MPAJA who were seen as the real liberators, not the British. When the army moved into some areas and the People's Committees were disbanded, some guerrillas felt their moment of triumph had been stolen by the returning British. Having spent years starving in the jungles and fighting the Japanese, they now found themselves facing fresh British and Indian troops who were still looking for the war. The soldiers' high-handed treatment of these resistance heroes led to numerous misunderstandings, which included the MPAJA fighters being roughly treated by Indian troops who mistook the MPAJA fighters for Japanese soldiers[82].

In his memoirs 60 years on, Chin Peng, who took over as the secretary general of the CPM in 1948, claimed that the ethnic violence was not caused by the communists:

> As early as July – before the first of the two atomic bombs dropped on Japan – Japanese troops, disguised as AJA (Anti-Japanese Army) guerrillas, went to a mosque in Johore and slaughtered a pig. This immediately inflamed Malay sentiments and they turned on the local Chinese villagers. Datuk Onn Bin Jaafar was at this time the district officer for Batu Pahat under the Japanese administration. Trouble spread from Batu Pahat to Yong Peng. The Malays were armed with *parang panjang* – the long knife. The Chinese villagers who became their targets were unarmed and desperately called on the AJA for support. We could not ignore their predicament and ordered in units of our army as a protection force. The British liaison officers (Force 136), who frankly didn't understand the root causes of the problem and were not prepared to listen, tried to prevent us from going. We ignored them. In the end, many liaison officers had no option but to move with us. We set up a line and told the Malays not to cross it. The Malays, believing their magic amulets would shield them from bullets, charged our lines. We shot. Some dropped. The rest hesitated, then retreated. We chased them into nearby *kampongs* and

> confiscated every *parang panjang* we could find. The major attack in the Batu Pahat area resulted in our forces actually arresting Datuk Onn and his assistant. In the event, Datuk Onn helped bring the violence to an end by speaking to the Malays. It was a very emotional time and nobody was willing to listen coolly to details of how the racial trouble began. The killing was on a very large scale. At least 1,000 died. Naturally, propaganda had it that the MPAJA was the primary cause. This is patently untrue. In numerous other racial instances at this time, Chinese bandits were the culprits. The CPM, of course, was blamed for their activities as well. Teluk Anson and Ayer Kuning were areas that suffered this way[83].

For many, however, it is hard to accept Chin Peng's denial of involvement in the racial massacres during the phoney surrender. Robert Callow, then a lieutenant with the 430 Madras Sappers & Miners' Forward Airfields Company, who had waded ashore with the rest of the ZIPPER troops on 9 September, and was working to restore the Klang airstrip, saw the vengeance wrought by the MPAJA:

> During that few weeks (before British military control was restored), the MPAJA were mainly concerned with finding supposed local collaborators with the Japanese to carry out summary trials and executions. Many shot bodies were found thrown afterwards into nullahs and left there for public attention to what had been done. In fact, the two adjacent wooden houses (beside the Klang - Port Swettenham road alongside the Klang airfield) which my Company occupied then had been vacated by one family group. We thought that they had merely fled but all their bodies were found later in the nullahs at Klang.
>
> However, the MPAJA did keep civil order for those first weeks but could not control the looting of Japanese stores, mainly by many Chinese and fewer Malays (who destroyed things rather than use them); while some Indians sensibly selected better items which they then sold![84].

The idea behind having clandestine operations in Malaya was to destabilise Japanese rule and defensive preparations in the country while providing effective intelligence for British forces planning to recapture Malaya. Although Force 136 was effective on both these counts through the agreements signed with the MCP and other smaller resistance groups, the limitations on its size and the separate agendas of the MCP and various other resistance groups meant that Force 136 did not have an effective force with which to control these groups once the war was over.

As long as the Japanese occupied Malaya, the MCP, the Chinese nationalists and the Malay resistance groups would put aside their differences and adopt the common aim of ousting the Japanese Imperial Army. However, once it became clear that the Japanese were on the way out, individual communal and political agendas began to resurface. The MCP, who agitated for greater political rights for Chinese in Malaya, a communist China and a communist state in pre-war Malaya, began to pursue their ideology again. The Chinese nationalists, who had worked with the communists in China and Malaya during the war, once again became their sworn enemies in the fight for China's future in the Malayan peninsula. The Malay nationalists were also now agitating for an independent Malaya under Malay rule and did not want the Chinese to have a greater say in Malayan politics; many had already joined up with Japanese groups willing to continue the struggle against the British. These separate and antagonistic agendas came to a head once Japanese control was removed as each group sought to fill the power vacuum. As Chin Peng notes:

> ...When there is talk about Malay units being pro-Japanese, Westerners again invariably fall into the easy trap of over-simplification. When we, as communist guerrillas worked with the British, none of us, for a single moment, considered ourselves pro-British. We were allies, but we had our own agenda. Likewise, following Japan's capitulation, a different set of circumstances presented themselves to us as far as the defeated army was concerned[85].

SEAC and Force 136 were in no position to control these disparate agendas, which had begun to surface during the phoney surrender period. Force 136, an espionage organisation, was obviously unable to quell the racial tensions and clashes that were emerging in the country. Although they were able to harness the various groups during the occupation, once their common goal had been achieved, it was impossible to get these groups to band together again. More worrying, the weapons that Force 136 had provided to these resistance groups would now be used against the local population and eventually against the British during the Emergency.

SEAC had not expected such a violent reaction from the various ethnic groups in the country. The interrupted transition of power from the Japanese to the British in Malaya meant that pre-war racial and political tensions, which had been controlled by earlier authorities and subsumed under a common goal during the Japanese occupation, was given free reign during the five weeks of the phoney surrender. The outpouring of ethnic violence and racial hatred in those few weeks, which were finally squelched upon the return of the British, had given elements within the MCP a taste of raw power and control. Such communal violence, almost unheard of before the war and now unleashed for such an extended period, would revisit the country less than three years later with the Communist Emergency of 1948.

Endnotes

1 Gough, Richard. *The Jungle was Red.* Singapore: SNP Panpac, 2003. 5.

2 SIS or MI6?. Secret Intelligence Service MI6 webpage. https://www.sis.gov.uk/our-history/sis-or-mi6.html, accessed 12 Oct 2011.

3 Brown, Anthony Cave. C: The Secret Life of Sir Stewart Graham Menzies, Spymaster to Winston Churchill. New York: Macmillan, 1987

4 Davies, Philip. MI6 and the machinery of Spying. Oxford: Frank Cass Publishers, 2004, P 131.

5 Callow, Robert. Email correspondence with the author, 13 December 2008, 9 March 2009.

6 Callow, Robert. Email correspondence with the author, 13 December 2008, 9 March 2009.

7 Callow, Robert. Email correspondence with the author, 13 December 2008, 9 March 2009.

8 Ibid. 5.

9 *Lim Bo Seng's Naval Contract, P.F. 146/8, Chungking, 19 October 1945, HS 9/1341/6.* London: The National Archives.

10 Ibid.

11 Ibid.

12 *KYBOC V COSEC NR 906, 15 November 1945, HS 9/1341/6.* London: The National Archives.

13 *Mr Tang. (Lim Bo Seng), HS 9/1341/6.* London: The National Archives.

14 Force 136 members in this chapter will be referred to by their given names, with aliases in brackets. Where they are referred to by their aliases (i.e. in quoted text), their given names will appear in brackets. *Ed.*

15 Ibid.

16 *Record of Activities of Tan Chong Tee (ZA/4), 27 September 1945, HS 1/107.* London: The National Archives.

17 Chapman, Colonel F. Spencer. *The Jungle is Neutral*. London: Chatto & Windus, 1949. 236.

18 Ibid. 236.

19 Ibid. 237.

20 Ibid. 239.

21 *Report on GUSTAVUS, HS 1/107*. London: The National Archives. Appendix D: 1.

22 *Report on OPERATION GUSTAVUS/PIRATE, HS 1/107*. London: The National Archives. 1.

23 *Report on GUSTAVUS, HS 1/107*. London: The National Archives. Appendix D: 2.

24 Ibid. Appendix D: 1.

25 Ibid. 2.

26 *Report on OPERATION GUSTAVUS/PIRATE, Record of Conference Held at Camp, 30–31 December 43, HS 1/107*. London: The National Archives. 1.

27 Chin Peng. *My Side of History*. Singapore: Media Masters, 2003. 100.

28 *Report on GUSTAVUS, HS 1/107*. London: The National Archives. 2.

29 *Report on OPERATION GUSTAVUS/PIRATE, HS 1/107*. London: The National Archives. 2.

30 *Report on GUSTAVUS, HS 1/107*. London: The National Archives Appendix D: 4.

31 *Record of Activities of Tan Chong Tee (ZA/4), 27 September 1945, HS 1/107*. London: The National Archives. 1.

32 Ibid. 2.

33 *Report on GUSTAVUS, HS 1/107*. London: The National Archives. 2.

34 Ibid. 3.

35 *Report on OPERATION GUSTAVUS/PIRATE, HS 1/107*. London: The National Archives. 2.

36 Chin, 2003. 106.

37 *Record of Activities of Tan Chong Tee (ZA/4), 27 September 1945, HS 1/107*. London: The National Archives. 3.

38 *Report on GUSTAVUS, HS 1/107*. London: The National Archives. Appendix D: 3.

39 *Record of Activities of Tan Chong Tee (ZA/4), 27 September 1945, HS 1/107*. London: The National Archives. 3.

40 *Chan Siak Foo, Wong Kwong Fai, Ho Wing Pun Report on Incident Leading to Arrest, 9 September 1945, HS 1/107*. London: The National Archives. 2.

41 *Report on GUSTAVUS, HS 1/107*. London: The National Archives. Appendix D: 3.

42 Chapman, 1949. 259.

43 *Report on GUSTAVUS, HS 1/107.* London: The National Archives. Appendix D: 3.

44 Ibid. Appendix D: 3.

45 *Record of Activities of Tan Chong Tee (ZA/4), 27 September 1945, HS 1/107.* London: The National Archives. 3.

46 Pang, Augustine and Angeline Song (eds.). "Meet Singapore's James Bond". *Chee Beng's Start Page*. 1998. [Internet]. Available from: <http://ourstory.asia1.com.sg/war/lifeline/bond7.html>.

47 Ibid.

48 *Record of Activities of Tan Chong Tee (ZA/4), 27 September 1945, HS 1/107.* London: The National Archives. 3.

49 Tan Chong Tee. *Force 136: Story of a WWII Resistance Fighter.* Singapore: Asiapac Books, 1995.

50 *Signal Sheet, HS 9/1341/6.* London: The National Archives.

51 Ibid.

52 Ibid.

53 Ibid.

54 Ibid.

55 *KBOC V COSEC NR. 432, 2 October 1945, HS 9/1341/6.* London: The National Archives.

56 *Letter to John Davis, 2 October 1945, HS 1/107.* London: The National Archives. 1.

57 *KYBOC V COSEC NR 1616, 4 October 1945, HS 9/1341/6.* London: The National Archives.

58 *KYBOC V COSEC NR 1994, 6 October 1945, HS 9/1341/6.* London: The National Archives.

59 *SRL 362/363, 10 December 1945, HS 9/1341/6.* London: The National Archives.

60 *From Kuala Lumpur, 13 December 1945, HS 9/1341/6.* London: The National Archives.

61 *SRL NO 637/8, 10 January 1945, HS 9/1341/6.* London: The National Archives.

62 *CAOG 9/337.* London: The National Archives.

63 Gough, 2003. 104.

64 Ibid. 114.

65 Ibid. 130.

66 Ibid. 131.

67 Ibid. 131.

68 Ibid. 131.

69 Ibid. 131.

70 Ibid. 132.

71 Ibid. 132.

72 *J.P.S. 180, G.25/4387, 6 August 1945, HS 1/328.* London: The National Archives. 1–3.

73 Ibid. 1.

74 Ibid. 1.

75 *Direction of Clandestine Operations after Japanese Capitulation, C.S.300.4/M, 15 August 1945, HS 1/328.* London: The National Archives. 1.

76 Gough, 2003. 141.

77 Ibid. 159.

78 Ibid. 159.

79 Ibid. 159.

80 Ibid. 160.

81 Ibid. 159.

82 Ibid. 170.

83 Chin, 2003. 127.

84 Callow, Robert. Email correspondence with the author, 13 December 2008, 9 March 2009.

85 Chin, 2003. 128.

Chapter 4

The Early Surrenders

In the week after the 15 August announcement of Japan's surrender, an uneasy silence prevailed as signals traffic among Japanese forces in Malaya came to a standstill.

Signal officers at SEAC, keen to implement TIDERACE, desperately needed to contact General Seishiro Itagaki, Commander of the 7th Area Army in Singapore, but all signals sent had been ignored by the Japanese forces.

Mountbatten had been so concerned that Singapore would not surrender that he sent out an urgent directive to all his commanders that should the circumstances warrant it, an urgent naval force should be launched at a moment's notice, ahead even of TIDERACE to recapture Singapore and Penang. Although there would be no assault troops as part of this new operation, tentatively codenamed TROPIC, Mountbatten called on the Allied Air commander-in-chief to provide sufficient air cover and transport to help achieve the objectives of the operation[1]. Although this plan was clearly impractical and was never carried out, the fact that Mountbatten would even have considered such an urgent recapture showed his high level of anxiety regarding the retaking of Singapore.

> At SEAC headquarters in Kandy, Captain Frank O'Shanohun, a recently-arrived SEAC Staff Signals Officer, was sent to Mountbatten at his residence in Peradeniya to tell him that Itagaki was not responding to SEAC signals, and to ask for further orders. They were joined by Colonel (later Brigadier General) John Anstey, the Deputy Head of the SOE India Mission (Force 136). Mountbatten was silent

for some moments then commented generally, "Well I suppose someone should go to Singapore and find out what he proposes to do". Turning to Anstey, he asked, "Who do you suggest we send?" There was a pause for a full minute following which Anstey turned to O'Shanohun and asked, "Are you doing anything at the moment?"[2].

As O'Shanohun recalls, he was to be dropped by Liberator aircraft on the Singapore race course at dawn. A small team of doctors would accompany him with about two tons of medical supplies and food[3].

When I left, we were still signalling the Japanese that Mountbatten was sending a senior British officer, me, to discuss the arrival of the British task force. However, in spite of repeated signals in clear, the Japanese did not reply so I had no idea what to expect once I landed.

It was that grey moment before daybreak when we arrived over Singapore (on 19 August 1945). There were no enemy fighters. No flak. Everything appeared quiet. As we overflew Singapore (I)sland, we saw the occasional fires as the kampongs began to wake up. The city was blacked-out but the racecourse was soon identified. As we passed over we could see it was empty. No apparent enemy reception committee.

After the aircraft circled once, I sat on the slide and waited. Then the green light came on. I felt a hard tap, more a push, on the back by the dispatcher and I was down that slide and into the dawn sky. Looking around me as I hung beneath the parachute's silk canopy, the city appeared asleep and I could see its empty blacked-out streets, which would have been bustling before the war. It was all rather eerie. Three minutes later, I hit the ground hard, some distance from the main stand.

A bit shaken, I stood up and discarded the parachute harness and looked around. I was alone in the middle of the racecourse without a Jap in sight. Then, as I began to walk towards the main stand, I saw movement as a Japanese officer stepped out of the shadows. This was it!

I kept on walking towards him and as I drew closer I saw a white band around his sleeve. A little later, when I heard the drone of the returning Liberator, I ran back and laid out white panels to show it was safe for the others to drop. After negotiating with the Japanese, one of the first places we visited was Sime Road civilian internment camp. I was soon told quite sharply by the crusty civilian doctors that

> I could take my medical team away. After more than three years in a Japanese camp, they knew all the internees' medical problems, I was told. "Just give us the medical supplies," they said, "and we can do the job ourselves"[4].

On 18 August, the day before O'Shanohun's arrival in Singapore, Itagaki had gone to Saigon to meet with Field Marshal Count Hisaichi Terauchi, where he was told in no uncertain terms to obey the surrender instructions of the Allied commanders. Itagaki had initially baulked at Terauchi's order to surrender and an early landing by Allied forces might have precipitated the stubborn Itagaki into ordering his 70,000-strong Singapore garrison and the 26,000 men in Malaya to resist. Worse still, a plan to massacre all the prisoners might have been carried out[5].

On 20 August, Itagaki met O'Shanohun in Singapore and, later that day, Itagaki signalled Mountbatten that he would abide by his emperor's decision and was ready to receive instructions for the Japanese surrender of Singapore. The next morning, close to a week after the Japanese emperor's announcement, newspapers in Singapore were allowed to carry the text of the emperor's speech, confirming what many already knew from listening to All India Radio broadcasts from Delhi on forbidden shortwave radios that had been hidden away. On 22 August, Itagaki held a meeting with his generals and senior staff at the 7th Army headquarters at Raffles College in Bukit Timah. He told his men that they would have to obey the surrender instructions and keep the peace.

That night, more than 300 Japanese officers and men committed suicide. Others deserted and travelled to Sumatra to join the anti-Dutch freedom movement or went over to the MCP in Johor with their weapons to continue the fight against the British[6].

On 19 August, a team of Japanese envoys had left Tokyo to discuss the surrender arrangements. Led by Lieutenant General Kalabi Takashiba, vice chief of the imperial Japanese army staff, they went to General Douglas MacArthur's headquarters in Manila. As the Tokyo team set off to see MacArthur, a personal representative from the emperor left to instruct General Hyotaro Kimura, commander of the Japanese Burma Army to surrender the Japanese forces there[7].

Plans were soon being made too, covering the surrender of Japanese forces in Java, New Guinea, the Solomons and those opposing General Chiang Kai Shek's (in *pinyin*, Jiang Jieshi) forces in western Hunan province. MacArthur agreed with British requests that the Japanese in Hong Kong surrender to the British Royal Navy's Rear Admiral Cecil Harcourt. On 20 August, Lieutenant General Sir Montague George North Stopford,

General Officer Commanding (GOC), 12th Army, ordered Kimura to make surrender arrangements.

Following Mountbatten's signal to Terauchi on 20 August, a Japanese delegation from Terauchi's headquarters in Saigon, led by his chief of staff (CoS), Lieutenant General Tokazo Numata, arrived at Ingahado Airfield outside Rangoon on 26 August, for talks before the signing of a preliminary surrender agreement. Terauchi was unable to attend any of the surrender negotiations, having recently suffered a stroke that had left him partially paralysed. Mountbatten's earlier date of 23 August for the Burma conference was thus pushed to 26 August in order to allow enough time for Terauchi's staff to make the logistical arrangements to attend the conference.

Six Spitfire fighters and a light spotter plane escorted the two silver-painted Japanese Topsy aircraft as they landed. The Japanese planes bore the specially agreed-upon green cross code markings on the underside of their wings.

Numata, short and wearing black-rimmed glasses, had served as the CoS of the Japanese 2nd Area Army in the Celebes before being appointed as CoS of the Japanese Southern Army in 1944[8]. Accompanying him was deputy chief of staff (DCoS) Admiral Kaigyo Chudo, who had commanded the 8th Section of the Japanese Navy General Staff and had been involved in the aborted plans to invade Australia[9]. Dressed in drab khaki uniforms, the two were accompanied by staff officer Lieutenant Colonel Moro Tomuria. The collars of their open white shirts were worn outside their tunics, their high field boots were immaculately polished, and all carried swords. They did not salute.

While the 22-strong Japanese team was being taken to a nearby tent to be searched for poison and weapons, a security team of British sergeants searched the aircraft. The delegation was then marched across to where Major General George William Symes, GOC, Southern Burma, was waiting to receive them. After a brief introduction, the Japanese were then driven to their accommodation by military policemen in three station wagons with the blinds drawn down. They were followed by an army three-tonner carrying their kit and rations of corned beef, rice, cucumber and raisins, which they had brought with them. The Japanese accommodation was enclosed by barbed wire and floodlit at night.

As the talks began in the Throne Room of Government House, it soon became clear that the Japanese team had come to negotiate and comment on Mountbatten's terms of surrender, rather than to sign it.

Lieutenant General Sir Frederick Arthur Montague Browning, Mountbatten's CoS, led the Allied team. Serving as the GOC of the British 1st

Airborne Division in North Africa from 1941 to 1943, Browning was GOC of the 1st Airborne Corps in Northwest Europe in 1944. Later that same year, he took over as Deputy General Officer Commanding (DGOC) of the 1st Airborne Army over Northwest Europe. Once the European sector was freed, he was attached to SEAC command for the closing chapter in the Pacific[10].

Irritated by the delays, Browning acted quickly and firmly. He allowed no discussion whatsoever of the actual terms laid down and allowed only questions of clarification and amplification. It took three long, drawn-out meetings with the Japanese delegates before a final draft was agreed upon. The preliminary agreement, originally to have been signed at 6.00pm on 27 August, was eventually signed at 1.00am on 28 August. Instructions were then sent to all Japanese senior field commanders through Terauchi to forthwith obey and assist the British commanders of the reoccupying forces.

The Throne Room of Government House, with the Union Jack, the Stars and Stripes, and the nationalist Chinese, Dutch and French flags draped from its balconies, and specially fitted with 12,000-candlepower floodlights, "looked like a Hollywood film set!"[11].

For the signing ceremony, a small table and three hard-backed chairs were set out for the Japanese, facing a long table for the Allied generals. Both sides had inkwells, pens and pencils but, significantly, only the Allies had erasers.

The three Japanese, Numata, Chudo and Tomuria, marched with dignity to the table, took off their caps and stood stiffly at attention while the press photographed them. The Allied delegates then entered the room from under a huge Union Jack.

Browning, dressed in a jungle-green bush shirt, came in last and sat down at the centre of the long table. After he had explained the terms of the agreement, Browning's deputy director of intelligence, Brigadier General John Gerald Nicholson, took the papers over to the Japanese. Numata took off his glasses before looking through the documents and then quickly dipped a pen into the inkwell and signed. Beside him, Chudo and Tomuria sat at attention, looking straight ahead with faces devoid of expression. The papers were returned to Browning who signed them, and then passed back to Numata for the affixing of Terauchi's seal. In less than 20 minutes, the ceremony was over.

The Burma conference was in effect the Japanese surrender of Southeast Asia. The terms listed in the appendices of the agreement set out how the Japanese would surrender but Mountbatten was at pains to make sure it was not portrayed as such because MacArthur was to have the honour of the 'first surrender' at Tokyo Bay while Mountbatten was to have his own moment of glory with the official surrender in Singapore on 12 September.

However, in a top-secret memo to his chiefs, Mountbatten admitted the significance of the Rangoon Agreement:

> The Japanese representatives signed at RANGOON a document which was in effect but not in name an instrument of surrender covering S.E.A.C. area, although, in order to comply with instructions I received from the Supreme Commander for the Allied Powers (MacArthur) not to sign any surrender papers before the TOKYO event, the document has been called a local 'agreement'[12].

Typhoons raging over Japan forced a delay in MacArthur's arrival to take the overall Japanese surrender. However, on 26 August, a massive American fleet sailed into Sagami Bay, just outside Tokyo Bay. After hurried preparations by engineers and communications specialists, MacArthur finally landed at Atsugi airfield on 30 August, together with leading elements of the American 11th Airborne Division.

The formal instrument of surrender of the Emperor of Japan, his government and his people was signed on a mess table on board the American battleship USS *Missouri* at 10.30am on Sunday, 2 September 1945. MacArthur was flanked by Lieutenant General Jonathan Mayhew Wainwright, who had surrendered the American forces to the Japanese at Corregidor, as well as by Lieutenant General Arthur Ernest Percival, former GOC, Malaya Command, who had surrendered the British and Commonwealth forces in Malaya to the Japanese in 1942.

With the official Japanese surrender over, it was now imperative for SEAC to not only take the surrenders in Malaya and Singapore but to reoccupy the territories urgently. Permission to execute Operation TIDERACE was given. The question now was how soon the British would be able to recapture Malaya and whether these non-assault-loaded forces would face fierce resistance from the Japanese army there.

Endnotes

1 *Operational Directive No. 37, OD/201/37, 15 August 1945, WO203/2308.* London: The National Archives.

2 Gough, Richard. *The Jungle was Red*. Singapore: SNP Panpac. 148.

3 Ibid. 150.

4 Ibid. 151.

5 Corr, Gerard. "The War was Over – but Where were the Liberators?". *The Straits Times Annual 1976*. Singapore: Times Publishing Bhd.49–52, 156.

6 Ibid. 51.

7 Fursdon, Major General Edward. "Without Saluting the Japanese Came to Bargain but Soon the Sun Set on Their Empire". *The Daily Telegraph*, 12 August 1985. 11.

8 Ammentorp, Steen. "Biography of Takazo Numata". *The Generals of WWII.* [Internet]. Accessed 28 January, 2005. Available from: <http://www.generals.dk/general/Numata/Takazo/Japan.html>.

9 Dunn, Peter. "Was there a Japanese Invasion Planned to Occur between Townsville and Brisbane in Queensland during WW2?". *Australia @ War.* [Internet]. Accessed 28 January 2005. Available from: <http://home.st.net.au/~dunn/japsland/invade02.htm>.

10 Ammentorp, Steen. "Biography of Sir Frederick Arthur Montague Browning". *The Generals of WWII.* [Internet]. Accessed 28 January 2005. Available from: <http://www.generals.dk/general/Browning/Sir_Frederick_Arthur_Montague/Great_Britain.html>.

11 Fursdon, 1985. 11.

12 *Mountbatten to Commanders in Chief, SAC(45) 14411, 29 August 1945, WO203/4917.* London: The National Archives.

Chapter 5

Operation TIDERACE

As he made last-minute preparations to implement TIDERACE, Rear (later Vice) Admiral Cedric Holland was keen to ensure that the recapture of Singapore was carried out quickly and efficiently.

A naval man through and through, Holland's father had also been an admiral in the Royal Navy with a long illustrious line of naval officers preceding him. With a sharp, hooked nose and a quick wit, Holland, known as 'Hookey' to his friends, had served his country in the First World War and was the British naval attaché for Western Europe, based in Paris, from 1938 to 1940. At the outbreak of the Second World War, he was put in command of the HMS *Ark Royal*. In June 1940, he joined HMS *Hood* and HMS *Foxhound* as part of Force 'H' in Gibraltar, where he acquitted himself admirably in the negotiations and operations against the French fleet at Oran. Promoted to the rank of Rear Admiral in 1942, he was Director of Signals at the Admiralty until 1943, when he was transferred to the East Indies fleet. On 1 June 1945, Holland was again promoted, this time to the rank of Vice Admiral.

> A year away from retirement at the age of 56, Holland was handpicked in early August 1945 by Admiral Arthur Power, the Commander-in-Chief of the British East Indies Fleet, to lead TIDERACE as the Naval Force Commander to recapture Singapore and act as the SEAC Naval Representative in accepting the initial Japanese surrender of Singapore aboard a warship in the city's harbour.

However, the Japanese had yet to agree to this initial surrender ceremony. The agreement signed in Rangoon only listed the official ceremony on

12 September and no mention was made of this separate agreement. As a result, the Japanese were caught unawares when on 30 August, Holland signalled the Japanese with instructions for meeting his delegation:

> The commanders of the Japanese Naval and Army forces at Singapore are to meet representatives of the Supreme Allied Commander Southeast Asia on board HMS *SUSSEX* at 0200 G.M.T. on 4 September, in position latitude 01 degs. 10', longitude 103 degs. 30'...
>
> ... The craft carrying the Japanese commanders will fly a large white flag. It is to have no ammunition or explosives on board and the breach blocks of its guns are to be removed before it reaches the rendezvous. No other shipping is to be within 10 miles of the rendezvous[1]...

In addition, the signal instructed the Japanese commanders to bring lists showing the position of all shipping, charts showing all minefields, berths occupied by ships and all obstacles to navigation. Maps were also requested showing the locations of all gun positions, fortifications and troops on the island as well as the positions of prisoner of war (POW) camps, dumps, stores, and radar and wireless equipment.

The HMS *Sussex* sailed from Trincomalee on 31 August 1945 at 11.30am at 16 knots. Major General Ralph Hone, head of the Civilian Administration Service Malaya (CAS (M)), had come aboard the ship the night before. On receipt of a signal from Vice Admiral (later Sir) Harold Thomas Coulthard Walker, Second-in-Command of the British East Indies Fleet (EIF), who was leading operation JURIST, Holland increased the speed of the fleet to 25 knots and headed for Penang[2].

However, just as this first force was leaving Trincomalee, the first British airmen had already 'retaken' Singapore.

Flight Lieutenant F.L. Andrews and Warrant Officer N.S. Painter from 684 Squadron, based in the Cocos Islands, were carrying out a photo-reconnaissance mission over Johor when suddenly the sustained roaring note of the engines changed in tone. Anxiously, Andrews scanned his instrument panel for an indication of what was wrong and diagnosed a fault in the constant speed unit.

Although the crew were not in immediate danger, they were faced with a difficult decision. Should they try to fly back across the Indian Ocean with the possibility of being forced to ditch, or risk a landing in Singapore? Although the war had ended, it was still unclear whether the Japanese in Singapore and Malaya would surrender peacefully. After some debate, they agreed to risk a landing.

Selecting the pre-war civilian aerodrome at Kallang, Andrews nosed the Mosquito plane down and then circled the area cautiously, trying to spot any danger before going into a final approach. There did not appear to be any craters in the landing strip and the Japanese, who had been watching the plane's circuits, made no aggressive gestures.

Armed soldiers ran out to meet the taxiing aircraft and Andrews and Painter followed the directions of the flag-waving marshals quite apprehensively, placing the Mosquito in a camouflaged dispersal bay. A few tense moments followed as the Japanese soldiers and airmen tried to make each other understood. However, the situation improved when an interpreter appeared, followed by a cheering crowd of prisoners of war (POWs) who had been working at the airfield. Arrangements were made for two of the POWs, who happened to be a British Royal Air Force (RAF) engineering officer and a fitter, to service the Mosquito. Although it was a type they had never seen before, the two managed to repair the constant speed unit. The two airmen spent a night as guests of their enemies, answering questions from the POWs who wanted news of the war. Although Allied doctors had been air-dropped into the Changi area on 30 August, the two airmen were the first British soldiers to land in Singapore. A terse signal was sent to SEAC informing them of the situation:

> From F/Lt. F.L. ANDREWS and W.O. PAINTER N.S. who made a forced landing at the COLON (Kallang) airfield SINGAPORE at noon today. Message reads: "Landed Colon airfield today due engine trouble"[3].

The next day, the Mosquito flew out of Singapore, ending the unofficial reoccupation of Singapore on 1 September 45.

The HMS *Sussex* along with part of the TIDERACE convoy arrived at Penang at 4.30pm on 2 September.

Late in the evening, Holland met with Vice Admiral Walker, who informed him of the Japanese surrender of Penang and handed over the Japanese minefield charts and other information brought up by Japanese officers from Singapore.

British naval forces had already been around Penang island for days. On 27 August, Vice Admiral Walker, aboard HMS *Nelson*, had led a British Task Group, which included HMS *Ceylon*, the escort carriers HMS *Hunter* and HMS *Attacker*, three destroyers and two Landing Ships Infantry (LSIs), out of port in Rangoon and set a heading for Penang, arriving there the next day.

During the 26 August discussions in Rangoon, Lieutenant General

Numata, Field Marshal Count Hisaichi Terauchi's chief of staff (CoS), had already cabled the 10th Area Fleet of the Japanese Southern Army in preparation for Walker's arrival:

> British naval units arriving off Penang, Sabang and possibly off West coast of Malaya, North and East coast of Sumatra forenoon 28 August. Aircraft and suicide craft ordered not to attack. Japanese guarantees security within harbour and coastal waters. British minesweepers commencing operations off Penang, Sabang, Malacca Straits and subsequently Singapore probably 28 August. Cooperate in supplying fresh water and vegetables to British fleet[4].

On the afternoon of 28 August, Walker met with junior Japanese naval and military representatives from Penang and made them sign an undertaking that no attack would be made on the British fleet off Penang[5]. This document was in effect another Japanese surrender, five days before the ceremony at Tokyo Bay.

After three more meetings, where the British forces ferreted out details on Japanese dispositions and locations in Malaya, Walker was poised to accept the Japanese surrender of Penang on the morning of 2 September 1945. However, when the Japanese representatives boarded the *Nelson*, their senior representatives were nowhere to be found. This was because the naval commander of Penang, Rear Admiral Jisaku Uozumi, had not yet received permission from Terauchi to sign the documents. Upon Walker's insistence, Uozumi eventually turned up for the meeting along with the Japanese Deputy Governor of Penang, Shigeru Mochinaga.

Uozumi was no stranger to the British Admiralty but Walker was surprised to see him wearing the British Distinguished Service Cross and Allied Victory Medal for his part as an ally in the First World War[6]. Serving as the captain of the Japanese cruiser *Haguro* in 1942, Uozumi had seen action at the Battle of the Java Sea where the remnants of the British and Dutch naval forces after the fall of Singapore and the Dutch East Indies faced superior Japanese naval forces in a last stand. The encounter ended with the almost total destruction of the Allied fleet. Uozumi had also served as a senior officer on the Japanese naval staff before being appointed naval commander of Penang island in August 1944. Ironically, the ship that he had commanded in victory barely two years before was sunk by the British East Indies fleet on 16 May 1945, just 45 miles southwest of Penang. Stepping on board the *Nelson*, Uozumi had clearly accepted the fate of the Japanese forces in Malaya. He apologised profusely but said he still had not received permission to sign the terms[7].

Walker, visibly upset, made the two Japanese representatives sign an undertaking that they would comply with the instructions of the British commanders following which Uozumi and Mochinaga departed on their naval vessel. A few minutes later, the Japanese vessel returned to the *Nelson*. On their way back to Penang, Terauchi had finally signalled Uozumi with his permission to sign. Thus, at 9.15pm on 2 September 1945, Uozumi and Mochinaga signed the surrender of Penang[8].

At 8.00am the following day, 480 British Royal Marines, known as Force Roma, landed on Penang island[9]. As the marines moved through the island to take over Bayan Lepas airfield and other installations from the Japanese, food riots broke out. The riots were eventually quelled but it was a clear sign of things to come[10].

Only at this point of the reoccupation did Terauchi cable Mountbatten with the message that he was agreeable to the Singapore shipboard discussions but not necessarily the signing of a surrender agreement:

> I presume the proposed conference to be held on board a warship on 4 September at Singapore is aimed to discuss the moving of a part of your forces as arranged in the preliminary agreement concluded at RANGOON. If this is the case I am ready to send my staff to attend the conference[11].

At 6.30am on 3 September, the *Sussex* sailed from Penang and contacted the TIDERACE convoy coming from Rangoon about two hours later. Up until then, everything was going according to plan. Then, the confusion began.

As part of SEAC's planning, the 15th Indian Corp was set to take over the land advance into Singapore. Lieutenant General Sir Alexander Christison, who had served in the First World War and had taken over temporarily as General Officer Commanding (GOC) of the British 14th Army in Burma, was appointed GOC, 15th Indian Corps.

As such, the 5th Indian Division, which was to take the surrender of the Japanese in Singapore, would now come under the 15th Indian Corps. The 5th Indian Division was led by Major General Eric Mansergh, who had served for many years in India and was fluent in Urdu. He had led the 5th Division in Burma as part of Operation MODIFIED DRACULA and now his division had been tasked with the Singapore surrender.

Christison, who had been at the surrender negotiations in Rangoon while the 15th Indian Corps was being reorganised, believed that as GOC, he would be the SEAC army representative and would now take the formal surrender of the Japanese, while his subordinate Mansergh would command the military reoccupation of Singapore. This meant that Holland would be both the SEAC naval representative and the naval force commander, and Christison would be the SEAC army representative and the military force commander while Mansergh would now be acting under his command instead of as the SEAC army representative.

Accordingly, before leaving Rangoon with the convoy on 28 August, Christison cabled Holland:

> I have assumed function of military force comd for operation TIDERACE vice comd 5 Ind Div now under my comd. Sailing with my Tac HQ in RMT DILWARA with first convoy. Propose come aboard HMS *SUSSEX* on arrival at KEPPEL Harbour unless you particularly require me aboard earlier.
>
> Procedure agreed here (Rangoon) yesterday as follows. On our arrival KEPPEL Harbour special Japanese liaison officer from Field Marshal COUNT TERAUCHI to Gen ITAGAKI will be summoned aboard *SUSSEX* where he will give us the situation and we as joint force commanders will give him our orders for ITAGAKI. As soon as we are satisfied we will put 5 Div ashore. NO landing to be permitted until leading tps 5 Div are established ashore. Please signal me to Naval HQ RANGOON your agreement above plan[12].

However, this message did not reach Holland before he departed Trincomalee and so he was unaware of the change in representatives when Holland's ship met the Rangoon convoy on 3 September. Thus, Holland was upset when he saw Christison board his ship:

> Here the General Officers Commanding of the 15th Corps and 5th Indian Division were transferred from SS DERBYSHIRE and DILWARA to HMS *SUSSEX*. It was not clear why the General Officer Commanding of the 15th Corps required a passage in HMS *SUSSEX*, since there had been no official signal from SACSEA nominating him as the Supreme Allied Commander's Army representative in place of the General Officer Commanding the 5th Indian Division[13].

Holland was unhappy that Christison had joined the party as an uninvited guest, one who would now outrank him at the negotiations with the Japanese. In his report, Holland questioned the need for having such high-level representation at the Corps level and the added complexity it entailed:

> The introduction of a corps headquarters at a later stage in the planning was a considerable complication, and served no useful purpose. 'TIDERACE' was a Divisional operation, and it was on

> that level that negotiations, entry and the development of the Island should have been executed[14].

More urgently, Holland had already signalled instructions to the Japanese before his departure from Trincomalee and Christison's contradictory instructions to the Japanese representatives in Rangoon over the Singapore surrender arrangements at the last minute had caused confusion on the Japanese side as the signal from Holland's Staff Officer to SACSEA HQ indicated:

> May have difficulty over PARLEYS on 4 September as BS3 (Vice Admiral Walker on board HMS *Nelson* in Penang) has been given a letter signed by the Japanese Army and Naval Commander at Singapore stating "They are not allowed to negotiate directly with the CINC British East Indies representative before the formal agreement is made between the SACSEA and the Supreme Commander of the Japanese Forces in the Southern Region". I have asked BS3 to inform Singapore that Conference on board HMS *SUSSEX* is being held by representatives of SACSEA and is for the purpose of arranging details based on the general agreement signed at Rangoon[15].

Furious, Holland held meetings with Mansergh to sort out the now-complicated situation and review the detailed plan for the entry of the reoccupying force into Singapore.

Christison, however, was concerned with what he felt were more pressing matters. Field Marshal William Joseph Slim, commander-in-chief of the Allied Land Forces, Southeast Asia had signalled him on the evening of 3 September with an intercepted Japanese message from the Japanese naval fleet in Singapore to Tokyo. The intercepted message read:

> The impression received by our representative who made the negotiations with the British navy in PENANG (from 28 August to 2 September) was that the British are extremely worried about our unrestricted movements and specially fear our special attack boats on the occasion of their occupation of Singapore. Since the primary objective of the agreement reached by the supreme army and navy commanders at Singapore and the British navy is to guarantee the safety of the above it would seem best to comply with this agreement. I believe that unreasonable demands such as that of today to the effect that all Japanese forces on Singapore (I)sland evacuate the island by 5 September are a reaction to the permission to wear swords granted by the above commanders[16].

Slim wanted to know if Christison had asked for swords to be handed in and the present status of negotiations. Holland's signal to the Japanese on 30 August called for the evacuation of Japanese troops by 5 September and Vice Admiral Walker had asked for Japanese swords to be handed in during the negotiations at Penang earlier in the week. Christison had not been involved in any of these instructions and was unaware that such instructions had been issued. He was now upset that he had to respond to Slim's query on the present status, which was not of his doing. It was obvious that Christison and Holland were at odds and each was unhappy with the unilateral actions of the other.

However, the most crucial part of the signal was the Japanese reference to the British fear of special attack boats. Although the signal indicated that the Japanese navy would not use them against the British fleet in Singapore, this did not mean that the TIDERACE fleet would not receive a rude shock from rogue naval elements when they moved into the outer Singapore roads the next day.

At about 9.00am on 4 September, Holland, Mansergh and Christison, all aboard the *Sussex*, arrived at the rendezvous point just outside Keppel Harbour and were met by Admiral Arthur Power, commander-in-chief of the British East Indies Fleet, who had arrived on the scene aboard the HMS *Cleopatra*. This was a fortuitous turn of events for Holland as it meant he would have support from his superior in determining who would hold the negotiations with the Japanese. In the end, however, Power convinced Holland to go along with Christison and hold the negotiations. In his own report, Power did not mention the disagreement but was at pains to portray the meeting among the commanders as cordial and that, "TIDERACE appeared to be running smoothly"[17]. Power left the *Sussex* just as the Japanese delegates were being escorted from their vessel.

The next few hours would determine whether the British takeover would be smooth or whether resistance would break out. Just after 8.00am, liaison officers on the *Sussex* reported that General Seishiro Itagaki and Vice Admiral Shigeru Fukudome were waiting to come aboard. This was a good sign. With the two top commanders coming aboard, it was unlikely that an attack was imminent. Nonetheless, all ships remained on alert.

The Japanese ships were kept waiting until about 10.00am when they were signalled over:

> General ITAGAKI and Vice Admiral FUKUDOME were brought on board at 1013 (hours), and were met by Captain A.F. de Salis (Captain of HMS *Sussex*)...and an armed officer escort...

> ... They were taken to a cabin (Major General Ralph Hone's cabin), where they left their swords, and were then brought into the Admiral's Dining Cabin. Here the British representatives were seated to receive the Japanese envoys, who were instructed to sit down facing them. They were given the terms to read...[18]

The terms of surrender were comprehensive[19] (see Appendix F: Part I). The Japanese forces on Singapore island and in Malaya were to be treated as "surrendered personnel" rather than as prisoners of war. In an order to his commanders, Mountbatten had made it explicit that it would be at his discretion whether Japanese forces would be made POWs or Surrendered Enemy Personnel. The reasons, he noted, were two-fold:

> a) It avoids any claim by the Japanese to the standard of treatment and privileges which should be accorded to P.W. (prisoners of war) under the Geneva Convention.
>
> b) It saves us from the embarrassment of having to deal with a large number of P.W. immediately capitulation (*sic*) takes place, and with which we have neither the forces nor the material resources to deal[20].

The Allied commanders also ordered that 100 large staff cars in "high-class condition" be made available for the use of the occupying forces. A further 500 lorries, with drivers, were to assemble in the dock area, and another 100 at the Kallang airfield on the day of occupation.

A curfew from sunset to sunrise was also imposed until further notice. Orders were also issued for all stocks of spirits and liquor shops to be sealed and guarded, and reports were also required of all epidemics or infectious diseases, the location of hospitals and laboratories, together with that of all Allied sick and wounded men. The Singapore Military Hospital (at Alexandra) would be emptied of all Japanese patients except those who were too ill to be moved. It would then be cleaned and made ready for use by the Allied medical services. In addition, interpreters and guides were to be available to help the landing forces[21] (see Appendix F: Part II).

Major General E.C. Mansergh, Commander of the 5th Indian Division, later to become Commander-in-Chief of British Land Forces.

A Japanese general was selected to report twice daily to Mansergh for orders and this would be the only official line of communication. The 28 Japanese generals who remained in Singapore were left housed in Raffles College on Upper Bukit Timah Road[22].

The two Japanese representatives took six hours to consider and negotiate the terms with the Allied representatives. They raised many points but in the end agreed to most of the instructions. At 6.05pm, Itagaki and Fukudome signed the Singapore Surrender document.

Holland noted that the agreement would not have been signed had it not been for the tough position taken by the Allied generals:

> In dealing with the Japanese, firmness pays. He will endeavour to spin out negotiations as long as possible, in order to save face, and will take advantage of any loophole to twist out of his obligations. A little determination will quickly get the Japanese down, but he has great resilience and will bounce up again if not held in his place. Many Japanese Naval Officers (like Fukudome) understand and speak English well, but they will not at first admit it[23].

Sixty years on, the original Surrender of Singapore and Surrender of Penang documents cannot be located at the National Archives in London, nor in files of the former Colonial, War or Foreign Offices. Although copies of the various texts have been found, the original with Itagaki and Fukudome's signatures and stamps are no longer part of the collection of files in which they should be located. The documents are believed to have been forwarded to SEAC Headquarters and then to the War and Colonial Offices but there the trail ends. No trace remains of who were the last officials in Whitehall to see these original surrender documents. The documents could have been removed so that they would not detract from the historical impact of the formal Japanese surrender on 12 September, or simply 'misplaced' in the last days of the war. However, the creation of these documents and the events they cover can no longer be hidden. Sixty years after the war, the secret surrenders have now come to light but the original documents that represent it have been lost in time. It will remain one of the last mysteries of the end of the war.

Although the surrender on board the *Sussex* was covered by the international press, most of Singapore was unaware of the momentous events happening in the seas off Singapore. As international publications and radio transmissions were prohibited within the country, much of the population of Singapore remained blissfully ignorant of the British return until their ships docked at Keppel Harbour. As the liberated newspapers would only begin publishing four days later (with most of the local journalists liberated only days before from internment camps and clearly not up to speed on what was going on) the first edition of *The Straits Times* made no mention of the Japanese surrender of Singapore aboard the *Sussex*. Even British newspapers with correspondents on board the *Sussex* did not report the event beyond a brief mention of British troops reoccupying the region[24]. The only item in *The Times* was a one-paragraph report on Power meeting Holland off Singapore. As a result, most of the people in Malaya and Singapore who lived through the war remember the 12 September ceremony as the official Japanese surrender of Singapore.

Although the 12 September ceremony is considered the only Japanese surrender of Singapore and Southeast Asia, this becomes problematic as Mountbatten, by his own account, admitted that the Rangoon Conference on 28 August was the effective surrender of Japanese forces in Southeast Asia, not in name but in action. Thus, all agreements following this would be local surrenders. Count Terauchi in Saigon and his field commanders throughout the region were well aware of the Rangoon agreement and the Japanese responsibility to adhere to the terms of the agreement. This is what followed in Penang on 2 September, when the garrison surrendered to the British followed by the Surrender Agreement signed aboard the *Sussex* on 4 September. With the signing of the document and the reoccupation of Singapore by the 5th Indian Division on 5 September, the communal violence in Singapore and Malaya, which had caused the deaths of so many, came effectively to an end[25]. Less than a day after the 4 September surrender, 35,000 Japanese troops were also evacuated from Singapore to prison camps in Johor[26]. With the ZIPPER landings begun on 9 September and the major cities and towns in Malaya under effective – but not 'official' – British military control by 11 September, the ceremony on 12 September was nothing more than just an additional floorshow.

Mountbatten had already shown with the reoccupation of Singapore on 5 September and the Malayan mainland on 9 September that the Allied forces had retaken Malaya with a superior force. It was clear to all Japanese military commanders that they would have to surrender and accept British military rule. Moreover, General Itagaki had signed the Singapore Surrender Agreement on 4 September on instructions from Count Terauchi. He then reprised that same role on 12 September. As a result, Mountbatten was only taking a purely ceremonial surrender of the Japanese forces in Southeast Asia on 12 September. The effective surrenders of Japanese forces had occurred in Rangoon on 28 August, when Terauchi's representative signed the terms of the Japanese Southern Army's instructions for surrender, and in Singapore on 4 September, when

Terauchi's military commanders signed the surrender of Singapore, ending communal violence in most of Malaya and with the detention of 35,000 Japanese troops within a day of the surrender.

By the evening of 4 September, most of the TIDERACE convoy had arrived in the waters off Singapore with a patrol of military launches established around the *Sussex* and its convoy from dusk until dawn.

It was a night filled with great tension and expectation as the huge naval fleet stood on the eve of liberating Singapore after three years of Japanese military occupation. Troops were placed on the highest degree of alert in case of any last ditch attempts by the Japanese to resist.

Just before dawn on 5 September 1945, the *Sussex* headed to the convoy waiting position in the Singapore Straits as the HMS *Attacker* carried out an air tactical reconnaissance at the request of the 5th Division. The Japanese minesweepers had been ordered to complete sweeping the channel to Singapore by 10.00am but as the Japanese vessels "proved slow and useless, they were told to keep clear"[27].

As the first British ships approached Raffles Lighthouse, six landing craft were lowered from the RFA *Dewdale* and troops boarded from HMS *Devonshire*. Embarkation was slow as the Indian troops had had only little practice in land mock-ups. Eventually, the group was ready and passed the *Sussex* at about 8.45am.

Mansergh, who was on the deck of the *Sussex*, addressed the troops through a loudhailer in fluent Urdu, wishing them good luck in the landings. The initial assault group was led by HMIS *Godavari* and HMS *Rotherham*, with four military launches on each wing and the *Sussex* in the rear giving gun support and acting as the headquarters ship of the assault commanders.

The 5th Division's diary recorded the landings in detail[28]:

> Full war precautions were taken. At seven o'clock on the 5 September, the landing craft, many of which had taken part in combined operations in North Africa and Europe, came alongside, and boatload-by-boatload the troops scrambled down the nets into them. By 8.30am the craft were ready in battle formation. On board, everyone felt a thrill of expectancy. How would the Japanese take the surrender? Would there be treachery?
>
> The first flight, which steamed in from a distance of some 25 miles, was composed of, on the left, the 3/9th Gurkha Rifles, and on the right, the 2/1st Punjab. (The) 123(rd) Brigade Headquarters travelled with the latter. And the 1/17th Dogras moved off to secure possession of certain islands – Pulau Brani, (Pulau) Blakang (*sic*) Mati,

On landing at Keppel Harbour, Brigadier Denholm-Young, 5th Indian Division, being met by a Japanese interpreter on General Itagaki's staff.

The first troops of the 5th Indian Division ashore were 'D' company of the 2/1st Punjab, under Major Niaz Mohammed Arbad.

Units of the 5th Indian Division landing at Keppel Harbour.

and Pulau Hantu, two miles south of Singapore harbour. These were occupied without incident at 10.30am. The rest of the convoy passed a series of these small islands, striking by their greenness, many of them only two hundred yards or so in length, with sandy beaches and palm trees, and a few white houses.

Then, Singapore itself appeared, no longer hidden from view by these islands that cover(ed) the approaches. Suddenly, the scene opened up, and the water line became visible in its wide semicircle, a mass of buildings along the front showing clearly against a dull and thundery sky. Soon after 11.00am (*sic*) the landing craft, in single file and with pennants gaily fluttering, passed *H.M.S. Sussex*, lying with her guns trained upon the city, and entered the harbour to berth, alongside the main wharfs.

In the dock area there were only a few civilians. But a small number of dockers and coolies gave a cheer and a wave of greeting, and several Chinese shouted from the roof of the customs sheds.

The first troops of the Division ashore were 'D' Company of the 2/1st Punjab, under Major Niaz Mohammed Arbad. The battalion was met by two senior Japanese officers who wore ceremonial swords and highly polished jackboots. All were standing rigidly to attention, at the salute. Behind them again was parked a line of glittering civilian cars, each with a booted chauffeur. On the main wharf, Brigadier

> Eric John Denholm-Young, Commanding Officer of the 123rd Indian Brigade, was met by one Major General Shimura who was staff officer to General Itagaki. And soon after midday, Denholm-Young held a conference with a number of senior Japanese officers, who showed themselves most helpful. All went as had been planned during the voyage, and no opposition was met.
>
> The battalions moved out fanwise from the docks and according to pre-arranged instructions occupied such key positions as arsenals, installations, airfields, the railway station, and camps. The Japanese officers, assisted by interpreters and by maps, showed our officers the dispositions of all enemy guards in Singapore itself.
>
> Meanwhile, 161(st) Brigade had landed at the West Wharf, near the Power Station, and were (*sic*) greeted by a lone Chinese boy, full of smiles. Led by the 4/7th Rajputs, they moved straight through northwards across Singapore Island to the naval base and causeway at Johor Bahru[29].

By dark, all personnel ships had been anchored in the Singapore roads and unloaded by a ferry service of military launches. *Sussex* and the nine other main ships of the force were berthed at Keppel, including *LCI 104*, the press ship, which brought the first Allied media into liberated Singapore.

That night, looting began to occur on the jetty and the captain of the *Sussex* responded by landing about 80 men to guard important stores that had been offloaded in the dock area. In the meantime, HMS *Rotherham* had begun disarming all Japanese military vessels in the harbour and its vicinity.

To boost morale, SEAC broadcast a special message from King George VI to the people of Singapore on all radio frequencies:

> Now that final victory over the forces of aggression has been achieved, I send to my peoples, and to the peoples under my protection in the Far East who have suffered the horrors of Japanese aggression, a message of real sympathy and heartfelt thanksgiving on their delivery.
>
> The thoughts of the Queen and myself have been constantly with you during your years of suffering so bravely borne, and with the dawn of the day of liberation we rejoice with you that the ties which unite my people everywhere will now be fully restored. I know full well that these ties of loyalty and affection between myself and my Far Eastern peoples have never been broken; that they have been maintained

> in darkness and suffering. The time has now come when their strength and permanence will again be displayed in calm before the whole world.
>
> The traces of a cruel and ruthless oppression cannot be wiped out in a day, and the work of restoration will be long and heavy, but it is a work in which we should be united in pride and in confidence, sure in the faith that security and happiness will, with God's help, be fully restored[30].

By midnight, Malayan time had once again been established in Singapore. The island was now an hour behind of Tokyo time, to which watches and clocks in Singapore and Malaya had been set to for the last three-and-a-half years.

On 6 September, day two of the reoccupation, Holland ordered the *Rotherham* and two military launches to retake the naval base in the northern part of the island while Japanese officers came on board the *Sussex* with plans to evacuate all Japanese naval personnel to Johor.

The reoccupation of Singapore was going according to plan. However, the chaotic conditions faced by the returning Allies would take months, if not years, to sort out. Three-and-a-half years of Japanese occupation had taken its toll and stepping ashore on recently occupied enemy territory, the British would now face much more than they had bargained for.

Endnotes

1 *From: F.O. Force 'N', 30 August 1945, WO203/2307.* London: The National Archives.

2 *Letter of Proceedings – Operation TIDERACE, 18 September 1945, ADM116/5562.* London: The National Archives. 2.

3 *Singapore Broadcast 31 1130 IST, GSI (s)/1, 31 August 1945, WO203/2435.* London: The National Archives.

4 *From: Lt. Gen. Numata T.O.O. 271115, 27 August 1945, WO203/2435.* London: The National Archives.

5 *JURIST Signal, 28 August 1945, WO203/4917.* London: The National Archives.

6 Kirby, Major General S. Woodburn. *The War Against Japan: The Surrender of Japan*, vol. 5. London: HMSO, 1969. 266.

7 *Proceedings of Operation JURIST, V.A.E.I.F. NO.737/743D, 13 September 1945, WO203/4675.* London: The National Archives.

8 Ibid.

9 Ibid.

10 Gough, Richard. *The Jungle was Red.* Singapore: SNP Panpac, 2003. 154.

11 *58108SIGS. Unclassified for S.O.inC., 2 September 1945, WO203/2435.* London: The National Archives.

12 *From TAC HQ 15 Ind Div, 28 August 1945, WO203/2308.* London: The National Archives.

13 *Letter of Proceedings – Operation TIDERACE, 18 September 1945, ADM116/5562.* London: The National Archives. 2.

14 *Letter of Proceedings, 18 September 1945, ADM116/5562.* London: The National Archives. p. 1.

15 *From: S.O. Force 'N', 3 September 1945, WO203/493.* London: The National Archives.

16 *1889 Int Secret Chritison from Slim, 3 September 1945.* London: The National Archives.

17 *Report of Proceedings – Commander-in-Chief, East Indies Station's letter, No.3001/ E.I.15002/45, 17 September 1945, ADM199/168.* London: The National Archives. 5.

18 *Letter of Proceedings – Operation TIDERACE, 18 September 1945, ADM116/5562.* London: The National Archives. 3.

19 *Instructions to the Japanese Forces under Command or Control of Japanese Commanders Singapore Area, 4 September 1945, ADM116/5562.* London: The National Archives. 1, Appendices A, B, C, D.

20 *C.S.300.4/M, 25 August 1945, WO203/4922.* London: The National Archives.

21 *Order of the Commander Occupying Force to the Japanese Commander of Singapore, 31 August 1945, WO203/2308.* London: The National Archives. 1–2.

22 Ibid.

23 *Letter of Proceedings, 18 September 1945, ADM116/5562.* London: The National Archives. 2.

24 "Surrender Ships from Singapore Met". *The Times*, 5 September 1945.

25 Chin Peng. *My Side of History.* Singapore: Media Masters, 2003. 128.

26 *Letter of Proceedings – Operation TIDERACE, 18 September 1945, ADM116/5562.* London: The National Archives. 3.

27 Ibid.

28 Brett-James, 1951.

29 Ibid.

30 "Message from the King". *The Times,* 6 September 1945.

Chapter 6

Reoccupation

The reoccupation of Singapore meant different things to different people. For liberators like Catherine Baker, her role in the historic reoccupation of Singapore came from out of the blue. A nurse based with the contingent of nurses (QARANC) in Bihar, India, looking after the wounded from Burma[1], Baker suddenly received top-secret orders:

> We were given orders... pack up your belongings and be ready to move to an unknown destination within 24 hours. Take what you can carry and the rest of the luggage will follow later...
>
> ... We were then transported to Calcutta by train and stayed in a transit camp before embarking on a hospital ship (with no patient) where we slept and ate in the wards. At Rangoon, we waited for three days (no shore leave) for orders to go to our final destination.
>
> We then sailed in a convoy of about 10 ships (ours the last one) in a dead-straight line down a narrow channel which had been mine-swept. We wore our life jackets as we watched the naval frigates acting like sheepdogs to ensure that there was no deviation from the narrow lane.
>
> We docked at Singapore, I think on 31 August (*sic*), as darkness fell and saw a desolate, ruined, unlit city. On the quayside were what appeared to be skeletal ragged and barefoot coolies: they were in fact our own prisoners of war.

> We disembarked the following day, to be taken by truck through deserted streets to our hospital 49 B.G.H. (49 British General Hospital, also known as the Singapore General Hospital) in which had been the civilian one. It was insect-ridden, filthy, ill-equipped and overrun by monkeys. There we prepared to receive wounded, diseased and emaciated patients from Changi and other jails.

By the time Japan had surrendered on 15 August, Southeast Asia Command (SEAC) realised it was no longer a matter of recovering prisoners and internees over a period of time as operations progressed, but of getting them evacuated simultaneously from all camps in the region. Estimates in the Official History listed close to 70,000 prisoners of war (POWs) in the Southeast Asia theatre with another 55,000 in Java, spread over 250 known camps[2].

By 12 August, Force 136 had carried out extensive clandestine reconnaissance in Malaya and provided SEAC with an initial breakdown of POWs in the various camps[3]:

> **SINGAPORE:** There are numerous camps scattered all over the island of Singapore and the total number of POWs is estimated as:

UK	2,700
Aust.	6,600
Ind.	5,600
Total	14,900

JOHORE:

MUAR	300 unknown POWs.
KLUANG	500 Ind. POWs.
ENDAU	? Unknown POWs.
JOHORE BAHRU	500 Aust. POWs.
BATU PAHAT	? Unknown POWs.

SELANGOR:

KUALA LUMPUR	2,500 Ind POWs.

NEGRI SEMBILAN:

PORT DICKSON	1,000 Unknown POWs.

> More recent information indicates the possibility of an unknown number of white POWs, believed Aust., in KUALA LUMPUR.
> There is also information, ungraded, that there are 1,000 Gurkha POWs at TANJONG RAMBUTAN, PERAK.

Liberated prisoners of war at Changi: The clothes they are wearing were provided by returning forces so that the first pictures of POWs would not cause morale problems.

As information like this began filtering in to SEAC headquarters, it was unclear how many POWs would have to be evacuated and what state they would be in. Thus the first phase of the rescue and evacuation operation, codenamed BIRDCAGE, was:

> The dropping by air of leaflets giving notice of the surrender of Japan to guards at POW camps, to the local population and to prisoners and internees. Leaflets in Japanese and the local language were to be dropped first on all known camps, main towns and concentrations of Japanese troops, followed about an hour later by leaflets in English giving instructions to prisoners and internees to stay in their camps until contacted so that food and medical supplies could be dropped to them, In the second phase (Operation MASTIFF), which was to follow as soon as possible after the leaflets had been dropped, food and medical supplies were to be dropped and medical and Red Cross relief teams with wireless sets and operators parachuted into known camps as quickly as possible[4].

While this was happening, Force 136 officers and 'E' parties (evacuation) that were operating in Malaya were to also contact the camps[5].

As soon as the initial drops had been completed, the RAF was tasked with keeping these camps resupplied by dropping special food, medical supplies, clothing and Red Cross stores:

> Liberator squadrons with experience of special duty (clandestine) operations were to be used for the long-range tasks since many of the

> camps were likely to be difficult to find. The short-range tasks were to be carried out by Thunderbolt, Dakota and Lysander squadrons as operationally convenient. The squadrons covering Malaya and Sumatra were to work from airfields in Ceylon and the Cocos islands, those covering western Siam from airfields around Rangoon, and those covering eastern Siam and French Indochina from airfields around Jessore (the original base for special-duty squadrons some 60 miles northeast of Calcutta)[6].

Despite the airlift, it was a desperate scene that greeted Baker and the relieving forces of the 5th Indian Division as they reoccupied Singapore on 5 September 1945.

> ... They (POWs) evinced no feelings of joy at being released after three-and-a-half years of starvation and misery. Just a quiet acceptance of the change of events.
>
> One patient, a merchant seaman, with stick-like legs and arms but an enormous pot belly due to beriberi, was given a drip of plasma for his dehydration but unfortunately the body could not take this life-saving fluid and he died. The ward was engulfed in misery. The patients knew he had fought to survive, giving encouragement to others, and now his life was ended when aid was at hand but to no avail...
>
> ... The following Sunday, a few of us were asked to open a ward in the third-class block in readiness to receive patients who were being flown in from Sumatra and were due to arrive in the afternoon. The ward had not been used by the Japs; the beds and mattresses were there, but little else. The filth was indescribable, and the mattresses alive with bugs and creepy crawlies. The kitchen was empty except for a refrigerator with the innards hanging out, and monkeys chattering and furious at being disturbed and ousted.
>
> It was hard work scrounging around for equipment. Chairs, lockers, kitchen utensils, anything we could lay our hands on, cleaning as best we could, and then putting sheets on infested mattresses. We were exhausted (and dirty!) when the men arrived. Half were stretcher cases; all weighed no more than 5 stone (32kg). I shall never forget their expressions when they came in. Wonderment, disbelief as they looked at the clean sheets (hiding the bugs!! And us nurses, sweaty and filthy in our khaki outfits). There was a stillness among them, but it was soon made evident that there was trouble brewing. There was

> a mixture of British POWs and Dutch Indonesian soldiers and there was resentment between them. Luckily, we managed to divide them by putting one lot in the beds on the veranda. We guessed the reason why there was this strong feeling between them but nothing was said.
>
> We had to be very careful with the food we gave them. Small amounts at a time. M and V (meat and vegetables) was the staple food and biscuits (no bread) but it was supplemented by Australian Red Cross parcels of tomotao (*sic*) juice, asparagus tips, and tinned fruit of all kinds with condensed milk and cream. Vitamins were given out three times a day, the 'brown smell' of them I remember so well that it brings back memories whenever I take them.
>
> We had to cope with men, after years of deprivation, cut off from news of family and home, suffering from malnutrition and the effects of cruelty, who now had to adjust to a normal way of living. Some hid their food in their lockers, in case. Some wept uncontrollably at times and some wanted to stand at attention if spoken to. Letters brought misery to some. Parents had died and, in one case, a wife had deserted him. It was a noiseless ward and not really happy as if the patients could not express their thoughts of release. They had obviously thought so much about the end of hostilities that it was almost an anticlimax, and their spirits had been deadened by all their sufferings.
>
> Amongst the patients was one of our staff who sat at the table for his dinner with six other patients. He left a piece of gristle on his plate. Without a word being said, this gristle was divided equally among the six. And woe betide if the food was not always equally divided. Two potatoes on one plate and only one on another could almost cause a riot. Everything, literally everything had to be equal, including time spent talking to a patient. The men did not talk about their experiences but neither did they ask any questions about events of the last three-and-a-half years. It was as if they had fought so long to survive and seeing their friends die from starvation that they just wanted both their bodies and brains to rest before they tackled their thoughts of home... and victory[7].

For the international press accompanying the TIDERACE convoy, covering these momentous events proved a formidable challenge. Douglas James Mackie, Traffic Manager for Cable and Wireless Ltd Singapore in 1941, and a team of eight technical staff were put in charge of helping the press contingent transmit their stories.

SEAC provided the journalists with a press ship, installed with a mobile cable office. Stories and photographs were to be filed and transmitted to Colombo, from where they would be retransmitted to the rest of the world. From the start, noted Mackie, the press faced numerous constraints:

> The vessel chose(n) for the Press ships (*sic*) was an LCI (L) (Landing Craft Infantry, Large), tonnage 300 and, of course, quite unsuited for the purpose. Out of this flat-bottomed reinforced biscuit tin, which was designed to transport troops for a maximum period of 36 hours, the R.N. 'Dockies' at Colombo made a reasonably comfortable floating wireless telegraph branch complete with cabin, mess-wardroom, instrument room, engine room, transmitter room, salt-water showers and the inevitable 'heads'.
>
> ... Space was my biggest headache, as the original passenger list showed 36 bodies. The sleeping-cum-baggage flat was 22-feet-by-26-feet, tapering to practically zero at the sharp end. Kit had, therefore, to be restricted to one kit bag per person.
>
> As planned, the Ceylon Force, the Rangoon Force, and the LCI Force joined at a point off Penang Island. En route down the Malacca Straits, I had a signal sent to the Flagship asking that the Press ship be berthed remote from other vessels for technical reasons. I suggested Telok Ayer Basin.
>
> As anticipated, I received a rocket from the Flagship asking me "not to send unnecessary signals" but I was not unduly disturbed by this reply.
>
> After many hours of movement outside Singapore while the fleet of over 100 vessels manoeuvred into position, we steamed majestically, line ahead with the Flagship leading into the Outer Roads. As we approached, our ship was signalled to leave convoy and proceed to berth three cable lengths off Telok Basin mole – a quick dividend to my signal. The value of this berth was that it is (*sic*) the nearest sea frontage to our C.T.O. (Central Telegraph Office) and about a quarter of a mile from it. We were anchored by 3.00pm, considerably in advance of the main fleet. After arranging for the hoisting of our Cable and Wireless flag, I asked the skipper to lower the dinghy and, with a SEAC Press observer, rowed ashore.
>
> As we steamed in, our transmitter was run up and Colombo was warned to stand by for heavy filing. Duties had been arranged and

> the operators were at their posts in the receiving Room (*sic*) below decks. By 6.30pm, the Navy, using ML's (*sic*) (military launches), had cleared away the jumble of Japanese tugs, fishing vessels, etc., from the mole to permit us to tie alongside.
>
> Then came the flood from the P.R.O. (Press Receiving Office). Placidity was replaced by intensity. Eight bodies stripped to the waist, sweating mightily in an atmosphere comparable to a steam room of a Turkish bath, could not cope. All staff were called on and the mess tables used for counting and preparing traffic.
>
> With one senior on the auto and control, the other three and myself could barely keep abreast of the counting, which in the best of conditions is slow work, with Press badly-typed on any old flimsy and plastered with inked-in amendments...
>
> ... My view, which was shared by the Assistant Director of Public Relations, was that it was better to limit the takes to 250 words per correspondent (there were about 80 of them) per day which would be duly delivered to the agencies and editors in time for going to press, rather than a few long takes to be delivered to some agencies to the indignation of the rest of the editors[8].

At a rate of 2,000 words an hour in the first four days of landings, more than 161,000 words were transmitted and the staff also radioed pictures of the landings to London[9]. Mackie made a trip to the old Cable and Wireless offices at Robinson Road to gather reinforcements but as the Associated Press reported, he faced the enemy head on:

> Mackie made a sortie to his old office and found a Japanese colonel sitting in his old office chair. With typical Scots brevity, he jerked a thumb and said, "Oot!" and the colonel 'ooted' at great speed. Then he called his old Sikh watchman and ordered him muster as many of the old Cable and Wireless staff who could be found. To his surprise and delight, 90 out of his 100 employees turned up. He said "No money, no food. Do you want to work?" The response was unanimous. So these loyal Chinese operators were installed in the Press Ship and started operating, telling the story of Singapore[10].

However, for local journalists, most of whom had been interned, freedom would have to come first before they could begin work. For Harry Miller, the pre-war chief reporter at *The Straits Times* and a civilian internee at Sime Road, the arrival of Allied troops on 5 September was a historic event:

> The troops, carrying arms strange to Singaporeans and wearing odd-looking camouflaged uniforms, climbed aboard innumerable trucks at the docks and began journeys to strategic points around the island. Those laughing, rifle-waving British, Indian and Ghurkha troops provided the exclamation point to the termination for Singapore of 1,328 days of Japanese occupation and terror.
>
> Neither the conquering heroes nor the people who welcomed them took the slightest notice of Japanese troops, who under British orders, stood on traffic control at important road junctions, a humiliating role for those men of *Bushido*.
>
> But for me and about 3,000 British civilian men, women and children who had been Japanese prisoners of the lowest calibre, and of the many more thousands of British military prisoners of war in vast camps around Singapore, that was our personal 'freedom day'.
>
> In Sime Road, our camp a few miles inland, bronzed but emaciated men, women and children, many wearing rags, gathered at midday round a specially erected flagpole near the entrance and watched a Union Jack hoisted over our few acres of once-Japanese land. It was a profound, intense and passionate moment and few attempted to hold back.
>
> It was with broken voices and choked throats that we tried to sing the national anthem. But the loudest voices in praise were from the women who, three-and-a-half years before had, with faces held high and shoulders firmly back, marched into Changi singing, "There'll Always Be An England". Now they were singing victoriously[11].

For Miller, it was suddenly back to work again. The call came for all released journalists and printers of *The Straits Times* to head for the offices in Cecil Street and augment the local staff. Robert Burns, the managing editor and now ex-internee, wanted the newspaper to be born again, but fast. It appeared on 7 September 1945, the paper's centenary year[12].

The hospital and medical conditions in Singapore were appalling. Although the new British Military Administration (BMA) in Malaya (announced by Mountbatten on 15 August but who only arrived with TIDERACE on 5 September) attempted to improve medical facilities, the main aim was to evacuate as many POWs as possible and only treat those who were in critical condition. Mountbatten's wife, Lady Edwina, as superintendent-in-chief, Nursing Corps and Divisions, St. Johns Ambulance Brigade, provided much support and visited numerous POW camps in the region. However, hospital conditions would take months to improve, as Baker noted:

> When we sisters first arrived at the hospital, we were given the old nurse's quarters, no beds, no furniture and no water except for a filthy trickle. But we did have rats galore. Our camping gear had been shipped with us and the canvas bed, bucket and wobbly bath were put into use. The water was undrinkable, pink and yellow tablets had to be put in jugs and it was still undrinkable! We managed to cadge pineapples to eat with our K rations. Our ration of cigarettes was used as money for we ate pineapples till our tongues were sore. We still only had our one suitcase with one change of clothes... We found that in our room of four sisters we had an Amah allocated to us and when we came off duty on the first day all our dirty clothes had been washed, ironed and mended. JOY! But the next day, she had disappeared. These conquerors had no money and away she went! As there was no money for a while, we bartered with our drink ration and ciggies for fruit.
>
> After the surrender, Tragedy (*sic*), as wood alcohol was being sold in popular cafes. First, one patient was admitted who dies and he was followed by others. If they survived, the optic nerve was damaged, resulting in blindness. Warning posters with thick black lettering were shown everywhere, but sailors off the ships and others did not heed them. As far as I can remember, it was never discovered where the drink came from but there were many casualties. And then it suddenly stopped[13].

By the end of September, close to 53,700 POWs and internees had been evacuated from Southeast Asia to India, Australia and the United Kingdom, with numbers increasing to almost 71,000 by October 1945. The majority were moved by sea from Singapore. By May 1946, 96,575 POWs and internees had been evacuated but, owing to the political situation in Java, it was believed that some 30,000 Dutch internees were still there[14].

Although the POWs and European civilian internees were being taken care of, the general population in Singapore, which had suffered just as badly through the occupation, was in desperate need of food and supplies.

> The main shopping areas were Chinese, and in the shops excited crowds of waving, cheering Chinese, particularly children, watched our troops arrive. Union Jacks were flying from buildings or being waved. The streets were empty of buses, trams and *tongas,* and the sole means of transport seemed to be a few rickshaws. So few were the Malays and Indians by comparison with the Chinese inhabitants that you might have thought yourself in China[15].

It was obvious to returning soldiers like Richard Munby that the local Chinese population had suffered terribly at the hands of the Japanese and that many wanted revenge[16]:

> For the past three or four years, the Chinese in particular have lived a life of inconceivable hardship and intense humility, many having been tortured into submission, and thousands have never lived to see the day of their city's liberation. Their joyous faces, their national flags which they sported on every possible occasion, their spotlessly clean clothes which they wore as if saved for the great day, the scorn and derisive laughter with which they greeted the hundreds of Japanese prisoners (under Indian guards – how they hate the Indians) who, as if planted there to be publicly jeered at, were filling in the trenches and taking down the barbed wire in the great open space in front of the Municipal Building (in preparation for the surrender ceremony at the Padang on 12 September 1945) – all these pointed without any doubt whatsoever to the fact that the Japs were despicable creatures, ill-behaved in every respect...

> ... we saw hundreds of Japs being marched under Indian guards to the green open space in front of the Y.M.C.A., and there made to fill in air raid trenches and clear debris under the eyes of a mocking crowd. The Japs passed within three feet of where I was standing and it was interesting to note the expressions on their face. Some showed signs of great humiliation and were probably unwilling tools forced to carry out their Government's orders; others were arrogant, brutal creatures to whom the catcalls and derision of the crowd meant not a thing. These are the men, if they can be sifted out, who should be made to pay for their country's merciless inhumanity. Each party of prisoners was under a Jap Major but orders were issued by a British Major to the Jap Major, who then carried on as "foreman first class". According to an intellectual Chinaman to whom I spoke, the Japs had made countless hundreds of his countrymen, men and women,

> including himself lie on this selfsame small open space for three days on end without food or water, herded together as cattle, and left exposed to the blazing tropical sun, hardly able to turn over. No wonder that hundreds of them wished to die, and had their wishes granted; no wonder that the spectators... were fierce in their hostility towards these defeated, though in many cases, unbroken, Japs.
>
> The Y.M.C.A. (Young Men's Christian Association), centre of goodwill and Christian relaxation before the war, was converted by the Japs into the vilest of *kempei* or *Gestapo* headquarters. Any one entering the walls of this building for interrogation – with one known exception, the Bishop of Singapore – never lived to see Liberation Day. Many were the heads, arms, legs and bodies strewn throughout the streets as warning to the citizens not to feed and succour our prisoners of war.

However, it was clear that as the end drew near, many of these torturers realised they would have to face Allied justice. For other Japanese officers, their warrior code, the *Bushido,* would not allow surrender. For these men, capitulation was not an option:

> Later, we had a walk along the seafront and in the luxurious lounge of the great Raffles Hotel, known to almost every traveller in the east, we disposed of a glass of iced water – all the beaming waiters had to offer in the way of food or drink. Only a few days before, according to the waiters, 300 Japanese officers had committed *hari kiri* in that very lounge when General (Seishiro) Itagaki had told them he was surrendering under orders from the Emperor. They held a farewell party at which a good deal of *saki* (*sic*) was drunk, then, leaning on their short swords, they hastily returned to their ancestors. A whole platoon of officers later blew themselves up with hand grenades[17].

Two days after the return of the British, the local population was in for another rude shock. After three-and-a-half years of occupation and rule by the Japanese, on Friday, 7 September, the BMA issued a Currency Proclamation declaring that:

> ... apart from $1,000 and $10,000 dollar notes, which had to be handed in and accounted for, all pre-war Malayan and Straits Settlements currency notes and coins would be legal tender. But it also gave the chief civil affairs officer discretion to authorise acceptance of other currencies. This proclamation was published in *The Straits Times* and

> also in the official *Malayan Times* newssheet, but the latter went on to explain this meant Japanese military 'banana' money was now worthless. Since this was virtually the only currency in circulation, the news threw the population into a panic. On Saturday, black market prices soared. Beef, which could previously be bought for 20 cents a *kati* (605g) or 150 Japanese Dollars on the black market, went up to $1,000 Japanese Dollars. The next day, when the full implication of the news had sunk in, no one would accept Japanese Dollars. By Monday (10 September) every shop, food stall and market was closed, and even people with Malayan currency could find nothing to buy...
>
> ... The BMA reacted quickly to the crisis. The chief civil affairs officer assured reporters that large quantities of Straits Dollar notes were available, everyone would be paid salary advances, and Allied servicemen were already spending their local dollars, so that soon there would be plenty of legal currency in circulation. At the same time, the first free rations of rice, sugar and salt were being distributed[18].

The reoccupation of Singapore and Malaya was clearly not going to be easy. It would take many months before some semblance of normalcy would return to the economy and for the next nine months, the BMA would provide the colony with its main lifeline. Now, the next major objective for SEAC troops was the reoccupation of the rest of Malaya. Operation ZIPPER was scheduled for 9 September and SEAC planners felt this final operation would be just as easy. Their overconfidence would ultimately lead to much confusion on the Malayan peninsula.

Endnotes

1 Baker, Catherine M.S. *Personal Papers, 96/34/11.* London: Imperial War Museum, 1996.

2 Kirby, Major General S. Woodburn. *The War Against Japan: The Surrender of Japan*, vol. 5. London: HMSO, 1969. 245.

3 *E Group/Force 136 Plan for Immediate Assistance to PWs in Malaya, T.W. 1460/E Gp., 12 August 1945, HS1/328.* London: The National Archives.

4 Kirby, 1969. 246.

5 *E Group/Force 136 Plan for Immediate Assistance to PWs in Malaya, T.W. 1460/E Gp., 12 August 1945, HS1/328.* London: The National Archives.

6 Kirby, 1969. 247.

7 Baker, 1996.

8 Stewart, Athole. "How History was Written at Singapore". *The Zodiac*, December 1945. 208.

9 "'Oot!' said Mackie and the Jap Colonel Fled". *The Zodiac*, November 1945.

10 Ibid.

11 Miller, H. "An End to 1,318 Days of Terror". *The Daily Telegraph*, 12 August 1985. 12.

12 Ibid.

13 Baker, 1996.

14 Kirby, 1969. 249.

15 Brett-James, Anthony. *Ball of Fire: 5th Indian Division in World War II.* Aldershot: Gale and Polden, 1951.

16 Munby, Richard. *SACSEA Surrender Mission to Singapore, 87/34/1.* London: The Imperial War Museum. 7.

17 Ibid. 8.

18 Turnbull, Mary. *Dateline Singapore: 150 Years of the Straits Times.* Singapore: Singapore Press Holdings, 1995. 136.

Chapter 7

Operation ZIPPER

In May 1945, Vice Admiral Lord Louis Mountbatten issued orders that set in motion the formulation of a plan for the invasion of Malaya, and instructed Lieutenant General Ouvry Lindfield Roberts, General Officer Commanding (GOC), XXIV Indian Corps, Rear Admiral BCS Martin (Flag Officer, Force 'W') and Air Vice Marshall Sir Percy Ronald Gardner (224th Group RAF), the Earl of Bandon, to execute the operation.

By 15 May, the Joint Planning Staff at Southeast Asia Command (SEAC) had come up with a plan for the recapture of Malaya and subsequently Singapore. The plan would call for an invasion of Malaya, codenamed Operation ZIPPER, which was scheduled for 9 September 1945, and the eventual recapture of Singapore, codenamed Operation MAILFIST, with seven divisions and three armoured brigades:

> In examining the advance on Singapore, the Force Commanders decided that, since stress had been laid on capturing the port and dock facilities at Singapore intact, the defeat of the Japanese army was merely incidental to the task and could be left to the stage subsequent to the capture of the island. In the operations leading up to the capture of Singapore, every effort should therefore be made to prevent the enemy from concentrating his forces on the island. Once a landing had been made in Malaya, it would be evident that the ultimate Allied objective was Singapore, which meant that surprise could only be achieved by the speed and method of advance. Since it might be possible to persuade the Japanese that the intention was merely to secure a bridgehead of sufficient size to cut their

> communications between north and south Malaya with a view to a relatively slow build-up and subsequent advance on Singapore, any action taken until the advance began should appear to support this intention but, once the advance did begin, it should be carried out at speed, full use being made of amphibious operations[1].

The plan would also call for the capture of advanced naval and air bases on Phuket island in Thailand (Operation ROGER) and Penang island in Malaya (Operation JURIST) before ZIPPER would be activated. The invasion of Singapore (MAILFIST) could occur immediately after ZIPPER was launched.

The recapture of Rangoon in May 1945 and the decision by Mountbatten to advance directly to Malaya, instead of first seizing Phuket, made it unnecessary to implement ROGER or to wait for forces from Europe to create the seven divisions needed. Mountbatten decided to launch ZIPPER from India with resources held by SEAC.

On 24 July, Mountbatten had just landed in Cairo, on his way to a meeting with British Prime Minister Sir Winston S. Churchill, when a telegram from the prime minister instructed him to fly directly to Berlin so that he could also meet with American President Harry E. Truman and his chiefs of staff[2].

That afternoon, he arrived in Berlin and went into a meeting with the combined chiefs of staff. After the meeting, the American chief of staff, General George C. Marshall, revealed to Mountbatten the top-secret plan to drop the atomic bomb on Japan. That evening, when Mountbatten dined alone with the prime minister, Churchill told him that in view of the imminent Japanese surrender, he should take all necessary steps to be prepared[3].

After dinner, Mountbatten sent an urgent signal to his deputy, Lieutenant General Raymond A. Wheeler, and his chief of staff, Lieutenant General (later Sir) Frederick Arthur Montague Browning, saying that there were strong reasons for thinking that Japan would surrender by mid August and that the prime minister wanted SEAC to have a plan ready for occupying Singapore, either direct, or through Port Swettenham and Port Dickson, the moment that Japan capitulated[4].

This new development meant that ZIPPER would no longer have the Singapore (MAILFIST) component. A new top-secret plan for the emergency capture of Singapore would have to be drawn up, giving birth to TIDERACE on 4 August 1945.

As for ZIPPER, Mountbatten noted that it would go on as planned on 9 September but as Japan was expected to surrender, there was no longer a need to assault-load Force W. This meant that ZIPPER would no longer be an invasion force but a reoccupation force.

With the completion of JURIST and TIDERACE on 2 September and 4 September respectively, ZIPPER was given the all-clear. The ZIPPER convoys set out from various ports in India for their landing beaches in the Port Swettenham-Port Dickson area. As the official history noted:

> During the voyage, the formations were given detailed orders regarding their areas of occupation and the procedure to be adopted towards Japanese who surrendered. The landings were to be carried out as rehearsed, except that there was to be no covering fire and a Japanese envoy would be at the Morib rest house with an officer of Force 136 at 6.30am to meet the commander of the 25th Division (Major General G.N. Wood) and the Brigadier General Staff of XXXIV Corps. The first landings were to be made on 9 September by 25th Division on the Morib beaches, 18 miles south of Port Swettenham, and by 37th Brigade of 23rd Division on the beaches west of Sepang, eight miles northwest of Port Dickson. Their immediate objectives were Kelanang airfield (on which 11th and 17th Spitfire Squadrons RAF were to be based) and the Sepang road junction respectively, both of which were a few miles inland from the beaches. After occupying the road junction, 37th Brigade was to move south to Port Dickson where the rest of the 23rd Division (Major General D.C. Hawthorn) was to land over the beaches south of the town on the 12th. Escorted by the battleships (HMS) *Nelson* and (HMS) *Richelieu,* the cruisers (HMS) *Nigeria,* (HMS) *Cleopatra* and (HMS) *Ceylon*, a carrier force consisting of the cruiser (HMS) *Royalist* and six escort carriers ((HMS) *Hunter,* (HMS) *Stalker,* (HMS) *Archer,* (HMS) *Khedive,* (HMS) *Emperor* and (HMS) *Pursuer*), with a screen of fifteen destroyers, the D-day convoys arrived off their respective beaches at daylight on 9 September, and the first flights of landing craft moved into their appointed beaches on time[5].

However, at this point things started to go wrong. By the first week of September 1945, the India Mission of the Special Operations Executive (SOE) had signalled the operational details for ZIPPER to its field units. Force 136 was left out of TIDERACE completely and so was not involved in the reoccupation of Singapore. 'P' Department at SEAC ordered Davis and his colleagues to the ZIPPER landing beaches.

Davis, along with Chin Peng (whom he had invited to view the landings), moved to Telok Datok, close to Morib Beach. This was a beach Davis knew well from pre-war holidays to the west coast. Dawn was still over the horizon. It was dark, the air warm and the beach was at its tropical best. There were neither Japanese defences nor troops, only broken-down trenches.

> Somewhere out at sea, in the darkness, we heard the sound of marine engines, then at first light we saw the fleet. The horizon was filled with ships, large and small, all shapes and sizes. Then, low-flying fighter aircraft swept over the empty beach waggling wings in a greeting, but the crew of a naval launch close to the beach looked them over and ignored us[6].

Later, on the road alongside the beach they saw the first landing craft, ahead of the main flotilla, surge towards the empty beach. As the boats drew close, Davis and Broadhurst (who had come over from northern Selangor) walked across the beach to meet the newcomers. One of the first men down the ramp was the beach master. Minutes later, a flotilla of landing craft hit the beaches, dropped their ramps and disgorged hundreds of Indian troops, jeeps, lorries and small amphibious DUKWs (an acronym derived

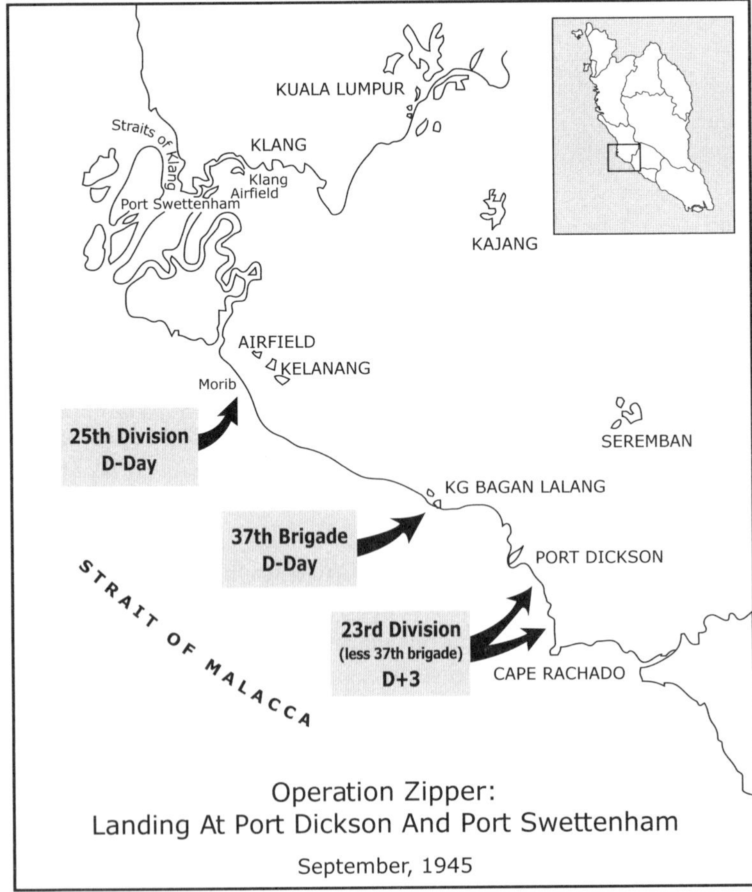

The ZIPPER landings in Malaya on 9, 10 and 11 September 1945.

from manufacturer General Motors Corporation's codes: 'D' for model year 1942, 'U' for amphibian, 'K' for all-wheel drive and 'W' for tandem axles). Immediately, the tranquil beach was transformed into chaos.

The invasion force was operating on Ceylon time and not on Malayan time, so it arrived an hour late on a receding tide. This left four large vehicles carrying DUKWs and smaller vessels stranded. In the growing disorder, the landing craft carrying bulldozers and heavy plant equipment beached at low tide, forcing vehicles to drive off ramps into the water to struggle ashore. Some became stranded and were towed up the beach past lorries stuck in the soft sand. Beyond the beach, tanks became trapped in ditches and those that did get off the landing area churned up and broke the roads. If it had been an opposed landing, observers at the landing noted, the initial wave would have been pinned down until reinforcements and higher tides freed them from their muddy traps[7].

The after-action reports for ZIPPER catalogued the problems:

> The three LSTs (Landing Ship Tanks) beached on ITEM sector at 8.30am to swim off DUKWS and to dry out. Although MUCK-A-MUCK roadway had been provided in LST, the Army Beach Group decided not to use it, as they considered the beach firm enough to take the traffic. As soon as vehicles drove off, however, the under-surface of the beach collapsed and vehicles bogged down on their axles. This meant that MUCK-A-MUCK had to be carried ashore to bridge the worst patches, and in the end, only 46 vehicles, exclusive of amphibians, were got ashore. It was impossible to clear four of these before the tide came up, and they were drowned.
>
> As soon as the treacherous nature of the beaches was discovered, unloading of LST's (*sic*) 280 and 1021 was stopped, as it was clear that to continue would result in the loss of many more vehicles[8].

To add to the farcical landing, the Japanese officer with the maps, who was supposed to turn up in the early morning, did not arrive until the afternoon. Eventually, a table was set out on the beach for the Japanese delegation to lay their maps and report the disposition of their troops.

At Port Dickson, a second invasion beach some miles down the coast, Captain G.P. Brownie headed the Force 136 reception committee:

> Seremban had emptied and the roads were choked with people, either walking or packed in bullock carts, old wood-burning lorries and cars. All full of families. It was a circus atmosphere, a carnival with roadside food stalls, puppet shows and entertainers.

> We were well behind the lines, using a five-figure code to keep the fleet informed of Japanese reactions. If things went wrong and the Japanese changed their minds, we would pinpoint targets for the big guns and aircraft. I understand the landing was a bit of a mess and the Japanese had to be called out to tow landing craft off the beaches[9].

Robert Callow, then a lieutenant with the 430 Madras Sappers & Miners' Forward Airfields Company, had expected ZIPPER to take place but not when and where it did. The young officer, who had special skills in explosives and was fluent in Chinese, Malay and Tamil, had been periodically detached from his unit and served with the ISLD in China, Burma and was carrying out operations along the Thai-Malayan border when he was recalled for ZIPPER:

> I had been evacuated from the Padang Besar area in July 1945 and subsequently a preliminary briefing indicated that I was likely to be part of the second reconnaissance (no doubt in a small group-mission) to survey the condition of Kelanang airfield for its suitability to receive light aircraft for vacating wounded...and this would take place simultaneously with a reconnaissance-survey by Royal Marines 'Special Forces' (in folding boats from a submarine) of water-depths along the proposed invasion-beaches. These missions were to take place in mid-September 1945... In view of the Emperor of Japan's surrender and change in occurrence of ZIPPER, neither reconnaissance was carried out – with ignorance of Morib's unsuitability[10].

Callow said that most of his regiment were unconcerned with their deployment in mid-August as they were told that ZIPPER was to take place sometime in November 1945, and so they thought that they were in for some practice landings ahead of the real operation:

> In the first week of August, I attended a briefing with my own 430 MS&M Company that, in the second week in August, we would embark in Madras on LST vessels for a practice beach-landing. We did in fact embark in Madras in mid-August but the then-intended practice-landing (Operation BUTTON, an initial element of ZIPPER) was to be on the beaches of India's Coromandel coast. The target there was to be RED beach and, since this was seen as something of a holiday-jaunt, we were completely unprepared for a possibly-opposed real invasion operation.

> Although a seasoned (Sapper) Lieutenant from ISLD missions, I had not weighed down my ammunition-pouches with ammunition for use against a non-existent foe. Instead they contained more-essential food to sustain me through the rigours of several days/nights of 'make-believe' combat. Thus, when instead of our LST (Landing Ship Tanks) sailing southwards to round Ceylon, I was horrified to find ourselves heading due eastwards across the Bay of Bengal – and, more especially when a Naval Destroyer passed to us new charts showing that RED beach was at Morib!!! There had been complete radio-silence since we had left Madras and we were unaware that, presumably due to the dropping of the two atomic bombs, BUTTON had become the real Operation ZIPPER. On arrival at Morib beach, I had to borrow a Sterling submachine-gun and its ammunition from the Navy!

However, Callow was not surprised at what he saw occur on the beaches of Morib:

> The cancelling of the original reconnaissance-missions had tragic effect. When our LST arrived at Morib, there were unknown sandbanks about 300-yards out to sea – and 20-feet-deep scoured channels between there and the beach proper. On the sandbanks, soundings showed that the water was only half-a-fathom (3 feet) deep and so six of our 3-tonner lorries drove off – and slid into the deep trough, drowning the drivers. The rest of the men and equipment in the LSTs had to wait nearly three hours until off-loading at the lowest tide. By which time the beach and the nearby roads were a soft quagmire! We eventually reached Kelanang after nightfall.
>
> I also have comic memories of a small group of fully-armed Japanese officers in a beach-top bungalow earnestly asking me to take them to the Beach Commander. I told them to await my return but, when I managed to report this to that Commander, he testily and brusquely told be to "Clear off! I have no time to bother about such nonsense at present!" I ordered the Japanese to stay where they were until someone came to collect them – what a shambles![11]

The biggest embarrassment ensued when a message had to be passed to the local Force 136 officer telling them to break cover, find the local Japanese commander and borrow his transport to get the landing party out of trouble. Although the official account noted that, "despite the chaos on the beaches, there is little doubt that had it been necessary to take Malaya by force of arms, Operation Zipper would eventually have achieved its object,"[12] it also outlined the great challenge that would be faced had there been actual opposition[13].

> It is equally true that... the invasion forces would have been very roughly handled and at least pinned to the beaches for some time. It is even possible that the troops landed on the Morib beaches might have had to be withdrawn[14].

Upon landing, the infantry, however, did not face such problems, and by 4.30pm, Port Swettenham and Klang had been occupied by troops moving by way of Telok Datok. A hundred Japanese guards handed Kelanang airfield over to the troops. After spending the night on the beaches of Morib without their equipment, the 25th Division moved to Klang on 10 September. However, it was still bedlam on the beach:

> Conditions on the beaches were chaotic, vehicles drowned in scores as there was no decent exit from the beaches, and roads became choked with ditched tanks which tore up the road surfaces and grass verges... A lack of vehicles ashore made movement of stores an impossible undertaking[15].

On 10 September, Port Dickson was occupied and Major General Douglas Cyril Hawthorn, GOC, 23rd Indian Division, landed and met with Force 136 members. The next day, Mountbatten, Roberts and the commander-in-chief of the Allied Land Forces, Southeast Asia, Field Marshal William Slim, visited the 25th Division in Klang before it moved inland to Kuala Lumpur, where XXXIV Indian Corps planned a ceremonial entry on 13 September. Reconnaissance of beaches south of Port Dickson showed a few south of Cape Rachado that were suitable for landing men and vehicles and the leading troops of the rest of the 23rd Division began to land there on 12 September.

Although ZIPPER finally managed to reoccupy Malaya, the lack of effective planning and alternative arrangements did not reflect well on a force that was trying to impress the enemy with overwhelming strength and superiority:

> Although it was realised that the information about the beaches might not be accurate, a risk was accepted that might have proved unjustifiable had the Japanese opposed the D-day landings with even a few battalions. There would in any case have had to be a quick and sound revision of the plan when it turned out that there was no

> possibility of the follow-up division being able to land at Morib as planned. Only good generalship could have avoided the delay that would have given the Japanese time to concentrate their available forces to oppose a breakout from the beachheads[16].

With the landing of ZIPPER, the British were once again in control of Malaya. However, that control would remain tenuous. The seeds of rebellion, which had been planted by the Malayan Communist Party (MCP) among the guerrilla forces during the occupation would now begin to blossom and the British would have a full-blown communist insurgency in their hands in less than three years after the end of the war. However, all this was still in the future. With the 'success' of ZIPPER, Mountbatten could now bask in the glory of the final Japanese surrender in Singapore that would occur on 12 September 1945.

Endnotes

1 Kirby, Major General S. Woodburn. *The War Against Japan: The Surrender of Japan*, vol. 5. London: HMSO, 1969. 69.

2 Kirby, 1969. 226.

3 Ibid.

4 Ibid.

5 Kirby, 1969. 268.

6 Gough, Richard. *The Jungle was Red*. Singapore: SNP Panpac, 2003. 157.

7 Ibid.

8 Sayer, Vice Admiral Sir Guy. *Operation ZIPPER, 311/13, 14 September 1945, P68*. London: The Imperial War Museum.

9 Ibid. 158.

10 Callow, Robert. Email correspondence with the author, 13 December 2008, 9 March 2009.

11 Callow, Robert. Email correspondence with the author, 13 December 2008, 9 March 2009.

12 Kirby, 1969. 270.

13 Stripp, Alan. *Codebreaker in the Far East*. Oxford: Oxford University Press, 1989. 176.

14 Ibid. 271.

15 Kirby, 1969. 269.

16 Ibid. 271.

Chapter 8

The Final Surrender in Singapore

On 9 September, Lieutenant General Sir Alexander Christison held a meeting with the army, navy and air force representatives to plan for the official Japanese surrender, which was to be held three days later at the Municipal Building in the heart of downtown Singapore.

Signals had already come in from units of the SEAC fleet that were arriving to participate in the ceremony on 12 September. Christison faced a major problem. The 5th Indian Division had no Caucasian British troops and so there would only be Indian faces at the moment of British triumph at the Padang. The planners felt that white faces were needed in order to boost the morale of the local population and to show that the British were still in charge. Accordingly, Rear (later Vice) Admiral Cedric Holland ordered shore leave to be given to the crew beginning on 8 September and by 12 September, more than 4,000 'British' libertymen were ashore for the surrender parade[1].

Although these libertymen were not involved in the actual liberation of Singapore and they did not face the same risk of death that each Indian soldier took on reoccupying Singapore, their presence at the parade was obviously aimed at taking the credit for the liberation. What clearly mattered was showing who was in charge. This myth of the White European as the ruler of the local populace needed to be propagated as it had been one of the key justifications for British colonial rule in Malaya and the special treatment and status accorded to the *Tuan*. On the resumption of British rule, a clear delineation had to again be drawn between the colonial masters and the subject races. It would be unacceptable if the local population began to believe that these Indian troops, similar in colour to them, were the actual liberators. This would obviously mean that the colonial masters were not as superior as they had claimed. As Holland later wrote:

> The 5th Indian Division had no British troops to show the flag, therefore libertymen were landed on the fourth day after entry, and on 12 September, 4,000 men were ashore for the Surrender Parade. This had an excellent effect upon the civilian population and helped CAS (M) (Civilian Administration Service Malaya) authorities to restore order[2].

By this time, instructions had already been relayed to the Japanese on preparations to house Mountbatten and his staff for the upcoming ceremony. In signals to SEAC on 31 August, the Japanese high command noted its preparations:

> Your msg No. 26 instructing us to make the SINGAPORE Government House ready for occupation by 5 Sept has duly been received here in SHONAN. Incidentally, we might add that we already started making the necessary preparations as laid down in your msg no. 24 prior to receiving this[3].

Richard Munby was a Sergeant in the Royal Signals attached to Mountbatten's personal staff. As part of the SACSEA's advance party, Munby and Mountbatten's personal staff landed at the Seletar Sea Plane Base on 9 September[4]:

> During the 10-mile drive to Singapore, we were greeted joyously by the crowds who had assembled to line the route; most houses and shops permanently displayed either the Chinese National Emblem or the Union Jack and many of the menfolk jumped to attention as we passed and saluted us, whilst the women and girls smiled charmingly, momentarily forgetful of their natural eastern modesty.
>
> Proceeding through the magestic (*sic*) gates and up the winding drive to Government House, we were soon confronted with one of the most beautiful and stately buildings imaginable. Outwardly at least, the Japs had treated Government House with due respect even to the extent of keeping the lawns and gardens in good condition. This of course was purely for their own convenience and advantage.
>
> Ascending the carpeted steps and entering the big reception hall, we were greeted by beaming, smartly dressed Chinese waiters, each

> carrying a tray containing glasses of most refreshing sherry. We were then taken up in a lift – lifts are very few and far between in the east – and whilst walking along the passages to our rooms we saw, and saw into, a number of stately chambers with cards on the door indicating that they were earmarked for our fellow guests, which included the Supremo, Generals Slim, Stopford, Christison, Dempsey, Carton de Wiart, Wheeler (USA), Leclerc (France), Feng Yee (China), Air Vice Marshal Cole (Australia), Air Chief Marshal Sir Keith Park, Admiral Sir Arthur Power; War Correspondents Tom Driberg, M.P., Alan Humphries, and the Marquis of Donegal, etc.
>
> We learnt that General Itagaki, the so-called "Tiger of Singapore" and commander of the Japanese forces in Malaya, had only vacated this palatial building with his staff three days previous to our arrival. Even so, not a vestige of Japanese occupation was visible, except that some of the annexes, including the Governor's library, had been pillaged, and that a number of third-rate Japanese cigarettes were found in the bedrooms, which the servants refused to smoke. I tried one and it proved rather American in flavour. In the library, searching amongst the remains, we found several most interesting and highly confidential documents, one or two of which had the signature of Queen Victoria and King Edward VII appended.

Mountbatten arrived on 11 September in preparation for the surrender ceremonies in the city. However, food remained a significant problem and even the supreme allied commander had to rely on military rations:

> There was no standing on ceremony. We all mixed freely with one another, equally sharing the discomforts of an acute shortage of water – one of the main reasons for the British collapse in Singapore in 1942 – and ate of the same meagre ration. It was rather amusing to watch the Supremo and Lady Louis – when she arrived – eating the same hard, butterless, dog biscuits about which the troops on exercise back in England used to grumble so incessantly[5].

Preparations for the ceremony were going into overdrive as a skeleton rehearsal was held on the Padang on the afternoon of 11 September to ensure there were no glitches during the event the following day.

However, as Munby relates, not everything for the supreme allied commander had gone according to plan:

The reality: Joyous scenes as the local populace welcome their liberators – not the British but MPAJA and Chinese nationalist resistance fighters, riding on lorries through downtown Singapore. Note the Chinese nationalist flag at the top left hand corner of the picture.

The fiction: Posed propaganda stills like these were taken to show the warm welcome the British received upon their return. Although the majority were happy to have the British back, the smiles would soon turn to sneers and looks of fear as the communist insurgency took hold of Malaya and Singapore less than three years after the end of the war.

> ...Lord Louis apparently had been looking over his white Admiral's uniform which he intended wearing for the Surrender Ceremony on the following day and found his medals and ribbons missing. He rushed up to our bedroom where he found his batman enjoying forty winks. On being hastily roused, the confused man explained rather haltingly that he had forgotten to pack the ribbons before leaving Kandy. The Supremo, I thought as I lay on my bed pretending to be asleep, retained an amazing degree of composure, merely mentioning that he would have a plane fly immediately back to Kandy for the ribbons and that meanwhile the batman would have to design a makeshift set from those he was wearing with his K.D. (khaki dress) uniform. Needless to say, the batman worked on the ribbons well into early morning, but the special plane just arrived in time back from Kandy, and the improvised set did not have to be worn for the ceremony[6].

The Japanese also faced similar problems. At about 4.30pm, Vice Admiral Yaichiro Shibata[7], commander-in-chief of the Japanese 2nd Southern Area Expeditionary Fleet, who was flying in for the surrender ceremony, landed at the wrong airfield, where he was met by the Special Correspondent from *The Sunday Despatch*, who then escorted him to his quarters.

By the evening of 11 September, Mansergh had arranged for more than 22,000 Japanese naval personnel to be transported in former enemy ships to holding camps around the Batu Pahat area in Johor. However, the shift was not easy. Japanese officers were trying to take with them much of what they had looted from Singapore prior to the Allied liberation. This enraged Mansergh so much that he instructed his men to ensure that all Japanese officers, regardless of rank, would from then on have the same baggage allowance as non-commissioned officers and that all bags were to be thoroughly searched before they were loaded onto the vessels[8].

All Japanese personal effects were thoroughly examined and the retained loot was thrown open to Allied prisoners of war (POWs). This, Holland noted in his report, fulfilled two requirements. It showed the POWs the Japanese were only being allowed to take strict service kit with them and it allowed the POWs to replenish their non-existent wardrobes.

The other challenge was evacuating as many POWs as possible from the island. Due to the lack of maritime transport, merchant navy ships had to be drafted in to help evacuate as many POWs as possible.

As dawn broke on 12 September 1945, there was a great sense of excitement in Singapore city. Streams of people began making their way to the Padang on foot, bicycles, rickshaws and wood-burning lorries. British Royal Marines lined the streets as the crowds filled the Padang, which was now level, the trenches having been filled in the day before by hundreds of Japanese surrendered personnel, who had worked double-time to complete the task in a day.

By about 10.00am, the Padang was packed, except for the square space in front of the Municipal Building where the Guard of Honour was drawn up. All vantage points had large groups of spectators. Any roof within sight of the Padang was packed with Chinese, Malay, Indian and Eurasian observers who were determined to see the historic event unfold before them.

In the bay, the Allied fleet consisted of the capital ships HMS *Sussex*, HMS *Nelson*, HMS *Richelieu* and numerous warships, which filled the harbour and inner roads. All the ships were gaily decorated in pennants and flags to mark the events taking place on the Padang. Fighter planes and bombers zoomed overhead as the troops began forming up for the event.

The sky was overcast as the guards of honour took to the Padang. The sun appeared only briefly through the clouds but the threatening rain held off.

The guards of honour comprised detachments from the 5th Indian Divison, commandos, gurkhas, Punjabis, Australian paratroops, detachments from the *Sussex* and other vessels of the Royal Navy as well as a British battalion of West Yorks. Flanking the steps of the Municipal Building were Royal Marines from HMS *Cleopatra* and just inside the building was a double file of men from the MPAJA, under the command of a British officer. "Slick and determined looking, they carried tommy and sten guns and with their khaki uniforms wore the peaked khaki caps bearing the three red stars"[9].

Harry Miller had a place inside the surrender chamber from which to cover the proceedings. Editor of *The Straits Times*, George Peet, who had also been interned, gave Miller the honour of covering the event. Breaking away from his straight, factual reporting style, Miller's report (although without a byline) in the special four-page issue described the scene thus[10]:

> The scene was set. Newsreel men and photographers from all over the world got ready. Commanders-in-Chief of the British Navy, Army and Air Force in South East Asia, the men who would have led their forces into action against the Japanese arrived.
>
> Cheering from the direction of Stamford Road told us that the Supreme Allied Commander himself was approaching.
>
> Ex-prisoners of war and ex-internees watching the spectacle – thus completing the cycle of the last three-and-a-half years – gave him a special cheer. He turned and saluted them.

> "Present Arms" rang out, and then the Royal Salute. A high-ranking naval officer, standing next to me, muttered, "Good!" when the parade clicked to a man. The National Anthem was played by the band of the Royal Marines. Various aircraft was (*sic*) heard. Then the bugles.
>
> That was a great moment indeed – to hear British bugles sounding again on the Padang, scene of so many historic events in the history of Singapore. "Order Arms!" Once again, the parade clicked to a man and the high-ranking officer again muttered "Good!". The polish and smartness of the parade was good to see. Lord Louis Mountbatten inspected the parade. He did it leisurely, stopping here and there to talk to a British Marine, a Dogra, a Punjabi, a Commando, a British soldier, a French soldier and so on until he reached a long line of British sailors. We had another thrill. 'Mosquito bombers' flew over in salute. Then there were cheers from the crowd as the big Sunderland flying boats, used on long-range reconnaissance and bombing missions, droned over, and finally some Dakota transports.
>
> Before Lord Louis had finished his inspection, hoots and jeers from the local crowds by the Singapore Cricket Club told us that the seven Japanese representatives had arrived. Dust flew up on the Padang as the crowds rushed in the direction of the High Street to see the Japanese step out of their cars, each of which bore a white flag. These officers lined up, one behind the other, and then escorted by men from the British, Indian, Chinese, Australian and American Forces, walked down the road, looking neither to the right or left, faces pale and expressionless under their cloth caps. They wore no swords.

General Seishiro Itagaki was followed by Lieutenant General Tokazo Numata, General Hyotaro Kimura, Vice Admiral Shigeru Fukudome, Vice Admiral Shibata, Lieutenant General Akita Nakamura, Commander of the 18th Area Army (Siam), and Lieutenant General Bin Kinoshita, Commander of the 3rd Air Army (Singapore)[11]. Miller continued with his report[12]:

> It was a tense moment. The crowd watched them grimly, wondering what were the thoughts in those bowed heads. They walked up the steps into the building, and past the Chinese Resistance Army, whose exploits in the jungles of Malaya had demoralised Japanese forces, and were taken to a room to wait until they were summoned to sign their surrender.

General Seishiro Itagaki and his fellow generals are led to the Municipal offices as the gathered crowds jeer at their former rulers.

Lord Louis Mountbatten finished his inspection, came up the steps smiling and saluting, to the cheers of the spectators on the balconies of the Municipal Building and went into a room, where he waited until he was informed that the Japanese representatives were standing, waiting for him to enter the signature room and formally surrender South East Asia to him.

Scene of so many important civic meetings which had produced decisions leading to the great development of Singapore in the old era, the Municipal Council Chamber yesterday became a stage for a drama of the most historical importance. The two great bronze chandeliers threw a soft light on the assemblage of representatives of Malayan communities. Government officers straight from the internment camps, officers and men of the British Dominions, Chinese, French and American forces, famous admirals, generals and air officers. Seated in the audience was the Sultan of Johore (*sic*), Sir Ibrahim, wearing a grey suit and a black Malay cap. His Highness told me afterwards, "I have never been so stirred. I have been glad to have been there to watch those fellows sign. I am proud to have had the honour of witnessing their formal surrender." Practically opposite him and in the front row of chairs situated immediately behind the table to be occupied by the Japanese was the Bishop of Singapore, The Right Rev. JL Wilson, a victim of imprisonment and torture by the Japanese Military Police.

The Official Surrender, 12 September 1945: The Japanese delegation stands at attention as Mountbatten arrives.

The Official Surrender: Mountbatten signs the Instrument of Surrender as the Japanese delegates look on impassively.

The Official Surrender: Mountbatten reads aloud the Instrument of Surrender as General William Slim (on Mountbatten's left), and Lieutenant General Raymond Wheeler (on Mountbatten's right), look on.

Also there was Mr L. Rayman, former President of the Singapore Municipality, and Mr Justice N.A. Worley, another victim of the military police. There were other men who had been captives. Mr E.C.H. Charlwood, the only Eurpoean representative of the legislative Council. There were leaders of Malayan communities, Dr Lim Han Hoe, Dr Moonshi, Mr Ong, Mr Koek and many others.

The Commanders-in-Chief and other representatives took their seats at a long table covered in green baize. From the galleries hung the flags of Britain, France, Holland, China, the United States, Australia, the Straits Settlements and the Federated Malay states.

Standing at the bases of the buff-coloured marble pillars were representatives of the fighting forces: a Gurkha, a Sikh, an Australian, a British airman, an English corporal, a Dutchman, a Chinese, an American and a rep of the 5th Indian Division.

All is ready. We are told that the Japanese delegates are about to come in, but we hear a request, "Please remain seated." The buzz of conversation dies down. There is silence, except (for) the whirr of newsreel cameras, as a door opens and in file the seven men headed by General Itagaki, and flanked by their army escort, one to each Japanese. They take their places at a table in front of the Allied

> representatives and remain standing, looking straight ahead. Their heads appear to have been recently shaved. The lights glint on bald pates.
>
> It is a very dramatic moment. They seat themselves amidst silence. Their escorts sit behind them. Lieutenant General Numata, Chief of Staff to Field Marshal Count Terauchi rises, opens a black dispatch case, extracts a document, walks to the front of General Itagaki, bows and puts it in front of him. It is General Itagaki's credentials as Count Terauchi's representative. It is time for the Supreme Allied Commander to enter. The audience and the Japanese stand. Lord Louis walks in and takes his seat between General Slim and Lieutenant General Wheeler.

Mountbatten, basking in the glory of the moment, reached for the document in front of him and read the opening statement that would go down in history[13]:

> I have come here today to receive the formal surrender of all the Japanese forces within the Southeast Asia Command. I have received the following telegram from the Supreme Commander of the Japanese forces concerned, Field Marshal Count Terauchi:
>
> "The most important occasion of the formal surrender signing at Singapore draws near, the significance of which is no less great to me than to your Excellency. It is extremely regretful that my ill-health prevents me from attending and signing it personally and that I am unable to pay homage to your Excellency. I hereby notify your Excellency that I have fully empowered General Itagaki, the highest senior general in Japanese armies, and send him on my behalf."
>
> On hearing of Field Marshal Terauchi's illness, I sent my own doctor, Surgeon Captain Birt, Royal Navy, to examine him, and he certifies that the Field Marshal is suffering from the effects of a stroke. In the circumstances, I have decided to accept the surrender from General Itagaki today, but I have warned the Field Marshal that I shall expect him to make his personal surrender to me as soon as he is fit enough to do so.
>
> In addition to our Naval, Military and Air Forces which we have present in Singapore today, a large fleet is anchored off Port Swettenham and Port Dixon (*sic*), and a large force started disembarking from them

at daylight on 9 September. When I visited the force yesterday, there were 100,000 men ashore. This invasion would have taken place on 9 September whether the Japanese had resisted or not, and I wish to make it entirely clear to General Itagaki that he is surrendering to superior force here in Singapore. I now call upon General Itagaki to produce his credentials.

Miller noted the pin-drop silence in the room as Mountbatten made the last statement:

He (Mountbatten) calls on General Itagaki to produce his credentials. These are handed to him. Lord Louis reads it out (See Appendix F: Part III). Then he says, "This is the Instrument of Surrender" He reads that out too (See Appendix F: Part III).

The Japanese remain immobile, except for one who twiddles his thumbs and twitches his feet. The others are impassive, looking straight ahead of them, three of them wearing horn-rimmed spectacles.

The Supreme Allied Commander reads, "Any disobedience of, or delay or failure to comply with orders and instructions may be dealt with as the Supreme Allied Commander, South East Asia may decide".

He finishes and Major General Penney places 11 copies of the instrument before General Itagaki. The Japanese officer takes his spectacles out of his pocket and puts them on. He reaches for the pen and dips it into the ink. He signs on behalf of the Supreme Commander, Japanese Expeditionary Forces, Southern Regions. The time is 11.10am.

General Itagaki reaches in his pockets again, bringing out a large seal and a tablet of vermillion wax. It is the large square seal of the Japanese Army that he sets on the table. He reaches in his pockets for the third time and produces a little leather case from which he extracts his own personal seal. He 'chops' the instrument with both. Major General Penney takes it up and passes it to the Supreme Allied Commander who puts his signature on it. The 11 copies are signed. All the while, all the other Japanese delegates look straight ahead. They do not look at General Itagaki who is the only one showing movement except for that same Japanese delegate who continues to

General Seishiro Itagaki signs the official surrender document, handing over Southeast Asia to the victorious Allies.

The Japanese delegation being led away to captivity after the surrender ceremony. Itagaki would be hanged as a war criminal in 1948.

display nervousness by twiddling his fingers and twitching his feet behind the table.

The instruments are all attested. Nine pens have been used by Lord Louis. He looks up at the Japanese and calls on them to withdraw. They stand, bow, and shuffle out. The signing has taken nine minutes. A signal is given, and all spectators move out to the balcony for the final ceremony of the morning. As we move out, we hear once again the jeers and catcalls of the crowd. It is the Japanese delegates departing.

However, Munby, who was on the steps of the Municipal Building, recalls the jeering differently[14]:

A very amusing incident occurred outside, as the Japs were marching away. Amongst the military detachments was one from Chiang Kai Shek's Chungking Army, and to one who is unaccustomed to seeing many troops of different nationalities massed together, the Jap uniform is not unlike the Chinese. Consequently, when the Japanese delegation moved off in the direction from which the Chinese Military Detachment had arrived, and the Chinese in the direction from which the Japs had arrived, a number of the local inhabitants were completely bamboozled. The Japs received tumultuous cheers, and the Chinese, loud, derisive laughter and boos.

Miller then observed Mountbatten heading towards the microphone at the head of the steps in front of the Municipal building where he

... announces to the parade that he has received the surrender of the Supreme Commander of the Japanese Forces. "I have accepted this surrender on behalf of all of you". When Lord Louis says that he has ordered Count Terauchi to report to him in person and that he does not intend to put up with "any evasion or trickery on the part of any defeated Japanese however important he may consider himself," the crowds cheer. He ends his address by telling the history of the Union Jack which is about to be hoisted.

Another stirring moment arrives. The band strikes up the National Anthem, the flag slowly moves upwards and spreads out. We see that the colours have faded, but it is the Union Jack. It is a never-to-be-forgotten moment. Throats are choked and eyes are misted. The red emblem of Japan during the last three-and-a-half years has stood for so much oppression and persecution. But freedom, liberty and justice

> prevailed. The Union Jack says that. The band plays the anthems of the United States, China, Holland and France.
>
> Dakotas fly over, the ceremony is over. The Supreme Allied Commander and others leave to ringing cheers from the crowd and troops.[15]

The crumpled Union Jack that now fluttered in the morning sun had 43 months earlier flown over Government House in Singapore. It had been pocketed by Malayan civil servant Mervyn Cecil Frank Sheppard (who later became Tan Sri Mubin Sheppard, a renowned historian and academic in Malaysia), a scholar-administrator, just as the Japanese were on the outskirts of Singapore city on 14 February 1942, and had remained in his possession throughout his captivity. "I put it inside my pillow. I wrapped a towel around it and there it remained for the rest of the Japanese Occupation"[16]. When the Japanese ordered that the Union Jack and the white flag should be carried through the streets of Singapore, Sheppard told them that there were no flags available, as they had all been burnt. In Changi, Sheppard's flag was draped over every coffin, always in great secrecy away from prying eyes, and so had been used countless times in the camp. "Not only was it faded, but ragged and torn in places"[17].

Later, the Union Jack was again flown over Government House. One of Mountbatten's aides, Lieutenant Colonel Guy Armstrong, the last of the delegation to leave Government House, took the Union Jack with him for safekeeping and this flag was subsequently used to drape the coffin of Armstrong's father and that of Lord Louis Mountbatten after he was assassinated by the Irish Republican Army (IRA) in 1979. Armstrong was later ordained, and served as the Vicar of Bagshot and Ripley in the 1970s. In 1993, he was awarded an Order of the British Empire (OBE). He died in 2002, taking with him the fate of the liberation Union Jack[18].

At the same time that the ceremonies at the Municipal Building were taking place, a similarly hidden Australian flag was raised over Changi Prison. The flag, which is now framed and held at the Returned Services League in Canberra, is displayed with a plaque that reads, "This important artefact was concealed in Changi Prison by Captain Strawbridge MBE, from 1942–1945. It was raised over the gates of the prison, the day of formal liberation in September 1945". Several Australian flags were secretly made of scavenged pieces of cloth by Australian POWs in various enemy camps. Some of these flags are now held by the Australian War Memorial[19].

However, not everyone was pleased with the ceremony at the Municipal Building. Admiral Arthur Power, a believer in procedure and protocol, was upset with the way the Press had done their job:

> It is with regret that I must place on record that the behaviour of the Press and cameramen during the parade was disgraceful, and marred the conduct of the proceedings. Subsequently, in the signing hall, the sides and galleries resembled batteries of searchlights. There was a great number of correspondents armed with cameras and sited in favourable positions for using them. As an example of their unseemly behaviour, one of these creatures came up to the signing table behind the Supreme Allied Commander and, from a range of a few feet, 'shot' him... I informed Rear Admiral Holland and, through him, Major General Kimmins of SACSEA's staff, that I hoped the Press, whilst being given good facilities, would not be allowed to make the scene resemble a football match. I much regret that no success attended my efforts, and many distinguished spectators have expressed to me their disgust[20].

On 13 September, another surrender ceremony was held in Kuala Lumpur. This time, it was to officially surrender the Japanese army in Malaya. Crowds had already gathered outside the Victoria Institution school in the early afternoon as the Japanese military officers were driven in with a few interpreters and a guard of Indian soldiers. The crowd jeered and booed on seeing the Japanese, who maintained a calm and unperturbed demeanour[21].

Lieutenant General Ouvry Lindfield Roberts, who had previously commanded the 23rd Indian Division in Burma and was now General Officer Commanding (GOC) of the 34th Indian Corps in Malaya, would take the formal surrender. He arrived with Captain E.T. Cooper of the Royal Navy; the Earl of Bandon, Air Vice Marshal Sir Percy Ronald Gardner; and several other military representatives.

The Guard of Honour, comprising men of the 2nd Punjab regiment, was drawn up just outside the front entrance. After inspecting the guard, Roberts waited in a classroom near the hall as the Japanese officers entered the hall, bowing low to the Union Jack at the entrance. Two rows of tables had been arranged for the two groups of representatives. The Japanese were handed a copy of the surrender document and the interpreters explained the contents to them. The main fact was that this was an unconditional surrender. The Japanese nodded in agreement. At this point, Roberts and his fellow commanders entered the room and took their places at the other table, facing the Japanese.

> Lieutenant General Teizo Ishiguro, Commander in Chief of the Japanese 29th Army, Major General Naoichi Kawahara, Chief of Staff and staff officer Colonel G. Oguri faced the SEAC representatives.

> General Ishiguro used a brush to sign the document, followed by Roberts who inked it with his pen. The surrender was completed in 20 minutes and by 2.30pm, the event was over[22].

Outside the school, the crowd had become restless but a large group of British, Punjabi, Baluchi and Gurkha troops maintained order. Loud cheers greeted the British staff cars as they were driven out of the school premises onto Shaw Road (now Jalan Hang Tuah). The Japanese had to put up with loud jeering and jibes hurled at them by the local population[23].

General Roberts then proceeded to the Selangor Padang (now Dataran Merdeka) where at 3.00pm he took the salute at a Victory Parade and march-past in which Allied forces and units of the Malayan People's Anti-Japanese Army (MPAJA) took part. Taking the salute with him were Force 136 members Spencer and Davis, who by then had already moved from the jungle and set up their headquarters in Kuala Lumpur more than three weeks past.

These were followed by a ceremony for the surrender of swords and firearms, which had not taken place earlier due to Japanese refusal when the signing of the Singapore surrender took place on the *Sussex* on 4 September.

The surrender of swords ceremony for the Japanese troops in Kuala Lumpur eventually took place at the old airport at Sungei Besi on the outskirts of Kuala Lumpur on 14 September 1945. Finally on 22 February 1946, General Itagaki along with his chief of staff and 14 other Japanese generals were brought up from Singapore to Kuala Lumpur and representing all Japanese troops in Malaya, surrendered their swords to Lieutenant General Sir Frank Walter Messervy, GOC, Malaya Command, at another ceremony held in Victoria Institution[24].

So Japanese dominance in Southeast Asia came to an end, 1,374 days after the first bombs fell over Singapore in the early hours of 8 February 1942, marking the beginning of the war in the Pacific. However, the end of the war did not mean the end of the challenges and problems faced by the peoples of Malaya and Singapore. The end of the war marked only the beginning of the struggles for independence that would mark the next two decades in the region.

From Mountbatten's remarks in the chamber and the way the ceremony played itself out at the Padang, it appeared obvious the surrender ceremony at the Municipal Building was being staged to save British face and pride. The loss of Singapore had been a devastating blow to British pride. Now was the time to erase memories of that ignominious defeat on 15 February 1942 when Lieutenant General Arthur E. Percival surrendered close to 100,000 British and Commonwealth troops to the 35,000-strong advancing Japanese army. Thus, the 12 September surrender ceremony was significant purely as a tool to restore British pride and status among the local population.

Just as Holland had insisted on having white faces at the parade, the 12 September surrender was meant to show the superiority of the British empire in race and force within the region. However, this had already been achieved with the effective surrender of Japanese troops in Singapore and the end of the communal violence with the signing of the Surrender Agreement on board the *Sussex* on 4 September. The landing of ZIPPER forces with the unofficial recapture of the key towns and cities in Malaya meant the British were back in control. As such, the 12 September ceremony had little, or only ceremonial, impact on the subject races. Peace had been restored in Singapore by 5 September and in most of Malaya by 11 September.

If it was hoped that the surrender ceremony would restore a pre-war acceptance of complete British superiority in Malaya, this was all but dashed less than a year later when plans for the Colonial Office's Malayan Union faltered, and was replaced with a federation. Within the next three years, the beginnings of a 12-year communist insurgency to overthrow British rule in Malaya took shape.

Endnotes

1 *Letter of Proceedings, 18 September 1945, ADM116/5562.* London: The National Archives. 3.

2 Ibid. 2.

3 *Singapore Broadcast 31 1130 IST, GSI (s)/1, 31 August 1945, WO203/2435.* London: The National Archives.

4 Munby, R. *SACSEA Surrender Mission to Singapore, 87/34/1.* London: The Imperial War Museum.

5 Ibid.

6 Ibid. 9.

7 *Ammentorp, Steen. "Biography of Yaichiro Shibata, Imperial Japanese Navy". The Generals of WWII.* [Internet]. Accessed 4 February 2005. Available from: <http://homepage2.nifty.com/nishidah/e/index.htm>.

8 *Letter of Proceedings – Operation TIDERACE, 18 September 1945, ADM116/5562.* The National Archives, London. 8.

9 "Japanese in Malaya Surrender in Singapore". *The Straits Times*, 13 September 1945. 1.

10 Ibid.

11 "Smooth Reoccupation of Singapore". *The Times*, 8 September 1945. 4.

12 Ibid.

13 *Instrument of Surrender of Japanese Forces in Southeast Asia, COS (45)229, 26 September 1945, CAB122/494.* London: The National Archives. Appendix A.

14 Munby, R. *SACSEA Surrender Mission to Singapore, 87/34/1.* London: The Imperial War Museum.

15 "Japanese in Malaya Surrender in Singapore". *The Straits Times*, 13 September 1945. 1.

16 Keay, John. *Last Post: The End of Empire in the Far East.* London: John Murray, 1997. 214.

17 Baker, C.M.S. *Personal Papers, 96/34/11.* London: Imperial War Museum, 1996.

18 "Obituary: The Rev. Guy Armstrong". *Daily Telegraph*, 15 January 2003.

19 Australian National Flag Association. "Timeline". *Australian National Flag Association.* [Internet]. Accessed 14 August 2004. Available from: <http://www.australianflag.org.au/timeline.php>.

20 *Report of Proceedings – Commander-in-Chief, East Indies Station's letter, No.3001/E.I.15002/45, 17 September 1945, ADM199/168.* London: The National Archives. 15.

21 Chung, Chee Min. "The Japanese Surrendered at the V.I. – TWICE!". *The Victoria Institution Web Page.* [Internet]. Accessed 14 August 2004. Available from: <http://www.viweb.freehosting.net/japsurr.htm>.

22 Ibid.

23 Ibid.

24 Ibid.

Chapter 9

Locations

The previous chapters in this book have dealt with the events surrounding the end of the war in Malaya and Singapore. This chapter deals with the locations in Singapore where many of these events occurred – locations that have become inextricably linked to our collective memory of that period and time.

The sites of these surrender events are sacred to many in the region and beyond. Although some are used for new purposes and others abandoned to time and decay, these locations remain crucial in telling the story of the end of the Second World War in Singapore. There exist many more locations, from the beaches at Morib and Port Dickson, to Victoria Institution in Kuala Lumpur, that are significant in marking the end of the war in the region. However, the stories of those locations will be told at another time. The ones that are mentioned here will focus on sites in Singapore, the crown colony that was the location of the final ceremonial Japanese surrender, and the effective centre of the Japanese forces in the Southern Region[1].

City Hall

The site where Lord Louis Mountbatten accepted the Japanese surrender of Southeast Asia, the Municipal Building in Singapore (later renamed City Hall upon independence), has long been associated with historic events on the island. Built in the 1920s on the site of the Europa Hotel, the Municipal Building was home to the Singapore municipality. The council chambers in the middle of the building first hosted the council

The City Hall: The backdrop to most civic events in the city, City Hall remains an iconic symbol of colonial Singapore. Used as municipal offices by the British and the Japanese, the buildings is most remembered as the background for the Japanese ceremonial surrender on 12 September 1945.

and later the legislative meetings of the colony. At the onset of the Second World War, the Padang, or field, in front of the building was the site of many Singapore Volunteer Corp parades and training sessions. On 16 February 1942, a day after Singapore fell, the new Japanese rulers ordered all European civilians in Singapore to gather on the Padang. After waiting there for several hours in the burning sun, they were force-marched into captivity at Changi. It was a desperate sight as women and children, many of whom were injured, struggled to keep up with the other civilians during the march. The Padang marked the beginning of internment for the European population in Singapore.

During the occupation, the Japanese municipality, or Syonan Tokubetsu, took over the building and the Padang was used by the Japanese military to punish locals. The Padang was also the site of an Indian National Army parade to mark the arrival of Subhas Chandra Bose in July 1943 as the new leader of the Indian independence movement in Southeast Asia. The Indian independence movement held several mass rallies at the Padang and another major INA parade was held when Japanese Prime Minister Hideki Tojo visited Singapore later that month. By the end of the war, the Japanese had forced locals to dig numerous trenches all over the field as air raid precautions, with barbed wire fences set up on the field. In the post-war period, the Padang became the centre of civic events, where in 1959, Singapore's first prime minister, Lee Kuan Yew, and the nation's Yang Di-Pertuan Negara, Yusof Bin Ishak, proclaimed the creation of the State of Singapore. The same field would in 1966 bear witness to the first National Day Parade, marking the birth of the Republic of Singapore a year earlier. Today, City Hall and the Padang remain bold reminders of the country's colonial past and of its more recent role in the independence of the republic.

Kranji War Memorial

The top of Kranji Hill in northwest Singapore was the site of a British military field hospital during the last weeks of the battle for southern Johor and Singapore. A cemetery was established by the British here as the main Christian cemetery was far away and there was no manpower to transport the bodies for burial at the Bidadari Christian Cemetery in Aljunied. During the occupation, the hospital was used as a prisoner-of-war (POW) camp and more bodies were added to the cemetery. At the end of the war, it was decided that Kranji would be turned into the main Allied cemetery on the island. The Commonwealth War Graves Commission (CWGC) redeveloped the site and today the Kranji War Cemetery is the final resting place of more than 4,000 Allied soldiers who gave their lives in the Second World War.

The Kranji War Memorial lies in the northern part of Singapore island, overlooking the Straits of Johor, also known as the Straits of Tebrau. It consists of war and military graves, memorials and a state cemetery. Although the cemetery is closed, a few plots remain for veterans who, having fought during the Malayan Campaign and/or survived the Japanese occupation, want to be buried with their comrades.

> The main feature of the Kranji War Cemetery is the Singapore Memorial. The memorial was constructed as a tribute to the men and women of the armed forces of the British commonwealth and empire who have no known grave. One of the memorials is dedicated to 789 British Indian army soldiers who died during the Malayan Campaign and were cremated. Others remembered here are those who also perished during the Malayan Campaign and in Indonesia as well as in subsequent captivity. These include a large number who died during the building of the Siam-Burma Death Railway, and also many who died at sea while being transported from Malaya into prison camps elsewhere. The memorial also pays tribute to men of the Commonwealth air forces who died during operations across Southeast Asia. This includes those who retreated from northern to southern Malaya, then to Sumatra and finally to Java, as well as those who helped liberate Burma[2].

The central avenue of the cemetery is built on a hill and slopes gently from the Stone of Remembrance near the entrance up to the Cross of Sacrifice, beyond which a short flight of steps lead to the terrace on top of the hill, on which the Singapore Memorial stands.

The Singapore Memorial has a flat roof that is supported by 12 columns, which are inscribed with names of the war dead. A great 80-foot pylon crowned by a star rises above the central axis of the roof. On a curved panel at the foot of this pylon are displayed these words[3]:

> On the walls of this memorial are recorded the names of twenty-four thousand soldiers and airmen of many races united in service to the British Crown who gave their lives in Malaya and neighbouring lands and seas and in the air over Southern and Eastern Asia and the Pacific but to whom the fortune of war denied the customary rites accorded to their comrades in death.

An additional inscription, "They Died for All Free Men", is engraved in Hindi, Urdu, Gurmukhi, Chinese and Malay.

At one end of the Singapore Memorial is a small, separate memorial to the 107 men who died in captivity and are buried in a single grave on the grounds of the Singapore General Hospital. At the other end, a similar memorial bears the names of 255 men buried in isolated places in Malaya, where their graves cannot be maintained.

Also buried at Kranji are the remains of Lieutenant Colonel Ivan Lyon, the daring leader of Force 136's Operation JAYWICK, which saw the destruction of more than 50,000 tons of Japanese shipping in Singapore harbour in 1943. A similar operation in 1944, codenamed RIMAU, ended in the death of Lyon and his team, five of whom were missing in action until 1994, when the remains of two were found. A solemn ceremony was held at Kranji two years later to inter Sub Lieutenant Gregor Riggs and Sergeant Colin Cameron with their fallen SOE comrades. The remains of the three men of Lyon's team still listed as missing in action, Lieutenant B.P. Reymond, Corporal C.M. Craft and Able Seaman F.W.L. Marsh, have yet to be found.

To the west of the main War Cemetery lie the remains of Commonwealth troops and their dependants who were buried in the Ulu Pandan and Pasir Panjang Military Cemeteries. When the British pulled out of Singapore in 1971, the lands on which these cemeteries were located were handed back to the Singapore Government. As the government needed the land for future development, the CWGC decided to accept all the graves for reburial at Kranji. This was done with the exception of the graves of stillborn babies, belonging mainly to those of the Gurkha troops in Singapore. These graves would be combined into a single mass grave at Kranji. This mass grave then ended up reinterred with those remains from Ulu Pandan and Pasir Panjang that could not be identified. In a note to the Foreign Office in 1972, the CWGC was amenable to the shifting of the remains:

> The spare ground at Kranji on the west side above the Caretaker's Quarters slopes away to the west and it would seem that a very satisfactory cemetery could be established here with entry from an un-made up road coming in from the south west behind the new State Cemetery. This roadway already runs over part of the Commission's land on its route to a rather ramshackle house just outside the SW corner of the Commission's boundary.
>
> Fencing and provisions of suitable gates and the siting of the Celtic Cross feature, now in Pasir Panjang, should not prove difficult and there is already a fence (with a small service gate), with a hedge inside, running along the war cemetery side[4].

Today, the Singapore State Cemetery sits next to the War Cemetery. The republic's first president, Yusof Ishak, and his successor, Benjamin Henry Sheares, are buried here. Groups of school children are often brought up to the Kranji War Cemetery, to show them what the previous generations had given up for future Singaporeans. On 15 February (Fall of Singapore), 25 April (ANZAC Day) and 11 November (Armistice Day) every year, memorial services are held at the cemetery to remember the sacrifices made by the few for the many.

Kranji War Cemetery: Most of the remains of the Allied War dead were centralised at the Kranji War Memorial by 1946 with the Commonwealth War Graves Commission building a large complex to house the remains. Today, Singapore's State Cemetery is located next to the War Cemetery.

Changi Prison

A trip to the Changi Prison complex is crucial for anyone who visits Singapore and wants to have an understanding of what happened to the colonial masters and parts of the civilian population during the Japanese occupation.

The story of Changi would fill several thick volumes. It was earmarked in 1927 to become a base for the Royal Artillery batteries, covering the eastern approaches to the Straits of Johor as part of the British defensive strategy for Singapore. However, the whole Changi area went through stops and starts in development from 1927 to 1941 as a result of political indecision and budget cuts at Whitehall.

With the fall of Singapore on 15 February 1942, the Japanese decided to turn the Changi complex into a huge POW camp.

Many do not realise that the prison, which has come to symbolise Changi, had not initially been used to hold POWs. Built in 1936, the new prison in Changi was meant to house 800 civilian prisoners. Shortly after the Japanese conquest of Singapore, the European community was gathered on the Padang and force-marched to Changi. The prison became home to mainly white, civilian internees – 3,000 men, and 400 women and children. For two years, they endured the brutality of their captors within the prison's stone walls. It was not until May 1944 that they were ordered out to make way for POWs.

Changi Prison: Prisoners marched into the compound behind these walls during the Second World War faced unimaginable hardship. Those liberated during the reoccupation were often extremely thin and malnourished.

Allied POWs had been located in various barracks throughout Changi, forcing close to 20,000 troops to live in abject squalor and hunger. As there was not enough space, crude tents and huts were fashioned to house this defeated army. Beginning early 1944, thousands more prisoners returned to the Changi area following the completion of the Siam-Burma railway.

The civilians were moved out of Changi Prison into an internment camp at Sime Road and 5,000 POWs were moved into the vacated cells, which were filthy and foul-smelling. Each cell had a concrete block in the centre that served as a bed for one prisoner. Two more prisoners slept on the floor on either side. One small window gave a little light while a hole in the floor served as a toilet. A further 12,000 POWs were concentrated in the surrounding area of the prison, living in camps made up of *attap* huts and rough accommodation. The Outram Road Jail was used as a punishment camp[5].

In addition to building the Siam-Burma Railway, many POWs from Changi were also forced to labour for two years to build the Changi airstrip for the Japanese, whose planes first started using the airstrip in 1944. It was very hard work in the searing heat as the men flattened mangrove swamps and built a rudimentary tarmac made of earth. Working 10 to 12 hours a day, suffering from starvation and disease, many died building the precursor to today's Changi International Airport.

By early August 1945, it was clear that the Japanese were losing as secret radios in the camps relayed news of Allied victories in the Western and Pacific theatres.

When Japan announced its unconditional surrender on 15 August 1945, POW work parties began returning to Singapore from other destinations, eager to return home. By early September, more than 17,000 men were congregated in and around the Changi prison compound. At about the same time, medicines and medics were parachuted in to assist the suffering men.

Changi continues to be a very significant reminder of man's inhumanity toward man. Although the main prison will be torn down by the end of 2005, the entry gate through which thousands of Second World War prisoners marched into Changi, never again to leave, will be preserved as a reminder of the grim days of the occupation.

The Japanese Cemetery

The Japanese Cemetery along Chuan Hoe Avenue was founded in 1891 as a burial ground that, until 1947, was exclusively Japanese. Almost 1,000 of early Singapore's Japanese community leaders and members are buried at the Shakkyozan Nihonji[6].

The Japanese Cemetery at Chuan Hoe Avenue holds the ashes of almost all Japanese troops who died during and after the end of the war.

During the Japanese occupation, the cemetery continued to be used for civilian Japanese burials while the Japanese military administration built two shrines, the Syonan Jinjya near MacRitchie Reservoir and the Syonan Chureito on Bukit Batok, to hold the ashes of Japanese soldiers who died in the Malayan Campaign and the battle for Singapore.

At the Chureito on Bukit Batok, a large pillar was erected with a shrine dedicated to the war dead. The Japanese also gave permission to British POWs to build a small wooden cross behind the pillar to pay tribute to the British and Allied troops who died in the Malayan Campaign and the fall of Singapore. When the British recaptured Singapore, sappers blew up the two shrines and the consolidated ashes were dumped at the Japanese cemetery.

The question subsequently arose as to who would be responsible for the remains of Japanese soldiers who died during the war and the remains of Japanese surrendered personnel who died before they could be repatriated to Japan. There was also concern over what would happen to the ashes of Japanese war criminals who were to be executed.

In a flurry of letters between the British Foreign Office, Commonwealth Office and War Office, no one could decide what to do with the remains or who would pay for the maintenance of the remains. The Foreign Office was of the view that the Japanese Government would have to bear the full cost:

> The limit of British responsibility in respect of any Japanese 'war graves' would appear to be physical maintenance, which would presumably be at the expense of the Japanese Government. Such maintenance, I suppose, would be on a scale commensurate with the

> amount of money which the Japanese were prepared to pay. If, to take the extreme case, the Japanese Government declared that they had no interest in the graves at all, and were not prepared to pay anything, we should no longer be under any moral obligation to see that the "graves... were treated with respect and suitably maintained".
> At the present moment the Japanese Government are not, I think, in a position to give us any foreign currency in exchange for services in respect of the graves. By the time the Peace Treaty is signed, there will presumably be some arrears to collect. I do not know whether this will amount to anything substantial.
>
> If it is desired to recover the expenses in question, it would seem to be desirable to ensure, as soon as possible, that the Japanese are aware that a claim will be made. This could, of course, be notified to them through the Supreme Commander for the Allied Powers in Tokyo. It is just possible that it might be thought worth covering the question in the Peace Treaty, by some general clause making it clear that the Japanese Government must be responsible for all past and future expenses in connexion (*sic*) with the maintenance of graves of J.S.P. (Japanese Surrendered Personnel) in Allied territory; and the same considerations presumably apply to the graves of Japanese who died during the occupation. I presume whichever Department undertakes the immediate responsibility of paying the caretakers would undertake to make suggestions for any such clause in the Peace Treaty which they might deem necessary[7].

As a result of this indecision at Whitehall and the inability to get the Japanese Government to commit funds, the local Japanese community along with the Singapore municipal authorities contributed funds for a very simple mass grave at the Japanese Cemetery. It was then that the ashes of more than 10,000 Japanese war dead from MacRitchie and Bukit Batok were deposited under two markers at the Japanese cemetery. Also interred there were the remains of 200 Japanese war criminals tried and executed in Singapore between 1946 and 1948. The Japanese Association in Singapore later contributed funds to landscape and build granite pillars over the tombs.

As mentioned in the previous chapter, Field Marshal Count Hisaichi Terauchi, commander-in-chief of the Japanese Southern Army, had suffered a stroke just before the Japanese surrender and was unable to sign the surrender document in Singapore on 12 September 1945 due to his weakened state. Although he did finally surrender himself and his two swords to Lord Louis Mountbatten in November 1945, Terauchi did not

SHRINE TO OUR WAR HEROES IN SYONAN-TO

Commemoration Of Battle For Singapore

(Domei)

CONSTRUCTION work has been started on the Syonan Shrine which will serve as a commemoration of the fall of Singapore into Nipponese hands.

It is also learned that a memorial dedicated to those Nipponese soldiers who sacrificed their lives in the battle for Singapore is also being constructed as well as other landmarks where our forces made successful crossings over the Johore Straits.

The Japanese Cemetery: The remains of Field Marshal Count Terauchi were buried beneath this tombstone, in a remote corner of the cemetery. It remains well tended close to 60 years after his death. On the right is a newspaper article published in the Syonan Shimbun *marking the erection of the two shrines in Syonan (Singapore) and another on Johor Baru's esplanade facing Singapore.*

The Syonan Chureito: The Japanese built a shrine on Bukit Batok to commemorate those who fell during the fierce fighting in Bukit Timah in the battle for Singapore. Allied POWs built a Cross behind the Japanese shrine to mark their dead as well. On reoccupation, the Allied forces blew up the shrine and the Syonan Jinjya shrine at MacRitchie, consolidating all Japanese remains at the cemetery in Chuan Hoe Avenue.

live very long after. When he died in 1946, his cremated remains were buried in a separate shrine at the Japanese Cemetery, where it is one of the most well-known graves.

The cemetery became a memorial park in 1987 and is currently maintained by the Singapore Japanese Association with donations from the Japanese community.

The Civilian Monument

Known affectionately as the "Chopsticks" monument due to its long, pillar-like structures, the Civilian Monument in downtown Singapore was built only in 1967. However, the history behind the setting up of the monument is tied to the end of the war and to Singapore's rocky road to independence.

In the late 1950s and early 1960s, as Singapore began redeveloping its land to meet the needs of its population and industry, contractors and workmen began finding huge mass graves all over the island. The mass graves were filled with the bodies of Chinese civilians who were killed by the Japanese in the opening days of the occupation. In what was known as the *Sook Ching* Operation, thousands of Chinese who were believed to have collaborated with the British before the war and those who appeared 'educated' or likely to put up a struggle against Japanese rule were rounded up at concentration points throughout the island. They were then taken in trucks to remote spots on the island where they were made to dig and stand in their own graves while the Japanese troops bayoneted or shot them where they stood.

The discovery of numerous mass graves created an enormous outcry among the Chinese community in Singapore and Malaya who demanded that the Japanese compensate them for the 'blood debt' that was owed to the peoples in the region. However, by this time, the Japanese Government had already signed a treaty with the Allied powers specifying that a full and complete compensation had been made. Consequently, in 1963, the Japanese Government took the position that no other compensation could be considered.

In and of itself, the issue could have been resolved quickly as, privately, the Japanese Government was willing to pay a certain amount of compensation. However, the Chinese Chamber of Commerce felt that any offer by the Japanese would have to match the 'donation' of 50 million Straits Settlements dollars that the Chinese community in Singapore had been forced to make to the Japanese during the occupation.

To complicate matters, the Japanese consul general in Singapore, Tanaka, did not appear to have the authority to settle the dispute on behalf of his government. However, the biggest complication was the fact that,

The Civilian Memorial: This memorial has come to symbolise the suffering of the general populace in Singapore during the Occupation. Its creation helped to repay a 'blood debt' that was demanded from the Japanese in compensation for the sufferings of a generation.

in 1963, Singapore was supposed to merge with peninsular Malaya, Sabah and Sarawak (British Borneo) as well as Brunei to become an independent and sovereign state in the Malaysian federation.

The day of merger, Malaysia Day, was, by the agreement of all parties involved, to fall on 31 August 1963. However, the Malaysian prime minister, Tunku Abdul Rahman, after meeting with the Indonesian and Philippine presidents between 30 July and 5 August, had agreed to postpone Malaysia Day to 16 September in order to give the United Nations time to ascertain the popular will in the Borneo territories on the proposition to join the Malaysian federation. The then prime minister of Singapore Lee Kuan Yew and chief ministers designate of Sabah and Sarawak were not consulted on this decision and as a result all three called on the Tunku to set up Malaysia on 31 August. Regardless, the Malaysian prime minister decided that Malaysia Day would be postponed to 16 September 1963[8].

Thus, Lee, who was in the midst of a political struggle with the Malayan Communist Party (MCP) for control of the hearts and minds of the populace and to garner support for the upcoming merger with Malaysia, declared Singapore's *de facto* independence on 31 August 1963. He said the PAP government would hold Singapore in trust until the formation of Malaysia. Lee called for unity and pledged the state's loyalty to the central Malaysian government[9]. In the same speech, Lee decided to turn the heat on the Japanese by announcing that as the Japanese had yet to settle the issue of the blood debt, the Singapore Government would now also take on the foreign relations portfolio of the state until Malaysia Day in an attempt to resolve the blood debt issue[10].

A day before Lee's speech, he had written to the British Colonial Secretary, saying that:

> ... one of the steps towards independence which he wishes to announce at a mass rally on 31 August is that Her Majesty's Government have

> delegated to the Government of Singapore complete powers in the matter of foreign relations "to the extent and in order that the Government of Singapore can between 31 August and 16 September settle the question of the nature and substance of the Japanese gesture of atonement for atrocities"[11].

The British Commissioner General for Southeast Asia, and later High Commissioner to Singapore, Sir George Nigel Douglas-Hamilton, the Lord Selkirk, cabled Whitehall that Lee's request would have a disastrous effect on British relations with Japan:

> If Lee attempts to turn the heat on, the Japanese will refuse to negotiate under pressure and will simply stand on the legal position under the Peace Treaty until things cool down. There would be no prospect of the early settlement which would be in everyone's interest.
>
> ... The fallacy in Lee's request lies of course in the fact that he has already for some time been exercising the powers he now suggests we should delegate as from 31 August, and indeed in his speech on 25 August gave some account of the way he had been doing so...
>
> ... If our position were distorted in any way by Lee in public utterances suggesting that he had received new powers, we would feel obliged to issue the statement ourselves to clear the record[12].

Three days later, Lord Selkirk submitted his report to London to explain the strategy adopted by the Singapore Government in negotiations with the Japanese:

> The Singapore claim against the Japanese for atrocities committed during the period of occupation is naturally getting a great deal of public support and whilst the leaders are all prepared to say privately they want a settlement, they are clearly not going to take a strong line advocating a limit to the amount which should be considered reasonable for Japan to pay.
>
> Lee is playing a very equivocable game and I am not surprised to learn that the Japanese view him with suspicion. The truth is that he wants to gain political kudos for himself by making a favourable settlement with the Japanese whilst he knows anything he agrees to will be denounced by his political opponents as totally inadequate. I believe he is genuinely out to get a settlement within this political setting.

> In the meantime, Lee has been very inaccessible to the Japanese Consul-General, Tanaka, and I have had the utmost difficulty in seeing him myself. He has been discourteous in public to the Japanese Consul-General. Although the communists may be trying to exploit the situation, the feeling among the Chinese is widespread; indeed hardly a family cannot recall a relative who disappeared...
>
> ... I have explained to the Singapore Ministers that there is no chance of blackmailing the Japanese Government. If they do not make a sufficient effort, they may find themselves with a continuing disagreement without any compensation. Lee is anxious to settle this himself with the Japanese Government; so far we have given him every chance to do so. I would not advocate our taking an open part in any negotiations. I believe that would complicate, rather than facilitate, matters but I have got to say that I think it is going to be very difficult to make a quick settlement below the figure of about $(Malayan) 50,000,000. This was the amount of the forced loan which the Japanese raised from the Chinese Chamber of Commerce during the occupation[13].

Speaking to one of the Japanese Consuls in Singapore, Lord Selkirk underlined the difficult position faced by the Singapore Government:

> We told the Consul that in our view it seemed increasingly unlikely that the Japanese Government would be able to achieve a settlement within the figure of $5 million; that however projects might be dressed up, they would be bound to be evaluated in monetary terms by the Chinese Chamber of Commerce; and that in the end they would have to be prepared to bargain seriously over the Chamber of Commerce figure of $50 Million[14].

However, more importantly, the Singapore Government had upped the ante on 3 September by asking the British legation to inform all visa-issuing authorities (until the merger occurred, visas for Singapore were supposed to be issued by British diplomatic posts around the world) that all Japanese visa applications were to be referred to Singapore. Lord Selkirk noted that from 16 September 1963 onwards, immigration would be a matter for the federal government in Kuala Lumpur but it was likely "to be some months before the federal government assumes control in Singapore. Until that time the status quo will be maintained and visa applications will continue in practice to be a matter for the Singapore Government"[15].

Pressure on Lee and the PAP government was also mounting, not only on the issue of Japanese reparations but also on whether Singapore would actually become a part of Malaysia. The PAP government was poised to hold local elections in Singapore five days after Malaysia Day[16]. The United Malay National Organisation (UMNO), the main political party in the Alliance coalition that made up the federal government in Kuala Lumpur, clearly wanted to break the PAP's control over the island. The communal parties in the Alliance, the Malaysian Indian Congress (MIC) and the Malaysian Chinese Association (MCA), had formed Singaporean versions of the mainland coalition to contest in the elections and UMNO clearly wanted their communal cousins to win. Although Lee had pledged Singapore's loyalty to the federal government in public, Lord Selkirk noted that he was actually willing to unilaterally declare Singapore's independence in September 1963:

> I saw Lee Kuan Yew this morning when he showed considerable intellectual arrogance, repeatedly referring to the stupidity (reference deleted) and of the Japanese Consul-General Tanaka...
>
> ... He still professes to be very anxious and determined to set up Malaysia but is worried whether it will hold together and insists on agreement being reached on the remaining conditions of Singapore's entry, which are now being discussed in Kuala Lumpur. If he does not get this settled by 12 September (nomination day for the Singapore elections), he will fight the election on programme for Singapore's independence and immediately ask for recognition by a number of countries as from 16 September. I did not discuss all that was involved in a declaration of independence but called on his co-operation (*sic*) in arriving at agreement with the Federation on the outstanding points. This he was willing to do and suggested that Goh Keng Swee should conduct these negotiations when he came back from Bangkok on 6 September instead of himself.
>
> He also promised to hold off anything which might damage relations during the period until 12 September but will attack the Malays wholeheartedly thereafter. He claims that if he does not get the points he has in mind, it will be because of the Malay intention to crush Singapore and he would be ashamed to accept the responsibility of entering Malaysia on these terms[17].

Lord Selkirk noted that Lee was fighting a battle for reparations and a larger battle for merger, both of which had a great impact on the way Singaporeans would vote in the coming elections. In dealing with reparations, it was clear that Lee was frustrated:

> In the course of my conversation with Lee Kuan Yew this morning, he referred to the Japanese problem and said he had done his utmost to lay it down for 15 months. But there was so little response from the Japanese that he had had to put himself at the head of the movement. He complained of some reference he said emanated from Japan that this matter would more easily be settled after Malaysia. The result of this has been that all parts of Malaysia have started agitating for Japanese compensation.
>
> I warned him of the danger of antagonising Japan which might lose (*sic*) their support for Malaysia at the United Nations and also of the danger of the communists getting hold of the whole movement, to which he agreed.
>
> He clearly found it very difficult to get on with the present Japanese Consul-General Tanaka, and I would strongly recommend that the Japanese Government should be encouraged to send someone here of stronger personality and with a better command of English if these negotiations are to be brought to fruition. At the present time, I do not judge the Prime Minister considers it worthwhile giving Tanaka a proper chance to do his job[18].

In the end, Singapore did join the federation on Malaysia Day, only to become an independent country two years later on 9 August 1965. As for the issue of reparations, Japan sent a new ambassador to Singapore but the negotiations continued long after the 16 September deadline Lee had set. It was not until 1966 that Japan and Singapore finally resolved the issue with a significant contribution made by the Japanese that resulted in the creation of the Civilian Monument. The monument was inaugurated on 15 February 1967, 25 years to the day that Singapore fell to the Japanese.

Even then, there was still controversy. The famous Chinese poet Pan Shou had been asked to write an epitaph for the Civilian Monument. The epitaph, written in Mandarin (translated into English and reproduced below), was scathing in its attack on the Japanese but clearly represented the feelings of the local Chinese community. However, the epitaph never saw the light of day and has long been forgotten, relegated as a curiosity in academic journals and books. Nonetheless, it remains a strong and poignant summation of the horrors that faced the Chinese community in Singapore and the desire for future generations to learn from it. Perhaps it will one day be installed at the location for which it was written[19]:

THIS MEMORIAL MARKS AN UNPRECEDENTED TRAGEDY IN THE HISTORY OF SINGAPORE

The occupation of Singapore by the Japanese Army between 15 February 1942 and 18 August 1945 was a dark and tragic epoch.

The people of Singapore were subjected to lashing, humiliation, enslavement and extortion. Under the pretext of "mass screening" (*Sook Ching*), the Japanese Army massacred tens of thousands of non-combatants in secrecy. God was ridiculed. Civilisation was buried, and the dignity of mankind trampled. Everywhere, tears flowed. Everywhere, blood splattered. And everywhere, terror reigned.

In January 1962, some of the remains of the civilian victims were first unearthed. This led to the setting-up of a committee by the Singapore Chinese Chamber of Commerce for conducting further investigation, for exhumation, as well as for the planning of the construction of a mass grave and a memorial for the remains. In July the same year, a permit for exhumation was obtained from the Authority. In March 1963, the Singapore Government allotted a four acre plot of land for the site of this Memorial Park. During the last four years, more and more remains of these victims were exhumed. In the meantime, as a result of the widespread response received from the public and the encouragement from the government who contributed to the Memorial Building Fund on the basis of a-dollar-to-a-dollar from the public, this memorial is (*sic*) eventually completed.

Now this memorial stands towering over the Equator, gazing at the ever-changing scenes of Southeast Asia and the world at large.

Now this memorial stands aloft at this hub of communication between the Eastern and the Western Hemispheres, beckoning friendly day and night to the passers-by of Southeast Asia and the world.

No one knows the exact number of our compatriots of the different races massacred during the dark days of the Occupation. Although countless sets of bones are already buried under the podium, it is most probable that they might represent only a fraction of the civilian victims massacred, whose number might be five or ten times greater. No one can list all our multiracial compatriots who were killed in the massacre. They deserve to be posthumously honoured as loyal, brave, virtuous and righteous men who have sacrificed their lives long before the independence of Singapore and should thus be enshrined in the spiritual foundation of the country.

The four towering columns of this memorial symbolise loyalty, bravery, virtue and righteousness, traits of which are reflected in the traditional harmony and solidarity of the multiracial, multicultural and multi-religious society of Singapore.

This memorial stands to prove that the people of Singapore were able to hold their own together in adversity and it also signifies their ever-readiness to share the common prosperity of the country in future.

Let this memorial echo the voice of the people of Singapore.

War is evil. Peace is sacred. The big and the strong nations want to live, so do the small and weak ones. The big and strong ones who oppress the small and weak ones will never escape condemnation and punishment on the final judgement of history. However, the best policy is to redress grievances amicably and not to generate enmity. The people of Singapore are always with the peoples of the world, including the people of Japan, who are peace-loving and who oppose aggression, imperialism and colonialism.

May the souls of the civilian victims of the Japanese Occupation rest in eternal peace and accept this epitaph dedicated to them by the people of Singapore.

"Tears stained flower crimson like
And blood tainted the blue ocean
Ye wandering souls who rise with the tide
Shall guard this young emerging nation."

The INA Monument

Set up by exiled Indian patriots with the help of the Indian community in Southeast Asia and support from the Japanese army, the Indian National Army (INA) was part of the Indian independence movement in Southeast Asia. The independence struggle against the British in India led many in the Indian diaspora to look for ways and means to liberate their country.

Before the start of the war, the Japanese were already encouraging Indian nationalism. During the Malayan Campaign, they recruited former British soldier Captain Mohan Singh to become commander of the newly created

INA. Although the INA was received warmly by the Indian community in Malaya, political infighting between Rash Behari Bose, an exiled Indian patriot in Japan, and Singh, as well as the Japanese demand to control the INA led to the dissolution of the first INA and Singh's detention.

The INA was resurrected under Subhas Chandra Bose, a staunch Indian nationalist and former president of the Indian National Congress. Bose had been in exile in Germany, where he had set up an Indian liberation army (Azad Hind Fauj) to fight alongside the Germans. After he grew disillusioned with German führer Adolf Hitler, Bose joined up with the Japanese in 1943, taking on the mantle of the Supreme Commander of the INA. Addressed as *Netaji,* or "Leader", Bose arrived in Singapore in July 1943 and within a month, had mobilised thousands of Indians in the region to fight for the freedom of their motherland. Through the Indian Independence League, Bose began to create a base of support and funds for the INA. On 21 October 1943, in the cinema hall at the Cathay Building, Bose declared the creation of the Free India Provisional Government (FIPG). With this act, Bose created a government and army in exile that would take over the running of India once the British were ousted by the Japanese.

Early Japanese successes meant that Bose could raise the tricolour Indian flag over Port Blair in the Andaman islands, the first Indian territory to come under the rule of the government-in-exile. However, this turned out to be just a symbol as the Japanese were the ones who wielded the real power. Not satisfied with such small wins, Bose wanted the INA to spearhead the fight against the British in Burma and to be the first ones to reach Indian soil. Although the Japanese did manage to capture Manipur and the INA did raise their flag on Indian territory, these successes were short-lived as the British managed to rout the Japanese forces, forcing them to begin their retreat in late 1944. By early 1945, it was clear that the Japanese had lost the battle for Burma and the Japanese army was in retreat. Many INA soldiers died in the retreat, even though most had served in the rear, because of the confusion and chaos that reigned.

Reports of these losses meant that Bose needed to boost the morale of Indians in Malaya and Singapore. Using funds the Indian Independence League had begun to raise in late 1944, the INA Memorial was built.

On 8 July 1945, Bose laid the foundation stone for the Memorial to the Unknown Soldier of the INA, located on the Esplanade in Singapore, a few feet from the British Cenotaph dedicated to the war dead in the First World War.

The memorial consisted of three joined pillars, inscribed in Urdu with the words *Ittefaq* (Unity), *Itmad* (Faith) and *Kurbani* (Sacrifice). At the ceremony, Bose spoke passionately to the assembled troops:

> The future generations of Indians who will be born, not as slaves but as freemen, because of your colossal sacrifice, will bless your names and proudly proclaim to the world that you, their forebears, fought and suffered reverses in the battle of Manipur, Assam and Burma, but through temporary failure you paved the way to ultimate success and glory[20].

However, on the return of the Allies, the memorial was destroyed by sappers from the 5th Indian Division. In its place, the British Military Administration built a memorial to Lim Bo Seng. The INA Memorial was

The INA Memorial: Built by public contribution, the memorial located on the Esplanade was unveiled by Subhas Chandra Bose on 8 July 1945. It came to symbolise the sacrifices made by the Indian populace for the Indian Independence movement. On the return of the Allies, it was blown up. These are some of the very few photographs which exist of the memorial. A sketch of the memorial has been etched on a bronze plaque, near the Lim Bo Seng memorial, commemorating the building of the INA memorial.

forgotten for close to 50 years before the Singapore Information and the Arts Ministry began installing plaques marking important Second World War sites in Singapore in 1992. Although the plaque for the INA Memorial does not list the location of the memorial, it provides recognition of the sacrifices made by the Indian community in Southeast Asia for the cause of freedom in India.

The Cathay Building

Prior to the Second World War, the Cathay building was the tallest structure in Singapore. It was home to rich tycoons and provided office space to big businesses in Singapore and Malaya. The Cathay was one of the only air-conditioned buildings in Singapore and had a state-of-the-art cinema at its base. The Malayan Broadcasting Corporation had one of its studios in the building while the British military occupied some of its suites as a wireless transmitting station.

During the Malayan Campaign, the building also housed the offices of the British Ministry of Information. As the battle for Singapore drew nearer, a top-secret radar unit was set up in the building to help coordinate radar traffic from air bases around the island and filter it to the Gun Operations Room at the Battlebox in Fort Canning.

On 15 February 1942, as one of the preconditions of surrender to the Japanese, the British were instructed to raise a Japanese flag and a white flag above the Cathay Building for 10 minutes to signal British acceptance of the surrender terms. When the flag was raised, it was shot at by British units, forcing it to be pulled down quickly.

With the fall of Singapore, the Japanese began using the Cathay Building for their propaganda units and broadcasting station. On 21 October 1943, Subhas Chandra Bose proclaimed the creation of the Free India Provisional Government (FIPG) in the cinema auditorium of the building. The very same auditorium was also the scene of frenzied discussions, following which the FIPG declared war on the United States of America and the United Kingdom.

Upon the reoccupation of Singapore by the British in September 1945, the Cathay Building was taken over as the headquarters of the supreme allied commander, Southeast Asia (SACSEA). Reverting to its owners in the late 1940s, the Cathay was refurbished and became an important location for post-war businesses in Singapore.

Today, the cinema and office buildings have been torn down and all that remains is the façade. Nonetheless, the site of the Cathay Building will always remain an important reminder of Singapore's not-so-distant wartime past.

Endnotes

1 Although the 29th Japanese Army had shifted its headquarters to Taiping in early 1945 in preparation for the expected Allied assault on Malaya, Itagaki as Commander of the 7th Area Army, which included the 29th Army, remained in Singapore.

2 Commonwealth War Graves Commission, The. "The Singapore Memorial: Introduction to the Register". *The War Dead of the British Commonwealth and Empire; The Register of the Names of Those who Fell in the 1939–1945 War and have No Known Grave.* London: The Commonwealth War Graves Commission, 1957. 17.

3 Ibid.

4 *DFE's Visit to Eastern and Pacific Regions (Delhi, Singapore, Melbourne) April 1972 – Singapore 11 April, 22 May 1972, FCO24/1291.* London: The National Archives.

5 Cooper, Carol. "South East Asia Under Japanese Occupation: The Story of Changi". *The Children (& Families) of the Far East Prisoners of War (COFEPOW).* [Internet]. Accessed 13 February 2005. Available from: <http://www.cofepow.org.uk/pages/asia_singapore_changi_story.htm>.

6 Lam, Pin Foo. "Japanese Settlers were Here Before the War". *The Straits Times: Life*, 25 February 1998. 2.

7 *F13687/13687/23, 17 October 1947, FO371/63826.* London: The National Archives.

8 Lau, Albert. *A Moment of Anguish: Singapore in Malaysia and the Politics of Disengagement.* Singapore: Times Academic Press, 1998. 17.

9 Ibid.17.

10 T*he Straits Times*, 3 September 1963.

11 *Colonial Secretary to Lord Selkirk. Signal No. 560, 30 August 1963, PREM11/4325.* London: The National Archives.

12 *Selkirk to Colonial Secretary. Signal No. 2540, 30 August 1963, PREM11/4325.* London: The National Archives.

13 *Selkirk to Colonial Secretary. Signal No. 632, 2 September 1963, PREM11/4325.* London: The National Archives.

14 *Selkirk to Colonial Secretary. Signal No. 636, 3 September 1963, PREM11/4325.* London: The National Archives.

15 Ibid.

16 Lau, 1998. 21.

17 *Selkirk to Colonial Secretary. Signal No. 641, 4 September 1963, PREM11/4325.* London: The National Archives.

18 *Selkirk to Colonial Secretary. Signal No. 642, 4 September 1963, PREM11/4325.* London: The National Archives.

19 National Heritage Board, National Archives of Singapore. *The Japanese Occupation 1942–1945: A Pictorial Record of Singapore During the War.* Singapore: Times Editions, 1996.

20 *Syonan Shimbun*, 9 July 1945.

Chapter 10

Postscript

The end of the war marked a new beginning for the region but it was one that would be filled with bloodshed and violent clashes as the former colonial subjects began their clamour for independence.

With the ceremonial end to the Far Eastern War on 12 September 1945, the British objective of recapturing and reoccupying their former colonies and possessions in Southeast Asia was met. From the beginning, the British had been under tremendous pressure to settle the situation in the Far East quickly. In March 1945, the Joint Intelligence Committee (JIC) had estimated that it would take at least another 12 months to force a Japanese collapse in the region. Moreover, the chiefs of Imperial General Staff agreed that the only way Britain could take part in the American-led CORONET and OLYMPIC operations to invade the Japanese home islands would be with the quick recapture first of Singapore and then Malaya. The British knew the Americans would not help in the reoccupation of their colonies because of their distaste for the British brand of colonialism. So the reoccupation of Malaya and Singapore would be a purely British affair and would tax British resources to the fullest. However, Britain was also keen to be seen as a key American partner in the invasion of Japan as this would give them a seat at the surrender table, reinforce the special relationship they shared with the US and ensure significant influence in any post-war settlement[1]. Thus, Japan's early surrender meant that British forces would not be forced to fight their way down the Malayan peninsula in order to retake Singapore and they could now take part in the occupation of the Japanese home islands.

However, Singapore had figured prominently on the minds of SEAC planners in Colombo for other reasons. The island fortress had been the symbol of British might in the region and its loss in 1942 was a severe blow to British pride and morale. The Japanese then used Singapore as their headquarters with the 7th Area Army based on the island. As such, it was imperative to British pride and strategy to capture Singapore as quickly as possible. Its recapture would symbolise to the Japanese the destruction of the heart of their southern forces and at the same time restore Britain's prestige in the region. The initial plan to recapture Singapore (prior to the Japanese surrender on 15 August) through ZIPPER meant a prolonged fight down the Malayan peninsula before Allied troops reached Singapore. The Japanese were aware of the British strategy and were in the midst of boosting their defences on Malaya's west coast when the war ended.

Now, it appeared even more imperative for SEAC to reoccupy Singapore quickly. The British wanted to ensure a total Japanese surrender and the fastest way to accomplish that was to capture the various Japanese headquarters in the region. Rangoon had fallen in July 1945 and the Japanese Burma army was now effectively destroyed. However, the forces in Malaya were still armed and fresh, a potential threat should Field Marshal Count Terauchi decide to continue the struggle in Southeast Asia.

However, the geopolitical necessity to have the Japanese government surrender first was clearly paramount to any other smaller surrender. Once the documents on board the USS *Missouri* were signed and sealed at Tokyo Bay, all other ancillary surrenders could take place. Although this delay was crucial to the last act of a world war, its repercussions for the people in Malaya and Singapore were tremendous. There was a span of three weeks between Emperor Hirohito's surrender announcement on Japanese Radio on 15 August and the eventual landing of the 5th Indian Division at Singapore's Keppel Harbour on 5 September. In the meantime, a state of virtual chaos had reigned in numerous towns and villages as well as in the Malayan countryside.

SEAC planners were taken aback when the phoney surrender period erupted into communal violence. Some violence would not have been unusual but the large number of revenge killings and lawlessness throughout the country was unexpected. Vice Admiral Lord Louis Mountbatten, keenly aware that the power vacuum had to be quickly filled, wanted Singapore recaptured at the earliest possible date. Once British power had been restored in Singapore, all other parts of Malaya would fall in line. Singapore remained a symbol of power in the peninsula and Mountbatten planned to use it as such.

Although the British had infiltrated clandestine outfits like Force 136 into the Malayan jungles, their main role was in working with resistance groups to destabilise Japanese rule and in providing ground intelligence for the returning British forces. Despite having very loyal support from local agents who risked their lives running spy networks, like Lim Bo Seng who gave his life for Force 136, these heroes were given only minimal recognition and that, more than three years after the war ended. Lim's network was supposed to be the foundation of spy rings in towns and villages throughout Malaya but the destruction of the network left Force 136 with no external source of information except the Malayan People's Anti-Japanese Army (MPAJA). By the end of the war, more groups were sent in to build jungle resistance forces. Restoring order and filling in a power vacuum were neither part of Force 136's mandate nor scope of operations. As such, Force 136 officers and men could only stand by and watch as much of the revenge killings by groups of the MPAJA and other resistance fighters took place. It was not until the first troops landed in Singapore on 5 September 1945 that the communal violence and killings of collaborators ended.

Moreover, the overriding priority for SEAC was not in restoring order in these towns or among the resistance groups but in reoccupying Malaya at a rapid pace. Greater focus was given to getting British troops into Malaya urgently and then leaving it to the field commanders to restore the peace in villages and towns throughout the peninsula.

The impact of the phoney surrender was far reaching. In taking over towns and villages throughout Malaya and exacting revenge on collaborators and ethnic groups during the three weeks of violence, the Malayan Communist Party (MCP) and the MPAJA were given a taste of real power and control. By setting up People's Committees and Central Committees in the open, the MCP had created a *de facto* government in the peninsula and became, in the eyes of many in the Chinese community, the true liberators of Malaya. This reputation would hold the MCP in very good stead when it began its armed struggle three years later as the goodwill among local Chinese leaders ensured the rebuilding of the MCP's secret army. Had there not been a phoney surrender period, the MPAJA would have remained in their jungle camps and would not have had that taste of self-government. It is unlikely that this would have prevented the MCP's eventual armed insurrection in 1948 but it could possibly have delayed the MCP's bid for power.

In reoccupying Malaya, Mountbatten needed to ensure that, in order for the official surrender ceremonies of 12 September to take place, the British had effective and almost total control of Malaya. This meant the reoccupation of Singapore by 5 September and the effective, though not official, reoccupation of Malaya by 11 September 1945.

Thus, the surrender of Singapore on 4 September came to play a much more crucial role in ending the war for the people of Malaya than the events of 12 September.

General Seishiro Itagaki's surrender agreement on board the HMS *Sussex* was effectively the Japanese surrender of Singapore. Within 24 hours of the signing, 35,000 Japanese troops had been moved across the causeway and had started building accommodation in concentration areas as outlined in the surrender orders. The removal of 35,000 frontline troops within a day clearly indicated the seriousness with which the Japanese took the agreement signed on board the *Sussex*. Therefore, the *Sussex* surrender marked the return of the British to Singapore and the Japanese handover of power. More importantly for the people of Singapore and Malaya, the disembarkation of the 5th Indian Division on 5 September as a result of the *Sussex* surrender put an immediate stop to the communal violence on the island and parts of the peninsula. Although most had not heard of the surrender ceremony, news of the British arrival in force spread quickly and this had the effect of immediately stopping the ongoing ethnic clashes. The populace believed that the British would now be the adjudicators of the numerous disputes and troubles plaguing the people.

From the outset, Lieutenant General Sir Alexander Christison and his fellow generals were concerned that the Japanese would not surrender. The TIDERACE force of one division, which had not been assault-loaded, was in no shape to carry out an invasion should Itagaki have decided to carry on fighting. If negotiations failed and fighting broke out, Christison and Rear (later Vice) Admiral Cedric Holland were under instructions not to engage the enemy but to retreat and hold back until they joined the ZIPPER forces which would land in central Malaya on 9 September. Until the *Sussex* surrender, SEAC was unsure as to whether the Japanese troops in Malaya would abide by the emperor's declaration and the Tokyo Bay Agreement. Thus, the *Sussex* surrender ensured, for SEAC, the unopposed ZIPPER landings five days later. Although ZIPPER forces far outnumbered Japanese troops in Malaya, the fact that they were also not fully assault-loaded meant that there would have been significant Allied losses and civilian casualties if the Japanese had resisted.

However, that is not to say the 12 September ceremonies were unimportant or insignificant. The events at the Municipal Building were crucial to closing the final chapter of a global conflict. It was important to have representatives of the various Allied powers accept the surrender from the commanders of the Japanese military in Southeast Asia. On the world's stage, it clearly signalled the complete and total victory of the Allied forces and provided a happy ending to close four years of warfare in the Pacific.

Photographs and newsreel footage of Mountbatten's acceptance of the Japanese surrender and pictures of the Supreme Commander Southeast Asia Command holding aloft his admiral's peaked cap as the crowds thronging the Padang cheered him on provided signal proof that the British had been restored to their rightful place and that the defeats early in the war were now a thing of the past and could now safely recede into memory.

However, to the people of Malaya, the ceremony was of little significance. Of greater concern was how to feed one's family now that Japanese 'banana' money was worthless and how to get life back to normal now that the British had finally returned. Although SEAC invited members of the MPAJA to take part in the 12 September ceremony and even awarded an OBE to the future Secretary General of the MCP, Chin Peng, in an attempt to appease and recognise the contributions of the communists, the MCP had other ideas and would begin brewing trouble less than a month after the war was over. The first communist-led dockworker's strike began on 21 October 1945 when 7,000 wharf labourers refused to work on ships in the Tanjong Pagar docklands. The situation was only resolved when the British Military Administration (BMA) began using Japanese surrendered personnel and a few British units as wharf labourers[2].

On the Japanese side, the emperor's announcement on 15 August 1945 came as a complete shock. The first reaction by Japanese Southern Army commanders was denial but as emissaries of the emperor met with Count Terauchi, General Kimura and General Itagaki, it became clear that the war was over. Generals like Itagaki found it hard to accept the surrender but, under orders from Terauchi, had finally agreed to comply. It was also not easy for Itagaki's commanders to accept that they had lost the war. Many of these officers subsequently committed suicide rather than surrender to the enemy.

During the three weeks of the phoney surrender period, Japanese commanders began to lose control of their men and the areas they were in charge of. The demoralisation that comes with being a member of a vanquished force meant the Japanese were hardly in a position to remain in command. Defeat made strange bedfellows as close to 200 Japanese soldiers decided to join the communist guerrillas whom they were fighting just days before, in a bid to continue the fight against the British. It was only when they found out that the MPAJA did not plan to fight the returning British that many Japanese soldiers returned to their units. Nonetheless, some stayed hidden in the jungles with the communists and when Chin Peng and the remnants of the MCP ended their struggle in 1989, two former Japanese soldiers emerged from the jungles with the communists[3].

At the end of the war, the Japanese were keen to develop nationalistic groups that would be a thorn in the side of the returning British. Their decision to help ally Malay nationalists with Indonesian freedom fighters like Sukarno was aimed at creating groups within Malaya that would fight against the return of the British. Although the majority of these groups disintegrated on the return of the British, the idea of Malay independence had begun to take root. When the colonial authorities introduced the idea of the Malayan Union, giving the Chinese rights of citizenship and reducing the power of the Malay Sultans, political parties like the United Malay National Organisation (UMNO) were formed in a bid to fight for Malay rights and independence.

Nonetheless, the Japanese were nothing if not thorough in ensuring their part in the surrender took place quickly and effectively. The Japanese had detailed evacuation plans drawn up within a day after the *Sussex* surrender and provided further plans for the evacuation of remaining Japanese personnel to prisoner camps on the islands off Indonesia. However, altruism had nothing to do with these moves. From the very beginning, Itagaki and Fukudome realised that the surrendered Japanese would face retribution from the local population, especially the resistance groups, and they wanted to ensure that their men would be repatriated to Japan alive. In order to do this, they would have to build camps and segregate themselves in remote areas far away from towns and villages. This was what Itagaki had proposed in the very first meeting with Holland and Christison on the *Sussex*. In the end, a vast majority of Japanese were relocated to these types of camps and from there, eventually to Japan.

Although many of the Japanese commanders and men were tried for war crimes, the majority of men who served in the region were released to go on with rebuilding their decimated country. However, the legacy of its occupation in Malaya would continue to haunt the Japanese government despite the signing of a peace treaty and war reparations to the Allied powers. The discovery of mass graves in Singapore and Malaya in the late 1950s and early 1960s led to a demand for compensation and accountability for the wartime atrocities committed in the region. Although the Japanese Government eventually made contributions to settle the 'blood debt', the issue became entangled in the politics of the proposed merger between Singapore and Malaysia, as well as the fledgling People's Action Party (PAP) and Lee Kuan Yew's bid to continue governing Singapore. Today, the blood debt still remains a very sensitive issue among Chinese communities in Malaysia and Singapore.

For the MCP, the end of the war marked the beginnings of its plans for an armed insurgency. In December 1943, the Secretary General of the MCP, Lai Teck, accompanied by his Perak state political commissar, Chin Peng, negotiated a treaty with Force 136 leaders Richard Broome, John Davis, Spencer Chapman and Lim Bo Seng for the MPAJA to work hand in hand with SEAC towards the restoration of British rule in Malaya. Lai Teck, who was a triple agent working for the British, Japanese and Chinese communists, agreed to plans for the MPAJA to create a resistance army with which to fight the Japanese. This army would be supplied with weapons, training and stores by SEAC, who would airdrop the supplies needed. Unbeknownst to the Force 136 members, Chin Peng revealed (in an interview in 1999) that the MCP had created two armies:

> We made an agreement with the British, to cooperate with them. But we must be prepared that, if the allied forces landed, we had to act on our own, to occupy as wide as possible an area and the towns... In order to have our freedom of manoeuvring, we must set up ourselves when the time comes to receive British arms. One day they would airdrop the arms, so our army must be divided into two forces, one called the 'Open Army' – that is to receive British arms and to cooperate with the British. The other portion, we called the 'Secret Army'. The Secret Army must not be known to the British. When the time came, and the British started to drop arms, we would pretend as if we were poorly armed. All the best weapons, automatic weapons, we would try our best to transfer to our Secret Army. And our best cadres, experienced fighters, would all be transferred to the Secret Army, to prepare for future fighting. In the Open Army we only keep a skeleton of experienced cadres to be the backbone of the Army...It seemed this was the only way to deal with the British. We cooperate with them on the one hand, to receive their aid, their military supplies, and on the other hand we still preserve our main force, under our control[4].

By August 1945, the MCP had established numerous MPAJA units throughout Malaya and provided the only real large-scale anti-Japanese resistance force on the peninsula. Although communist leaders wanted to take an "enhanced military posture" against the Japanese, Lai Teck insisted that the MCP concentrate more on organising labour. As a triple agent, he had to ensure that the Japanese were protected while he organised labour to serve the interests of the Chinese Communist Party and, at the same time, keep the MPAJA from beginning an armed struggle against his British handlers[5]. So it came to pass that by the end of the war, the MCP controlled labour unions throughout Malaya and Singapore.

However, once the Japanese surrender was announced, MPAJA regiments that did not receive directives on Lai Teck's new change of tack began occupying towns and villages throughout the country. This gave the MCP leaders their first taste of governing and ruling. Following the September surrender, the MPAJA disbanded its open army, while burying much of the war material supplied by Force 136, to be dug up and used later. By 1947, Lai Teck found his position untenable and fled with the coffers of the MCP. He was subsequently killed in Bangkok and Chin Peng took over as the new leader of the party.

However, Chin Peng was to claim later that he had not initially pushed for an armed struggle but that he had instead "resolved, along with my fellow Politburo members and the Central Committee, merely to enhance the political format we were following. As I saw it, the requirement was for subtle readjustments" [6].

Chin Peng also claimed that the Malayan Emergency did not start in June 1948 with the killing of three British planters in Sungei Siput. He argues that it began on 21 October 1945 when British troops were called in to disperse a huge labour demonstration in Sungei Siput, Ipoh and Batu Gajah. He noted that in Sungei Siput and Ipoh, the troops were ordered to fire directly into the crowds. He claimed that 10 demonstrators were shot dead in Sungei Siput and three more in Ipoh. "In Batu Gajah, the emotions were so high that the British civil affairs officer was cornered in the court house and surrounded by 500 furious demonstrators. Troops were ordered to rescue him," he said[7].

The British Government had by then begun enacting ordinances to close down the MCP-controlled unions and had developed plans for a Malayan Union. The proposal was made in 1946 with the intention to create a union of Malaya, composed of all the former federated and unfederated states, including Penang. Singapore would be left out of this mix and become a crown colony, due in part to the large Chinese population on the island. If Singapore were to have been included in the union, the population of immigrant Chinese would then clearly outnumber the Malays, leading to increased friction over the racial ratio. The union also proposed equal voting rights for all races and citizenship for the Chinese.

After numerous riots and strikes, colonial authorities abandoned the plan for the union. By 1948, a compromise federation was set up in Malaya. The MCP, however, remained dissatisfied, as it believed the citizenship rights did not go far enough. Moreover, it was constantly being attacked by colonial authorities who had attempted to close down the MCP's offices. In March 1948, the decision was made at the MCP's Singapore party offices at Queen Street to begin an armed struggle. As Chin Peng noted, "Finally, we came to the conclusion that the Lai Teck policy, stopping the armed struggle, and only struggling for self-government, was wrong". The precipitating factor for armed insurrection was the planned introduction of the Trade Union Ordinance Amendment of 31 May 1948, which would ban the MCP's trade unions:

> ... So, in that case how do we respond? We consider that as a full-scale attack. If they ban our trade union, or in some other way paralyse

> our trade union or perhaps they openly banned our party and arrested us. Then, how to respond? In the last resort, we have to launch armed struggle[8].

By June 1948, the Malayan Emergency had begun, as the secret army began remobilising their forces and digging up the hidden arms and weapons. A general plan of attack throughout the peninsula was launched in 1949[9]. The Emergency would last 12 years with more than 25,000 casualties on both sides[10].

Thus, the end of the war clearly signalled the beginning of independence movements throughout Southeast Asia. In the Dutch-controlled East Indies, Sukarno and Hatta declared an independent Indonesia shortly before the end of the war. After four years of Nazi occupation, the Dutch were in the midst of rebuilding their cities and were in no position to recover their colonies as quickly as the British. As a result, the Netherlands East Indies was administered by a British military governor for more than a year before the Dutch were able to resume control of their colonies. The British military administration in Indonesia witnessed the beginnings of the bloody fight for independence with several hundred troops killed in violent clashes with Indonesian nationalists. In 1946, the British handed power back to the Dutch colonial authorities, having received a huge black eye for their efforts at recolonising the country.

Although the British did manage to regain their colonies and start reestablishing their power, it was obvious that the days of colonial rule were numbered. Although both countries faced differing scenarios and struggles in their path to independence, the experiences in Indonesia and particularly in Malaya would plague the British for the next two decades, with insurgencies, confrontations and independence struggles eventually leading to the independent nations of Indonesia, Malaysia and Singapore.

The impact of the end of the war and its repercussions still resonate today; in the form of architectural artefacts as well as in how societies in the region were impacted and changed by British reoccupation policy, clandestine groups, the communal violence and the eventual surrenders that purportedly ended the war but which really marked the beginning of more violence to come. Such elements obviously shaped post-war attitudes towards the British and some of the nationalist groups fighting for the hearts and minds of the local populace. Today, countries like Singapore, Malaysia and Indonesia appear very far removed from those war-torn ruins of 60 years ago. However, many issues like race relations, Malay rights and the place of the Chinese community in these countries still continue to be informed by the events of those times. Nonetheless, the return of the British in 1945 and their rule in Malaya till the early 1960s meant that stability and progress had also returned, a model that has been modified extensively by each country but adhered to in principle by present-day governments in Malaysia and Singapore. That these countries today were able to have the freedom over the last 60 years to evolve in their own ways and forms remains a testament to those who gave their lives and those who persevered in the belief that victory, liberty and independence would surely come.

Endnotes

1 Baxter, Christopher. "In Pursuit of a Pacific Strategy: British Planning for the Defeat of Japan, 1943–45". *Diplomacy & Statecraft*, vol. 15, no. 2, June 2004. 258.

2 Chin, Peng. *My Side of History*. Singapore: Media Masters, 2003. 141.

3 Hack, Karl & Chin, C.C. (eds). *Dialogues with Chin Peng: New Light on the Malayan Communist Party*. Singapore: Singapore University Press, 2004. 95.

4 Ibid. 106.

5 Chin, 2003. 162.

6 Ibid. 193.

7 Ibid. 142.

8 Hack & Chin, 2004. 135.

9 Ibid. 144.

10 Hagan, Max. "Open Letter to My Daughters". *National Malaya & Borneo Veterans Association UK*. [Internet]. Accessed 10 December 2004. Available from: <http://www.nmbva.co.uk/paddy%20articles.htm>.

Appendix A: Chronology of Events, August–September 1945

4 August	The deputy to Vice Admiral Lord Louis Mountbatten, Supreme Allied Commander, Southeast Asia (SACSEA), Lieutenant General Raymond Wheeler, orders planners at Southeast Asia Command (SEAC) to devise an emergency plan to recapture Singapore quickly.
8 August	Operation TIDERACE is born.
15 August	Emperor Hirohito of Japan announces in a radio broadcast the end of hostilities and Japan's surrender.
18 August	General Seishiro Itagaki, Commander-in-Chief of the 7th Area Army in Singapore, flies to Saigon to meet with Field Marshal Count Hisaichi Terauchi, Commander-in-Chief of the Southern Army, to discuss the surrender order. Terauchi orders him to comply. Mountbatten declares the institution of a British Military Administration (BMA) in Malaya led by Major General Ralph Hone. However, the BMA does not begin operations in Malaya till the landings on 5 September.
19 August	SEAC Staff Signal Officer, Captain Frank O'Shanohun, parachutes into Singapore's racecourse to discuss Itagaki's surrender. Japanese delegates leave Tokyo for the Manila headquarters of General Douglas MacArthur, Supreme Allied Commander, South West Pacific Command. Japanese delegates also meet with General Heitaro Kimura, Commander-in-Chief of the Burma Area Army, ordering him to surrender.
20 August	Itagaki meets O'Shanohun and signals SEAC that he will abide by the surrender terms. In a signal sent in the clear, Mountbatten orders Terauchi to send representatives to surrender talks in Rangoon on 23 August. Terauchi signals Mountbatten that he is unable to send his staff due to lack of transport and preparation time and both sides eventually set the date for 26 August.
21 August	Newspapers in Singapore are finally allowed to print the Emperor's surrender message. X-Day for Operation TIDERACE.
22 August	More than 300 Japanese officers and men in Singapore commit suicide rather than face surrender to the Allies.

26 August	Terauchi's delegates, led by his Chief of Staff, Lieutenant General Takazo Numata, arrive in Rangoon for surrender talks.
27 August	Surrender talks take place in Rangoon with Japanese representatives initially arguing about the terms for surrender.
28 August	Japanese delegates finally sign the surrender agreement at 1.00am in the Throne Room, Government House, Rangoon. Vice Admiral Harold Walker arrives in the waters off Penang Island and begins negotiations with the Japanese to surrender the island and get more details on enemy dispositions in Malaya.
2 September	General Douglas MacArthur accepts the formal Japanese surrender on board the USS *Missouri* in Tokyo Bay, Japan. At 9.15pm, the Japanese garrison commander in Penang, Rear Admiral Jisaku Uozumi, surrenders to Vice Admiral Walker on board HMS *Nelson*.
4 September	General Seishiro Itagaki and Vice Admiral Shigeru Fukudome sign surrender terms on board HMS *Sussex* in Keppel Harbour, handing over Singapore to SACSEA's naval and military representatives, Rear (later Vice) Admiral Cedric Holland, Naval Fleet Commander and Lieutenant General Sir Alexander Christison, GOC, 15th Indian Corps.
5 September	Major General Eric Mansergh, Commander of the 5th Indian Division, and his troops land at Singapore's Keppel docks and assume control of Singapore. Communal violence in most parts of Malaya ceases as a result.
9 September	Operation ZIPPER is carried out as the 34th Indian Corps begin landing on Morib Beach.
10 September	Remaining ZIPPER forces land in the Port Dickson area.
12 September	Mountbatten accepts the formal Japanese surrender at a nine-minute ceremony in the Municipal Hall in Singapore, followed by a flag-raising and parade at the Padang. Itagaki represents Terauchi, who is too ill to attend.
13 September	ZIPPER forces, led by the 25th Indian Division march into Kuala Lumpur with Lieutenant General Ouvry Roberts, GOC, 34th Indian Corps, accepting the Japanese surrender from Lieutenant General Teizo Ishiguro, Commander of the Japanese 29th Army, at Victoria Institution.

Appendix B: List of Operations

BUTTON
A British military plan to practise amphibious landings planned for Malaya ahead of the ZIPPER landings, on the beaches of India's Coromandel coast. The plan was aborted in mid-August following Japan's surrender and the decision to implement ZIPPER immediately.

CARPENTER/MINT
Force 136 blind-landing three miles off Tanjong Balau, on the east coast of Johor on 5 October 1944, to contact, arm and train any local resistance. Two weeks later, MINT, a joint SOE/Inter-Services Liaison Department (SIS) operation to spy on the naval base in Singapore, landed at the same location.

CORONET
Plan for the invasion of the Japanese island of Kyushu, led by American forces with the participation of the British.

CULVERIN
A British military operation with the objective of capturing north Sumatra that was never put into action.

DRACULA
A British military operation, involving an amphibious landing at Rangoon, to recapture Japanese-occupied Burma.

FUNNEL
Force 136 airdrop of supplies and trained Malay resistance fighters close to the Tapah/Bidor Road on 25 February 1945.

GUSTAVUS I, II, III, IV and V
British Special Operations Executive Force 136 operations to infiltrate Malaya and set up clandestine resistance networks (beginning with Perak) during the Japanese Occupation.

JAYWICK
An operation undertaken by Force 'Z' under Lieutenant Colonel Ivan Lyon to sneak into Keppel Harbour in Japanese-occupied Singapore and destroy enemy shipping.

JURIST
A British military plan to capture advanced naval and air bases on the island of Penang in Malaysia. Initially part of ZIPPER, it was eventually implemented under TIDERACE.

MAILFIST
A British assault plan to retake Singapore as part of ZIPPER. This was later replaced by TIDERACE.

MARKET GARDEN
A combined airborne and ground offensive launched by Allied forces in Holland that, had it succeeded, would have ended the Second World War by Christmas 1944.

MODIFIED DRACULA
A scaled-down version of Operation DRACULA, successfully executed, with the British arriving in Rangoon in May 1945.

OLYMPIC
Plan for the invasion of the Japanese island of Honshu led by the American forces but in which the British participated.

RIMAU
Another operation, similar to JAYWICK, in which Force 'Z' destroyed enemy shipping in Singapore Harbour.

ROGER
A British military plan to capture advanced naval and air bases on the island of Phuket in Thailand as part of ZIPPER that was never implemented. A modified version of ROGER was used to minesweep the Andaman Sea and as a feint for TIDERACE.

TIDERACE
An emergency reoccupation plan for the recapture of Singapore and Penang ahead of Operation ZIPPER.

TROPIC
Contingency British naval operation with the objective of recapturing Singapore and Penang that was never implemented.

ZIPPER
A British amphibious assault plan for the west coast of Malaya.

Appendix C: Operation ZIPPER, Order of Battle[1]

Headquarters 14th Army
Headquarters XXXIV Corps

CORPS TROOPS:
11th Cavalry
25th Dragoons
18th Field Regiment Royal Artillery
208th Field Regiment Royal Artillery
6th Medium Regiment Royal Artillery
86th Medium Regiment Royal Artillery
1st Indian Medium Regiment
8th Sikh Light Anti-Aircraft Regiment
9th Rajput Light Anti-Aircraft Regiment
1st Heavy Anti-Aircraft Regiment, Hong Kong & Singapore Regiment Royal Artillery

FORMATIONS:
5th Indian Division
23rd Indian Division
25th Indian Division
26th Indian Division
50th Indian Tank Brigade
3rd Commando Brigade
5th Parachute Brigade

ENDNOTES

1 "Operation Zipper: The Invasion of Malaya, August 1945, Order of Battle". *Orbat.com* [Internet] Available from: <http://orbat.com/site/history/historical/malaysia/operationzipper.html>.

Appendix D: Ships Anchored in Singapore Roads During the Ceremony of Surrender, 12 September 1945[1]

CLEOPATRA (Commander-in-Chief's vessel)

Battleships:
NELSON (Vice Admiral, East Indies Station)
RICHELIEU

Cruisers:
SUSSEX (Flag Officer, Force 'N')
CUMBERLAND
ROYALIST
CEYLON

Headquarters and Depot Ships:
KEDAH (Flag Officcr, Malaya)
BULOLO (Flag Officer, Force 'W')
SANSOVINO
BARRACUDA, HMIS
MULL OF GALLOWAY (Captain, Coastal Forces, East Indies Station)

Destroyers:
TARTAR
SAUMAREZ
MYNGS
FARNDALE
RELENTLESS
PALADIN
BLACKMORE
VERULAM

Escort Vessels:
GORLESTON (Captain, East Indies Escort Force)
LOCH SCAVAIG
LOCH LOMOND
DART
CAUVERY, HMIS
GODAVARI, HMIS
KALE
AWE

Submarines:
SIBYL

Surveyor Ship:
CHALLENGER

Landing Ships & Craft:
Landing Ships, Tank, 11, 165, 199, 302, 321 and 324
Six landing craft from Force 'W'

Royal Fleet Auxiliary Ships:
DEWDALE
ORANGELEAF
CROMWELL

Hospital Ships:
ORANJE
MANUNDA
KARAPARA

Merchant Ships:
RAJULA
DERBYSHIRE
DEVONSHIRE
CHESHIRE
HIGHLAND BRIGADE
THALMA
PASHA
PAKHOI
CITY OF DERBY
JALAVEIRA
ITAURA
MORETON BAY
MANELLA

Minesweepers:
PELORUS (Captain, Minesweepers, Forward Areas)
FRIENDSHIP
VIRILE
GOZO
LENNOX
PERSIAN
POSTILION
MELITA
IMERSAY
LINGAY
PICKLE
RECRUIT
RIFLEMAN

CHAMELEON
PINCHER
PLUCKY
DECCAN, HMIS
PUNJAB, HMIS
BIHAR, HMIS
ROHILKHAND, HMIS
KUMAON, HMIS

ENDNOTES

1 *Report of Proceedings – Commander-in-Chief, East Indies Station's Letter, No.3001/E.I.15002/45, 17 September 1945, ADM199/168.* London: The National Archives. Enclosure No. 1.

Appendix E: List of Notable Personalities

THE ALLIES

The British

Armstrong, Lieutenant Colonel Guy Lionel Walter
Born in 1918, Armstrong served as staff officer in the Imphal campaign and was posted to Southeast Asia Command (SEAC) Headquarters (HQ) in Ceylon. He moved with Vice Admiral Lord Louis Mountbatten to Singapore after the Japanese surrender and retired as Second-in-Command of the 16th Parachute Brigade in 1960. Ordained in 1961, he served as Vicar of Bagshot and Ripley. He died on 14 December 2002.

Attlee, Clement Richard
Born in 1883, Atlee swept into power in the 1945 British General Election, giving the Labour Party its largest victory at the polls. He was prime minister of Britain (1945–1951) for six years and led the Labour Party until 1955, remaining active in the House of Lords until his death in 1967.

Auchinleck, Field Marshal Sir Claude John Eyre
Born in 1884, Auchinleck was Commander-in-Chief (CinC), India (1940–1941), before serving as CinC, Middle East Command (1941–1942), and then as temporary General Officer Commanding (GOC), 8th Army in North Africa (1942), before reprising his role as CinC, India (1943–1947), becoming Supreme Commander in India and Pakistan in 1947. Auchinleck died in 1981.

Brooke, Field Marshal Sir Alan
Born on 23 July 1883, he joined the British army and served in Ireland and India before going to France in 1914. In June 1940 Brooke played a leading role in the evacuation of British troops at Dunkirk. Alan Brooke was appointed Chief of Imperial Staff in December 1941. Promoted to Field Marshal in January 1944, he was created Baron Alanbrooke of Brookeborough in September 1945. He died on 17 June 1963.

Browning, General Sir Frederick Arthur Montague
Born in 1896, Browning served in North Africa and Northwest Europe (1941–1945) before being appointed SEAC Chief of Staff (CoS) (1945–1946). He later served as Military Secretary in the War Office (1946–1948) before retiring in 1948. He died in 1965.

Christison, Lieutenant General Sir Alexander Frank Philip
Born on 17 November 1893, Christison had served in the First World War and rose to the rank of Brigadier in 1941. He served as the GOC, 33rd Indian Corps, in Burma (1942–1943) before taking over as GOC, 15th Indian Corps (1943–

1945). Christison was then appointed temporary GOC, 14th Army in Burma (1945), before taking over as CinC, Allied Land Forces Southeast Asia (1945). After concluding his role in TIDERACE, Christison became Allied Commander of the Dutch East Indies (1945–1946) and General Officer Commander-in-Chief, Northern Command (GOCinC) (1946–1947), and appointed Aide-de-Camp to the King (1947–1949) before retiring in 1949. Christison died on 21 December 1993.

Churchill, Winston Leonard Spencer
Born in 1874, Churchill is considered one of the greatest of British statesmen. A soldier and a journalist before he entered politics, he was elected twice as the prime minister of Britain (1940–1945, 1951–1955). Churchill received the Nobel Prize for literature in 1953 and was knighted in the same year by Queen Elizabeth II. He died on 24 January 1965.

Eden, Sir Anthony Robert
Born in 1897, Eden won the Military Cross at the Battle of the Somme in 1916. He became Under-Secretary for Foreign Affairs (1931–1934) and served as Foreign Secretary (1935–1938) until he resigned in 1938. He then served again as Foreign Secretary under Churchill (1940–1945) and became deputy leader of the opposition until 1951 when he again served as Foreign Secretary. Eden disagreed with Prime Minister Neville Chamberlain about the way to deal with Fascism in Europe and in 1938 he resigned from office. When Churchill took over from Chamberlain in 1940, Eden was reappointed as Foreign Secretary. After the Labour Party victory in the 1945 General Election, Eden became deputy leader of the opposition. The 1951 General Election saw the return of a Conservative government and once more Eden became Foreign Secretary. He later replaced Winston Churchill as prime minister (1955–1957). Created Earl of Avon in 1961, he died in 1977.

Gardner, Air Vice Marshal Sir Percy Ronald, the Earl of Bandon
Born on 30 August 1904, Gardner became a Squadron Leader in 1936 and served as Air Officer Commanding, No 244 Squadron, in 1944. He was involved in the air invasion plans for ZIPPER and, after serving in various theatres, was promoted to Air Marshal in 1957 before taking over as CinC, Far East Air Force. In 1959, he was promoted to Air Chief Marshal and became Commander, Allied Air Forces Central Europe (1961), before retiring in 1964. He died on 8 February 1979.

Harcourt, Admiral Sir Cecil Halliday Jephson
Born in 1892, Harcourt served in the First World War before becoming Director of Admiralty's Operations Division (1939–1941). He then commanded the HMS *Duke of York* and was Flag Captain of the Home Fleet (1941–1942), later becoming the Flag Officer Commanding the 10th, 12th and 15th Cruiser Squadrons in North Africa and Italy (1942–1944). He was then appointed Naval Secretary to the First Lord of the Admiralty (1944–1945) before becoming Flag Officer Commanding, 11th Aircraft Carrier Squadron, on board HMS *Venerable* (1945). Upon the Japanese surrender, he was put in charge of the force which accepted the Japanese surrender of Hong Kong on 30 August 1945. He was later appointed CinC and Head of Military Administration Hong Kong (1945–1946), becoming

Flag Officer (Air) and Second-in-Command, Mediterranean Fleet (1947–1948), and Second Sea Lord (1948–1950) and was promoted to the rank of Admiral in 1949 before being appointed Commander-in-Chief, The Nore (1950–1952). Harcourt retired in 1953 and died on 19 December 1959.

Holland, Vice Admiral Cedric Swinton

Born in 1889, Holland served in the First World War with the Grand Fleet at Scapa Flow. Naval Attaché for France, Holland, Belgium, Spain and Portugal (1938–1940), Holland took command of the aircraft carrier HMS *Ark Royal* in May 1940 (1940–1941). He later played the role of chief negotiator in discussions with the French during the Mers el Kebir affair (1940). He was subsequently appointed Director of Naval Communications (1942–1943), during which he was promoted to the rank of Rear Admiral. Attached to SEAC HQ (1943–1945), he was promoted to Vice Admiral in 1945 before being appointed as Naval Force Commander for TIDERACE and SEAC's naval representative at the Singapore surrender on board his flagship, the HMS *Sussex*, on 4 September 1945. Holland retired from active service in 1946 and died on 11 May 1950.

Hone, Major General Sir Herbert Ralph

Born in 1896, Hone was Attorney-General of Uganda (1937–1940) and Commandant of the Ugandan Defence Force (1940) before serving as Chief Political Officer in the Middle East and the War Office. Following his appointment as Chief Civil Affairs Officer, Malaya (1945–1946), Hone took on the responsibility of developing plans for the British Military Administration (BMA) in the country and the eventual restoration of a civil administration in the peninsula. Hone arrived in Singapore with TIDERACE and took over as head of the BMA. On handing over power to the civilian government, he was appointed Secretary-General to the Governor-General of Malaya (1946–1948) before being made Governor and CinC of North Borneo (1949–1954). He was then appointed as the head of the Legal Division at the Commonwealth Office (1954–1961) and continued to serve in this role for five more years after his retirement in 1956. Hone died in 1992.

Leese, Lieutenant General Sir Oliver William Hargreaves

Born in 1894, Leese served as Deputy Chief of Staff (DCoS) to the British Expeditionary Force in France in 1940 and was made GOC of the 15th Division in 1941. He also served as GOC for the Guards Armoured Division (1941–1942) and 30th Corps in North Africa (1942–1943) and the 8th Army in Italy (1943–1944) before being appointed CinC, Allied Land Forces South-East Asia (1944–1945), where he was partly involved in preparations for ZIPPER and the Burma campaigns. He took over as GOCinC, Eastern Command in 1945, retiring in 1946. Leese died in 1978.

Mansergh, General Sir Eric Carden Robert

Born in 1900, Mansergh was appointed Commander of the Royal Artillery 5th Indian Division (1943–1944) and served in Burma where he was made GOC, 11th East African Division (1945). He was later appointed GOC, 5th Indian Division (1945–1946), during which time he led the 5th Division in the reoccupation of Singapore on 5 September 1945. Mansergh was then appointed CinC, Dutch

East Indies (1946–1947), before returning to the War Office where he was later appointed Military Secretary to the Secretary of State for War (1948–1949). Mansergh then served as CinC, Hong Kong (1949–1951), before becoming CinC, Allied Powers Forces Northern Europe (1953–1956). He was later made CinC, British Land Forces (1956–1959), a post he held until his retirement in 1959. Mansergh died in 1970.

Martin, Vice Admiral Sir Benjamin Charles Stanley
Born in 1891, Martin had served in the Somali Campaign in 1908 and in the First World War. He was Captain of HMS *Dorsetshire* (1939–1941) during the Second World War and was involved in the sinking of the German battleship *Bismarck.* Martin then served as Commodore in charge of Naval Establishments in Durban (1942–1943) before retiring in 1944. Called back into service, he was attached to SEAC HQ. He was later appointed Flag Officer Force 'W' on board HMS *Bulolo,* as part of MODIFIED DRACULA. As Commanding Officer (CO) of the close-covering group, he was involved in the Rangoon landings off Ramree Island in February 1945. Martin was also involved in developing plans for ZIPPER. He was promoted to the rank of Vice Admiral (Retd.) in 1948. Martin died on 3 June 1957.

Messervy, General Sir Frank Walter
Born in 1893, Messervy served in the military as an Instructor at the Staff College in Camberley (1932–1936) before being stationed in East and North Africa. He become Acting Chief of Staff, Middle East Command, in 1942 and subsequently served as GOC of the 43rd Armoured Indian Division (1942–1943), the 7th Indian Division (1943–1944) and the 4th Indian Corps in Burma (1944–1945). He assumed the role of GOC, Malaya, in 1945. He later served as GOCinC, India (1946–1947), and as CinC, Pakistan army (1947–1948), before retiring in 1948. Messervy died in 1974.

Mountbatten, Admiral Lord Louis Francis Albert Victor Nicholas
Born on 25 June 1900, Mountbatten was the younger son of Admiral of the Fleet, the 1st Marquess of Milford Haven and Princess Victoria (daughter of Louis IV, Grand Duke of Hesse, KG, and Princess Alice, Queen Victoria's Daughter). He was known as Prince Louis Francis of Battenberg until 1917 when his father relinquished the German title and assumed the surname of Mountbatten. CO of the HMS *Illustrious* in 1939, he was appointed Commodore, Combined Operations (1941–1942), before becoming Chief of Combined Operations. He then became a member of the British Chiefs of Staff Committee (1942–1943) before being appointed Supreme Allied Commander Southeast Asia Command (SACSEA) (1943–1946). After the war, he was made Viscount Mountbatten of Burma (1946) for his role in Southeast Asia and a year later became Viceroy, and subsequently Governor General, of India. For his services in India, he was made 1st Earl Mountbatten of Burma (1947) and served in various capacities in the Admiralty, being promoted to Admiral of the Fleet in 1956. Upon retirement, Mountbatten assumed the post of First Sea Lord and Chief of Naval Staff (1955–1959). He then served as Chief of the UK Defence Staff and Chairman of Chiefs of Staff Committee (1959–1965). He was killed on his boat on 27 August 1979 in Donegal Bay, Ireland, by a bomb planted by the Irish Republican Army (IRA).

Penney, Major General Sir William Ronald Campbell
Born in 1896, Penney served as Deputy Director of Military Intelligence at the War Office (1939–1940) and as CO of the 3rd Brigade (1940–1941) before serving as Chief Signal Officer in the Middle East and for the 18th Army Group (1941–1943). He then served as GOC, 1st Division, in North Africa and Italy (1943–1944) before becoming Director of Military Intelligence, SEAC (1944–1945). He later became Assistant Controller of Supplies in the Ministry of Supply (1946–1949) before retiring in 1949. He died in 1964.

Percival, Lieutenant General Arthur Ernest
Born in 1887, Percival had served in Malaya as a General Staff Officer 1 (1936–1938) before serving in the UK and France. In 1940, he was appointed GOC, 43rd Division, and Assistant Chief Imperial General Staff at the War Office. He returned to Malaya in 1941 to serve as GOC, Malaya Command, where he is unfairly remembered as the general who lost the Malayan Campaign and who surrendered more than 100,000 British and Commonwealth troops to Lieutenant General Tomoyuki Yamashita on 15 Febrary 1942 at the Ford Motor Factory in Singapore. A prisoner of war (1942–1945), Percival retired in 1946 and was closely associated with the Far East Prisoners of War Association as well as the Red Cross until his death in 1966.

Power, Admiral Sir Arthur John
Born on 12 April 1889, Power did not see action in the First World War but was appointed CO of the HMS *Ark Royal* when the ship was under construction in 1938. Serving as the ship's First CO and Flag Captain, he was also Chief Staff Officer to Rear Admiral, Aircraft Carriers, Home Fleet (1938–1940). Briefly serving in the Admiralty and in Malta, Power was appointed Vice Admiral Commanding 1st Battle Squadron & Second-in-Command, Eastern Fleet (1943–1944), before becoming CinC, East Indies Station (1944–1945). After the war, he served in the Admiralty and in the Mediterranean before being promoted to Admiral of the Fleet in 1952 and being appointed Allied CinC, Channel and Southern North Sea Command (1952–1953). He retired in 1953 and died on 28 January 1960.

Roberts, General Sir Ouvry Lindfield
Born in 1898, Roberts served as Deputy Director of Military Operations & Intelligence, India (1939–1941), and as General Staff Officer 1, 10th Indian Division (1941), as well as CO, 20th Indian Brigade (1941). Appointed Brigadier General Staff, IV Corps (1943), he was later made GOC 23rd Indian Division, Burma (1943–1945). Prior to ZIPPER, he was appointed GOC, XXXIV Corps, Malaya (1945). After the war, he became a Deputy Adjutant-General in the War Office (1945–1947) and served as GOC, Northern Ireland; CinC, Southern Command, and finally as Aide-de-Camp General to the Queen (1952–1955). Roberts retired in 1955 and died in 1986.

Slim, Field Marshal Viscount William Joseph
Born in 1891, Viscount Slim served in Africa and the Middle East before becoming the GOC, Burma Corps, in 1942. He was then appointed GOC, XV Corps, Burma (1942–1943), before being made GOC, 14th Army, Burma (1943–1945). He then replaced Leese as CinC, Allied Land Forces Southeast Asia (1945) and

was made Commandant of the Imperial Defence College after the war (1946–1947). Although he retired in 1948, he was recalled to serve his country as Chief Imperial General Staff (1948–1952), ending his career as Governor-General and CinC of Australia (1952–1960). He died in 1970.

Stopford, General Sir Montague George North
Born in 1892, Stopford served in France at the beginning of the war and was made GOC, XII Corps (1942–1943), before taking over as GOC, XXXIII Indian Corps, in Burma (1943–1945). He was also GOC, 12th Army, Burma (1945). Later he was appointed CinC, Allied Land Forces Dutch East Indies (1945–1946) and CinC, South-East Asia Land Forces (1946–1947) before serving as GOCinC, Northern Command (1947–1949) and also as Aide-de-Camp General to the King (1947–1949). He retired in 1949 and died in 1971.

Walker, Admiral Sir Harold Thomas Coulthard
Born on 18 March 1891, Walker served in the First World War and began his service in the Second World War as Flag Captain of the HMS *Barham* and as Chief Staff Officer to Vice Admiral Commanding, 1st Battle Squadron, in the Mediterranean (1939–1940). He then served in the Admiralty before becoming Rear Admiral Commanding, 5th Cruiser Squadron (1944), and was then appointed Flag Officer Commanding, 3rd Battle Squadron, and as Second-in-Command, East Indies Station (1944–1945). He later served as Vice Admiral Commanding, British Naval Forces in Germany, and as Chief British Naval Representative in the Allied Control Commission (1946–1947) before retiring in 1947. He was promoted to the rank of Admiral (Retd.) the following year. Walker died on Christmas Day 1975.

The Americans

MacArthur, General of the Army Douglas
Born in 1880, MacArthur served as CinC, South-West Pacific Area (1942–1945), and was CinC, US army forces in the Pacific (1945), as well as CinC, Allied Forces of Occupation, Japan (1945). After the war, MacArthur was made CinC, US Forces Far East (1947–1951), as well as CinC, UN Forces, Korea (1950–1951), retiring in 1951. MacArthur died in 1964.

Marshall, General of the Army George Catlett
Born in 1880, Marshall served as CoS, VIII Corps, in France (1918) and was CoS, US army (1939–1945). Retiring from the military in 1945, he was appointed Secretary of State in 1947. He is known for the Marshall Plan, which helped provide economic aid to post-Second World War Europe. He was also Secretary of Defense (1950–1951). He retired in 1951 and died in 1959.

Truman, Harry S.
Thirty-third president of the United States, Truman took over after President Franklin Delano Roosevelt died in office on 12 April 1945. Truman retired from public life in January 1953 and died on 26 December 1972.

Wainwright, Lieutenant General Jonathan Mayhew

Born in 1883, Wainwright was Commanding General, I Philippine Corps, in Philippines in 1942 and as MacArthur escaped to Australia, took on the role of CinC, Far East, before surrendering to the Japanese. A prisoner of war (1942–1945), Wainwright was on board the HMS *Missouri* with Percival in Tokyo Bay to witness the Japanese surrender on 2 September 1945. Wainwright was made Commanding General of the 4th Army (1946–1947) before retiring in 1947. He died in 1953.

Wheeler, Lieutenant General Raymond Albert

Born in 1885, Wheeler served Mountbatten as Deputy Commander-in-Chief, SEAC (1944–1945). He was also CinC, US Burma-India Theatre of Operations (1945), and was tasked by Mountbatten to come up with a quick plan to recapture Singapore. He later served as Chief of Engineers (1945–1949) before retiring in 1949. Wheeler died in 1974.

SPECIAL OPERATIONS EXECUTIVE (SOE) AND FORCE 136 MEMBERS AND AFFILIATED FIGURES[1]

Anstey, Brigadier John

Born on 3 January 1907, Anstey, who was a Territorial Army Officer in the Somerset Light Infantry and a well-liked junior manager in the Imperial Tobacco Company, had served in the War Office and in the SOE in the beginning of the Second World War before being promoted to the rank of Colonel and sent to Delhi in November 1944 as Deputy Head of the SOE India Mission/Force 136. After the war, Anstey was promoted to the rank of Brigadier and was awarded a Commander of the Order of the British Empire (CBE).

Broadhurst, Lieutenant Colonel Douglas Keith

Born on 28 June 1910, 'Duggie' Broadhurst served in the pre-war Malayan Police Force and joined Force 136 during the Second World War.

Broome, Major Richard Neville

Born on 19 June 1916, Broome was a District Officer in Perak when war broke out and became an original member of the SOE's Oriental Mission in Singapore. He later escaped the fall of Singapore with Davis and played a key role in clandestine operations in Japanese-occupied Malaya. After the war, Broome was Secretary of the Chinese Section of the BMA.

Chapman, Lieutenant Colonel Frederick Spencer

Born on 10 May 1907, Chapman served at the 101ST guerrilla warfare school in Singapore. Sent behind enemy lines to organise reconnaissance and sabotage operations, he helped build up Force 136 in the Malayan jungles. At the end of the war he was promoted to the rank of Lieutenant Colonel and awarded a Distinguished Service Order (DSO). He went back to a career in teaching but as retirement approached, he was under increasing pressure from health and financial worries. Chapman shot himself on 8 August 1971.

Chin Peng
Born in Setiawan, Perak on 21 October 1924, Chin Peng (Ong Boon Hua) eventually led the Malayan Communist Party (MCP) in the late 1940s. Fleeing to the jungles of Thailand after losing the war against the Malaysian government, he continued to lead the MCP in exile, finally signing a peace agreement with the Malaysian government in 1989 At the time of writing, Chin Peng is yet again petitioning the Malaysian government to allow him to end his exile in Thailand and return to Malaysia, which has allowed many of his compatriots back in. The long-standing refusal to grant Chin Peng's applications to return to the country is partly due to his role in the 12-year communist insurgency and the racial massacres of 1945.

Chua Koon Eng @ Choy/Bill
Owner of a few fishing boats on Pangkor Island, Chua was key in ensuring the network's rendezvous with Force 136's submarines. Chua broke under interrogation by the Japanese military police, the *Kempeitai*, and revealed the names of the agents in the network. His betrayal led to Lim Bo Seng's eventual capture. As gratitude for his cooperation, the Japanese put all fishing boats on Pangkor Island under Chua, who survived the war.

Davis, Major (later Colonel) John L. H.
Like Broadhurst, Davis had also served in the pre-war Federated Malayan States Police Force and was a member of the SOE's Oriental Mission in Singapore. He, along with Broome, escaped the fall of Singapore and helped run agents and a clandestine organisation in Malaya. Davis played a key role in negotiations with the Malayan Communist Party (MCP) after the war but retired in 1947 before returning to Malaya to serve as a District Officer. He advised British forces during the Malayan Emergency.

Ivory, Lieutenant Colonel Basil Gerritsen
Born on 25 May 1901, Ivory was commissioned in the Royal Artillery (Territorial Army). He is believed to have served with the SOE in China and arranged the terms of service for Lim Bo Seng but not much else is known about his wartime role as his files are still classified.

Li Han Kwang/Lee Han Kwong @ Lee Ah Cheng/Lee Tsing
A nationalist Chinese who had joined Force 136, Lee was initially tasked with coordinating the monthly rendezvous but because of a clash with Davis, Lee became demoralised. However, his escape from the *Kempeitai* showed his resourcefulness. After the destruction of the network, Lee remained in the jungle camp for the rest of the Occupation.

Liang Yuan Ming @ Lee Chuen/Lee Choon
Another nationalist Chinese who joined Force 136, Liang was infiltrated into Malaya on 12 September 1943 as part of GUSTAVUS IV, led by Richard Broome. He remained in the jungle camps and served as a signals operator, the role for which he had been trained.

Lim Bo Seng @ Tan Choon Lim/Tang/Ah Lim
Born on 27 April 1909, Lim was trained by Force 136 to lead the Perak spy network. Captured after one of his agents broke under interrogation, Lim died on 29 June 1944. It took the British Government more than three years after the war to recognise Lim's contribution with a reduced version of a promised pension to his widow and seven children. Lim is a national hero in Taiwan and Singapore.

Lung Chiu Ying @ Ah Long/Ah Loong
Another resourceful Force 136 agent, Lung replaced Li Han Kwang as the main rendezvous contact and went along with Chua to make the meetings with the monthly submarine visits. However, he was unable to make contact with the submarines from January to March and was on his way to the April rendezvous when he met Li on the way out of the jungle camp and was thus not captured. He survived the war.

Mackenzie, Colin Hercules
Born on 5 October 1898, Mackenzie was appointed head of the SOE India Mission in 1942 and was made Commander of Force 136 when the name of the organisation was changed.

Moh Wing Pun @ Muk Ching/Mok Kee/Lee
An ethnic Chinese journalist who worked for the Japanese in the Ipoh Information Department during the Occupation, Moh was recruited into the underground resistance movement in Malaya by Lim Bo Seng. He was the Force 136 representative in Ipoh and was captured with Lim along Gopeng Road as they tried to escape from the Japanese cordon that was tightening around Force 136 members. Tan Chong Tee had accused Moh of collaborating with the Japanese but action was never taken on this allegation.

Tan Chong Tee @ Lim Soong/Tan Thiam Seng/Ah Lim
A Force 136 agent recruited by Lim Bo Seng in Chungking, Tan was stationed in Lumut. He was also captured by the Japanese. Tan survived the end of the war and wrote his memoirs, describing the events surrounding the destruction of the spy ring. Tan went on to become a Singaporean hero on the badminton court.

Tan Kong Cheng @ Kong Ching
One of the first locals to begin helping the Force 137 spy network, Tan and his wife were eventually responsible for conveying food to the agents.

Wu Chye Sin @ Goh Meng Chye/Ah Ng/Wong Kwong Fai
Described by Davis and Broome as one of their best and most resourceful agents, Wu was also having an affair while operating as an agent for Force 136, a fact that upset some of his colleagues. He survived the war and was awarded an Order of the British Empire (OBE) for his services.

Yi Tian Song @ Tan Sek Fu/Tan Shi Fu/Chan Siak Foo
Recruited by Lim Bo Seng in Chungking, Yi arrived in Malaya on GUSTAVUS IV as well. Trained as a signal operator, he was based at Tapah. He was later captured by the Japanese but survived the war.

THE JAPANESE

Chudo, Admiral Kaigyo
DCoS to Field Marshal Count Terauchi, Chudo had commanded the 8th Section of the Japanese Navy General Staff and had been involved in the aborted plans to invade Australia.

Fukudome, Vice Admiral Shigeru
Commander of the 10th Area Fleet, Fukudome had been Director of the 1st Section (Plans and Operations) of the Japanese naval staff at the time of the attack on Pearl Harbour. He was one of the officers principally responsible for planning the destruction of the American fleet. Fukudome was executed as a war criminal in 1948.

Ishiguro, Lieutenant General Teizo
Appointed GOC, 28th Division (1940–1943), Ishiguro was later made GOC of the 6th Army (1943–1944). He ended his career as CinC of the Japanese 29th Army in Malaya (1944–1945).

Itagaki, General Seishiro
Born in 1885, Itagaki was CO of the 33rd Regiment in China (1928) and became DCoS of the Kwangtung army in Manchuria in 1934. A year later, he became CoS and then served as GOC, 5th Division, in China. He subsequently served as Minister of War (1938–1939) and then as CoS, China Expeditionary Army (1939–1941). He served a major portion of the war as CinC of the Chosen Army in Korea (1941–1945) and as CinC, 17th Area Army, in Korea before being posted as CinC, 7th Area Army, in Singapore as well as the Japanese Governor of Johor State. After signing the 4 September and 12 September surrenders, Itagaki was tried, condemned to death and hanged as a war criminal in 1948.

Kimura, General Hyotaro
Kimura was appointed Vice War Minister (1941–1944) and was also a member of the Supreme War Council (1943) before being appointed Commander of the Japanese army in Burma (1944–1945). Kimura was executed as a war criminal in 1948.

Numata, Lieutenant General Tokazo
CoS of the Japanese 2nd Area Army in the Celebes, Numata was later appointed as CoS of the Japanese southern army (1944–1945).

Terauchi, Field Marshal Count Hsiaichi
CinC of the Japanese southern army, Terauchi based his final headquarters in Saigon in 1944. He had suffered a debilitating stroke early in 1945 and as a result of its after-effects, was unable to surrender to Mountbatten in Singapore in September 1945. Mountbatten accepted Terauchi's surrender in Saigon in November 1945 before the Field Marshal was transferred to Singapore where he died in 1946. His ashes are located in a special shrine at the Japanese Cemetery in Singapore.

Tojo, General Hideki
Born on 30th December 1884, Tojo became head of the Kwantung army's military police in September 1935, following which he was appointed CoS to the Kwantung army (1937–1938). In July 1941, Tojo was appointed Minister of War and became prime minister on 16th October 1941. Tojo also held the posts of Minister of War, Home Minister and Foreign Minister. From February 1944, he was also CinC of the General Staff. He ordered the attack on Pearl Harbour on 7 December 1941. Tojo resigned from office July 1944 and tried to kill himself by shooting himself in the chest as Allied forces tried to arrest him in 1945. Tojo survived, was tried as a war criminal and executed on 23 December 1948.

Uozumi, Rear Admiral Jisaku
Having served in the First World War, Uozumi was Captain of the Japanese cruiser *Haguro* in 1942. He saw action at the Battle of the Java Sea where the remnants of the British and Dutch naval forces were destroyed by a superior Japanese naval fleet. Uozumi had also served as a senior officer on the Japanese naval staff before being appointed Naval Commander of Penang Island in August 1944.

THE INDIAN NATIONAL ARMY (INA)

Bose, Rash Behari
An Indian independence leader, Bose had gone into exile in Japan after a failed attempt to assassinate the Viceroy of India, Lord Hardinge, on 23 December 1912. Bose was one of the founders of the Indian Independence League and played a key role in setting up the first INA. After a fallout with Mohan Singh, he ran the movement by himself until Subhas Chandra Bose's arrival.

Bose, Subhas Chandra
An Indian nationalist leader, Bose was president of the Congress Party but later broke ranks with Mahatma Gandhi and Jawaharlal Nehru. Bose fled to Germany and set up the Azad Hind Fauj, which fought with the Wehrmacht in North Africa. Following Japan's victory in the Far East, Bose came to Asia to assume command of the Indian Independence movement. He set up an Indian government-in-exile and believed the men of the INA would be able to liberate India through the battle in Burma. With the Japanese routed in Burma and the war lost in August 1945, Bose was attempting to fly to Russia when his plane is believed to have crashed in Formosa. Bose was said to have been killed. Many do not believe this and hold that he survived the end of the war. Nonetheless, the INA was disbanded and the men repatriated.

Singh, Captain Mohan
A member of the Indian army, Singh was captured during the Malayan Campaign and was convinced to lead the first INA. However, he disagreed with Rash Behari Bose and felt the Japanese were using the INA to achieve their own aims. He tried to disband the first INA, following which he was put under house arrest, where he remained until the end of the war.

CIVIL ADMINISTRATORS AND DIPLOMATS

Lee Kuan Yew

Born on 16 September 1923, Lee led Singapore to independence and served as its first prime minister. He led the country through merger and then separation from Malaysia and then made the republic an economic superpower. In 1990, he stepped down as prime minister though he remained in the cabinet as senior minister and, later, minister mentor.

Selkirk, Lord, Sir George Nigel Douglas-Hamilton, 10th Earl of Selkirk

Born on 4 January 1906, he succeeded in 1940 as the 10th Earl of Selkirk. He became the UK Commissioner General for Southeast Asia (1957–1963) and UK Commissioner for Singapore (1963). He was also the UK Council Representative for Seato from 1960 to 1963. For services rendered, he was made Knight of the Order of the Thistle (KT) and Knight Grand Cross of the Order of St Michael and St George (GCMG) and awarded the Grand Cross of the British Empire (GBE). Selkirk died on 24 November 1994.

Tunku Abdul Rahman

Known as the Father of Malaysian Independence, he was born on 8 February 1903. The seventh son and twentieth child of Sultan Abdul Hamid Halim Shah, the 24th Sultan of Kedah, the Tunku became Chief Minister of the Federation of Malaya in 1955 and the country's first prime minister at independence in 1957. He remained prime minister after Sabah, Sarawak and Singapore joined in 1963 to form Malaysia and after Singapore separated in 1965. Following the 1969 racial riots, the Tunku resigned as prime minister in 1970. He died on 6 December 1990.

ENDNOTES

1 Details on SOE personnel are sketchy as most personnel files are still classified.

Appendix F: Reproductions of Original Documents (Part I)

INSTRUCTIONS TO THE JAPANESE FORCES UNDER THE COMMAND OR CONTROL OF JAPANESE COMMANDERS SINGAPORE AREA

(Courtesy of the National Archives, London)

On board H.M.S. SUSSEX in position
01° 10' North, 103° 30' East.

4th September, 1945.

Sir,

I have the honour to report that the enclosed Agreement was signed at 1805 FG in the Admiral's fore-cabin on board H.M.S. SUSSEX. The original has been sent to the Supreme Allied Commander South East Asia by General Sir Philip Christison. One copy was handed to General Itagaki, General Commanding 7th Area Army and the other copy to Vice-Admiral Fukodome, Commander-in-Chief of the 10th Zone Fleet.

I have the honour to be, Sir,
Your humble and obedient servant,

Rear-Admiral.

Admiral Sir Arthur J. Power, K.C.B., C.V.O.
Commander-in-Chief East Indies Station.

INSTRUCTIONS TO THE JAPANESE FORCES UNDER COMMAND OR CONTROL OF JAPANESE COMMANDERS SINGAPORE AREA.

1. The Japanese Commanders, Singapore Area, being fully aware that all Japanese Sea, Land, Air and Auxiliary Forces have already been surrendered unconditionally at Tokio by the Japanese Government to the Allied Powers, and that hostilities have ceased, do hereby agree to put into force immediately certain measures to prepare for the acceptance of the surrender of the Japanese Forces in the Singapore Area. You are required to confirm by appending your signatures and seal below that the definitions given in Appendix "A" are understood, and that you will carry out the following instructions as directed in Appendices "B" and "C" attached.

2. These definitions and instructions are drawn up in the English language, which is the only authentic version. In any case of doubt as to the intention or meaning, the decision of the Supreme Allied Commander, South East Asia, is final.

3. Since the Japanese Commanders of the Singapore Area have had no instructions or orders as yet regarding saluting and the surrender of Officers' swords from the Supreme Japanese Commander, Southern Region, paragraph 6, Appendix "B" and paragraph 2 (c) Appendix "C" are temporarily held in abeyance until such instructions and orders are received by them.

XXXX) Representing the
Rear-Admiral) Supreme Allied
XXXX) Commander, South
Lt. General) East Asia.

XXXX

4th September, 1945

XXXX

APPENDIX "A"

DEFINITION OF TERMS USED IN THE INSTRUCTIONS CONTAINED IN APPENDICES "B" AND "C"

1. "The Singapore Area" means the area bounded on the North by a line including Mersing, KLUANG, Batu Pahat, on the South by the latitude of 00 30' North and on the East and West by the longtitude of 102 54' E and 105 00' E, but not including Sumatra.

2. "Japanese Forces" means all Japanese Army and Naval Forces.

3. "Japanese Army Forces" means all Japanese Land and Army Air Forces, including Administrative Troops, Para-Military organisations ancillary forces, Security Police, and Japanese Allied Forces in the Singapore Area, or under the command or control of the Japanese Army Commander, Singapore.

4. "The Japanese Army Commander" means the Senior Japanese Army Officer in the Singapore Area.

5. "Japanese Naval Forces" means all Japanese Naval ships and craft and all Naval personnel controlled by the Japanese Army or Naval Commander.

6. "Naval ships and craft" means all vessels of the Japanese Navy or Merchant Navy or controlled by the Japanese Army or Naval Commader. It includes submarines, auxiliary craft, coastal forces, tugs and powered harbour craft.

7. "Naval personnel" means all Japanese Naval and Mercantile personnel, Naval Air Force and Base personnel, and other personnel controlled by the Japanese Naval Commander.

8. "The Japanese Naval Commander" means the Senior Japanese Naval Officer in the Singapore Area.

9. Any orders issued regarding the Singapore Area in the name of the Senior British Naval or Army Commander by any British Officer or Subordinate Commander will be regarded as the Orders of the Supreme Allied Commander, South East Asia.

A P P E N D I X "B"

INSTRUCTIONS TO BE CARRIED OUT BY 0200 GREENWICH MEAN TIME ON WEDNESDAY, 5TH SEPTEMBER, 1945.

MAINTENANCE OF LAW AND ORDER AND FEEDING OF CIVIL POPULATION.

1. The Japanese Army and Naval Commanders Singapore will be responsible for the maintenance of law and order and the prevention of looting, and the maintenance of all essential public services, and for the care and feeding of the civil population until such time as the British Forces assume control.

2. The existing rationing and price control systems will be continued until further orders, and all books and documents thereto will be preserved and handed over intact.

3. To assist to maintain order and preserve public safety, the Military and Civil Police Forces and the Military, Naval and Civilian Fire Brigades will remain at their posts in a state of readiness.

MAINTENANCE OF JAPANESE FORCES.

4. The Japanese Army and Naval Commander Singapore will continue to be responsible for the maintenance of their Forces until such time as this responsibility is assumed by the British Commanders.

DISCIPLINE OF JAPANESE FORCES.

5. Japanese Commanders, at all levels, will be informed that, pending further instructions, they will be responsible for the maintenance of discipline among their own personnel, providing that no sentence of death or corporal punishment will be put into force without prior reference to the local Allied Commanders, who must not be below the rank of Brigadier or equivalent Naval rank. Should any Japanese commit offences against local inhabitants in the area, those actually committing the offence and their immediate and formation commanders will be subject to disciplinary action.

6. All Japanese Military and Naval personnel of whatever rank will salute all Allied Officers. Failure to do this will be an offence and will be dealt with. Allied Officers will return salutes.

PROHIBITION OF DESTRUCTION

7. All demolitions, destruction, damage and sabotage of all kinds whatsoever are prohibited. In particular, the following are to be placed under guard until taken over by British Forces:-

(a) Arms, equipment, tanks, vehicles, artillery, ammunition, explosives all warlike stores, and all supplies.

(b) Fortifications and their armaments, field works.

(c) All aircraft and equipment, and airfields.

(d) All signal communications of all kinds; all broadcasting stations, equipment and facilities.

(e) Civil stores, all food stocks, stocks of raw and prepared opium, all stocks of liquor and spirits, all land, water and air transportation and communication facilities and equipment, public utilities, workshops, and harbour facilities.

(f) All documents, records, archives, cyphers and codes, both Military and Civil. This is to include those prior to the Japanese occupation and during it.

(g) Charts of minefields, booby traps and other dangerous obstacles and Survey Maps.

(h) Plans of fixed and field defences.

(i) All stocks of petrol, oil, lubricants and other fuel.

(j) All stocks of material, whether raw or prepared.

(k) All ships and craft of any kind operated by the Japanese Forces.

(l) All radar stations and equipment, including detecting and counter-acting equipment.

8. The Japanese officers in charge of the guards placed in accordance with the preceding paragraph will be held personally responsible for the condition of installations, equipment, stores, buildings and papers in their care.

STAND FAST

9. All movements of Japanese Forces will cease except as ordered by the British Commanders, and to comply with paragraph headed "Withdrawal of Japanese Forces".

10. All aircraft will be grounded, and will remain grounded except as ordered by the British Commanders.

11. Any movements of troops, naval ships and craft, or aircraft without the authority of the British Commanders will be treated as a hostile act.

WITHDRAWAL OF JAPANESE FORCES.

12. All Japanese Forces will be evacuated from the areas marked "A", "B", "C", "D" and "E" on the attached map, and in addition the area to the South and inclusive of the Stamford Canal as far West on the junction of Paterson Hill Road and Grange Road, thence Irwell Bank Road - Kimsong Road to the Singapore River and the Cathay Buildings.

13. All Japanese Forces on Singapore Island will be withdrawn, in accordance with instructions to be issued, into the area on the mainland bounded on the North by the general line, all inclusive Mersing - Kluang, Batu Pahat and on the South by exclusive the Road Pontian Kechil - Skudai - Tebrau - Masai.

14. All Japanese Forces under command or control of 46 Division will concentrate within the above area.

15. The minimum forces necessary to maintain law and order, guard dumps, installations, public services, warehouses, etc., and to prevent looting and sabotage, will be left in evacuated areas. On being relieved by Allied Forces these guards will be despatched to join their parent units under arrangements made by the Allied Forces.

16. "Prove safe" parties of Japanese will be required, and will be left behind in the evacuated areas.

17. Every member of the Japanese Forces, including auxiliary personnel and police, who are left behind in any evacuated area, will wear a white arm band.

18. A small Japanese Military Staff, limited to 20 persons in all, for Adminstrative purposes, will remain in Area "A" for work with the Allied Force Headquarters. In addition, 30 English-speaking Japanese will be made available for interpretation and to act as guides for the Allied Forces. These interpreters will be located with the staff mentioned above, available to be called forward as required.

COMMUNICATIONS

19. (a) All communications in code and cypher are prohibited.

(b) All signal communications, other than those permitted in paragraph (c) below are prohibited.

(c) Communications in clear between Army and Naval Commanders, Singapore, and their subordinate commanders may continue, subject to such supervision as the British Commanders may decide.

(d) No W/T transmitters are to be used without the authority of the British Commanders.

MILITARY TRANSPORT

20. All Japanese motor transport, including civil transport requisitioned by the Japanese Forces, will be concentrated in Motor Transport Parks within the evacuated area "A", and 100 lorries, on Kallang Airfield, with drivers available and filled with petrol and oil. Allied Forces will take over control of all such Motor Transport.

21. All the above vehicles will have a white flag flying.

22. No Civil or Military vehicles will move within the evacuated area on the day of occupation, except those used in the handing over proceedings and others authorised by the British Commanders.

ORDER OF BATTLE

23. The Order of Battle and Location Statementsoof all Japanese Forces located in the Singapore Area, as defined in Appendix "A" will be submitted to Headquarters 15th Ind. Corps on the first day of occupation.

CURFEW

24. A curfew, confining all persons to their houses and forbidding any movement outside, from 1800 hrs. to 0600 hrs. will be enforced until further orders, starting on the day of occupation. The Japanese Commander will be held responsible for the promulgation of the Curfew to all personnel, including the civilian population, on the first day of the occupation.

NAVAL SHIPS AND CRAFT

25. No personnel are to leave their ship or craft and Commanding Officers are to be on board to hand over their ships.

26. All special attack craft are to be rendered harmless and placed under guard.

27. All guns are to be unloaded and the breech blocks are to be removed and placed alongside the guns.

NAVAL SHIPS AND CRAFT - (CONTD.)

28. All torpedoes are to be unloaded and their warheads removed.

29. All explosives are to be struck down to the magazine; the magazines are to be locked and the keys held by the Commanding Officers.

30. Japanese ships and craft are to hoist and keep flying until further orders, a white ensign over their national flag. If this is not possible, a black flag only is to be flown at the masthead.

31. All minesweeping Forces are to keep their full crews and equipment on board, and are to be at the disposal of the British Naval Commander for the clearance of minefields. All ammunition in minesweepers is to be thrown over the side.

PRISONERS OF WAR AND INTERNEES

32. (a) The Japanese Commander will ensure the protection, good treatment, care and feeding of all Prisoners of War and Internees until such time as the British Commanders take over the responsibility.

(b) Ensure that all APWI are relieved forthwith of all forms of work.

(c) All records concerning Prisoners of War and Internees are to be kept intact and handed over to the British Army Commander.

CIVIL PRISONERS

33. All occupants of the civil prisons are to remain there, and the prisons are to be kept under guard. All records in connection with the occupants are to be kept intact and handed over to the British Army Commander.

HOSPITALS

34. All hospital staffs are to remain at their hospitals in charge of their patients until further orders are given. All drugs and equipment in hospitals will be left in position.

HEADS OF SERVICES

35. The Senior Representative of the Port Organisation, Civil Administration and Public Utility Services are to remain at their posts, and are to be instructed to assist in maintaining their particular service, and preventing sabotage.

36. The existing Japanese Civil Administration (including the Shonan Special Municipality) and all Japanese concerned therewith, will continue to function and remain at their posts until further orders.

TECHNICIANS.

37. All technical personnel of dockyard, port installations, public utility services and wireless stations will remain at their posts.

PILOTS

38. All the local port and harbour pilots are to be held at the disposal of the British Naval Commander.

PORT LABOUR

39. All available stevedores, gangers, and in addition 1,000 unskilled labourers to work the port will be made available at one hour's notice on instructions from the British Commanders.

TREATMENT OF RESISTANCE FORCES

40. All personnel of all resistance and guerilla forces in all areas occupied by the Japanese Forces shall be treated by the Japanese Forces as if they were Allied Forces. All reprisals against such personnel, and all acrion which may harm or injure them is prohibited.

INFECTIOUS DISEASES

41. Japanese Commanders will be responsible for disclosing forthwith the nature, type and extent of outbreak of any infectious diseases within the territory under their control, and for ensuring that all possible steps are taken to prevent any spread of such diseases.

FINANSE

42. (a) All Treasuries, Banks and Financial Houses, whether State or private, will cease forthwith.

(b) All coin, notes, species, valuables of any kind (including bonds and securities) and all books of account and business documents to be safeguarded.

(c) The printing and issue of all further paper currency in prohibited.

POSTS AND TELEGRAPHS

43. All public business is to cease forthwith and premises to be closed to the public. No further handling of postal and telegraphic matter will take place. All stocks of stamps, currency,

POSTS AND TELEGRAPH - (CONTINUED)

postal and telegraphic matter, records and books of accounts to be safeguarded.

NEWSPAPERS, ETC.

44. The publication of all newspapers and other forms of propaganda will cease forthwith. All printing presses will be closed and safeguarded and their whereabouts disclosed.

APPENDIX "C"

FURTHER ACTION REQUIRED BY THE BRITISH COMMANDERS

DISARMAMENT

1. All Japanese Forces will disarm and will move to the concentration areas mentioned in Appendix "B", paragraph 13.

2. All Japanese Forces will disarm in accordance with the following principles:-

(a) Weapons, after cleaning and oiling, and ammunition will be put in central dumps each for not less than one battalion or equivalent where possible.

(b) Dumps will be guarded. These guards may retain rifles on the minimum scale necessary but not automatic weapons or grenades.

(c) All officers' weapons, including swords, will be given up whenever their unit or formation as a whole disarm.

(d) Japanese Commanders will arrange disarmament of all subsidiary forces armed by them, and will be responsible that the personnel of such forces are not permitted to disperse. In particular, the INA will remain in their units or formations under their own officers.

NAVAL SHIPS AND CRAFT

3. British parties will board all ships and craft and will inspect them removing breech blocks and such material as they deem necessary. Thereafter, a daily inspection of ships will be carried out by officers of the British Navy.

4. The provision of necessary supplies to Japanese personnel in ships and craft will be arranged by the British Naval Commander.

5. Orders for the disposal of ammunition will be issued later.

6. The crews of all ships and craft, except minesweepers, will be reduced to one-fifth complement, the disembarked personnel being removed to the area mentioned in Appendix "B" paragraph 13.

JAPANESE, GERMAN AND ITALIAN NATIONALS.

7. Lists will be compiled without delay in English of all German and Italian Nationals, whether Naval, Military, Air Force or Civil, and Japanese civilians, showing full names, sex, age, occupation, and place of residence in Singapore and in Japan or Germany or Italy. No such personnel will leave the Singapore Area.

8. All Japanese, German and Italian businesses (other than those essential to the life of the community) will cease public business forthwith. Premises will be closed to the public, and all cash, goods, stock in trade and books of accounts will be preserved.

9. Lists in English of all Japanese, German and Italian businesses in the Singapore Area will be compiled showing the name and nature of the business, address of the business permises, name of the manager or owner, number and names of Japanese, German and Italian employees, address of Head Office in Japan, Germany, Italy or elsewhere.

10. All German and Italian civilians not engaged on public services or work essential to the life of the community, are to remain in their residences until further orders.

MEDICAL

11. The Japanese Medical Authorities will

(a) Produce details of the sanitary arrangements and apparatues in existance.

(b) Produce detailed malaria charts of Singapore Island.

(c) State the location of all hospitals, laboratories, medical stores and installations.

(d) Give the names and locations of all Allied sick and wounded, who are in Japanese medical care, other than those in Prisoner of War Camps.

(e) Ensure that the Singapore General Hospital, located at New Bridge Road, will be emptied of all Japanese patients by 1130 Greenwich Mean Time on the day of occupation, except those unfit to be moved. The hospital will be clean and in every way fit for immediate use. All other property vacated by the Japanese will be left clean and ready for use.

RESTITUTION OF PROPERTY.

12. Everything of every nature whatsoever that may have been requisitioned, taken or otherwise acquired by the Japanese in territories occupied by Japanese Forces, or in territories which they have entered, shall be surrendered and restored in accordance with the direction of the Supreme Allied Commander, South East Asia.

Appendix F: Reproductions of Original Documents (Part II)

ORDERS OF THE COMMANDER OCCUPYING FORCE TO THE JAPANESE COMMANDER OF SINGAPORE

(Courtesy of the National Archives, London)

No Action
File
TOP SECRET
SACSEA Mission
221
31 Aug 45

ORDERS OF THE COMMANDER OCCUPYING FORCE'
TO THE JAPANESE COMMANDER OF SINGAPORE.

94

(a) All JAPANESE Forces to be withdrawn from SINGAPORE Island by hours on the day of occupation. Your order of battle and location statements of all troops under your command will be submitted to this Headquarters by hours on the day of occupation. Prior to their departure all arms and equipment to be left dumped in areas. This to include all small arms, automatics, grenades, dahs and all ammunition and stores connected therewith.

(b) All guns to have the breech blocks removed.

(c) Tanks to be parked in unit areas.

(d) Only minimum guards to be left on these dumps and parks to ensure their safety and good order.

2. (a) Every member of all branches of the JAPANESE Forces and their Puppet Forces remaining on the island to wear a white arm band.

(b) Personnel not surrendering will be outlawed, and escaping surrendered personnel will be severely dealt with.

3. The JAPANESE will be held responsible for the maintenance of Law and Order and for any looting or destruction prior to the arrival and taking over of the occupying Force.

4. (a) The minimum force necessary will remain in SINGAPORE Town and Island area to maintain Law and Order, to guard dumps, installations, public services, ware houses, docking equipment and to prevent all looting or sabotage.

(b) The existing JAPANESE civil administration (including the SHONAN Special Municipality and the Police) will continue to function, and all JAPANESE concerned therewith will remain at their posts until further orders.

(c) All Japanese and Civil Port Authorities and personnel will remain at their posts and will have ready all available stevedores, gangers and the necessary unskilled labour to work the port.

(d) All technical personnel who are operating company, public or other installations including Wireless Telegraphy, water, lighting, gas, sanitation etc., will remain until the occupying Force takes over control of the said installations.

5. (a) All gun sites and guns to be disclosed.

(b) All mines, booby traps to be disclosed and removed by JAPANESE personnel under supervision of occupying Force.

(c) "Prove Safe" parties of JAPANESE will be required (from the force in 4 (a) above).

(d) All hospital staffs to remain at their hospital until further orders.

(e) All Port Installations including cranes etc., to be handed over in good condition.

(f) A responsible guard or caretaker will be left in every building vacated by the JAPANESE Forces to ensure its safe keeping and to prevent looting.

(g) All BRITISH and JAPANESE administrative records will be safeguarded and their locations disclosed. None will be destroyed. This order includes, in addition to all other records:-
(i) The records of the British Custodian of Enemy Property, and of the Japanese Custodian of Property, the former including all records under the Trading with the Enemy Act.

3/8(a)

/To Sheet TWO .. 2/

221a

Sheet TWO .. 2 95

(g) (continued)

(ii) All Survey maps, charts and plans.
(ii) All titles and records of the Land Office, including all records of dealings with lands and of the issue of title to lands, during the Japanese occupation.

(h) All cash and currency, including money orders and stamps held in bulk by the Japanese Armed Forces and the Civil Administration will be frozen and further instructions as to it's disposal will be issued later.

6. (a) All JAPANESE motor transport including civil requisitioned by JAPANESE to be collected in Motor Transport Parks under guards and to be handed over in good condition.

(b) Of the motor transport specified in 6(a) above 500 lorries with drivers will be collected at Dock area by hours on the day of occupation and 100 lorries at KALANG Airfield. All these lorries and vehicles to have a white flag flying.

(c) 100 large staff cars in high class condition to be available on the second day of oc-cupation for use by occupying Force.

(d) No civil or military vehicles other than the above will move on the day of occupation except those used in the handing over proceedings.

(e) CLEMENCEAU AVENUE will be cleared of all vehicular and pedestrian traffic from dawn on the second day of occupation until further orders.

7. Arrangements to be made for the local civil authorities to be available from hours onwards on the day of occupation to contact the Commander of the occupying Force.

8. A curfew confining all inhabitants to their houses and forbidding any movement from sun set to sun rise will be enforced until further notice starting on the day of occupation, except for personnel employed on essential services who must have a signed permit.

9. All stocks and stores of spirits, liquor shops, breweries etc., will be closed and guarded. Any other large supplies will be dis-closed.

10. All JAPANESE flags or tokens will be removed.

11. (a) A small JAPANESE Headquarters for Administrative purposes will remain in SINGAPORE Town for work with Force Headquarters.

(b) Four similar Headquarters will be required to work with minor formations in the Island Area and will be ready to move immediately when so ordered.

(c) In each of these Headquarters 20 interpreters and guides will be available.

12. No JAPANESE Officer above the rank of MAJOR will be employed in contact with disarmed JAPANESE and/or Puppet Forces. These will be concentrated under orders of the Commander, Occupying Force.

13. (a) The where-abouts and numbers of all Allied Prisoners of War and Civil Internee Camps, permanent and temporary, will be disclosed.

(b) You will report by hours on
(i) Numbers by nationalities giving in each case their location.
(ii) The number of sick at each location which cannot be moved.

(c) (i) All Allied prisoners will be relieved forthwith of all forms of work.
(ii) They will be fed by you until taken over by the occupying Force.
(iii) You are responsible that they come to no harm until taken over by the occupying Force.

To Sheet THREE ... 3

2216

96

Sheet THREE ... 3

14. ( ) Responsible representatives of the following departments will be available by hours on day of occupation and will be in possession of all relevant information in connection therewith:-

(a) Engineer Services.

(b) Supply (Food)

(c) Supply (Petrol)

(d) Inter-communication and Signals.

(e) Railways.

(f) Prisoners of War and Civilian Internees.

BGS (O)
GSO 1 (S)
G II (X)
G III (X) 1
G III (X) 2
G III (X) 3
G II (N)
G III (N) 1
G III (N)
G II (S)
G III (S)

15. (a) A JAPANESE Medical Officer, with an interpreter with medical knowledge will be included in the Headquarters detailed in paragraph 11(a) above.

He will produce full details of the following matters relating to SINGAPORE Town and Island.

(i) The presence of any epidemic, endemic or infectious diseases and the measures taken to control them.
(ii) The sanitary arrangements and apparatus in existence.
(iii) Detailed malaria charts of SINGAPORE ISLAND.
(iv) The locations of all hospitals, laboratories, medical stores and installations.
(v) The names and locations of all Allied sick and wounded who are in JAPANESE Medical care (other than those in Prisoners of War Camps.)

(b) (i) SINGAPORE General Hospital located at NEW BRIDGE STREET will be emptied of all JAPANESE patients except those unfit to be moved, before occupation of the island by the Force.
(ii) This hospital will be cleaned and in every way prepared for immediate use by the Medical Services of the Force.
(iii) A small staff, with technical interpreters, will remain to operate the water supply, lighting, heating, disinfecting, electricity and X ray apparatus and equipment.

(c) All other hospitals vacated by the JAPANESE Forces will be left clean and ready for use.

16. No aircraft will leave the ground.

17. All aircraft, stores and air-field equipment will be guarded and kept in good condition.

18. JAPANESE troops leaving the Island will take three days food with them, all other supplies, civil and military, will be guarded until arrival of the occupying Force and then handed over intact.

19. All JAPANESE Commanders will be held personally responsible for the behaviour and discipline of the troops under their immediate command.

20. If any doubt or dispute arises as to the meaning or interpretation of these orders, the decision of the Commander, Occupying Force will be final.

The English version of these orders are the authentic text.

E. Mansergh

MAJOR GENERAL.
COMMANDER OCCUPYING FORCE.

Appendix F: Reproductions of Original Documents (Part III)

INSTRUMENT OF SURRENDER OF JAPANESE FORCES IN SOUTHEAST ASIA

(Courtesy of the National Archives, London)

3/43 (P) 21A

SECRET. **Copy No.** 39

C.O.S. (45) 229.

26th September, 1945.

CHIEFS OF STAFF COMMITTEE.

INSTRUMENT OF SURRENDER OF JAPANESE FORCES IN SOUTH-EAST ASIA.

NOTE BY THE SECRETARY.

THE annexed copy of the Instrument of Surrender of Japanese forces under the command or control of the Supreme Commander, Japanese Expeditionary Forces, Southern Region, within the operational theatre of the Supreme Allied Commander, South East Asia, as signed at Singapore at 0341 hours G.M.T. on the 12th September, 1945, is circulated for information and record.

At Appendix " A " is a copy of the Supreme Allied Commander's statement made prior to the actual signature of the Instrument of Surrender, together with a copy of General Itagaki's credentials at Appendix " B."

(Signed) L. C. HOLLIS.

Offices of the Cabinet and Minister of Defence, S.W. 1,
26th September, 1945.

ANNEX.

INSTRUMENT OF SURRENDER OF JAPANESE FORCES UNDER THE COMMAND OR CONTROL OF THE SUPREME COMMANDER, JAPANESE EXPEDITIONARY FORCES, SOUTHERN REGIONS, WITHIN THE OPERATIONAL THEATRE OF THE SUPREME ALLIED COMMANDER, SOUTH-EAST ASIA.

1. In pursuance of and in compliance with :

(*a*) the Instrument of Surrender signed by the Japanese plenipotentiaries by command and on behalf of the Emperor of Japan, the Japanese Government, and the Japanese Imperial General Headquarters at Tokyo on the 2nd September, 1945;

(*b*) General Order No. 1, promulgated at the same place and on the same date;

(*c*) the Local Agreement made by the Supreme Commander, Japanese Expeditionary Forces, Southern Regions, with the Supreme Allied Commander, South-East Asia, at Rangoon on the 27th August, 1945;

to all of which Instrument of Surrender, General Order and Local Agreement this present Instrument is complementary and which it in no way supersedes, the Supreme Commander, Japanese Expeditionary Forces, Southern Regions (Field-Marshal Count Terauchi), does hereby surrender unconditionally to the Supreme Allied Commander, South-East Asia (Admiral the Lord Louis Mountbatten) himself and all Japanese sea, ground, air and auxiliary forces under his command or control and within the operational theatre of the Supreme Allied Commander, South-East Asia.

2. The Supreme Commander, Japanese Expeditionary Forces, Southern Regions, undertakes to ensure that all orders and instructions that may be issued from time to time by the Supreme Allied Commander, South-East Asia, or by any of his subordinate Naval, Military or Air Force Commanders of whatever rank acting in his name, are scrupulously and promptly obeyed by all Japanese

[30578]

2

sea, ground, air and auxiliary forces under the command or control of the Supreme Commander, Japanese Expeditionary Forces, Southern Regions, and within the operational theatre of the Supreme Allied Commander, South-East Asia.

3. Any disobedience of, or delay or failure to comply with, orders or instructions issued by the Supreme Allied Commander, South-East Asia, or issued on his behalf by any of his subordinate Naval, Military or Air Force Commanders of whatever rank, and any action which the Supreme Allied Commander, South-East Asia, or his subordinate Commanders, acting on his behalf, may determine to be detrimental to the Allied Powers, will be dealt with as the Supreme Allied Commander, South-East Asia, may decide.

4. This Instrument takes effect from the time and date of signing.

5. This Instrument is drawn up in the English language, which is the only authentic version. In any case of doubt as to intention or meaning, the decison of the Supreme Allied Commander, South-East Asia, is final. It is the responsibility of the Supreme Commander, Japanese Expeditionary Forces, Southern Regions, to make such translation into Japanese as he may require.

Signed at Singapore at 0341 hours (G.M.T.) on the 12th September, 1945.

(Signed) SEISHIRO ITAGAKI,
for *Supreme Commander,*
Japanese Expeditonary Forces,
Southern Regions.

[Seal.]

(Signed) LOUIS MOUNTBATTEN,
Supreme Allied Commander,
South-East Asia.

[Field-Marshal Count Terauchi's Seal.]

APPENDIX "A."

STATEMENT BY SUPREME ALLIED COMMANDER, SOUTH-EAST ASIA, MADE AT SURRENDER CEREMONY HELD IN THE MUNICIPAL BUILDINGS, SINGAPORE, ON 12TH SEPTEMBER, 1945.

"I HAVE come here to-day to receive the formal surrender of all the Japanese forces within the South-East Asia Command. I have received the following telegram from the Supreme Commander of the Japanese forces concerned, Field-Marshal Count Terauchi :—

> 'The most important occasion of the formal surrender signing at Singapore draws near, the significance of which is no less great to me than to your Excellency. It is extremely regretful that my ill-health prevents me from attending and signing it personally and that I am unable to pay homage to your Excellency. I hereby notify your Excellency that I have fully empowered General Itagaki, the highest senior general in Japanese armies, and send him on my behalf.'

On hearing of Field-Marshal Terauchi's illness, I sent my own doctor, Surgeon Captain Birt, Royal Navy, to examine him, and he certifies that the Field-Marshal is suffering from the effects of a stroke. In the circumstances I have decided to accept the surrender from General Itagaki to-day, but I have warned the Field-Marshal that I shall expect him to make his personal surrender to me as soon as he is fit enough to do so.

In addition to our Naval, Military and Air forces which we have present in Singapore to-day, a large fleet is anchored off Port Swettenham and Port Dixon, and a large force started disembarking from them at daylight on the 9th September. When I visited the force yesterday, there were 100,000 men ashore. This invasion would have taken place on the 9th September whether the Japanese had resisted or not, and I wish to make it entirely clear to General Itagaki that he is surrendering to superior force here in Singapore.

I now call upon General Itagaki to produce his credentials."

3

APPENDIX "B."

Credentials of General Itagaki.

(Translation.)

I, the undersigned, hereby authorise General Seishiro Itagaki, Commander of the Imperial Japanese Seventh Area Army, to make, for and in the name of myself, arrangements and sign an instrument or instruments, with the Supreme Commander of the Allied Forces, South-East Asia, concerning the formal surrender of all the Imperial Japanese Army, Naval, Air and Auxiliary Forces which are under my command or control and are within the operational theatre of the Supreme Allied Commander, South-East Asia.

Done at Saigon this 10th day of the 9th month of the 20th year of Showa, corresponding to the 10th of September, 1945, of the Christian era.

(L.S). HISAICHI TERAUCHI,
Field-Marshal, Count, Supreme Commander of the Imperial Japanese Force, Southern Region.

[Seal.]

Selected Bibliography

Primary Sources

Great Britain, The National Archives (Public Records Office), London

ADM116 Admiralty: Record Office: Cases. 1852–1965.

ADM199 Admiralty: War History Cases and Papers, Second World War. 1922-1968.

CAB79 War Cabinet and Cabinet: Chiefs of Staff Committee: Minutes. 1939–1946.

CAB81 War Cabinet and Cabinet: Committees and Sub-committees of the Chiefs of Staff Committee: Minutes and Papers. 1939–1947.

CAB119 War Cabinet and Cabinet Office: Joint Planning Staff: Correspondence and Papers. 1939-1948.

CAB122 War Cabinet and Cabinet Office: British Joint Staff Mission and British Joint Services Mission: Washington Office Records. 1940–1958.

CAOG9 Crown Agents for Oversea Governments and Administrations: Finance Departments: Registered Files, Funds, Loans and Investments. 1860–1981.

DEFE2 Combined Operations Headquarters, and Ministry of Defence, Combined Operations Headquarters later Amphibious Warfare Headquarters: Records. 1937-1963.

FO371 Foreign Office: Political Departments: General Correspondence from 1906. 1906–1966.

FCO24 Commonwealth Office, Far East and Pacific Department and Foreign and Commonwealth Office, South West Pacific Department: Registered Files (H and FW Series). 1967–1974.

HS1 Special Operations Executive: Far East: Registered Files. 1940–1947.

HS9 Special Operations Executive: Personnel Files (PF Series). 1939–1946.

PREM4 Prime Minister's Office: Confidential Correspondence. 1934–1946.

PREM11 Prime Minister's Office: Correspondence and Papers.1944–1964.

WO193 War Office: Directorate of Military Operations and Plans, later Directorate of Military Operations: Files concerning Military Planning, Intelligence and Statistics (Collation Files). 1934-1958.

WO203 War Office: South East Asia Command: Military Headquarters Papers, Second World War. 1932–1949.

WO259 War Office: Department of the Secretary of State for War: Private Office Papers. 1937-1953.

Great Britain, Imperial War Museum, London

Baker, C.M.S. *Personal Papers. 96/34/11.*

Brown, Lieutenant A. P. G. RNVR. *Personal Papers. 92/27/1.*

Cazalet, Vice Admiral Sir Peter. *Papers.*

Findlay, Major R.J. *Personal Papers. 91/13/1.*

Horne, Captain J.E.T. *Personal Papers. 83/53/1.*

MISC 53 (799). "To All Allied Prisoners of War".

MISC 223 (3215). "Instructions to the Japanese Forces Under Command Or Control of Japanese Commanders, Singapore Area".

Munby, R. *Personal Papers. 87/34/1.*

Sayer, Vice Admiral Sir Guy. *Personal Papers. P68.*

Secondary Sources

Official Histories

Kirby, Major General S. Woodburn. *The War Against Japan,* vols. 1 to 5. London: HMSO, 1965.

Books

Attiwell, Kenneth. *The Singapore Story.* New York: Doubleday, 1960.

Ban, Kah Choon & Yap Hong Kuan. *Rehearsal for War: The Underground War Against the Japanese.* Singapore: Horizon Books, 2002.

Barber, Noel. *A Sinister Twilight: The Fall of Singapore 1942*. Boston: Houghton Mifflin, 1968.

Braddon, Russell. *The Naked Island*. London: Werner Laurie. 1952.

Brett-James, Anthony. *Ball of Fire: 5th Indian Division in World War II*. Aldershot: Gale and Polden, 1951.

Brooke, Field Marshal Alan F., Lord Alanbrooke, 1st Viscount, Baron Alanbrooke Of Brookeborough. *War Diaries 1939–1945: Field Marshall Lord Alanbrooke. Edited by Alex Danchev and Daniel Todman*. London: Weidenfeld and Nicolson, 2001.

Bryant, Arthur. *Triumph in the West 1943–1946*. London: Collins, 1959.

Chapman, Lieutenant Colonel F. Spencer. *The Jungle is Neutral*. London: Chatto & Windus, 1949.

Cheah, Boon Kheng. Red Star Over Malaya: Resistance & Social Conflict during and after the Japanese Occupation, 1941-1946 (Third Edition). Singapore:Singapore University Press, 2003.

Chin, Kee Onn. *Malaya Upside Down*. Singapore: Jitts, 1946.

Chin, Peng. *My Side of History*. Singapore: Media Masters, 2003.

Churchill, Sir Winston S. *The Second World War*, vols. 1 to 6. Boston: Houghton Mifflin, 1950.

Commonwealth War Graves Commission, The. *The War Dead of the British Commonwealth and Empire; The Register of the Names of Those who Fell in the 1939–1945 War and have No Known Grave; The Singapore Memorial: Introduction to the Register*. London: The Commonwealth War Graves Commission, 1957.

Eden, Anthony R., 1st Earl of Avon, Viscount Eden of Royal Leamington Spa. *The Eden Memoirs: The Reckoning*. London: Cassell, 1965.

Falk, Stanley. *Seventy Days to Singapore*. New York: G.P. Putnam's Sons, 1975.

Farrell, Brian and Sandy Hunter (eds.). *Sixty Years On: The Fall of Singapore Revisited*. Singapore: Eastern Universities Press, 2002.

Gough, Richard. *The Jungle was Red*. Singapore: SNP Panpac, 2003.

Hack, Karl and C.C. Chin (eds.). *Dialogues with Chin Peng: New Light on the Malayan Communist Party*. Singapore: Singapore University Press, 2004.

Harrington, Joseph D. *Yankee Samurai: The Secret Role of Nisei in America's Pacific Victory*. Detroit: Pettigrew Enterprises, 1979.

Keay, John. *Last Post: The End of Empire in the Far East.* London: John Murray, 1997.

Kratoska, Paul H. *The Japanese Occupation of Malaya 1941-1945.* London: Hurst & Company, 1998.

Lau, Albert. *A Moment of Anguish: Singapore in Malaysia and the Politics of Disengagement.* Singapore: Times Academic Press, 1998.

Low, Ngiong Ing. *When Singapore was Syonan-To.* Singapore: Eastern Universities Press, 1973.

Mitchell. Austin. *Election '45.* London: Fabian Society, Bellew Publishing, 1995.

Morrison, Ian. *Malayan Postscript.* London: Faber & Faber, 1943.

National Heritage Board, National Archives of Singapore. *The Japanese Occupation 1942–1945: A Pictorial Record of Singapore During the War.* Singapore: Times Editions, 1996.

Owen, Frank. *The Fall of Singapore.* London: Michael Joseph, 1960.

Percival, Lieutenant General Arthur E. *The War in Malaya.* London: Eyre & Spottiswoode, 1949.

Show, Clara. *Lim Bo Seng: Singapore's Best-Known War Hero.* Singapore: Asiapac Books, 1998.

Smyth, John. *Percival and the Tragedy of Singapore.* London: Macdonald, 1971.

Stripp, Alan. *Codebreaker in the Far East.* Oxford: Oxford University Press, 1989.

Tan, Chong Tee. *Force 136: Story of a WWII Resistance Fighter.* Singapore: Asiapac Books, 1995.

Turnbull, Mary. *Dateline Singapore: 150 Years of the Straits Times.* Singapore: Singapore Press Holdings, 1995.

Articles

"'Oot!' Said Mackie and the Jap Colonel Fled". *The Zodiac,* November 1945.

"Japanese in Malaya Surrender in Singapore". *The Straits Times,* 13 September 1945.

"Obituary: The Rev. Guy Armstrong". *Daily Telegraph,* 15 January 2003.

Baxter, Christoper. "In Pursuit of a Pacific Strategy: British Planning for the Defeat of Japan, 1943–45". *Diplomacy & Statecraft,* vol. 15, no. 2, June 2004.

Corr, Gerard. "The War was Over – but Where were the Liberators?". *The Straits Times Annual 1976*. Singapore: Times Publishing Bhd., 1976.

Fursdon, Major General Edward. "Without Saluting the Japanese Came to Bargain but Soon the Sun Set on Their Empire". *The Daily Telegraph,* 12 August 1985.

Lam, Pin Foo. "Japanese Settlers were here before the War". *The Straits Times – Life,* 25 February 1998.

Miller, Harry. "An End to 1,318 Days of Terror". *The Daily Telegraph,* 12 August 1985.

Roberts, Major Frank. "With the Beach Groups in Malaya". *The Malayan Daily News*, 22 October 1945.

Stewart, Athole. "How History was Written at Singapore". *The Zodiac,* December 1945.

Newspapers

Syonan Shimbun, 1944–1945.
The Straits Times, 1945–1975.
The Malayan Tribune, 1945–1948.
The Times of London, 1945–1946.

Websites

Ammentorp, Steen. "Biography of Seishiro Itagaki". *The Generals of WWII.* Accessed 28 January 2005. Available from <http://www. generals.dk/general/Itagaki/Seishiro/Japan.html>.

Ammentorp, Steen. "Biography of Sir Alexander Frank Philip Christison". *The Generals of WWII.* Accessed 28 Jan 2005. Available from <www.generals.dk/general/Christison/Sir_Alexander_Frank_Philip/Great_Britain.html>.

Ammentorp, Steen. "Biography of Sir Frederick Arthur Montague Browning". *The Generals of WWII.* Accessed 28 January 2005. Available from <http://www.generals.dk/general/Browning/Sir_Frederick_Arthur_Montague/Great_Britain.html>.

Ammentorp, Steen. "Biography of Takazo Numata". *The Generals of WWII.* Accessed 28 January 2005. Available from <http://www.generals.dk/general/Numata/Takazo/Japan.html>.

Australian National Flag Association. "Timeline". *Australian National Flag Association.* Accessed 14 August 2004. Available from <http://www.australianflag.org.au/timeline.php>.

Chung, Chee Min. "The Japanese Surrendered at the V.I. – TWICE!". *The Victoria Institution Web Page.* Accessed 14 August 2004. Available from <http://www.viweb.freehosting.net/japsurr.htm>.

Cooper, Carol. "South East Asia Under Japanese Occupation: The Story of Changi". *The Children (& Families) of the Far East Prisoners of War (COFEPOW).* Accessed 13 February 2005. Available from <http://www.cofepow.org.uk/pages/asia_singapore_changi_story.htm>.

Dunn, Peter. "Was there a Japanese Invasion Planned to Occur between Townsville and Brisbane in Queensland during WW2?". *Australia @ War.* Accessed 28 January 2005. Available from <http://home.st.net.au/~dunn/japsland/invade02.htm>.

Fildew, L.G. *Looking back at Singapore 1945-1946.* Accessed 15 August 2004. Available from <http://www.geocities.com/lesfil2000/mypagetoo.html>.

Green, Ken. "Memories of Stoke-on-Trent People – Ken Green". *Stoke-on-Trent.* Accessed 10 September 2004. Available from <http://www.thepotteries.org/memories/green_ken5.htm>.

Houterman, Hans. *World War II Unit Histories and Officers.* Accessed 12 February 2005. Available from <http://houterman.htmlplanet.com/home.html>

Malaya Historical Group. "Operation Zipper". *Malaya Historical Group: Malaya – Wrecks Research Group: Malaysian Military & Aviation Research & Project.* Accessed 26 August 2004. Available from <http://www. geocities.com/malaya_hg/ops_zipper.htm>.

Nishida, Hiroshi. *Imperial Japanese Navy.* Accessed 4 February 2005. Available from <http://homepage2.nifty.com/nishidah/e/index.htm>.

Pang, Augustine and Angeline Song (eds.). "Meet Singapore's James Bond". *Headlines, Lifelines: Chee Beng's Start Page.* Accessed 15 November 2004. Available from <http://ourstory.asia1.com.sg/war/lifeline/bond7.html>.

Taylor, Ron. "Charles Thrale Paintings". *East Anglia Net.* Accessed 10 August 2004. Available from <http://www.ean.co.uk/Data/Bygones/ History/Article/WW2/Painting_the_Horror/html/body_charles_thrale_paintings_15.htm>.

Watson, Graham. "Operation Zipper: The Invasion of Malaya, August 1945". *Orders of Battle.* Accessed 30 January 2005. Available from <http://orbat.com/site/history/historical/malaysia/operationzipper.html>.

Wong, Marjorie. "Force 136 in Malaya: An Excerpt from 'The Dragon and the Maple Leaf'". *Burma Star Association.* Accessed 10 August 2004. Available from <http://www.burmastar.org.uk/136malaya.htm>.

Picture credits

Romen Bose: Page 264, 266 (all)

Brett-James, Antony, *Ball of Fire: 5th Indian Division in World War II* (Aldershot: Gale and Polden, 1951): Page 207, 211 (both), 212

Chapman, Lieutenant Colonel F. Spencer, *The Jungle is Neutral* (Singapore: Times Editions – Marshall Cavendish, 2005): Page 157 (both)

Imperial War Museum: Page 133, 139, 218, 245, 246 (both), 247, 250 (top)

Gough, Richard, *The Jungle as Red* (Singapore: SNP Panpac, 2003): Page 176

Marshall Cavendish International (Asia): Page 261, 268

Courtesy of The President and Mrs S.R. Nathan: Page 276 (all)

Tan, Chong Tee, *Force 136: Story of a WWII Resistance Fighter* (Singapore: Asiapac Books, 1995): Page 170, 171

Yap, Siang Yong, Romen Bose, Angeline Pang, Kuldip Singh, Lisa Lim & Germaine Foo, *Fortress Singapore: The Battlefield Guide* (Singapore: Times Editions – Marshall Cavendish, 2005): Page 241 (both), 250 (bottom), 258, 262.

www.geocities.com/malaya_hg/ops_zipper.htm: 232

Every effort has been made to trace and credit the sources of photographs and illustrations used. Please contact us if there have been any inadvertent errors or omissions.

KRANJI

THE COMMONWEALTH WAR CEMETERY AND THE POLITICS OF THE DEAD

Contents

	Preface to the First Edition	341
Chapter 1	Introduction	343
Chapter 2	The Beginning	359
Chapter 3	The Commonwealth War Graves Commission	365
Chapter 4	Building Kranji	371
Chapter 5	The Japanese War Dead	383
Chapter 6	The Civilian Memorial	395
Chapter 7	Those Remembered in Kranji	411
Chapter 8	The Kranji Military Cemetery	432
Chapter 9	The State Cemetery	437
Chapter 10	Kranji Today	443
Appendix A	Layout of Kranji Cemetery	450
Appendix B	Layout of the Japanese Cemetery	451
Appendix C	Documents showing location of Japanese graves and cemeteries in British-controlled territories	452
Appendix D	Blueprints of Kranji Cemetery	454
	Selected Bibliography	457

Preface to the First Edition

It was a sunny day in December 1991 when I first stepped foot in the Kranji War Cemetery. I was expecting a gloomy patch of grass filled with ruined headstones and overgrown grass, a cemetery that represented the chaos of a war fought close to 50 years before. I was in for a surprise.

What greeted me was an immaculately kept memorial to the brave young men and women of the British Empire, who had laid down their lives in defence of a common good. The well-trimmed grass and stone sculptures took my breath away. Upon climbing to the top of the Cemetery, I was greeted by what I thought was an enormous palace with aeroplane-like wings forming the roof of the structure and highlighted by a pointed star at the top, but with no doors enclosing the "building". Upon further inspection, I saw names, thousands upon thousands inscribed neatly in ever dizzying rows and columns. The grounds were enormous and all the headstones were lined in neat rows. As I surveyed the view from the top, the headstones appeared like serried ranks of soldiers lined up for a final parade of honour, with the Johore Straits forming the backdrop to this eternal parade.

This, I thought, was truly a fitting monument to the war dead. I wondered then whether I could get hold of a book to tell me of the history of this remarkable place and about the men and women who were buried on this hillside. I looked all over but all that I could find were vignettes and brief descriptions of Kranji and its occupants. I decided that I would rectify this situation immediately. Fifteen long years later, the book is now complete. However, it does not just cover the Commonwealth cemetery. From the start, I wanted to examine what the tradition of remembrance was for the various groups that went through the war. The book discusses in depth how the Kranji War Cemetery and Military Cemetery came about and examines some of those who are buried here. However, it also goes on to examine how the vanquished commemorated their dead as well.

For the very first time, this book shows a picture of the steps and entrance to the Syonan Chureito as it looked upon Singapore's liberation in September 1945 just days before it was blown up by British sappers. The book also tells the story of Japanese shrines to their war dead in Singapore and how monuments to Japan's militarism were built right under the noses of the reoccupying Allied forces. It then goes on to relate how the civilian populace in Singapore wanted to commemorate their war dead and the uphill challenge faced by the Chinese community in settling the controversial "blood debt" issue and building a multi-racial civilian monument, all in the midst of a communist insurgency and a bid for independence from their colonial masters.

This book would never have been possible had it not been for the continual support from my wife Brigid and my daughters Lara and Olive. My mum and dad must also be thanked for their continual encouragement to persevere with this project despite work and household commitments. I would also like to thank my uncle M.K. Dutta for his constant support and introduction to many of his friends who witnessed the events in this book. I must also thank the National Library Board in Singapore and staff at the Lee Kong Chian Reference Library for giving me a tour of the new building and also providing me access to several books which I did not know existed locally. I owe a great debt of gratitude to Makeswary Periasamy, Timothy Pwee and Bonny Tan for their help and in providing me access to the amazing state-of-the-art research facility at the new National Library. I would also like to mention several others who have helped greatly in getting this book published: Kevin Blackburn, Edmund Lim, Brian Farrell, Jeyathurai Ayadurai, Ling Cheng Lai, Chandra Mohan, Lionel Skinner, Lara Torvi and Trish Carter.

I hope this book on Kranji will not only provide an easily readable guide to the cemetery but also help generate interest in further research into the issues raised within these pages.

Romen Bose
21 January 2006

Chapter 1

Introduction

His hands were tied to his back as blood oozed down his soot-covered face. The flow from the cut above his eye was not serious. But the festering wound in his stomach, from a Japanese bayonet thrust days before, was.

Forced to crouch on the dirt floor along with several of his men, Gunner Walter Ernest Brown was surrounded by the dead as the stench of the rotting and burned flesh filled the evening air. Overrun by Japanese soldiers three days after the enemy formed a bridgehead in the mangrove swamps off Singapore's northwestern coast, Brown's regimental headquarters had effectively disintegrated in the face of the overwhelming force and fierce hand-to-hand fighting in the jungles off Jurong.

It had been a very long fight for his field regiment, from northern Johor all the way to the hillocks of northwestern Singapore Island. In the meantime, the mighty Australian Imperial Force (AIF), which had so boldly fought the Japanese in Bakri and Muar, had become a rag-tag bunch, barely able to hold off the offensive thrusts of the Imperial Japanese Army.

Since the beginning of the Malayan Campaign on 8 December 1941, the losses had mounted and Major General Gordon Bennett, commander of the AIF in Malaya, promised a tough fight once the Japanese came face to face with the might of the Aussies.

However, the tactical errors and mistakes throughout Malaya Command and among field commanders meant that retreat became the order of the day, as the Japanese took command of the sky and sea, while their troops inched ever closer to the capture of Singapore. Within 70 days, the battle for Singapore was over. By 15 February 1942, close to 125,000 British and Commonwealth troops were prisoners of the Japanese.

Thirteen days after the surrender and the Allied prisoners of war were being continually brutalised by the victors.

Brown was disgusted. He wanted to fight but there was no more fight left. In his 56 years of existence, he had seen such demoralisation only once before. It was almost a lifetime ago, in much colder circumstances and where a similar stench of death permeated the battlefield.

In another battle, in another world, 23 years before, it had been so similar and yet so very different. The smell of the battle was constant but there was no question of defeat. On the fields of the second battle of the Somme in France during the summer of 1918, demoralisation was also rife but there was also a strong will to fight.

After capturing a German trench during a night operation near Villers Bretonneux, Corporal Brown and his men had come under intense sniping on the morning of 6 July 1918. On hearing that his regiment was planning to take out the sniper's dugout later in the morning, he had decided then and there to charge the post in a bid to disable it before more of his men were killed. Acting alone, he ran like a madman, dodging heavy fire from the enemy before reaching the dugout unscathed.

Holding out a Mills grenade, he ordered the Germans to come out or face being blown up. The first German to rush out slammed into Brown and all hell broke loose. It was a bloody fight as both men struggled against each other in the open while guns from both sides opened up on the two.

Brown managed to take the advantage and strangled his opponent. As the German officer lay limp at the entrance to the dugout, observed by the rest of his men, slowly, yells of "Kamerad" came from inside the dugout and a German officer along with 11 other ranks began straggling out. The Germans immediately surrendered to Brown who then led his new prisoners back to the British lines as other German gun positions continued to fire on the group.

For his courage under fire, Brown received a Victoria Cross and was decorated by King George V at Sandringham exactly three months later. Promoted to the rank of Sergeant and demobbed after the war, Brown, who was born in New Norfolk, Tasmania on 2 July 1885, had done his duty for King and Country[1]. Married in July 1932 with eight VC winners as guards of honour, it seemed a happy ending for a brave soldier[2].

Wally Brown then carried on life as a grocer for the next eight years. But when the clouds of war appeared once again, Brown decided to re-enlist, this time as a Gunner in the Royal Artillery. He gave his age as 39 instead of 54 and was attached to the 2/15th Field Regiment. Brown and his mates arrived in Singapore in July 1941. Equipped with 3" mortars, the 2/15th was a highly trained unit. Although the 2/15th was supposed to be equipped with 25-pounders, they were only armed with their real weapons on 25 November 1941, barely two weeks before the Japanese invasion[3]. Training was provided in the middle of December and the unit had barely a month's practice before being engaged by the vanguard of the Japanese army. The lack of training meant the unit faced an uphill challenge. This was a common problem faced by numerous units during the campaign.

So now it was on 28 February 1942 that Walter Ernest Brown, VC and his fellow gunners were trapped on Singapore, facing the wrath of a victorious enemy. Not one to take things quietly, Brown wanted to escape. His previous attempts at escaping led to the bayoneting and brutal assault. However, he would not give up. Today would be his final attempt. Managing to untie himself when the Japanese guards were not looking, Brown crawled away from the rest of the men. Slowly, he pulled himself into a standing position and began to run towards the jungle behind the temporary POW camp.

Brown made it to the jungle. Or maybe he didn't. He could have died of his bayonet wounds, all alone in the jungle or he could have been shot in the back by his pursuing Japanese captors. Then again, on 15 February 1942 when Singapore was about to be surrendered to the Japanese, Brown could have been last seen picking up some grenades and walking towards the enemy saying, "No surrender for me"[4]. No formal or eyewitness records exist of Brown's last hours nor have any witnesses to his death come forward as yet. Moreover, we still do not know the location of his mortal remains or whether he was buried where he fell. The last day of this VC's life remains unwritten.

Gunner Walter Ernest Brown VC, seen here in a photograph taken at the end of the First World War.

His wife Maude, who lived in Carlton, New South Wales, mourned his passing as did Brown's family but there was never an official obituary for this hero. For many years, no one knew whether he was a POW or had died in captivity. The 1947 edition of Who's Who in Australia listed him as, "missing, presumed dead, February 1942"[5].

Who he was and the life he led

has long been forgotten and all that remains of Walter Ernest Brown is a name etched on a wall, known as the Singapore Memorial in the Kranji War Cemetery in Singapore.

Brown, along with over 29,000 other men and women are commemorated here on perfectly manicured grounds in the northwestern part of Singapore island.

Brown's life and death form part of the story of Kranji – the story of the ultimate sacrifice made by Australians, Britons, Indians, New Zealanders, Canadians, Dutch, Americans, Malaysians and Singaporeans during the Second World War in the region. It is also the story of the many Japanese whose ashes are buried on the island, who came as victors in the early part of the war and who never left these shores. This book attempts to tell these stories in the hope that future generations can learn from the sacrifices made by both sides, so aptly expressed on the Kohima War Memorial in Burma:

WHEN YOU GO HOME, TELL THEM OF US AND SAY:
'FOR YOUR TOMORROW WE GAVE OUR TODAY'

The complex at Kranji is divided into three sections, namely the Kranji War Cemetery, the Kranji Military Cemetery and the Singapore State Cemetery. The Commonwealth War Graves Commission (CWGC) maintains the War and Military Cemeteries while the State Cemetery is maintained by the Singapore Government.

The Kranji War Cemetery

Built on the slopes of a hill, the cemetery houses the remains of 64 First World War servicemen and 4,458 Second World War troops along with 850 unidentified graves[6]. The following is an explanation of the various sculptures and monuments erected at Kranji as well as how to identify individual tombstones in the cemetery.

Kranji, like most other war cemeteries administered by the Commonwealth War Graves Commission, is closed to any new burials, even if the person to be buried has died of causes attributable to his war service or present day strife. However, an exception is made for remains which are found and known to be of servicemen who died during the First or Second World War.

Headstones

One of the first things that greet visitors to Kranji are the immaculate white tombstones marking each grave in the war cemetery. The Commission's headstones, which are copyrighted, were decided on by a committee of artists which included D.S. MacColl, then Keeper of the Wallace Collection; Sir Charles Holmes, then Director of the National Gallery and MacDonald Gill, an authority on the lettering of inscriptions[7].

The engraved headstone above an identified grave is the normal type of commemoration provided by the Commission. Occasionally, such markers are not used and commemoration is instead made on a memorial or some other type of marker. This usually occurs when the grave is not in a Commission plot and is already marked by a privately owned memorial, or it is a privately owned grave and permission to erect a Commission memorial has been withheld, or where the burial is in a common grave, and in the most extreme circumstances, where the grave is unmaintainable.

Not all Commission headstones were the same. The ones at the Chungkai and Kanchanaburi War Cemeteries in Thailand are a semi-recumbent bronze plaque placed on a pedestal.

The standard headstone is two feet eight inches high. Many considerations prompted Sir Fabian Ware, founder of the Commonwealth War Graves Commission, to insist on having this form of a headstone as the standard marker as opposed to a cross. This is because it allowed the details of the dead to be shown. Topmost on the stone is an emblem, normally the badge of the regiment or service for British or British Indian Army troops (the Maple Leaf for Canadians; the badge of the Australian Imperial Force for the Australians; the Fern Leaf for New Zealanders; the Springbok for South Africans and the Caribou for Newfoundlanders). Over 1,500 different national, regimental and departmental corps badges are inscribed on the CWGC's headstones worldwide.

Below the emblem is the service or regimental number (usually omitted for officers). The serviceman's rank is given, initials (the first names, if requested by the next of kin), surname and the official abbreviation of any military decorations. Below this is the name of the service or regiment, followed by the date of death, and age (if known). Beneath this, a religious emblem like a Cross, Star of David or Crescent is placed based on the wishes of the next of kin.

The Commission also invited the next of kin to provide a personal inscription of up to 60 letters (with the exception of the New Zealand government which decided against this for their troops, although some New Zealander graves in France do have them)[8].

An example of a headstone would be that of H.R. Ross (pictured). Ross' details as given in the Commission's database are as follows:

Name: ROSS, HAROLD ROBERT
Initials: H R
Nationality: United Kingdom
Rank: Lieutenant
Regiment: General List
Secondary Unit Text: attd. 'Z' Special Unit
Age: 27
Date of Death: 16/10/1944
Service No: 325365
Additional information: Son of Thomas Spinks (formerly Lieut,.Col. Indian Medical Service) and Irene Leefe Ross. (Nee Robinson)
Casualty Type: Commonwealth War Dead
Grave/Memorial Reference: 27. A. 15.
Cemetery: KRANJI WAR CEMETERY

The headstone, however, only has Ross' rank, surname and initials, followed by his unit and his date of death, underlined by a Cross. The Commission holds much more information on individuals than there is enough space to inscribe on a headstone. Although the Commission does not have such comprehensive information on all individuals it commemorates, the Second World War entries are normally more comprehensive compared to those of the First World War. The location of Ross' remains (27.A.15) is read as plot 27, row A, headstone number 15.

Lieutenant H.R. Ross' headstone.

Throughout the cemetery, the rows of headstones are also set into concrete headstone beams, which lie invisible below ground keeping the headstones upright and aligned giving a uniform and symmetrical look to the cemetery[9].

The exigencies of war and the speed with which the Japanese moved down the Malayan peninsula meant that many records were lost. During the Occupation, incomplete records were kept by the Japanese and many Allied servicemen were executed in secret and their remains were never identified. As such, some remains are only partially identifiable and the Commission marks them

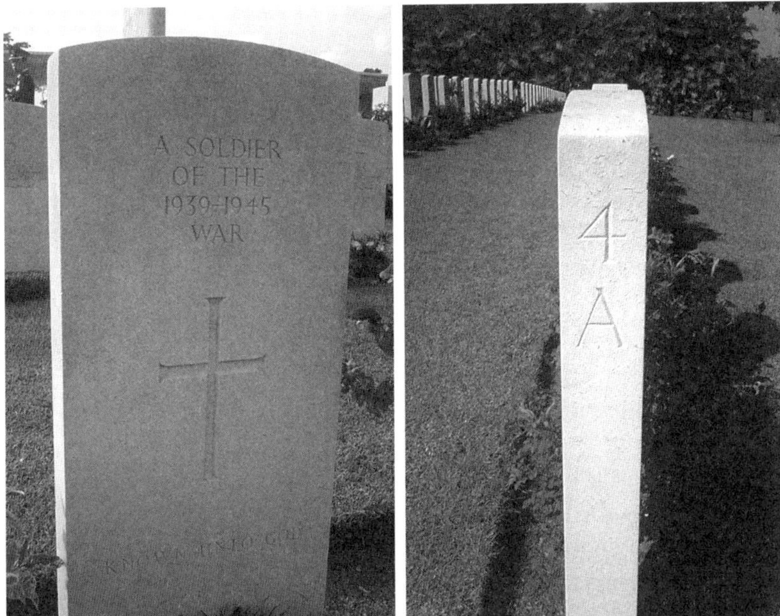

Left: The grave of an unidentifiable soldier bears the inscription "Known Unto God". Right: The inscription on the side of this headstone identifies it as being located in Plot 4 and Row A. Such numbering on the first and last headstones in each row lets visitors identify headstones easily.

with as much information as it has. Some read, "A Sergeant Australian Imperial Force" or even, "A Captain Royal Artillery, 12th February 1942". A large number of graves are totally unidentified and the Commission uses a standard formula for such markers. The inscription usually reads, "A Soldier (Sailor or Airman) of the 1939–1945 War (Cross) Known Unto God".

The phrase, "Known Unto God" was chosen by Rudyard Kipling and appears on all headstones marking the graves of those unidentified by name. In a number of instances, the top of the headstones are inscribed with the words, "Buried near this spot", which means that there is a group of graves in the immediate area but it is not clear who is buried in which grave.

The headstones themselves were initially made of Portland stone but as the stone is porous, it has now been replaced with Botticino limestone from Italy, which is impervious to the humidity and therefore lasts longer in a tropical climate.

In addition to the headstones, there are also five memorials situated in the cemetery marking the various war dead whose remains are located elsewhere.

The Cross of Sacrifice

Blomfield's Cross stands in front of the main aerofoil of the Singapore Memorial.

Designed by Sir Reginald Blomfield, the Cross, just like the Memorial Stone, can be seen in Commonwealth War Cemeteries worldwide. There are four sizes based on the size of the cemetery and the number of graves it contains. The Crosses range from slightly under 15 feet to just under 30 feet for the largest Cross and are considered to be among the best proportioned memorials of their kind[10].

The Cross stands on an octagonal block (weighing about two tons in the largest types), and rests on three steps. The two arms are in one piece and together measure about a third of the height of the Cross, measured from the base of the shaft. The shaft is also in one piece from the pedestal block to under the arms. The downward pointing bronze sword mounted on the cross stands out, similar to old armour and weapons hung against a wall.

However, the sword's symbolism is open to many interpretations. Some look at the sword and its hilt as being the Cross and the stonework as its frame while others see the sword as an offering up in sacrifice of those who died by the sword.

Initially, the Commission wanted to ensure that each architect would be free to design a special Cross of Sacrifice suitable in his view for the particular cemetery in which it was to stand, but public opinion so strongly supported Blomfield's Cross that it has been used wherever possible. The minimum number of burials to qualify for a Cross is normally 40 but there have been exceptions as in the case of the Falkland Islands and the Royal Engineers Grave at Zillebeke, near Ypres[11].

Memorial Stone

Designed by Sir Edwin Lutyens, it is found in nearly all large cemeteries containing more than 400 war dead. It provides, "an altar-like point of focus for ceremonies and one which is acceptable to all faiths". For this reason, it is frequently the spot at which wreaths are laid since Christians, Jews, Muslims, Hindus and non-believers all take it for what it is: a permanent memorial of dignity and beauty. However, at Kranji, the wreaths are

The Memorial Stone at the entrance to the Kranji War Cemetery.

normally laid at the top of the hill, at the Dedicatory Inscription of the Singapore Memorial. Both sides of the Memorial Stone bear the inscription, "THEIR NAME LIVETH FOR EVERMORE". These words were picked by Rudyard Kipling from the Bible, which reads, "Their bodies are buried in peace; but their name liveth for evermore"[12]. The memorial was close to Lutyen's heart and he described it as:

> A great fair stone of fine proportions, 12 feet in length, lying raised upon three steps...all its horizontal surfaces and planes are spherical and parts of parallelspheres, 1,801 feet, 8 inches in diameter, and all its vertical lines converging upwards to a point some 1,801 feet, 8 inches, above the centre of these spheres[13].

Dedicatory Inscription to the Singapore Memorial

Preceding the Singapore Memorial is a U-shaped panel inscribed with the following words:

1939–1945
ON THE WALLS OF THIS MEMORIAL ARE RECORDED THE
NAMES OF TWENTY FOUR THOUSAND SOLDIERS AND
AIRMEN OF MANY RACES UNITED IN SERVICE TO THE
BRITISH CROWN WHO GAVE THEIR LIVES IN MALAYA AND
NEIGHBOURING LANDS AND SEAS AND IN THE AIR OVER
SOUTHERN AND EASTERN ASIA AND THE PACIFIC BUT TO
WHOM THE FORTUNE OF WAR DENIED THE CUSTOMARY
RITES ACCORDED TO THEIR COMRADES IN DEATH
THEY DIED FOR ALL FREE MEN

The inscription panel has been used as the main site for commemoration ceremonies for the last two decades as its location allows the gathering of large numbers of veterans and their families during the commemoration ceremonies and events held at Kranji. Although most memorial ceremonies were originally held at the Cenotaph just opposite the Padang in downtown Singapore, this tradition ended upon Singapore's independence when all commemorations shifted to Kranji. This was because holding similar ceremonies at two different locations diluted the commemoration efforts and with the pullout of the British, there was no longer a large enough critical mass of servicemen and families who would attend these two events.

The Dedicatory Inscription Panel to the Singapore Memorial.

The Singapore Memorial

At the top of Kranji Hill is what is described as a great winged memorial. Looking like the wings of an aeroplane, the roof of the Singapore Memorial reaches to a height of 80 feet and is surmounted by a star. On the panels below are inscribed the names of over 24,000 men and women who have no known grave.

Of these, 6,800 came from Britain; 1,400 from Australia; 12,000 from India and 1,000 from Malaya (which includes the Federated Malay States Police Force). The majority of those listed died in the Malayan Campaign and in Netherlands East Indies (Indonesia) or during subsequent captivity. A large proportion also includes those who died building the Siam-Burma Death Railway and others who lost their lives at sea while being shipped from Malaya to prison camps elsewhere. Of the airmen named, 2,500 came from the UK; 191 from Canada; 200 from Australia; 60 from New Zealand; five from South Africa; six from Malaya and 50 from India. Their final resting places are even more widely scattered than the infantry, covering the whole of south and eastern Asia and its surrounding waters. Of the land forces, the regiment most represented are the Royal Artillery (UK) with 2,235 names; the 2/19th Battalion (Australia) with 246; the 14th Punjab Regiment (India) with 866 and the Malay Regiment (Malaya and Singapore) with 229[14].

Listed on this Memorial are the names of more than 250 servicemen whose graves are unmaintainable and whose remains lie in cemeteries throughout Malaya (Malaysia).

The Unmaintainable Graves Memorial

Standing at the western end of the Singapore Memorial, it lists more than 250 servicemen who lost their lives in Malaya, and due to the exigencies of war, whose graves were located in civil cemeteries and where permission was not given to relocate the remains to Kranji where maintenance of these graves could be assured. These also include graves that could not be moved due to religious reasons. On the Memorial are inscribed these words:

THESE SOLDIERS DIED SERVING THEIR COUNTRY
AND LIE BURIED ELSEWHERE IN MALAYA

The Cremation Memorial

Located immediately behind the Singapore Memorial, the Cremation Memorial lists close to 800 war dead, mostly from the British Indian Army, whose remains were cremated in accordance with their religious beliefs. The Memorial is inscribed with the following words:

IN HONOUR OF THE OFFICERS AND MEN
WHO DIED IN BATTLE AND WHOSE
MORTAL REMAINS WERE COMMITTED TO FIRE

The various units inscribed on the Memorial include: Royal Indian Army Service Corps, Royal Hong Kong & Singapore Artillery, Indian Armoured Corps, 16th Light Cavalry, 3rd Cavalry, 16th King George

V Own Lancers, Royal Regiment of Indian Artillery, The Royal Bombay Sappers and Miners, King George V's Own Bengal Sappers and Miners, Queen Victoria's Own Madras Sappers and Miners, Indian Engineers, Indian Signal Corps, 1st Punjab Regiment, 2nd Punjab Regiment, 3rd Madras Regiment, 6th Rajputana Rifles, Indian Grenadiers, 7th Rajput Regiment, 5th Mahratta Regiment, 5th Mahrati Light Infantry, 11th Sikh Regiment, 10th Baluch Regiment, 9th Jat Regiment, 8th Punjab Regiment, 12th Frontier Force, 17th Dogra Regiment, 18th Royal Garwhal Rifles, 19th Hyderabad Regiment, Kumaon Regiment, 1st Kumaon Rifles, The Bihar Regiment, 9th Gurkhas, 1st King George V's Own Gurkha Rifles, 2nd Edward VII's Own Gurkha Rifles, 4th Prince of Wales' Own Gurkha Rifles, 5th Royal Gurkha Rifles, 7th Gurkha Rifles, 8th Gurkha Rifles, Indian Medical Department, Indian Hospital Corps, Indian Army Medical Corps, Indian Army Veterinary Corps, Indian Army Ordnance Corps, Corps of Indian Electrical and Mechanical Engineers, Indian Army Corps of Clerks, Indian Army Postal Services, Indian General Service Corps, Indian Pioneer Corps, Corps of Military Police (India), Intelligence Corps (India), 1st Hyderabad Infantry, Jind Infantry, 1st Battalion Mysore Infantry, 1st Battalion Patiala Infantry (Rajindra Sikhs) and Federated Malay States Police Force[15].

The headstone of a Muslim soldier who served in the Royal Indian Army Service Corps and who died slightly over a month after the end of the war in the Far East.

The Civil Hospital Grave Memorial

Standing at the eastern end of the Singapore Memorial, it marks the fate of numerous wounded civilians and servicemen who were brought to the hospital in the last days before the fall of Singapore. Before the war, an emergency water tank had been dug in the grounds of the hospital and due to the intense shelling and the lack of burial space, more than 400 bodies are believed to have been placed in the tank with slaked lime sprinkled over the remains to reduce the stench and hasten decomposition. After the war, it was decided that as individual identification of the dead would be impossible, the grave would be left undisturbed. It was suitably marked, consecrated by the Bishop of Singapore and a cross in memory of all of

This memorial marks the more than 400 soldiers and civilians who died in the last days of fighting and whose remains were placed in a mass grave at the Civil Hospital (Singapore General Hospital).

those buried there was erected over it by the British military forces. Out of the 400, the 107 Commonwealth military casualties buried in the grave are commemorated on the Civil Hospital Grave Memorial. The words incribed on the memorial reads:

THE SOLDIERS WHOSE MEMORY IS HONOURED
HERE PERISHED IN CAPTIVITY IN FEBRUARY 1942
AND LIE BURIED IN ONE GRAVE IN THE GROUNDS
OF SINGAPORE CIVIL GENERAL HOSPITAL

Opposite Block 8 of the Singapore General Hospital in Outram Road, lie the remains of the more than 400, which is still marked by a refurbished cross and memorial stone. The words inscribed on the plinth read:

BENEATH THIS CROSS LIE 94 BRITISH,
6 MALAYAN, 5 INDIAN, 2 AUSTRALIAN SOLDIERS
AND 300 CIVILIANS OF MANY RACES,
VICTIMS OF MAN'S INHUMANITY TO MAN,
WHO PERISHED IN CAPTIVITY IN FEBRUARY 1942.
THE SOLDIERS ARE COMMEMORATED BY NAME
AT KRANJI WAR CEMETERY

The Chinese Memorial

Located in Plot 45, the Chinese Memorial marks a collective grave for 69 Chinese members of the British and Commonwealth forces, who were killed as a result of the "Sook Ching" massacre of the Chinese community in Singapore during the first weeks of the Japanese Occupation in February 1942. The words inscribed on the memorial read:

THE MEN WHOSE NAMES ARE RECORDED ON THESE
PANELS PERISHED IN CAPTIVITY IN FEBRUARY 1942
AND LIE BURIED HERE IN ONE GRAVE WITH
TEN COMRADES WHOSE NAMES ARE NOT KNOWN

The men buried in the collective grave were part of the Royal Army Medical Corps, Dalforce, Pioneers Corps, Royal Air Force, Singapore Volunteer Corps, Chinese Labour Corps and the Straits Settlements Volunteer Force.

A memorial marking the collective grave for 69 Chinese members of the British and Commonwealth forces.

Kranji Military Cemetery

Built in 1975, the Kranji Military Cemetery houses a substantial non-world war collection of 1,378 burials (servicemen and their families), which were relocated from the Pasir Panjang and Ulu Pandan cemeteries that became unmaintainable upon the British military withdrawal from Singapore in 1971. Unlike the War Cemetery, the Military Cemetery is still open for new burials but only a select few qualify for the stringent criteria for burial at Kranji. In 2005, 50 First and Second World War graves were shifted from the Bidadari Christian Cemetery in Aljunied to Kranji for re-interment as the Bidadari Cemetery made way for redevelopment. These graves had been left undisturbed for over 60 years according to the wishes of the next of kin till the cemetery was removed.

A Celtic Cross is one of several distinctive sculptures in the military cemetery which is different in tone and presentation from the war cemetery. A British and Commonwealth Garden of Remembrance was also set up for the ashes of those servicemen and family members whose remains were no longer marked or unidentifiable. The stone plaque in the Garden reads:

Site of the former Pasir Panjang Military Cemetery at Dover Road. These pictures were taken in 1995 by Brian Houldershaw, who served in Singapore in the 1960s.

IN MEMORY OF BRITISH AND COMMONWEALTH
SERVICEMEN AND CIVILIANS AND MEMBERS OF
THEIR FAMILIES FORMERLY BURIED IN PASIR
PANJANG AND ULU PANDAN CEMETERIES
WHOSE ASHES NOW LIE IN THIS GARDEN

A Gurkha Garden of Remembrance was also built for the ashes of mainly stillborn babies of Gurkha servicemen from the Ulu Pandan and Pasir Panjang Cemeteries which were consolidated in one site. The inscription on the stone reads:

IN MEMORY OF GURKHA OFFICERS AND SOLDIERS OF
THE BRIGADE OF GURKHAS AND THEIR WIVES
AND CHILDREN FORMERLY BURIED IN PASIR
PANJANG AND ULU PANDAN CEMETERIES
WHOSE ASHES NOW LIE IN THIS GARDEN

Although the descriptions in this chapter provide a brief introduction to the cemetery at Kranji, the actual building of the cemetery and the issues involved with commemorating the war dead would take over 12 years to solve before the Kranji War Cemetery came into being. Over the next few chapters, the story of the Commonwealth War Graves Commission and the quest to commemorate the British, Commonwealth, Japanese and local war dead unfolds.

Endnotes

1 *Brown, W.E. VC Papers, VC Box 6,* London: Imperial War Museum.

2 *Daily Mirror* (London), 12 July 1932; "War Hero Married", *Sydney Morning Herald,* 6 June 1932.

3 Whitelocke, Cliff. *Gunners in the Jungle: A story of the 2/15 Field Regiment, Royal Australian Artillery, 8 Division, Australian Imperial Force.* Eastwood, New South Wales: The 2/15 Field Regiment Association, 1983, p. 50.

4 ANZAC Day Commemoration Committee, "List of Australian Winners of the Victoria Cross". ANZAC Day Commemoration Committee 2005. [Internet]. Accessed 27 September 2005. Available from: <http://www. anzacday.org.au/education/medals/vc/austlist.html>

5 *Brown, W.E. VC Papers, VC Box 6,* London: Imperial War Museum.

6 Commonwealth War Graves Commission. "Kranji War Cemetery and the Singapore Memorials". *Commonwealth War Graves Commission.* [Internet]. Accessed 26 September 2005. Available from: <http://www. cwgc.org/cwgcinternet/ publications.htm>

7 Ward, G. Kingsley. & Gibson, Major Edwin. *Courage Remembered:The story behind the construction and maintenance of the Commonwealth's Military Cemeteries and Memorials of the Wars of 1914-1918 and 1939-1945.* London: HMSO, 1995, p. 66.

8 Ibid. p. 66.

9 Ibid. p. 55.

10 Ibid. p. 55.

11 Ibid. 55.

12 Ecclesiasticus Chapter 44, Verse 14. The Bible.

13 Ibid. p. 54.

14 Ibid. p. 164.

15 Stubbs, Peter W. "Singapore Cremation Memorial" *KRANJI,SINGAPORE War & Military Cemeteries* [Internet]. Accessed 26 September 2005. Available from: <http://www.petrowilliamus.co.uk/kranji/kranji.htm>

Chapter 2

The Beginning

Before 1939, Kranji Hill was occupied as a temporary military camp, and during the Malayan Campaign the area was reorganised into an ammunition magazine[1]. 2/26 AIF set up their battalion headquarters on the hill on 31 January and stayed there till the battalion retreated on 10 February 1942. The camp was then overrun by the invading Japanese later in the day. The camp was a series of huts located in the middle of a rubber plantation, at the thirteenth milestone on the main Singapore-Johore Road. After the fall of Singapore, it was used as a hospital for Indian troops and eventually became a field hospital for the Indian National Army (INA), a Japanese-sponsored Indian independence movement that was attempting to overthrow the British in India. The INA occupied the "hospital", which was barely equipped to deal with any serious injuries. However, the hospital was abandoned in 1944 when most of the INA troops were shipped to Burma for the Imphal Campaign.

At the same time, the men who had survived the Siam-Burma Death Railway were being sent back to Singapore. In order to make space for the returning POWs, the civilians who occupied the main civilian prison at Changi were moved to the Sime Road Internment Camp while a large number of sick and injured POWs were to be moved to Kranji. As one prisoner noted,

> ...combatants were to move to the civil criminal gaol at Changi, hospital patients and holders of the Red Cross card to huts around the gaol and that a 1,200-bedded hospital would be opened at Kranji to accommodate the surplus.

> All patients requiring a month or more in hospital would be sent to Kranji. Acute surgery would be undertaken at Changi. A weekly service of ambulances or lorries would run between Changi and Kranji. Most of these arrangements failed to materialize. Transfers took place three times monthly, then twice monthly and in July 1945 ceased altogether[2].

Major F.W. Bradshaw of the 148 Field Regiment RA from the British 18th Division was appointed Commander of the new hospital at Kranji. The doctors included Captain V.R. Jackson (RAMC), Captain J.B. Burgess (Army Dental Corps) and Captain P.K. Betty (2/2 Gurkhas). They were assisted by Lieutenant R.G. Fletcher (Gordons), Second Lieutenant A.G.R. Makepeace (Bedfordshire and Hertfordshire Regiment) and Second Lieutenant F.J.P. Coles (Royal Army Service Corps)[3].

Bradshaw dealt directly with the Japanese Army and not through the Malaya Command headquarters at Changi[4]. The Japanese commander of the area was a non-commissioned officer (NCO), a "severe disciplinarian whose behaviour gained him a place in the list of war criminals"[5]. Under his command were 40 Koreans as well as 20 Indians who had been part of the earlier INA hospital. The Indians appeared to be so embarrassed by the conflict between their old and new loyalties that they were eventually transferred to the main INA camp in Nee Soon[6].

A Japanese medical officer was appointed overall in command of the camp but he had little or no authority. The Japanese NCO demanded large working parties for labour unrelated to the hospital or medical duties. These had to be provided under the threat of a cut or even stoppage of rations[7].

In order to accommodate the 1,200 beds and some 400 staff, 50 huts were allocated. These were in fairly good repair and well off the ground with attap walls and roofs. The advance party of Royal Engineers and hygiene personnel repaired the huts, laid on electrical lighting, extended the water points and prepared an emergency operating theatre. By June 1944, there was running water in all the wards, which were all now wired for electrical light, the current being provided by an old Army field set[8]. The operating theatre and specialist departments were well-stocked. Replenishments of drugs and dressings were obtained from the central stores at Changi every quarter but drugs like emetine and insulin were never available.

As in Changi, the hospital was sub-divided into Australian and British wings. Chaplains and welfare officers were also among the 50 officers and 425 Other Ranks (ORs) of the approved hospital staff for the British wing. The band and the concert party staged performances thrice weekly until July 1945 when they were forbidden. There were three camp libraries but its contents were badly mutilated when the "trick of splitting the leaves of books for the manufacture of cigarette paper was mastered"[9].

A main kitchen cooked for 800 and a special-diet kitchen for 200. Yet another cookhouse catered for sick officers. Three other kitchens were available. The whole camp was enclosed in a double wire fence[10]. 1,600 bedstands, about 1,300 blankets and a few sheets were brought from Changi. By the end of the year the number of serviceable blankets had fallen to 1,000 and the hospital linen had ceased to exist. Clothing and footwear were worn out and the men were dressed in rags[11].

Forty-five-year-old Reverend Gilbert John Marion Chambers had served as a Chaplain 4th Class with the 35th Light Anti-Aircraft Regiment and was captured in Singapore at its fall. Serving at Changi, Selarang and Great World internment camps, he was eventually moved to Kranji as noted in his diary of 28 May 1944,

> Left at 0930hrs by IJA bus for Woodlands Camp, ex 51 Searchlights camp. We were all supposed to have moved, but this was cancelled except officers and patients & some staff. But in the afternoon the whole hospital was moved, & the consequent confusion was appalling. I enjoyed the drive over. The town looks empty, but the inhabitants better fed & happier looking than I anticipated. Padres Wearne, Paine, Daniels, Wheeler, RC Hugh Jones, P Jim Ward, RC Pugh, RC Andrews & myself. Evening meal Rice stew with meat @ 23.00hrs[12].

However, even the spiritual mentors of the men had their differences within four days of their arrival at Kranji, as Chambers noted on 1 June 1944:

> At our conference Daniels accepted the principle of cooperation, & the cutting out of competition. Decided that Evening Sunday service should be in the Theatre, & that they should alternate; 1 C/E (Church of England) one O/D (Other Denomination). That we should all attend each service. ie next Sunday service C/E Daniels preach. We have asked him to explain what we have in mind to die hards, as we will to our own. D (Daniels) was not over enthusiastic, hence the compromise reached. I think it is a satisfactory one, provided we get a good mid week Evensong going. PW (Padre Wearne) & I are to meet today to discuss ward visiying (*sic*) etc. – Food excellent to begin with, relapsed & is on the up grade. I have never eaten such quantities of rice in my life! Patients have just ½ our ration. Almost riots in TB & Eye wards yesterday[13].

And the right of ministering to the men was also argued over as Chambers noted on 3 June 1944:

> On Thursday as I wrote, PW (Padre Wearne) and I met. Paine was late so Wearne & I got going. W opened by saying he thought my position was 'Most Awkward'. I asked why & how he thought so? He began a long story of complaint, going right back to our start at Selarang, in the course of which he called me 'An incompetent Priest', & insisted that I had exaggerated the value of the Roberts Hospital St Lukes (which held the murals painted by Stanley Warren and which had been forcibly taken back by the Japanese by then). I brought him back to his original statement. He said it was awkward because Col Collins refused to have any dealings with me; Anything I might require must come to the CO (Major Bradshaw) through him. I thought that the ACG (Assistant Chaplain General) had made my position perfectly clear. I came on the suggestion of Col Dillon himself, to do a Chaplain's job, & that I had this in writing. W. replied that if this was so I should show the letter at once to the CO. I replied that I had no intention of doing so, unless I felt called on to do so by an order preventing me from doing a Chaplain's job in the hospital by the CO or anyone else. The existance (*sic*) of this letter cleared the air, & the subject of my position was dropped. W. accepted without further question my right to work as a Chaplain here.
>
> There is no doubt that had the ACG insisted on my seniority, I should have been in an intolerable position with the CO. & W.(Wearne) & D (Daniels) would have united against me. We then fell to clearing up outstanding grievances, which he did with much fullness, & I not so bluntly. I had to think of the future & it would have been silly to foul the pitch. With Ps assistance we even cleared up the 'Incompitant (*sic*) Priest'. The following working arrangement was agreed. 1. W to have all dealings with the CO. & I was not to be jealous of this, or think him pushy. He's more than welcome, if he plays fair. 2. W to have spiritual responsibility for all hospital personell (*sic*). Plus TB Ward. 3. I am to take entie (*sic*) spiritual responsibility for all the patients including Officer's Ward. The figures are BGH (Battalion General Hospital) Patients 557 plus 65 Officers TBW (TB Ward), BGH Staff 416 plus TBW[14].

Chambers would not be there to celebrate mass at the end of the war. He died on 13 July 1945, less than a month before Emperor Hirohito announced Japan's surrender on 15 August 1945. He is buried at 14. B. 14.

In May 1945, a small quantity of Red Cross clothing became available. Individual personal equipment consisted of an enamel mug or milk tin, an enamel plate or a mess tin and a spoon.

One of the patients in hospital, a member of the Straits Settlements Volunteer Force, had been a rubber planter prior to the war. Under his direction and with approval from the Japanese, a 200-tree plantation nearby was taken over and a rubber factory was established. The factory supplied rubber sandals, soles for boots and raw latex for repairs.

Once a month the Japanese allowed the collection of palm fronds while fatigue parties also collected coconuts on their journeys. With the fronds and coconut husks, a broom factory was started[15].

In addition, the hospital at Kranji, like the one in Changi, had begun to maintain a cemetery for those who died. The rudimentary cemetery at Kranji would be the beginning of the Kranji War Cemetery. After the reoccupation of Singapore in 1945, the small hospital cemetery at Kranji was developed into a more permanent war cemetery by the Army Graves Service when it became evident that a larger cemetery at Changi, which had been maintained by the British and Australian Imperial Force, could not remain undisturbed.

In 1946, after much controversy and delays, the graves were moved from Changi to Kranji, as were those from the Buona Vista prisoner of war camp. Many other graves from all parts of the island were then transferred to Kranji, together with all Second World War burials from Saigon Military Cemetery in French Indo-China (now Vietnam), and graves of both world wars from Bidadari Christian Cemetery in Singapore, sites where permanent maintenance was not possible.

However, it would take another 11 years before the Commonwealth War Graves Commission would be able to set up the Kranji War Cemetery. It was an uphill task for an organisation that was created in the fields of France during the First World War.

Endnotes

1 Crewe, F. A. E. *"Medical Narrative of Campaign in Malaya", 20 October 1953, WO222/138.* London: The National Archives.

2 *Chambers, Rev G.J. Papers, 91/35/1,* London: Imperial War Museum.

3 Ibid.

4 Ibid.

5 Ibid.

6 Ibid.

7 Ibid.

8 Crewe, F. A. E. *"Medical Narrative of Campaign in Malaya", 20 October 1953, WO222/138.* London: The National Archives.

9 Ibid.

10 Ibid.

11 Ibid.

12 *Chambers, Rev G.J. Papers, 91/35/1,* London: Imperial War Museum.

13 Ibid.

14 Ibid.

15 Crewe, F. A. E. *"Medical Narrative of Campaign in Malaya", 20 October 1953, WO222/138.* London: The National Archives.

Chapter 3

The Commonwealth War Graves Commission

The Commonwealth War Graves Commission (CWGC) is responsible for maintaining cemeteries and memorials for over 1,750,000 war dead in 140 countries and territories.

When war broke out in 1914, Fabian Arthur Goulstone Ware was 45 years old. Too old to be accepted for army duty, he tried quickly to get to the front lines, reaching Lille in France as Commander of the Mobile Unit, British Red Cross Society[1]. This unit was a collection of daring novices who drove civilian vehicles and often collected wounded men and stragglers. Officially, they were under the direction of the Joint War Committee of the British Red Cross and the Order of St John of Jerusalem. In September 1914, Lord Kitchener had suggested that the committee send such a mobile unit to search for missing soldiers along the line of retreat between the Aisne and Ourcq rivers. During the First Battle of Ypres the unit was attached to the French I Cavalry Corps, and later to the French X Corps behind Arras, showing its mettle by transporting many wounded from the war zones to the hospitals[2].

As Ware went about his duties, he began to note the names of the British war dead and the locations of their graves. He was alone in this as there was no previous Army policy of noting and maintaining grave sites. There were very few marked graves from the Battle of Waterloo or the Crimean War. Although army regulations ordered the clearance of battlefields and the proper disposal of the dead, fluid battle conditions meant that little recording was done. During this period, dead servicemen's graves were marked with a wooden cross after burial by their comrades, but no official record existed. As a result, when military units moved from area to area, details of the dead men's burials were soon lost[3].

As commander of the Mobile Unit, Ware negotiated the supply of more ambulances and rations from the Red Cross Society in London but prevented his unit from becoming part of the new Army Medical Corps. In October 1914, a visit by a Red Cross Adviser led to the first extension of the unit's work into the noting of graves to help the Red Cross in tracing the missing and the dead. As a result, the registration of graves began to take place as sites were now installed with permanent markers and thus began being maintained[4].

The new approach was noted by General Sir Neville Macready, Adjutant-General of the British Expeditionary Force. Worried about the growing public demand in Britain that British war graves should not be neglected, Ware was able to convince Macready that an organisation had to be established to ensure proper marking and recording of graves, and that his unit was the right one for this burgeoning task. Macready assisted the Commander-In-Chief Sir John French, in obtaining War Office approval for the creation of a graves registration organisation as a key part of the expeditionary force. So, on 2 March 1915, Ware's unit was given this new mandate under the title of Graves Registration Commission[5].

Although still part of the Red Cross, the Commission was attached to the Adjutant-General's office and Ware was given the local rank of a temporary major. However, with some 27,000 registrations during 1915, it was obvious that the Commission had to leave the Red Cross, becoming an integral part of the Army on 6 September 1915.

Of historic significance to how all future war remains would be treated, Ware was insistent that the Adjutant-General order equality of treatment for the fallen[6]. An order in April 1915 established equality of treatment after an equality of sacrifice. What this meant was that exhumations for repatriation were forbidden not only on the grounds of hygiene but also because 'of the difficulties of treating impartially the claims advanced by persons of different social standing'[7]. These two important principles of equality of treatment and no repatriation were thus observed in the Second World War as well.

Families of dead servicemen were also requesting photographs of the graves of their loved ones. As most of the landscape was war-torn and very bleak, the Commission attempted to improve the surroundings with grass and a few simple flowers. This was the beginning of the Commission's extensive horticultural work in the cemeteries. Ware felt that as the next of kin could not look after the graves, an official service would have to do it. If no official body was authorised to care for the graves once the war was over, a commercial outfit might step in with more interest in the bottom line than care for the remains of the war dead[8].

In January 1916, Ware was involved in the establishment of the National

Committee for the Care of Soldiers' Graves, with the Prince of Wales as President. At the same time, the British Treasury agreed to meet the cost of the upkeep of the graves, unaware of the enormous expenses it would incur in future[9].

By now, many theatres of war had opened up and to manage these wider responsibilities, Ware was promoted to temporary Lieutenant Colonel and appointed Director-General of the newly created Directorate of Graves Registration and Enquiries. His office was moved to London in May 1916 and he was provided with a staff of 700[10].

The numerous 'unknown' graves were of concern to Ware as many next of kin would have no place of remembrance for the fallen soldier. He introduced a new form of double identity disc made of compressed fibre and this greatly helped in identifying the dead in future combat. These discs were also used in the Second World War[11].

Another of the Commission's defining policies was the provision, whenever possible, of a marked grave for every "unknown solider". This was a significant policy for up to 50 per cent of the dead in Belgium were unknown and some 40 per cent in France, something which is only too clear in some cemeteries.

As the number of burials grew, so did the work of Ware's unit. Eventually, he lobbied for the National Committee for the Care of Soldiers' Graves to become a permanent organisation under Royal Charter, with its own funds, staff and overseen by Britain's Secretary of State for War and commissioners from Britain and each of the Dominions[12].

The Prince of Wales had become a big supporter of Ware's work and had demonstrated much interest in Ware's project from the very beginning. The Prince felt strongly that the National Committee's work was essential as a concrete tribute to those who had made the ultimate sacrifice for the Empire. In 1917, King George V made Ware a Companion of the Order of St Michael and St George (CMG) in recognition of his work and dedication[13].

The Prince of Wales also sent a minute to the Imperial War Conference, with his endorsement of Ware's memorandum that proposed the creation of 'an Imperial organisation to care for and maintain in perpetuity the graves of those who have fallen in the War, to acquire land for the purpose of cemeteries and to erect permanent memorials in the cemeteries and elsewhere'[14]. With a few amendments, the draft charter was approved. On 13 April 1917, a resolution recommending its adoption was moved by Canada's Prime Minister, Sir Robert Borden. A Royal Charter was granted on 21 May 1917, establishing the Imperial War Graves Commission, with the Prince of Wales as its head and Brigadier General Fabian Ware as its vice-chairman[15].

By Armistice Day on 11 November 1918, the IWGC had dealt with over a million British and Commonwealth dead[16]. In between the wars, Ware dedicated his time to building proper cemeteries and memorials to commemorate the fallen with dignity and in perpetuity. For the rest of his life, Ware (eventually promoted to the rank of Major-General) continued his dedicated work in the commemoration of the war dead. Although the founder of the Imperial War Graves Commission (which changed its name to the Commonwealth War Graves Commission in 1960), Ware served as its vice-chairman from 1917 till 1948, a year before his death on 28 April 1949 at the age of 80. He was buried at Holy Trinity Church at Amberley and stone tablets in his memory were installed at Gloucester Cathedral and Westminster Abbey. He was also granted the signal posthumous honour of having his grave marked by a standard Commission war-pattern headstone to which he was not officially entitled.

Today, the CWGC's work still continues close to 60 years after its founder's death. The landscapers, horticulturists and gardeners continue to maintain their 'amazing gardens' and take pains to avoid the depressing appearance of many civilian cemeteries. The cemeteries were planted under the advice of Captain Sir Arthur Hill, then Director of the Royal Botanical Gardens at Kew[17]. Trees and bushes were planted to brighten the dull landscape while headstone flower borders were laid out to break up the large number of headstones. Paths and spaces between the blocks and rows were sown with grass which made the cemetery very green and inviting, a place for contemplation and meditation, not of depression.

Maintaining war cemeteries and monuments worldwide does not come cheap. Initially, in accordance with the Imperial War Conference resolution of 1918, the cost was borne by the participating governments in proportion to the number of graves each required, a system which is still used today. The chart below shows the proportions contributed in 1937 and in the 1980s by each Commonwealth country. The changes in funding reflect subsequent political changes and the combining of graves from the First and Second World Wars in order to arrive at a total[18].

Government	**Percentage (1937)**	**Percentage (1980)**
United Kingdom	81.53	77.81
Canada	7,78	9.88
Australia	6.35	5.91
New Zealand	1.81	2.1
South Africa	1.14	2.07
India	1.02	2.23
British West Indies	0.23	-
Newfoundland	0.14	-
Total	**100.00**	**100.00**

By 1925 the participating governments agreed to contribute to an Imperial War Graves Endowment Fund of £5 million to provide money for permanent maintenance. The fund was completed in 1940[19]. The UK, which had spread its contributions over a longer period than most of the other governments, donated an additional sum to enable the fund to provide an income of £218,000 a year, which was at that point in time estimated to be sufficient to preserve the agreed standard of maintenance.

However, by the end of the Second World War, annual expenditure for maintaining the First World War Graves alone had exceeded the income of the Endowment Fund. The excess and the whole of the amount needed to meet the costs of the Second World War graves are now provided by annual contributions by participating governments in the proportions shown in the chart[20]. Annual outgoings in the early 1990s exceeded £20 million, with a staff of over 1,300 worldwide.

However, in 1945, the challenge facing the CWGC was the quick building of war cemeteries in which to inter the war dead of the last six years. The proposed cemetery at Kranji in Singapore was only one of several that the CWGC had planned for the Far East. Nonetheless, it would prove to be one of the most challenging ones to set up, taking close to 12 years before it would be officially opened.

Endnotes

1 Longworth, Philip. *The Unending Vigil: A history of the Commonwealth War Graves Commission.* London: Constable, 1967, pp. 1-16.

2 Ibid.

3 Ibid.

4 Ward, G. Kingsley. & Gibson, Major Edwin. *Courage Remembered:The story behind the construction and maintenance of the Commonwealth's Military Cemeteries and Memorials of the Wars of 1914-1918 and 1939-1945.* London: HMSO, 1995.

5 Ibid. p. 55.

6 Longworth, Philip. *The Unending Vigil: A history of the Commonwealth War Graves Commission.* London: Constable, 1967, p. 14.

7 Ward, G. Kingsley. & Gibson, Major Edwin. *Courage Remembered:The story behind the construction and maintenance of the Commonwealth's Military Cemeteries and Memorials of the Wars of 1914-1918 and 1939-1945.* London: HMSO, 1995.

8 Ibid.p. 56.

9 Longworth, Philip. *The Unending Vigil: A history of the Commonwealth War Graves Commission.* London: Constable, 1967, p. 16.

10 Ibid. p. 17.

11 Ibid. p. 46.

12 Ibid. p. 24.

13 Ward, G. Kingsley. & Gibson, Major Edwin. *Courage Remembered:The story behind the construction and maintenance of the Commonwealth's Military Cemeteries and Memorials of the Wars of 1914-1918 and 1939-1945.* London: HMSO, 1995, p. 45.

14 Ibid. p. 60.

15 Longworth, Philip. *The Unending Vigil: A history of the Commonwealth War Graves Commission.* London: Constable, 1967, p. 28.

16 Ibid. p. 208.

17 Ibid. pp. 66, 21.

18 Ward, G. Kingsley. & Gibson, Major Edwin. *Courage Remembered:The story behind the construction and maintenance of the Commonwealth's Military Cemeteries and Memorials of the Wars of 1914-1918 and 1939-1945.* London: HMSO, 1995, p. 57.

19 Ibid. p. 56.

20 Ibid. p. 56.

Chapter 4

Building Kranji

With the end of the war in the Far East, the Army Graves Services (AGS) under the Allied Land Forces South East Asia (ALFSEA), temporarily in charge of the war remains, decided to centralise the various war graves in Singapore, which had been located next to the numerous POW camps throughout the island. As the huge cemetery at Changi, which had been set up by the Australians and the British, was unmaintainable due to its proximity to military installations and facilities, it was decided that the hospital cemetery at Kranji would be extended and all war remains consolidated on this hilly site. By mid-1947, the AGS had managed to transfer most of the war dead to Kranji, along with remains from Buona Vista POW camp and the Bidadari Christian Cemetery (some war graves, however, were left at Bidadari and were only transferred in 2005, when the Bidadari Cemetery was redeveloped). In addition, war graves at the Saigon Military Cemetery in French Indo-China (Vietnam) were also relocated to Kranji.

The IWGC was aware of this consolidation of graves and was involved in the initial discussions but was unable to take over the cemetery at Kranji due to the slow progress by the AGS. This came to a head when former POWs who came back to Singapore, saw the "mess" at Kranji. A Reuters wire report, carried in London newspapers on 9 January 1948 caused great consternation at the War Office and with the IWGC:

> SINGAPORE TUESDAY – Protests against the condition of Woodlands (Kranji) War Cemetery, Singapore where more than 4,000 Allied servicemen who died during the war have been

> reinterred, were made today to newspapers here by local residents. One British Ex-Prisoner of War in a letter to *The Straits Times*, said: "Ex-Prisoners of War appear to know that the cemeteries at Changi, which during the Occupation were carefully tended by half-starved POWs unfit for heavier duties, and were left by them with trimmed grass graves, lawns, paths and hedges, flowering trees and shrubs, are now just torn-up weed covered wastes; and that the remains of their comrades have been transferred to a bare neglected hillside".
>
> The writer, "On behalf of those comrades at whose burial I assisted", urged that the authorities concerned should be persuaded to take an immediate active interest in the cemetery.
>
> An officer of the War Graves Commission said the Commission would take over Woodlands Cemetery, "when the Army Graves Service is ready to hand over"[1].

The report caused an immediate query by the War Office into the delays at Singapore. No satisfactory reply was given. It became of such great concern that the issue was raised in the House of Commons three months later when the Secretary of State for War was asked for assurance that, "proper steps are being taken to identify and maintain the graves of soldiers who lost their lives in Malaya and the Far East area"[2]. Despite this, not much action was taken to speed up the process, so much so that the IWGC was forced to respond to the allegations made.

In a note to the Colonial Secretary in Singapore, it claimed that, "taking over from the Military Authorities has been delayed from time to time on such grounds as the future of the Chinese Mass Grave Singapore, tenure of land, documentary questions, structural matters etc". The IWGC planned to, "take over KRANJI Cemetery on a Stage I basis – i.e. for horticultural treatment and structural maintenance – in the very near future"[3]

As the debate on the speed of work at Kranji continued, another mass grave was discovered. Before the war, an emergency water tank was dug in the grounds of the Civilian General Hospital (Singapore General Hospital). In the last hours before Singapore fell to the invading Japanese, the tank was used as a common grave for the dead from the hospital and corpses that were brought to the hospital in far greater numbers than could be dealt with. The dead were placed in the water tank and treated with lime. Several hundred bodies were disposed of in this manner.

The tank and its contents went unnoticed during the Occupation and upon liberation, the hospital was occupied by the British military, which did not know of the tank's existence. It was not until a year after liberation that the government medical department took over and it was almost another year before the fate of the bodies was discovered. Orders were immediately given that the ground, which had been used as a sports pitch, should be left undisturbed. More than 400 bodies were believed to have been buried in the tank. Although mainly filled with civilians, battle records indicate that more than 101 British and Commonwealth servicemen were also buried there. However, the lime treatment meant that the bodies had disintegrated beyond recognition and the identity discs that were famously thought up by Sir Fabian Ware, "were not worn or did not survive four years burial in Singapore soil"[4].

In a telegram to the Secretary of State for the Colonies, Singapore Governor Sir Franklin Charles Gimson noted that the IWGC, "will not accept any remains in a War Graves cemetery unless they can be definitely proved to be remains of persons entitled to War Graves burial"[5]. However, the Governor said that the IWGC would note the names of the servicemen in a future war memorial at Kranji. Nonetheless, he lobbied the IWGC to set up a common memorial to the soldiers and civilians at the general hospital despite the fact that the majority of remains were that of civilians.

While negotiations with the IWGC continued, Gimson, with help from the Singapore Base District, set up a memorial to the dead on the site of the graves and by 27 September 1948, the area was converted into a simple garden.

> Three long years later, the IWGC, ...after a lot of discussion with the local administration...decided that they must permanent mark this grave in situ... It was represented to the Commission that to abandon the site would offend local feeling. The Commission accordingly had their architect design a memorial...The memorial (was) designed to commemorate 103 British soldiers but nothing is known of the names of the civilians. The design consists of an octagon with four large panels and four small panels. It provides for a dedicatory inscription for the army burials on one of the large panels and for another inscription for the civilian deaths on a similar panel on the opposite side. The remaining panels bear the names of the soldiers, but the names of civilians will not be inscribed. The inscription proposed for the Army dead is:
>
> THE BRITISH SOLDIERS WHOSE MEMORY IS HONOURED HERE WERE MADE PRISONERS OF WAR BY THE JAPANESE ARMY AND DIES IN THIS PLACE IN FEBRUARY 1942.
> THEIR GLORY SHALL NOT BE BLOTTED OUT[6]

However, when the IWGC asked Gimson's government to contribute one-quarter of the £700 cost of building the memorial, which had been instigated by the Governor himself, the Colonial Secretary in Singapore reported that, "there is no public interest in the matter whatever and that it would not therefore seem possible for the Singapore Government to contribute financially to the proposed memorial but that they have no objection to its erection or to the design and inscription suggested"[7].

Surprised by the Governor's politicking, the IWGC, in a letter to the Colonial Office, complained that, "normally, the Commission cannot put up memorials on isolated graves of this kind. It is a very peculiar case and it was only because of the pressure from Singapore earlier that we considered marking this grave in this way. We would very much prefer to put up a tablet with the names of the soldiers in a suitable place in Kranji War Cemetery where it can be properly looked after by our people"[8].

As a result, the Civil Hospital Grave Memorial was built at Kranji, while a simple plaque was eventually installed at the base of the cross at the general hospital, which now reads:

BENEATH THIS CROSS LIE
94 BRITISH, 6 MALAYAN, 5 INDIAN, 2 AUSTRALIAN SOLDIERS
AND 300 CIVILIANS OF MANY RACES,
VICTIMS OF MAN'S INHUMANITY TO MAN,
WHO PERISHED IN CAPTIVITY IN FEBRUARY 1942.
THE SOLDIERS ARE COMMEMORATED BY NAME
AT KRANJI WAR CEMETERY.

At this time, the Church of England in Singapore was also looking to commemorate the war dead. The loss of the Archdeacon of Singapore Graham White and his wife during the Occupation was still strongly felt and the Church elders wanted to build something in honour of White's contributions.

Roping in the Bishop of Singapore, the Australian Commissioner and even the war heroine Elizabeth Choy, the then Archdeacon Woods enlisted the help of Gimson in putting out an appeal to raise $250,000 Malayan dollars in order to build a War Memorial Hall (now known as the North Transept) adjoining St Andrew's Cathedral. As a result, in The Times of London on 18 March 1952, the Governor of Singapore made an appeal to the many in the UK, "who remember this land with affection and who value the friendships contracted here". He noted that, "they will share with us our desire for the development of the spiritual and social service of this city and will wish to be associated with this memorial and to give contributions for its erection"[9].

The personal appeal by the Governor of Singapore caught the Colonial Office by surprise as they were not aware that the Governor had endorsed the building of a separate memorial to the war dead from the one that the IWGC was building at Kranji.

After asking for more details from the Colonial Secretary in Singapore, it was discovered that the memorial was actually to be a "Christian Social Centre in the heart of Singapore…to provide a centre for Christian youth work…as well as a library and a centre for the activities of the Christian Church in this area"[10].

Nonetheless, Archdeacon Woods felt it was of sufficient significance that he wrote to Buckingham Palace in order to solicit a Royal Message from the Queen for the opening of the Memorial Hall. Upon finding out from the Palace that such a request had been made directly to the Sovereign, the Secretary of State for the Colonies wrote to Gimson asking for clarification as to why a simple hall should deserve a Royal Message and why the request had not been made by the Governor as the representative of the Colony.

Red-faced, Gimson cabled back that the Archdeacon had taken it upon himself to make the request for the message without consulting the government and that regardless, the Singapore Government would not have made such a request in the first place as the hall was not significant enough to warrant a message from the Queen. Gimson noted that he had had words with the Archdeacon following which the request for the message had now been withdrawn. The Queen's principal private secretary acknowledged the Governor's reply to the issue and noted in his letter to the Secretary of State that the Governor's intervention had saved the Palace embarrassment as it would not have been able to respond to such a request[11].

In the end, the $250,000 was raised and together with funds already collected for Archdeacon White's memorial, the memorial hall was built in 1952 and remains an important place for the church's present activities.

By the mid-1950's progress on building the war cemetery and memorial at Kranji had speeded up and by the middle of 1956, it was clear that the official opening ceremony could be planned for the first half of 1957. However, the political scenario in Malaya and Singapore had changed considerably in that last decade. Where in 1945 there were welcoming smiles for the returning British, 1955 saw Malaya in the midst of a communist insurgency with a strong nationalist Malay movement calling for independence from Britain. Although there was limited autonomy when the Federation of Malaya was created in 1948, Malayan political parties like the United Malays National Organisation (UMNO) and their partners in the Alliance coalition wanted all-out independence.

Following the Alliance's landslide victory in the first Federal Elections in

1955, Tunku Abdul Rahman Putra Al Haj was appointed Chief Minister of the Malayan Federation.

The drafting of the Constitution of the Federation of Malaya was the beginning of a new Malayan government after Britain agreed to give independence to Malaya during Constitutional talks in 1956. The British formed a Working Committee to draft the Constitution, consisting of British representatives, advisors from the Conference of Rulers and Malayan political leaders. January 1956 saw the Tunku lead a delegation to London to discuss the Federal Constitution and negotiate a date for Malayan independence. Three months later, a Commission chaired by Lord Reid was set up to formulate a draft and refine the Constitution of the Federation of Malaya.

The Commission sought the views of various political parties, non-political organisations and individuals on the form of government and racial structure appropriate for the country, finally basing its decision on an Alliance memorandum. The memorandum, aimed at inter-communal conciliation as well as the political realities facing the Malays, highlighted five main non-negotiable demands, namely the position of the Malay Rulers, Islam as the official religion of the Federation, the position of the Malay language as prime in the Kingdom and the special rights of the Malays as well as equal citizenship.

The Constitutional Commission's Working Committee authorised the draft in early 1957 as the Constitution of the Federation of Malaya which would commence on the nation's independence on 31 August 1957. When Singapore, Sabah and Sarawak joined Malaya in 1963, several provisions in the Constitution were amended and the country's name was changed to Malaysia[12].

In Singapore, the situation was also just as precarious for the colony was also on the road to independence. However, the path had been much more rocky and unstable.

The colonial government in 1953 appointed Sir George Rendel to head a commission to review Singapore's constitution in order to create a complete political and constitutional structure designed to allow Singapore to develop as an autonomous state within a larger country with which it might ultimately be part of, namely the Federation of Malaya. As such, the commission recommended partial internal self-government for Singapore, with the United Kingdom maintaining control over internal security, law, finance, defence and foreign affairs. It also recommended a single-chamber, 32-member Legislative Assembly, of whom 25 would be elected, and a nine-member council of ministers that would act as a cabinet along with a Chief Minister to run the government. However, the Governor would retain his power to veto legislation. Accepting the Commission's proposals, the British government implemented the Rendel Constitution in February 1954, with elections scheduled for the Legislative Assembly in April 1955.

At the same time in July 1954, two former members of the Singapore Labour Party, Lim Yew Hock and Francis Thomas as well as a prominent lawyer, David Saul Marshall, formed a new political party, called the Labour Front. A member of Singapore's minuscule Jewish community, Marshall had studied law in Britain and fought with the Singapore Volunteer Corps during the Japanese invasion. As a POW during the Occupation, he had worked in the Hokkaido coal mines. A staunch anti-colonialist, Marshall campaigned for immediate independence within a merged Singapore and Malaya, the abolishing of the Emergency regulations, the Malayanisation of the civil service within four years (by which time locals would be in a position to take over from colonial officials), multilingualism and Singapore citizenship for its 220,000 Chinese immigrants.

In November 1954, the People's Action Party (PAP) was formed at a gathering of 1,500 people in Victoria Memorial Hall. Created by a group of mainly British-educated middle-class Chinese who had returned to Singapore after studying in post-war Britain, the PAP was led by 31-year-old Lee Kuan Yew, as Secretary General, Toh Chin Chye, Goh Keng Swee, and S. Rajaratnam. The PAP sought to attract a following among the mostly poor and non-English-speaking Chinese community. Lee had worked as a legal adviser to several trade unions and had earned a reputation for honesty and gained strong support from unionists. Lee had also helped defend Chinese students arrested during the 1954 student demonstrations protesting national service. Through his work with the unions and student groups, Lee made friends with anti-colonialists, non-communists and communists alike.

Present at the PAP's launch were the Tunku as President of UMNO, and Tan Cheng Lock, President of the Malayan Chinese Association (MCA). The PAP sought the repeal of the Emergency regulations, union with Malaya, a common Malayan citizenship and the Malayanisation of the civil service. However, the PAP planned to gain independence first, through support from the Chinese-educated public and the communist-controlled trade unions. It calculated that a united front with the communists was necessary to end colonialism. As such, it declared itself non-communist, neither pro- nor anti-communist, in a bid to put off until after independence any clash with the communists.

The 2 April 1955 contest saw the Labour Front win 10 of the 25 seats, forming a coalition government with the UMNO-MCA Alliance (whose leaders were present at the PAP's formation) which had won three seats. Three ex-officio members and two nominated members joined the coalition, forming a group of 17 in the 32-member assembly. The Progressives won only four seats and the loyalist Democratic Party just two, in a clear rejection of colonial rule and politics. The PAP had won three of the four seats it had contested, with Lee and Lim Chin Siong both winning seats. Lim had the backing of organised labour and led the pro-communists in the party while Lee led the non-communist wing.

The newly elected Labour Front government, with David Marshall as Singapore's first chief minister, faced serious problems from the very beginning. The communists had launched a campaign of strikes and student protests in a bid to destabilise the government. The Hock Lee Bus Riots broke out on 12 May when police attempted to break up an illegal gathering by striking bus workers and Chinese school students. Four people were killed and 31 injured in that single incident, which became known as "Black Thursday". Although the government arrested some students, Marshall was forced to eventually back down and agreed to the registration of the Singapore Chinese Middle School Students' Union because he supported the student's dissatisfaction with the colonial education system. Although the students agreed that one of the pre-conditions of registration would be to keep out of politics, the communist leaders of the union had different ideas[13].

Marshall also faced a constant conflict with the colonial government over his need to run the colony independent of the Governor. So, when Governor Sir Robert Brown Black refused to allow Marshall to appoint four assistant ministers, he threatened to resign unless Singapore was given immediate self-government under a new constitution. This crisis forced the Colonial Office to agree to hold constitutional talks, known as the Merdeka Talks in London in April 1956. Marshall led a 13-member delegation consisting of members of all the legislative parties which also included Lee and Lim. The Colonial Office offered to grant Singapore full internal self-government but wanted to control foreign affairs and internal security. They proposed a Defence and Internal Security Council, with three delegates each from Britain and Singapore, to be chaired by the then British Commissioner-General in Southeast Asia and future British High Commissioner in Singapore, who would have the casting vote in case of a tie. Marshall was unwilling to give the High Commissioner the casting vote with the talks breaking down. He had promised that he would resign if he did not obtain internal self-government. Once the delegation returned to Singapore, Marshall resigned in June 1956 and was succeeded by his deputy, Lim Yew Hock[14,15].

While these political scenarios were playing out, the Duke of Edinburgh had paid a Royal visit to Malaya in late 1956. Although he received a warm welcome in Malaya, the Duke's visit to Singapore was cancelled at the last minute at the insistence of Lim's new government because of the unstable political situation in the colony. As a result, the Kranji War Cemetery and Memorial's completion could not have come at a more inopportune moment.

The Duke of Gloucester, as Chairman of the IWGC was keen to attend the official opening of the cemetery and provide royal support in the establishment of the cemetery, as was the case for any of the Commission's major cemeteries throughout the world. In addition, as Colonel-in-chief of the Royal Army Service Corp and the Rifle Brigade, which were stationed in Malaya, he also planned to visit the Federation. However, a royal visit at such a time was considered ill-advised. In a two-page telegram to the Secretary of State, the British High Commissioner to the Federation of Malaya, Sir Donald Charles MacGillivray, wrote:

> ...it is not unlikely that some quarters would fail to recognise that it was pure coincidence that the two visits should fall within such a short time of each other, and both within ten months of independence, and would suspect a deliberate design to stimulate loyal sentiment, just at a time when the whole question of status of the Crown in Malaya is in question. The report of the Constitutional Commission is likely to be published in February (1958), and this may well be followed by bitter controversy in regard to the future of the Settlements and their connection with the Crown. It would not be an appropriate time for a Royal Visit[16].

In Singapore, Black was also concerned:

> I consulted the Chief Minister (Lim Yew Hock) and his colleagues in Council this morning. On the whole, I gained the impression of embarrassment...We are still in the middle, I might almost say at an early stage, of our struggle with the Chinese Middle Schools. I do not write off the possibility of further trouble in connection with the action which we may have to take. There still remains a feeling of tension, arising out of the recent rioting and the action against the leaders of subversion. The end of February is the time to which politically conscious people in Singapore will now be looking forward, because they expect that we shall have started or be about to start further constitutional talks...There may be political demonstrations at that time engineered by opposition parties, just as there were demonstrations before the last conference in April. Ministers have also suggested that it would be most unfortunate indeed if having had to request the cancellation of the visit of the Duke of Edinburgh, it became necessary to cancel, at short notice, the visit of the Duke of Gloucester. We cannot rule out the possibility, also, that a visit by the Duke in February might have

political repercussions and, of course, it would be distressing if political factions in Singapore planned demonstrations or a boycott, as they might well do, at the time of the Duke's visit[17].

As a result of the political instability in Malaya and Singapore, there would be a very unusual situation where no high-level representation from the UK would be made at the opening of an Imperial War Graves Commission cemetery. The Colonial Office left the responsibility to the Governor to act as the Queen's representative and as the Guest of Honour for the event. The cable from the Air Ministry to the Commander-in-Chief Far East Air Forces in Singapore reflected Whitehall's position:

...Decided that in view of local political situation, transport considerations etc, army and air councils will not Repeat not be represented from UK. It is requested that you will be good enough to attend ceremony as the representative of the Royal Air Force in your capacity as C In C F.E.A.F. You will rank in precedence below His Excellency the Governor and C In C F.E.L.F. (Commander In Chief, Far East Land Forces) but above Commonwealth representatives...[18]

Regardless, the ceremony went ahead on 2 March 1957, with the Australians sending Lieutenant General Gordon Bennett, who had led the AIF in the Malayan Campaign, to the event[19]. As *The Times* reported:

Those who stood yesterday in the early sunshine on this rise and looked north across the shimmering Straits of Johore, with the blur of Malaya behind, appreciated the beauty of the service in which the music was played by the band of the 2nd Battalion, The Royal Welch Fusiliers, the combined bands of the 1st Battalion, 2nd Gurkha Rifles, and the No.2 RAF regimental band, and the pipers of the 1st Battalion, The King's Own Scottish Borderers.

The lamentations of a very old Chinese woman; the small thud of a soldier who fell on his face in the heat; the clink of flag rings against the memorial walls; the incantations of a Buddhist priest robed in yellow; and far above, so far as to make the machines inaudible and invisible, the sight of vapour trails of RAF jet aircraft writing their inscription in the sky – all these were part of the scene of which one was subconsciously aware.

At 8.30am, the Governor, Sir Robert Black, was received by Air Chief Marshall Sir Arthur Longmore, vice-chairman of the Imperial

War Graves Commission. He ascended the hill, and, after the royal salute, inspected the guards of honour which were drawn up on either side of the cross of sacrifice which stands before the memorial. The officiating clergy, with Canon V.J. Pike, chaplain-general to the forces, at one end of a long row and Muslim, Hindu, and Buddhist representatives at the other end, were presented[20].

The Governor then unveiled the inscription to the Singapore Memorial, which bore the phrase, "They died for all Free Men". In his speech, Black said, "that simple sentence tells us why this multitude of men and women, of differing faiths and races but united in the service of their King, were faithful unto death. The traditions they so worthily upheld live on in the hearts and minds of those who follow them"[21]. The Correspondent for *The Times* then reported that there was a

> ...roll of drums seven times. The faces of the 13 columns of the memorial, on which the names of the missing are inscribed, were unveiled – the buglers sounded Last Post, the pipers played Lochaber No More, the chaplain-general read the dedication, and the buglers followed with Reveille.
>
> After prayers had been said and blessings pronounced, six soldiers and six airmen and one sailor marched on to hand wreaths to the Governor, representatives of the Dominions and heads of the Services. A Chinese soldier was the bearer to the Chief Minister of Singapore[22].

With the last wreath laid and many more placed by private citizens and representatives of numerous towns in the UK, the ceremonial opening of Kranji was complete. Kranji now provided some form of closure to the relatives and families of the Allied forces who lost their lives in the Second World War. However, for the vanquished Japanese, it would be a very different story.

Endnotes

1 "'Weed-Covered War Graves' Protest". REUTERS WIRE REPORT, 8 January 1948, CO323/1897, London: The National Archives.

2 *HANSARD, 25 March 1948, CO323/1897*, London: The National Archives.

Kranji Preparations, 1011/16/D.A., 1 June 1948, CO323/1897, London: The National Archives.

4 *From Governor To S of S, 6649/10/47, 9 February 1948, CO323/1897,* London: The National Archives.

5 *From Governor To S of S, 6649/10/47, 9 February 1948, CO323/1897,* London: The National Archives.

6 *IWGC, A/43510, 4 May 1951, CO323/1897,* London: The National Archives.

7 *IWGC, A/43510, 4 May 1951, CO323/1897,* London: The National Archives.

8 *IWGC, A/43510, 4 May 1951, CO323/1897,* London: The National Archives.

9 "A Singapore Memorial", *The Times* of London, 18 March 1952.

10 *St. Andrew's Cathedral War Memorial Hall Appeal pamphlet, 1952, CO1022/368,* London: The National Archives.

11 "Decision not to ask the Queen for a message on the occasion of the unveiling of the new Singapore War Memorial", various correspondence, CO1022/368, London: The National Archives.

12 Government of Malaysia. "History of the Constitution" Centre of Government Information and Service [Internet]. Accessed 29 September 2005. Available from: <http://mawar.www.gov.my/MYGOV/BI/Directory/Government/AboutMsianGov/GovConstitution/HistoryConstitution/>

13 *The Straits Times*, 4 June 1956.

14 U.S. Library of Congress. "Road to Independence" Library of Congress website [Internet]. Accessed 29 September 2005. Available at: < http://countrystudies.us/singapore/10.htm>.

15 On 11 April 1957, Lim Yew Hock and Alan Lennox-Boyd, Secretary of State for the Colonies would finally sign an agreement to allow the island colony of Singapore to govern itself under a new constitution agreed in London, after four weeks of discussions. The constitution would come into effect some time after 1 January 1958 when the colony would be known as the State of Singapore. Britain, however, would remain in charge of external affairs and defence.

16 *From Federation of Malaya to S of S, Personal No. 81, 12 November 1956, CO1032/73,* London: The National Archives.

17 *Personal & Confidential, Government House Singapore, 10 November 1956, CO1032/73,* London: The National Archives.

18 "Unveiling of Singapore Memorial", 1461/S.4.(C) Jan. 10, 10 January 1957, AIR2/12484, London: The National Archives.

19 "Tribute to 24,000 Service Men", *The Times* of London, 2 March 1957.

20 "Singapore Memorial Unveiled", *The Times* of London, 4 March 1957.

21 "24,000 Honoured in Singapore", *The Telegraph*, 4 March 1957.

22 "Singapore Memorial Unveiled", *The Times* of London, 4 March 1957.

Chapter 5

The Japanese War Dead

During the Malayan Campaign, the Imperial Japanese Army had also suffered heavy losses in the 70 days prior to the Fall of Singapore. Once the island was captured, plans were under way to locate their war dead at the newly constructed Syonan Chureito on top of Bukit Batok, one of the highest points in Singapore, where the ashes of the Japanese fallen during the campaign to take Singapore would now be enshrined. Built using POW labour, the Syonan Chureito was a 12-metre tall wooden pillar with Japanese prayers to the war dead inscribed on its side. The Japanese also gave permission to British POWs to build a small wooden cross behind the pillar to pay tribute to the British and Commonwealth troops who died in the Malayan Campaign and the Fall of Singapore.

One of the few known photographs of the Syonan Chureito shown from the base of the steps on Bukit Batok. The picture, taken in 1945, shows a wooden entrance at the top of the stairs leading on to the shrine at the top. Today, only the stairs remain at the location while the top of the hill has been converted into a transmitting station.

Bukit Batok was significant as it overlooked the Ford Motor Factory, where Lieutenant General Arthur Percival, General Officer Commanding, Headquarters Malaya Command, had surrendered over 125,000 British and

Commonwealth troops to Lieutenant General Tomoyuki Yamashita on the evening of 15 February 1942. The hill was also located in the the Bukit Timah area, where some of the heaviest fighting on the island took place.

The Japanese military administrators also decided to build a Shinto State Shrine opposite the Singapore Golf Club, near the banks of the MacRitchie Reservoir. Known as the Syonan Jinjya, it replaced the earlier Daijingu shrine in Ang Mo Kio as the principal Shinto State Shrine on the island. Accessed by a wooden bridge across the reservoir, the Jinjya was modeled on the Ise Grand Shrine in Japan and was also used for the worship of the Japanese war dead and propagation of Japanese imperialist ideologies[1]. In his book, *Syonan – My Story*, Mamoru Shinozaki, who had been appointed head of the Japanese municipal government's Welfare Department, described the opening of the Shrine:

> Wearing the official uniform of a thousand years ago, in black to indicate his high rank, Mayor Odate performed the opening ceremony early in 1943. Other officials wore red and blue uniforms in accordance with their rank. They all wore wooden shoes. Generals, admirals, senior officials and businessmen were all in attendance. So were community leaders and priests of other faiths. They all followed the manner of the Japanese at prayer. I explained to them that the ceremony showed respect for the ancestors of the Japanese Emperor. 'You can learn something about Japanese customs from this ceremony,' I told them. 'You do not betray your religion.'[2]

The military and Japanese officials would regularly worship the Japanese Emperor and the deified spirits of their fallen comrades at the Chureito and Jinjya. As Blackburn and Lim point out, the shrines were used to convey the message that Japan had "liberated" the Asian countries from European colonists, and was "benevolently" guiding the destinies of its Asian "brothers". The nationalist rhetoric was in contrast to the brutal subjugation with which the Japanese militarists enforced the new "East Asia Co-Prosperity Sphere" in the region. They used Shintoism to uphold an imperial hierarchy with the Emperor at its head, who was believed to have descended from the Sun Goddess Amaterasu, the ancestor of Jimmu, founder of Japan's unbroken imperial dynasty since 660 BC. The Jinjya was dedicated to Amaterasu.

After Japan surrendered to the Allies in 1945, the Japanese destroyed these monuments according to their own rituals, rather than have the British desecrate them[3]. However, the Japanese did not touch the Allied POW Cross. Major Edward Williamson, the commanding officer of the 5th Indian Division's Royal Engineers had been instructed to blow up the shrine, two days after landing in Singapore on 5 September 1945. To his amazement, he found the cross intact. His men blew up whatever was left of the shrine but left the cross alone. However, the POW cross disappeared shortly after and no one is sure of what has happened to it since[4].

Upon re-occupation in 1945, one of the guiding principles of South East Asia Command, under the leadership of Vice-Admiral Lord Louis Mountbatten, who had been appointed Military Administrator of Singapore and head of the British military administration in the region, was the need to bring Japanese war criminals to justice and to repatriate Allied POWs as fast as possible. Japanese concerns for their war dead were not a priority for his administration.

Slightly more than a month after the official Japanese surrender in the municipal building in Singapore, Count Hisaichi Terauchi, Commander-

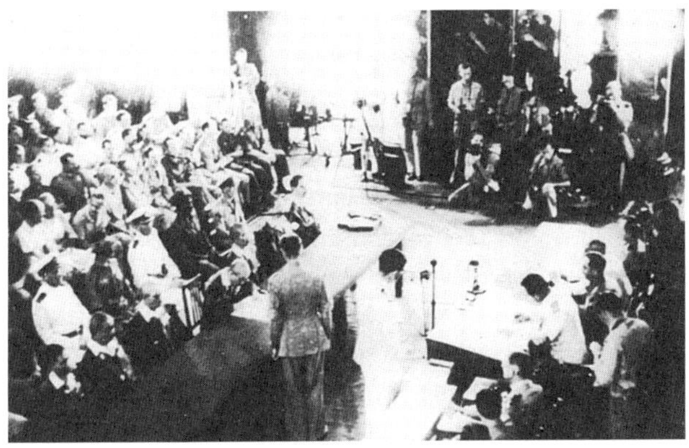

Top: The scene in the Municipal Chamber as Vice-Admiral Lord Louis Mountbatten, Supreme Allied Commander, South East Asia Command (SACSEA), signs one copy of the Surrender Document while General Itagaki is busy signing other copies. Above: The dejected Japanese delegation leaving the surrender ceremony under guard.

in-Chief of the Japanese Southern Forces, who was bed-ridden in Saigon (Ho Chi Minh City) and as a result unable to surrender in person at the 12 September ceremony, sent an urgent signal to Mountbatten. In it, he requested permission for the Japanese to, "excavate the ashes of dead soldiers and send them to JAPAN commencing with 1,996 personnel buried temporarily in JAPANESE burial place in SINGAPORE"[5].

Mountbatten's Chief of Staff demurred:

> Please inform Field Marshal TERAUCHI that BRITISH dead are not being conveyed to U.K. or Dominion of origin. JAPANESE will accordingly not be allowed to take the ashes of their dead back to Japan[6].

On reading the curt reply to Terauchi's request, Esler Denning, Mountbatten's Chief Political Adviser, asked SEAC administrators to reconsider:

> I am sorry but I simply cannot understand the logic of this reply. Assuming that the real reason is not the question of shipping, the intention of the refusal would appear to be purely to be nasty to the Japanese to whom the recovery and suitable disposal of the ashes of their relatives who have fallen in the war is as important as it would be for the relatives of a British soldier who had died in battle to know that he had had a proper Christian burial and that his grave would be cared for. This signal seems to suggest that it is because the Japanese do not permit it that the British dead are not being conveyed to U.K. or the Dominions.
>
> I think that this action is likely to cause unnecessary bitterness among the Japanese and in any case I would suggest that this matter, in which equal treatment in regard to all territories where Japanese soldiers have been killed should be given, should, therefore, be referred to the Supreme Commander for the Allied Powers[7].

Brigadier John Gerald Nicholson, SEAC's Deputy Director of Intelligence, discussed the matter with Mountbatten's Chief of Staff, Lieutenant General Sir Frederick Arthur Montague Browning, who was also SEAC's Director of Intelligence. Guided by the IWGC's principle of equality of treatment and no repatriation for British and Commonwealth servicemen, Browning decided that the Japanese remains would stay in Singapore. In a note to Denning, Nicholson said that, "in light of our conversation this morning with the Chief of Staff, I doubt if there is any further action I can take"[8].

Although Browning had considered the IWGC's policy on no repatriation, he clearly had a narrow interpretation of the complementary policy of equality of treatment. Browning's understanding of equality meant that both sides would have their remains kept in Singapore. However, this did not stretch to equal burial locations and cemeteries.

Unlike in northern France, where the Allies allowed the Germans to build cemeteries like La Cambe and St Desir De Lisieux to commemorate their war dead, SEAC did not appear to be interested in what the Japanese surrendered personnel did with the ashes of their war dead as long as they were not taken out of Singapore and did not cost SEAC any money.

Therefore, the question also subsequently arose as to who would be responsible for the remains of Japanese soldiers who died during the Second World War and the remains of the Japanese surrendered personnel who died before they could be repatriated to Japan. There was also concern over what would happen to the ashes of Japanese war criminals that were to be executed.

In a flurry of letters between the British Foreign Office, Commonwealth Office and War Office, no one could decide what to do with the remains or who would pay for the maintenance of the remains. The Foreign Office was of the view that the Japanese Government would have to bear the full cost:

> The limit of British responsibility in respect of any Japanese "war graves" would appear to be physical maintenance, which would presumably be at the expense of the Japanese Government. Such maintenance, I suppose, would be on a scale commensurate with the amount of money which the Japanese were prepared to pay. If, to take the extreme case, the Japanese Government declared that they had no interest in the graves at all, and were not prepared to pay anything, we should no longer be under any moral obligation to see that the "graves... were treated with respect and suitably maintained".
>
> At the present moment the Japanese Government are not, I think, in a position to give us any foreign currency in exchange for services in respect of the graves. By the time the Peace Treaty is signed, there will presumably be some arrears to collect. I do not know whether this will amount to anything substantial.
>
> If it is desired to recover the expenses in question, it would seem to be desirable to ensure, as soon as possible, that the Japanese are aware that a claim will be made. This could, of course, be notified to them through the Supreme Commander for the Allied Powers in

> Tokyo. It is just possible that it might be thought worth covering the question in the Peace Treaty, by some general clause making it clear that the Japanese Government must be responsible for all past and future expenses in connexion (*sic*) with the maintenance of graves of J.S.P. (Japanese Surrendered Personnel) in Allied territory; and the same considerations presumably apply to the graves of Japanese who died during the occupation. I presume whichever Department undertakes the immediate responsibility of paying the caretakers would undertake to make suggestions for any such clause in the Peace Treaty which they might deem necessary[9].

As a result of this indecision at Whitehall and the inability to get the bankrupt Japanese Government to commit funds, the role of war commemoration then passed to the Japanese Cemetery in Singapore, which had previously been a civilian cemetery.

The Japanese Cemetery along Chuan Hoe Avenue was founded in 1891 as a burial ground for Japanese prostitutes, also known as Karayuki-san. Almost 1,000 of early Singapore's Japanese community leaders and residents were buried at the Shakkyozan Nihonji[10].

Japanese Surrendered Personnel, who were being used as manual labourers by the British, decided they would take it upon themselves to commemorate their war dead. From 1945 to 1947, 40,000 Japanese surrendered personnel were kept at camps in Singapore, because of a shortage of shipping as well as the fact that SEAC was busy repatriating Allied POWs using all available vessels. This captive Japanese labour was used to repair the war damage on the island.

A group of them decided to build tombstones and memorials marking the Japanese militarist view of the war and their work remained undisturbed by the British authorities who could not read the Japanese inscriptions on the memorials and who were too busy rebuilding the city[11]. These surrendered

The Japanese Surrendered Personnel formed labour groups and were used by the returning British to repair the city. Men from a similar workgroup were involved in building the shrines and memorials to the Japanese war dead at the Japanese Cemetery.

personnel viewed their compatriots who were being tried for war crimes as martyrs and patriots. Many perceived their own ill-treatment as prisoners of the British as evidence that the British were not interested in justice but only in taking revenge on the vanquished, disregarding the murderous treatment that the Japanese military had meted out to Allied POWs only weeks before. This was the version of the past that the surrendered Japanese soldiers told in stone in the Japanese Cemetery, with the British authorities largely unaware of what they were doing[12].

The surrendered Japanese first put the remains from the Chureito in ten small jars which they then placed in the Chamber of Bones at the Japanese Cemetery[13]. The Chamber of Bones had been built at the Japanese Cemetery before the war, and had on one side a Buddhist dharma wheel and a steel gate at the back. It was meant to temporarily store the ashes of the dead before burial. Only two jars remain of the original ten used for the Japanese war dead[14].

As noted earlier, Field Marshal Count Hisaichi Terauchi, Commander-in-Chief of the Japanese Southern Army, had suffered a stroke just before the Japanese surrender and was unable to sign the surrender document in Singapore on 12 September 1945 due to his weakened state. Although he did finally surrender himself and his two swords to Lord Louis Mountbatten in Saigon in November 1945, Terauchi died in Malaya on 12 June 1946. His cremated remains were buried in a separate shrine at the Japanese Cemetery. This, according to Blackburn and Lim, gave the Japanese prisoners an opportunity to put up the kind of memorials they wanted with little, if any, interference from the British authorities.

The Cemetery at Chuan Hoe Avenue holds the ashes of Japanese troops who died in the region during and after the end of the war. Their remains were consolidated here.

The shrine of Field Marshal Hisaichi Terauchi, who died shortly after the Japanese surrender, is located in a separate site at the cemetery.

Terauchi's tombstone and three other distinctive memorials in the Japanese Cemetery were completed by three Japanese prisoners in April 1947. The first was a memorial for army and navy personnel (*rikukaigun gunjin gunzoku ryukon no hi*), the second, a memorial to the martyrdom of patriots (*junnan resshi no hi*), while the third was a memorial for the work team members who died at their posts (*sagyotai junshokusha no hi*)[15].

The martyrdom of patriots memorial was for the Japanese who committed suicide after Japan's surrender or who were executed as war criminals by the British. In his book on the building of these memorials, Hajime Fujita noted that the ground around the the martyrdom of patriots memorial was "consecrated" by soil from Changi Prison, where the war criminals had been executed, smuggled out by Japanese interpreters[16].

The principal builders of the three large stone monuments were carpenter Kunio Higashitsuji, and stonemasons Tomokatsu Mizuya and Tokiyaki Tetsuka. In creating Terauchi's tombstone, rock was taken from Singapore and Kota Tinggi. The inscription reads, "Southern Troop Commander General Terauchi, Built by the Southern Troops Work Team in April 1947". Work on the tombstone progressed in secret while the three were interned at the Jurong work camp. Later, Japanese volunteers transported these four tombstones to the Japanese cemetery. It took two days to erect the tombstones in the cemetery and the entire process to build and install the monuments took three months[17]. All the while, the British remained in the dark.

The Japanese also built another memorial to commemorate the Japanese war criminals who were hanged at Changi, known as a memorial to the ashes of 135 martyrs (*junnan nokotsu hyaku sanju go chu*). In addition, there is also a memorial to the 79 war criminals hanged in Kuala Lumpur, Penang and Malacca. Both memorials appear to have been made of wood but were replaced by the Japanese government with a stone monument in 1955[18].

However, once the British repatriated all the Japanese in 1948, no Japanese were allowed back into Singapore or Malaya for fear of their war past. The Singapore government took over ownership of the cemetery and left it disused. Even the caretaker, who had been maintaining the cemetery since 1944 was not paid but nonetheless, continued looking after the graves. In return for his dedication and as a token of their appreciation to Zhang Ya Gong, the Japanese Association later allowed Zhang to be buried in the cemetery, one of only a handful of Chinese styled tombs in the cemetery[19].

This policy towards the Japanese dead in Singapore remained until the Official Peace Treaty was signed with Japan in 1951. However, it was not goodwill and friendship but a political trade-off that allowed the Japanese to re-establish their consulate and presence in Singapore in 1952.

By November 1952, the Japanese Government had appointed Ken Ninomiya as the first post-war Japanese Consul-General to Singapore. At the behest of the Japanese Government, one of Ninomiya's first tasks was to find out the fate of Japanese war remains in Singapore, as the Japanese surrendered personnel's handiwork had yet to be discovered by either the Japanese government or the British. Upon locating the remains, the aim was to repatriate the ashes of the dead.

In addition, the Japanese Government, emulating the IWGC, had also set up a Graves Registration Team that was to travel throughout Asia and even the US in a bid to locate various Japanese remains, identify and finally repatriate them to Japan. The first expedition would be to the US, the second would head for Borneo, Okinawa and the Philippines, the third would go to Indochina and Java while the fourth would proceed to Guadalcanal, Attu and Burma and the fifth would go to China and Manchuria. Although Malaya and Singapore were not mentioned, they would also be part of the plan[20]. As a result, the British Embassy in Tokyo, upon finding out about Ninomiya's orders in a news report, cabled London:

> Kyodo News Agency has recently referred to a report said to have been sent by Ken Ninomiya, the Japanese Consul-General in Singapore, about the Japanese cemetery outside Singapore. According to the Agency (*sic*) Ninomiya states that the area is covered in deep grass and shrubs although a Chinese is being paid 20 dollars to look after the cemetery. 399 grave posts have apparently been identified in addition to the remains of about 60 others placed in a charnel house and there is said to be an additional tomb where about 10,000 others, including civilians, are buried. In reply, the Japanese Ministry of Foreign Affairs has apparently instructed the Consul-General to take measures to have the cemetery cleaned and Kyodo reports that after consulting with the Repatriation Board they intend to negotiate with the Singapore authorities about bringing back these remains to Japan[21].

This was the first that the Colonial Office had heard of the issue. The Secretary of State urgently cabled Singapore Governor Sir John Fearns Nicoll and his colleagues in the region for advice on whether the British government should allow these visits. However, even if these local governments did not agree with Japanese wishes there would still be no option for the British but to comply as a complicating factor for the British government was the fact that the rights to maintain the Commonwealth War Cemetery in Yokohama, Japan were up for renewal:

> The Imperial War Graves Commission have under consideration a treaty with the Japanese Government regarding rights to maintain the Commonwealth War Cemetery at Yokohama. The negotiations are being carried out by the Australian Department of External Affairs, and the Commission has learned that it is almost certain that the Japanese Government are about to ask for certain rights to visit and collect Japanese graves in Commonwealth territories. I am advised that these rights, if denied or delayed, will have an adverse effect on the negotiations of the treaty...[22]

The Australian negotiating team was led by Sir Esler Denning, Mountbatten's former Chief Political Adviser, who had appealed in 1945 to allow the Japanese to repatriate their ashes from Singapore but who was overruled by Mountbatten's Chief of Staff, Frank Browning, on the grounds of equality of treatment. It was thus, ironic, that the man who was willing to repatriate the ashes in 1945, would now see permission granted to repatriate those remains but in return for a guarantee on maintaining the Commonwealth graves in Japan using as the basis of the exchange, the principle of equality of treatment[23].

Meanwhile, Nicoll, unaware that Japanese surrendered personnel had built various memorials to their war dead and had entombed the ashes in question at the Japanese Cemetery in Singapore, cabled back:

> I agree in principle to proposed visit for the purpose of identification of graves of Japanese interred here, but strongly recommend that any such visit should be made as inconspicuous and by as few persons as possible.
>
> It is not clear, however, whether any useful purpose would be served by such a visit. Only one Japanese cemetery is known here, and this is a pre-war civilian cemetery. I understand that all Japanese war dead were cremated during the occupation period and their ashes sent back to Japan. I suggest, therefore, that the Japanese be asked if they have any information about the location of graves of war dead here, since it will be necessary to arrange for the team to have access to the graves[24].

By the middle of 1953, the British government had identified most of the Japanese graves within their colonies with the exception of the ones in Singapore, of which they remained unaware. The list (see Appendix C) prepared by the British Far East Land Forces was forwarded to the War

Office for transmittal to the Australian negotiating team in working out a final deal with the Japanese.

Regardless of the outcome of the negotiations, Ninomiya and his consular team managed to identify the various war tombs in the cemetery and began gathering support from the newly established post-war Japanese community in Singapore for the maintenance of the cemetery.

However, the Japanese government eventually decided it would not remove the remains of the Japanese war dead to a separate cemetery nor would they repatriate the ashes. This was because the Japanese surrendered personnel had put in so much effort to erect a memorial to their fellow soldiers and as such the memorial was a type of a shrine in itself as well as the fact that all ashes had been entombed in one single mound which made any form of identification impossible.

In 1955, the Japanese Government allocated funds to Ninomiya to restore parts of the war memorials and graves in the cemetery. However, it was not until 1969 that the Singapore government handed back ownership of the cemetery to the re-formed Japanese Association which was now tasked with maintaining the cemetery[25]. Burials continued until 1973 when the Singapore government passed an ordinance preventing the further expansion of 42 cemeteries on the island. The Japanese Cemetery then took on the role of a park for the appreciation of history and for its natural flora and fauna. The cemetery was gazetted as a memorial park in 1987 and is still visited by Japanese veterans and tourists who continue to pay homage to their war dead in Singapore.

Although the Japanese and British both constructed memorials to their dead, it was not till 1966 that an official monument to civilians was constructed in Singapore. This was in no small part due to the political minefield that had grown around the building of a Civilian Memorial in Singapore.

Endnotes

1 Blackburn, Kevin and Lim, Edmund. "Singapore's Little Japan and Its Japanese Cemetery" in *Spaces of the Dead: A Case from the Living*, Ed. Kevin YL Tan, Singapore: Singapore Heritage Society, 2006.

2 Shinozaki, Mamoru. *Syonan - My Story*. Singapore: Marshall Cavendish Editions, 2005, p. 118.

3 Blackburn, Kevin and Lim, Edmund. "Singapore's Little Japan and Its Japanese Cemetery" in *Spaces of the Dead: A Case from the Living*, Ed. Kevin YL Tan, Singapore: Singapore Heritage Society, 2006.

4 Author Interview with E. Williamson, Singapore, 8 September 2005.

5 Commission No.1 SAIGON to SACSEA, COS 57, 18 October 1945, WO203/5637, London: The National Archives.

6 SACSEA to COMMISSION NO.1 SAIGON, NGS 297, 25 October 1945, WO203/5637, London: The National Archives.

7 To Brigadier Nicholson, 8/68/45, 27 October 1945, WO203/5637, London: The National Archives.

8 C.P.A. 8/68/45, 31 October 1945, WO203/5637, London: The National Archives.

9 F13687/13687/23, 17 October 1947, FO371/63826. London: The National Archives.

10 Lam, Pin Foo. "Japanese Settlers were here before the War". *The Straits Times: Life*, 25 February 1998. 2.

11 Blackburn, Kevin and Lim, Edmund. "Singapore's Little Japan and Its Japanese Cemetery" in *Spaces of the Dead: A Case from the Living*, Ed. Kevin YL Tan, Singapore: Singapore Heritage Society, 2006.

12 Ibid.

13 Ibid.

14 Ibid.

15 Ibid.

16 Ibid.

17 Ibid.

18 Ibid.

19 Ibid.

20 "Japanese War Dead", 1853/17/52, 19 November 1952, CO1032/3, London: The National Archives.

21 Ibid.

22 "Japanese War Graves", GEN62/137/01, 12 January 1953, CO1032/3, London: The National Archives.

23 CONFIDENTIAL, No.467 (FJ 1851/15), 17 November 1953, CO1032/3, London: The National Archives.

24 "War Graves", No.35, 16 January 1953, CO1032/3, London: The National Archives.

25 Blackburn, Kevin and Lim, Edmund. "Singapore's Little Japan and Its Japanese Cemetery" in *Spaces of the Dead: A Case from the Living*, Ed. Kevin YL Tan, Singapore: Singapore Heritage Society, 2006.

Chapter 6

The Civilian Memorial

While the British, Commonwealth and Japanese governments took care of their war dead, the civil population in Singapore did not have any such luxury. In the 1950s and early 60s, there was no monument in Singapore to mark the loss incurred by the Chinese community and the various other races living on the island. The only local monument was to the late Chinese nationalist hero Lim Bo Seng, who lost his life in clandestine operations with the British-led Force 136 in the jungles of Malaya. Even this was paid for mainly by funds from the Chinese nationalist government in Chungking and with token contributions by the British authorities in Malaya.

As Singapore began redeveloping its land to meet the needs of its population and industry, contractors and workmen began finding mass graves all over the island. These graves were mostly filled with the bodies of Chinese civilians who were killed by the Japanese in the opening days of the occupation. In what was known as the "Sook Ching" Operation, thousands of Chinese who were believed to have collaborated with the British before the war and those who appeared "educated" or likely to put up a struggle against Japanese rule were rounded up at concentration points throughout the island. They were then taken in trucks to remote spots on the island where they were made to dig and then stand in their own graves while the Japanese troops bayoneted or shot them where they stood.

In the late 1940s, Chinese businessman Tan Kah Kee had set up a committee to estimate the cost of the war damage and to identify the Chinese war dead. By early 1951, a Joint Appeal Committee of Japanese-massacred Chinese was set up to look into the deaths and to demand reparations from the Japanese. A typical discovery of remains became front page news in Singapore and even made it to the pages of newspapers in the UK, as reflected in the find in 1951 of 1,300 graves, which was then reported in *The Times*:

> Representatives of the War Graves Inquiry Services and "Joint Appeal Committee of Japanese-massacred Chinese" to-day located in the Siglap and Bedok suburbs, about seven miles along the east coast road from Singapore, the graves of about 1,300 soldiers, volunteers, and civilians, mostly Chinese, who were massacred by the Japanese on February 22, 1942. They were assisted by two Chinese who escaped the massacre and a third Chinese on whose small-holding some of the graves were dug. The graves were mostly in an undulating country site which had become known locally as the "valley of the dead." The majority of the victims were civilians. The military dead, numbering perhaps 200, will later be exhumed for reinterment at Kranji War Cemetery[1].

However, the Appeal Committee's compensation claims were filed after the Japanese government had signed the official Peace Treaty in San Francisco in 1951, and under which it had discharged all its obligations for reparations after making payments to signatories of the treaty. As Malaya and Singapore were not signatories to the treaty, there would be no compensation per se.

The issue died down in the 1950s although sporadic discoveries of civilian remains continued. However, the discovery of numerous mass graves in 1962 would create an enormous outcry among the Chinese community in Singapore and Malaya who demanded that the Japanese compensate them for the "blood debt" that was owed to the peoples in the region.

The British Foreign Office viewed these protests anxiously as they were aware that legally the Japanese did not have to make any further reparations:

> The liability of Japan in respect of losses arising out of the Pacific war was fixed finally in the Treaty of Peace with Japan of September 8, 1951...In Article 14(b) of the Treaty the Allied Powers waived all reparations claims of the Allied Powers, other claims of the Allied Powers and their nationals arising out of any actions taken by Japan and its nationals in the course of the prosecution of the war (underlined in original) except as otherwise provided in the Peace Treaty. No compensation is provided under the Treaty for personal injury or death, wherever suffered. We might in certain circumstances,

> however, be prepared to discuss the situation with the Japanese and possibly encourage them to make some gesture of reparation[2].

As the Japanese Government had already discharged its liabilities under the Peace Treaty, it took the position that no other compensation could be considered.

In and of itself, the issue could have been resolved quickly as, privately, the Japanese Government was willing to pay a certain amount of compensation. However, the Chinese Chamber of Commerce felt that any offer by the Japanese would have to match the "donation" of 50 million Straits Settlements Dollars that the Chinese community in Singapore had been forced to make to the Japanese during the Occupation.

Moreover, the political landscape in Singapore would continue to influence the issue.

A founding member of the PAP in 1954, Lim Chin Siong was the leader of the pro-communist faction within the PAP. Detained along with several other pro-communists after the Chinese Middle School Riots in 1956, he was released in 1959 after the PAP won its first general election. However, due to ideological differences, he broke ranks with Lee Kuan Yew (who was then trying to eliminate left-wing radicals in the party) and formed the Barisan Sosialis Party on 17 September 1961.

The Special Branch in Singapore, although at the time still under the control of the British, provided the Singapore government with a security intelligence briefing on Lim and the communist stance towards the "blood debt" issue:

> ...the discovery of the bones of Chinese war victims in the course of building operations, has resulted in the Chinese Chamber of Commerce undertaking the exhumation and re-burial of the remains of other Chinese murdered by the Japanese. Presumably intended deliberately to inflame the emotions thus aroused, a rumour (by the communists) has circulated that these atrocities were the outcome of Malay collaborations with the Japanese. It so happens that a reminder of the Chinese struggle against the Japanese was contained in a speech by LIM Ching-siong (*sic*) in December last year (1961) when he said that merger on the terms of the PAP's White Paper would reduce Singapore's citizens to the status of a "conquered people", using the term that had been employed to describe the condition of the people at the time of the Japanese occupation of China (paragraph 8 of 12/61). Since LIM Ching-siong's speeches are used for instructional purposes at cadre training classes, this move to equate the Malays with the Japanese may gain ground. Peking Radio has

> broadcast an account of the action taken by the Chinese Chamber of Commerce[3].

As such, the discovery of the graves in 1962 caused great concern. The British High Commission cabled London with the news of the new find:

> 49 mass graves have been found but no attempt at systematic exhumation has been made so far, and it is not possible to estimate how many were buried in each grave. Singapore Government confirm our impression that, although exact site of graves may not have been known, this is not evidence of hitherto unknown atrocity[4].

Within hours, London cabled back what they suspected was the action that led to the graves and what the High Commissioner's response to the Singapore government should be:

> It seems highly probable that atrocity to which present discovery is related is that described in the record of one of the Japanese war criminal trials in the following terms.
>
> Seven and a half mile stone East Coast Road. Between 18th and 20th February, 1942, all Chinese residence (*sic*) of the Gaylang (Geylang) District were rounded up and assembled at Teluk Kurau English School. There, following a conference addressed by Lt. Col. Oishi (head of the Kempeitai) and attended by Lieutenant (now Major) Onishi these Chinese were screened by various Kempeitai officers including Lieutenant Onishi. Certain categories were then placed to one side and removed on 23rd February by lorry to seven and a half mile East Coast Road where they were led off the road to prepared trenches and killed by machine gun fire. Those killed numbered about five hundred.
>
> In March, 1947, seven Japanese officers including Oishi and Onishi were tried by a British Military Court in Singapore upon charges of being concerned in the massacre of large numbers of Chinese civilian residents of Singapore between 18th February and 3rd March, 1942. All seven officers were convicted, two including Oishi being sentenced to death and the remainder including Onishi to life imprisonment. The death sentences were carried out at Changi Gaol on 26th June, 1947...
>
> ...In replying to Singapore Government it would seem advisable to point out that although no monetary reparation to individuals for

> Japanese war crimes against Singapore civilians could be exacted justice was done as described above to persons who were responsible for them[5].

However, it was not an issue of justice being done but one of justice being seen to be done. The Chinese community was outraged in 1947 when so few Japanese were made to pay the ultimate price for such heinous crimes, with a large number of the accused escaping the hangman's noose. Thus, it was no surprise that when the issue of justice was resurrected, there had to be a certain element of compensation for some of the justice that did not appear to have been meted out.

Then Singapore Deputy Prime Minister Toh Chin Chye met with Japanese Consul General Maeda to resolve the issue and the Japanese consul suggested the building of a park and memorial costing about $1 to $2 million Straits dollars, with the Singapore government providing the land free of cost. The Japanese government was willing to make a gesture of atonement on the clear understanding that it did not constitute reparations, as it had discharged all its obligations for reparations under the terms of the 1951 Peace Treaty.

In May 1962, then Singapore Prime Minister Lee Kuan Yew visited Japan and the Japanese again offered to build the park. Lee did not commit himself to the Japanese proposal but said he would consult the Chinese Chamber, which had mobilised immense support on the issue. The Japanese, however, thought it was a done deal. They even sent a new Consul General to Singapore.

Hiroto Tanaka, however, would have a much harder time than his predecessor. Upon consultation with the Chamber, Lee told Maeda before he left that the memorial park was not enough and that the Chamber, led by rubber magnate Ko Teck Kin (right), was demanding compensation of at least $50 million Straits dollars. Ko had been elected President of the Chamber in February 1960. Although Maeda told Lee that Japan had paid its debts under the Peace Treaty, Lee countered that the treaty was signed at a time when Singapore was "was under the yoke of a colonial power and that the local Chinese had not received any of the material benefits of the Treaty"[6].

Moreover, the Singapore government announced in March 1963 the launching of a public appeal for funds to build a $750,000 memorial and park for Japanese war victims. The Singapore government would match public subscription dollar for dollar, with the first day's collection amounting to more than $109,000[7]. Instead of being a purely Chinese memorial to the Chinese community, Lee wanted the Civilian Memorial to be a multi-racial commemoration to all locals who lost their lives during the war. Moreover, negotiations for Japanese compensation, which had originally been handled between the Japanese government and the Chinese Chamber of Commerce now moved to a higher level as it had now become a bilateral issue between the two governments.

Lee's enemies were determined to exploit these sensitive negotiations. Ong Eng Guan was another founding member of the PAP. An Australian-educated accountant, Ong was a firebrand Hokkien orator who could inspire crowds and support from the Chinese community. Voted in as the first Mayor of Singapore, he removed all the symbols of colonial rule from City Hall, banishing the Speaker's Mace from the legislative chamber. He also removed from public view the tattered Union Jack used in the British surrender in 1942 and again on liberation in 1945, and which was on display in the City Hall chambers. The flag, which hung for many years in Charterhouse at Eton, is now kept in the collection of the Imperial War Museum[8].

As Mayor, Ong emphasised basic issues like hawker's demands, water standpipes, proper drainage for villagers and went about "cutting white civil servants down to size". His performance and anti-colonial antics worried Lee but it made him very popular among the masses and especially in his constituency of Hong Lim.

In December 1960, Ong resigned from the Assembly after alleging nepotism by Lee and another minister, and was expelled from the PAP. Resigning his seat in Hong Lim, Ong formed the United People's Party and won the by-election there with a 73 per cent majority. In 1963, Ong attempted to use the reparations issue as a lever against the government. In a report to Lee, the Special Branch noted,

> Ong Eng Guan, Chairman of the United People's Party, was reported in June to be attempting to exploit the delay of the Japanese Government to provide compensation for the families of Singapore Chinese massacred during the war through an appeal to Chinese communal sentiments. In the 16th June issue of his paper "BERSATU" he called on the Chinese Chamber of Commerce to hold a mass rally and demand the boycott of Japanese goods. He accused the PAP Government of deliberate delaying tactics on this issue until it could get rid of its responsibilities on the establishment of Malaysia[9].

In 1963, Singapore was to merge with peninsular Malaya, Sabah and Sarawak (British Borneo) as well as Brunei to become an independent and sovereign state in the Federation of Malaysia.

The day of merger, Malaysia Day, by the agreement of all parties involved, was to be 31 August 1963. However, the Malaysian Prime Minister, Tunku Abdul Rahman, after meeting with the Indonesian and Philippine presidents between 30 July and 5 August, had agreed to postpone Malaysia Day to 16 September in order to give the United Nations time to ascertain the popular will in the Borneo territories on the proposition to join the Malaysian Federation. Lee and the Chief Ministers designate of Sabah and Sarawak were not consulted on this decision and as a result all three called on the Tunku to set up Malaysia on 31 August. Regardless, the Malaysian Prime Minister decided that Malaysia Day would be postponed to 16 September 1963[10].

Thus, Lee, who was in the midst of a political struggle with the Malayan Communist Party (MCP) for control of the hearts and minds of the populace and to garner support for the upcoming merger with Malaysia, declared Singapore's de facto independence on 31 August 1963. He said the PAP government would hold Singapore in trust until the formation of Malaysia. Lee called for unity and pledged the state's loyalty to the central Malaysian government[11].

In the same speech, Lee decided to turn the heat on the Japanese by announcing that as the Japanese had yet to settle the issue of the blood debt, the Singapore Government would now also take on the foreign relations portfolio of the state until Malaysia Day in an attempt to resolve the blood debt issue[12].

Just days before, on 25 August, the Chinese Chamber of Commerce organised a rally of close to 100,000 of all races at the Padang to demand Japanese reparations. Lee decided to lead the rally. In his cable to London, the British High Commissioner reported Lee's remarks:

> (Lee) regretted that the present Japanese Consul-General (Tanaka) was so insensitive and so prosaic in his approach to this issue. "I do not know why the former Consul-General (Maeda) of Japan was recalled. He knew more about this matter, particularly the feelings of the people on this issue and the perils it holds for Japan. I hope his recall was purely coincidental and not a deliberate change of policy. For if the Japanese government were to be insensitive and unimaginative in their approach, then they stand to lose a great deal in this part of the world. I hear that the Japanese Government fears repercussions in the rest of S.E. Asia, with the exception of these territories, the Japanese Government had settled with independent national Governments. But for these territories, they settled with the British Government. Not unnaturally, the British can never have the

> same intense feelings about what happened to the civilian population in 1942 as we have". He hopes that the Japanese, being a practical people, would come to realise the wisdom of coming to terms with the national representatives of the people of Singapore, Malaya, North Borneo and Sarawak, and even Hong Kong. It was now up to them if they wished to participate in the lucrative commerce and industry of Malaysia[13].

The rally also passed three resolutions:

> 1. That the people of all races in Malaya, Sabah, Sarawak and Singapore should join in united action against Japan to press for satisfactory settlement of the "Blood Debt" – compensation for atrocities committed against the civilian population during the Japanese Occupation.
>
> 2. That failing satisfactory settlement of the "Blood Debt" by the Japanese Government, the people should carry out a non-co-operation campaign against the Japanese.
>
> 3. This meeting requests the Government of Singapore not to issue any new entry permits to Japanese nationals if there should be no settlement of the "Blood Debt"[14].

As the British High Commissioner noted, the "Blood Debt" issue had now moved from being one affecting just the Chinese community to one that was embraced by all communities and something with which Lee could win the hearts and minds of the nation instead of just the Chinese. However, Japanese alienation would mean economic disaster for the country:

> Lee Kuan Yew for his part has found himself in a very difficult position. This is an issue which can potentially unite all races and groups in Singapore. On the other hand, the Government have a very big interest in encouraging Japanese investment here, which is very important for their industrialisation programme[15].

Nonetheless, Tanaka was being very tardy in responding to Lee's requests and provided inadequate and general responses to the proposals put forth by the Singapore government. As a result, a day before Lee's "independence" speech on 31 August 1963, he had written to the British Colonial Secretary, saying that:

> ... one of the steps towards independence which he (Lee) wishes to announce at a mass rally on August 31 (*sic*) is that Her Majesty's Government have delegated to the Government of Singapore complete powers in the matter of foreign relations "to the extent and in order that the Government of Singapore can between August 31 (*sic*) and September 16 (*sic*) settle the question of the nature and substance of the Japanese gesture of atonement for atrocities"[16].

The British Commissioner General for Southeast Asia, and later High Commissioner to Singapore, Sir George Nigel Douglas-Hamilton, the Lord Selkirk, cabled Whitehall that Lee's request would have a disastrous effect on British relations with Japan:

> If Lee attempts to turn the heat on, the Japanese will refuse to negotiate under pressure and will simply stand on the legal position under the Peace Treaty until things cool down. There would be no prospect of the early settlement which would be in everyone's interest.
>
> ... The fallacy in Lee's request lies of course in the fact that he has already for some time been exercising the powers he now suggests we should delegate as from August 31, and indeed in his speech on August 25 gave some account of the way he had been doing so...
>
> ... If our position were distorted in any way by Lee in public utterances suggesting that he had received new powers we would feel obliged to issue the statement ourselves to clear the record[17].

Three days later, Lord Selkirk, in his report to London, explained the Singapore Government's strategy in negotiating with the Japanese:

> The Singapore claim against the Japanese for atrocities committed during the period of occupation is naturally getting a great deal of public support and whilst the leaders are all prepared to say privately they want a settlement, they are clearly not going to take a strong line advocating a limit to the amount which should be considered reasonable for Japan to pay.
>
> Lee is playing a very equivocable game and I am not surprised to learn that the Japanese view him with suspicion. The truth is that he wants to gain political kudos for himself by making a favourable settlement with the Japanese whilst he knows anything he agrees to will be denounced by his political opponents as totally inadequate.

> I believe he is genuinely out to get a settlement within this political setting.
>
> In the meantime, Lee has been very inaccessible to the Japanese Consul-General, Tanaka, and I have had the utmost difficulty in seeing him myself. He has been discourteous in public to the Japanese Consul-General. Although the communists may be trying to exploit the situation, the feeling among the Chinese is widespread; indeed hardly a family cannot recall a relative who disappeared...
>
> ...I have explained to the Singapore Ministers that there is no chance of blackmailing the Japanese Government. If they do not make a sufficient effort, they may find themselves with a continuing disagreement without any compensation. Lee is anxious to settle this himself with the Japanese Government; so far we have given him every chance to do so. I would not advocate our taking an open part in any negotiations. I believe that would complicate, rather than facilitate, matters but I have got to say that I think it is going to be very difficult to make a quick settlement below the figure of about $(Malayan) 50,000,000. This was the amount of the forced loan which the Japanese raised from the Chinese Chamber of Commerce during the occupation[18].

Speaking to one of the Japanese Consuls in Singapore, Lord Selkirk underlined the difficult position faced by the Singapore Government:

> We told the Consul that in our view it seemed increasingly unlikely that the Japanese Government would be able to achieve a settlement within the figure of $5 million; that however projects might be dressed up, they would be bound to be evaluated in monetary terms by the Chinese Chamber of Commerce; and that in the end they would have to be prepared to bargain seriously over the Chamber of Commerce figure of $50 Million[19].

However, more importantly, the Singapore Government had upped the ante on 3 September by asking the British legation to inform all visa-issuing authorities (until the merger occurred, visas for Singapore were supposed to be issued by British diplomatic posts around the world) that all Japanese visa applications were to be referred to Singapore.

Lord Selkirk noted that from 16 September 1963 onwards, immigration would be a matter for the Federal Government in Kuala Lumpur but it was likely "to be some months before the Federal Government assumes control in Singapore. Until that time the status quo will be maintained and visa applications will continue in practice to be a matter for the Singapore Government"[20].

Pressure on Lee and the PAP government was also mounting, not only on the issue of Japanese reparation but also on whether Singapore would actually become a part of Malaysia. The PAP government was poised to hold local elections in Singapore five days after Malaysia Day[21].

The Federal Government in Kuala Lumpur was formed mainly by the United Malay National Organisation (UMNO) and communal parties, the Malaysian Indian Congress (MIC) and the Malaysian Chinese Association (MCA). These parties formed Singaporean versions of the mainland's Alliance coalition. UMNO clearly wanted their communal cousins to win and thus break the PAP's control over the island. Although Lee had pledged Singapore's loyalty to the Federal Government in public, Lord Selkirk noted that he was actually willing to unilaterally declare Singapore's independence in September 1963:

> ... He still professes to be very anxious and determined to set up Malaysia but is worried whether it will hold together and insists on agreement being reached on the remaining conditions of Singapore's entry, which are now being discussed in Kuala Lumpur. If he does not get this settled by 12th September (*sic*) (nomination day for the Singapore elections), he will fight the election on programme for Singapore's independence and immediately ask for recognition by a number of countries as from 16th September (*sic*). I did not discuss all that was involved in a declaration of independence but called on his co-operation (*sic*) in arriving at agreement with the Federation on the outstanding points. This he was willing to do and suggested that Goh Keng Swee should conduct these negotiations when he came back from Bangkok on 6th September (*sic*) instead of himself.
>
> He also promised to hold off anything which might damage relations during the period until 12th September (*sic*) but will attack the Malays wholeheartedly thereafter. He claims that if he does not get the points he has in mind, it will be because of the Malay intention to crush Singapore and he would be ashamed to accept the responsibility of entering Malaysia on these terms[22].

Lord Selkirk noted that Lee was fighting a battle for reparations and a larger battle for merger, both of which had a great impact on the way Singaporeans would vote in the coming elections. In dealing with reparations, it was clear that Lee was frustrated:

> In the course of my conversation with Lee Kuan Yew this morning, he referred to the Japanese problem and said he had done his utmost to lay it down for 15 months. But there was so little response from the Japanese that he had had to put himself at the head of the movement. He complained of some reference he said emanated from Japan that this matter would more easily be settled after Malaysia. The result of this has been that all parts of Malaysia have started agitating for Japanese compensation.
>
> I warned him of the danger of antagonising Japan which might lose (*sic*) their support for Malaysia at the United Nations and also of the danger of the communists getting hold of the whole movement, to which he agreed.
>
> He clearly found it very difficult to get on with the present Japanese Consul-General Tanaka, and I would strongly recommend that the Japanese Government should be encouraged to send someone here of stronger personality and with a better command of English if these negotiations are to be brought to fruition. At the present time, I do not judge the Prime Minister considers it worthwhile giving Tanaka a proper chance to do his job[23].

In the end, Singapore did join the Federation on Malaysia Day, only to become an independent country two years later on 9 August 1965. As for the issue of reparations, Japan sent a new ambassador to Singapore but the negotiations continued long after the 16 September deadline Lee had set. It was not until 1966 that Japan and Singapore finally resolved the issue. The local press noted that the Civilian Monument was built with the $150,000 raised by the Chinese Chamber of Commerce and the Singapore Government, although sources involved in the episode say that there was a significant Japanese contribution to the final construction bill. The monument was inaugurated on 15 February 1967, 25 years to the day that Singapore fell to the Japanese.

Even then, there was still controversy. The famous Chinese poet Pan Shou had been asked to write an epitaph for the Civilian Monument. The epitaph, written in Mandarin (translated into English and reproduced below) was scathing in its attack on the Japanese but clearly represented the feelings of the local Chinese community. However, the epitaph never saw the light of day and has long been forgotten, relegated as a curiosity in academic journals and books. Nonetheless, it remains a strong and poignant summation of the horrors that faced the Chinese community in

Singapore and the desire for future generations to learn from it. Perhaps, one day it will be installed at the location for which it was written[24]:

THIS MEMORIAL MARKS AN UNPRECEDENTED TRAGEDY IN THE HISTORY OF SINGAPORE

The occupation of Singapore by the Japanese Army between 15 February 1942 and 18 August 1945 was a dark and tragic epoch.

The people of Singapore were subjected to lashing, humiliation, enslavement and extortion. Under the pretext of "Security Screening" (Sook Ching), the Japanese Army massacred tens of thousands of non-combatants in secrecy. God was ridiculed. Civilisation was buried, and the dignity of mankind trampled. Everywhere, tears flowed. Everywhere, blood splattered. And everywhere, terror reigned.

In January 1962, some of the remains of the civilian victims were first unearthed. This led to the setting-up of a committee by the Singapore Chinese Chamber of Commerce for conducting further investigation, for exhumation, as well as for the planning of the construction of a mass grave and a Memorial for the remains.

In July the same year, a permit for exhumation was obtained from the Authority. In March 1963, the Singapore Government allotted a four-and-a-half acre plot of land for the site of this Memorial Park. During the last four years, more and more remains of these victims were exhumed. In the meantime, as a result of the widespread response received from the public and the encouragement from the Government who contributed to the Memorial Building Fund on the basis of a-dollar-to-a-dollar from the public, this memorial is (*sic*) eventually completed.

Now this Memorial stands towering over the Equator, gazing at the ever-changing scenes of South-East-Asia (*sic*) and the world at large.

Now this Memorial stands aloft at this hub of communication between the Eastern and the Western Hemispheres, beckoning friendly day and night to the passers-by of Southeast Asia and the world.

No one knows the exact number of our compatriots of the different races massacred during the dark days of the Occupation. Although countless sets of bones are already buried under the podium, it is most probable that they might represent only a fraction of the civilian victims massacred whose number might be five or ten times greater. No one can list all our multiracial compatriots who were killed in the massacre. They deserve to be posthumously honoured as loyal, brave, virtuous and righteous men who have sacrificed their lives long before the independence of Singapore and should thus be enshrined in the spiritual foundation of the country.

The four towering columns of this Memorial symbolise loyalty, bravery, virtue and righteousness, traits of which are reflected in the traditional harmony and solidarity of the multiracial, multicultural and multi-religious society of Singapore.

This Memorial stands to prove that the people of Singapore were able to hold their own together in adversity and it also signifies their ever-readiness to share the common prosperity of the country in future.

Let this Memorial echo the voice of the people of Singapore.

War is evil. Peace is sacred. The big and the strong nations want to live, so do the small and weak ones. The big and strong ones who oppress the small and weak ones will never escape condemnation and punishment on the final judgement of history. However, the best policy is to redress grievances amicably and not to generate enmity. The people of Singapore are always with the peoples of the world, including the people of Japan, who are peace-loving and who oppose aggression, imperialism and colonialism.

May the souls of the civilian victims of the Japanese Occupation rest in eternal peace and accept this epitaph dedicated to them by the people of Singapore.

"Tears stained flower crimson like
And blood tainted the blue ocean
Ye wandering souls who rise with the tide
Shall guard this young emerging nation."

Endnotes

1 "Singapore Victims of Japanese", The Times of London, 14 September 1945.

2 "Japanese mass graves", No. 1481/3, 8 March 1962, CO1030/1401, London: The National Archives.

3 SECRET, SUMMARY OF SECURITY INTELLIGENCE – SINGAPORE No. 2/62, R.214(84), February 1962, CO1030/1401, London: The National Archives.

4 "Japanese Reparation", NO.126, 9 March 1962, CO1030/1401, London: The National Archives.

5 "Japanese Reparations", NO. 113, 9 March 1962, CO1030/1401, London: The National Archives.

6 "Reparations", LAW/6431. 1497/5/63., 6 June 1963, CO1030/1722, London: The National Archives.

7 Ibid.

8 Bradley, James. The Tall Man Who Never Slept: A tribute to Cyril Wild. Bognor Regis: Woodfield Publishing, 1997, p.176-183.

9 SECRET, SUMMARY OF SECURITY INTELLIGENCE – SINGAPORE No. 6/63, FED 111/63/04, June 1963, CO 1030/1722, London: The National Archives.

10 Lau, Albert. *A Moment of Anguish: Singapore in Malaysia and the Politics of Disengagement.* Singapore: Times Academic Press, 1998. 17.

11 Ibid.17.

12 *The Straits Times,* 3 September 1963.

13 "Anti-Japanese Rally", No.603, 26 August 1963, CO1030/1722, London: The National Archives.

14 "Japanese Compensation", LAW/6431 Pt. B., 22 August 1963, CO1030/1722, London: The National Archives.

15 Ibid.

16 *Colonial Secretary to Lord Selkirk. Signal No. 560, 30 August 1963, PREM11/4325.* London: The National Archives.

17 *Selkirk to Colonial Secretary. Signal No. 2540, 30 August 1963, PREM11/4325.* London: The National Archives.

18 *Selkirk to Colonial Secretary. Signal No. 632, 2 September 1963, PREM11/4325.* London: The National Archives.

19 *Selkirk to Colonial Secretary. Signal No. 636, 3 September 1963, PREM11/4325.* London: The National Archives.

20 Ibid.

21 Lau, 1998. 21.

22 *Selkirk to Colonial Secretary. Signal No. 641, 4 September 1963, PREM11/4325.* London: The National Archives.

23 *Selkirk to Colonial Secretary. Signal No. 642, 4 September 1963, PREM11/4325.* London: The National Archives.

24 Pan, Shou. 1976. "Memorial Epitaph to the Civilian Victims of the Japanese Occupation", translated by C.M. Wong. *Journal of the South Seas Society.* [Internet]. Accessed 26 August 2004. Available from: <http://www.knowledgenet.com.sg/singapore/shf/e_journal/articles/EJV1ART005.htm>.

Chapter 7

Those Remembered at Kranji

Every name inscribed on the walls of the memorial at Kranji and on the gravestones located in the cemetery's expansive lawns has a story to tell. The enormous sacrifices made by these men and women in the defence of the island and in the following occupation deserve great respect and more importantly, remembrance.

As one wanders through Kranji, there are some names and stories that have always stood out and this chapter examines a few of these individuals who are buried or commemorated by name at Kranji. It is not a comprehensive listing of all the heroes buried here as that would cover almost everyone commemorated at Kranji.

It is interesting to note that the youngest serviceman to be buried at Kranji was Lance Naik Papayya, of the Indian Pioneer Corps. The son of Kammajojappa and Chinnamma, of Kottala, Kurnool, India, Lance Naik Papayya died on 15 August 1946 at the age of 16, from wounds suffered at the end of the war. This would mean that Papayya would have been about 14 years old when he signed up with the IPC in 1944. He is buried at 27. B. 10.

The oldest to be buried at Kranji was Sapper Leslie Reginald Edmett of the Johore Volunteer Engineers. Edmett, who lived with his wife Mabel in Kota Tinggi before the war, succumbed to dysentery and cholera on 10 January 1945, at the age of 68. He is buried at 36. A. 1. Other interesting burials include that of Vice-Admiral Ernest John Spooner, the Senior Naval Officer in charge of Naval Establishments. On Friday,13 February 1942, Spooner and Air Vice-Marshal Conway Walter Heath Pulford (Air Officer Commanding, RAF) along with numerous others escaped Singapore in an armada of small ships and boats. However, the boat carrying them was

Left: The headstone of Lance Naik Papayya, the youngest soldier buried at Kranji.
Right: The headstone of Sapper L.R. Edmett, the oldest soldier buried at Kranji.

attacked and beached on a small island north of Banka Island. Two months later, the starving survivors surrendered but both Spooner and Pulford did not make it. Spooner is buried at 27. B. 4 while Pulford is buried in a collective grave at 31. D. 1-17.

Lieutenant Colonel Ivan Lyon and 'Z' Special Unit

One of the more intriguing burials at Kranji deals with the remains of Lieutenant Colonel Ivan Lyon of the Gordon Highlanders and the men he led on a sabotage mission into enemy-occupied Singapore.

In September 1943, 11 Australian and four British army and navy commandos raided Japanese shipping in Singapore harbour, sinking seven ships and despite enormous odds, made it back to Australia[1].

Codenamed Operation JAYWICK after the toilet cleaner used for flushing out toilets, the Singapore raid was conceived by Lyon. A member of the Oriental Mission of the Special Operations Executive based in Singapore, he had escaped from the island when it fell to the Japanese in February 1942 and knew the waters to its south. A former local fishing vessel, which had been captured off Singapore in December 1941 and sent to Australia, was renamed the *Krait* and used in transporting the raiding party to Singapore[2].

The raid was planned by Special Operations Australia (SOA) and most of the raiders came from its 'Z' Special Unit. The plan was to sail the *Krait* to an island off Singapore and then three teams of two men would paddle two-man canoes into Keppel Harbour, attach limpet mines to Japanese ships and blow them up as the team made its way back home. The plan was very risky and viewed by many as a suicide mission.

The *Krait*, a very slow wooden-hulled vessel, was disguised as a Malay fishing boat and its crew of Caucasians stained their skin in an attempt to look Malay. The *Krait* was about 20 metres long and crammed with 11 commandos, three collapsible canoes, limpet mines, communications equipment, weapons and supplies. On 1 September 1943, the *Krait* slipped out of Exmouth Harbour (used by the US Navy as a submarine base) heading north towards the Netherlands East Indies (Indonesia).

On 19 September 1943, after searching for a suitable base for its three canoe teams, Lyon pulled into a small, hilly, jungle-clad island known as Pandjang, where the six-man team and their canoes as well as equipment were offloaded at dusk. By dawn, the 11 other members of the raiding party sailed away in the *Krait* for the next 10 days towards Borneo and back again, hoping to avoid detection by enemy aircraft and ships[3].

After narrowly avoiding detection by a Japanese patrol boat, Lyon and his team left their island hideout and paddled towards Singapore in the night. Hiding out on islands, they finally reached the island of Subar, 11 km from Singapore and launched their raid. Although their canoes were weighed down by limpet mines the six men managed to evade enemy vessels and reached the target area. Undetected, they attached limpet mines to several vessels, dumped excess equipment and tried to get as far away from Singapore before the mines blew up Japanese shipping early on 26 September 1943. They reached their hideout shortly before dawn, hearing the explosions. Seven

The grave of Lieutenant Colonel Ivan Lyon

Japanese transport ships had been sunk, with over 39,000 tons of Japanese shipping damaged[4].

Over the next few nights, the team paddled towards their rendezvous point. After midnight on 2 October, the first two commandos were picked up by the *Krait*. They waited several hours but the remaining four did not make the rendezvous. The *Krait* then set sail. The missing four had missed the *Krait* in the darkness and ended up on the wrong beach. They saw the *Krait* sailing off and thought they were stranded deep in enemy territory. However, their fellow commandos decided to give the four missing canoeists one more day and returned that night, successfully retrieving them.

The return journey was long and hazardous as several enemy patrol boats and aircraft were evaded in addition to local fishing vessels whose crews might report a suspicious vessel to the Japanese. The vessel entered Exmouth Harbour on 19 October 1943. The daring raid had been a spectacular success. Most of the raiding party were decorated or mentioned in despatches. The *Krait* is now preserved in Australia and is on display at the Australian National Maritime Museum in Sydney.

However, not happy with the success of JAYWICK, Lyon planned another raid the following year. Operation RIMAU would be similar to JAYWICK. The new operation would also destroy Japanese shipping in the Singapore Harbour by attaching limpet mines to enemy ships. The attack was scheduled for the night of 10 October 1944.

The codename Operation RIMAU (which means "tiger" in Malay) was chosen as a Malayan tiger was tattooed on Lyon's chest. RIMAU was originally part of a larger operation codenamed HORNBILL that was aimed at attacking Japanese shipping in Singapore and Saigon (Ho Chi Minh City). However, HORNBILL was abandoned when resources were diverted to the invasion of Europe but plans for RIMAU still went ahead.

Again led by Lyon, the plan this time was for a submarine to drop the team off at a designated area off the Netherlands East Indies instead of sailing in from Australia as with JAYWICK. The men would then seize a local fishing boat and enter Keppel Harbour undetected. Upon entering the harbour, special one-man motorised submersible canoes, known as 'Sleeping Beauties', would be used to plant the limpet mines on the Japanese ships. The operation's base camp would be on Merapas Island in the Riau Archipelago where the men would rendezvous with the pick-up submarine.

On 11 September 1944, 23 British and Australian members of Z Special Unit left Garden Island Naval Base near Perth on HMS *Porpoise*. Amongst the RIMAU group were six former members of JAYWICK. On 28 September, the *Porpoise* stopped a local junk, the *Mustika*, and took over the vessel. The RIMAU team boarded her, loaded operational stores, explosives and equipment onto the junk and sailed for Singapore on 1

October 1944. On the way, Lyon stopped at Merapas Island and left some men and equipment as his rear base.

It was now that things began to go wrong. On the afternoon of 10 Oct 1944, just hours before the scheduled raid was to take place, a Japanese police patrol vessel spotted the *Mustika* and approached it. One of the RIMAU commandos panicked and opened fire on the patrol vessel. With the operation compromised, Lyon aborted the raid and ordered his men to head for Merapas Island – the rendezvous point with the *Porpoise* that was scheduled for the night of 7 November 1944[5].

The *Mustika* was then blown up together with its secret stores. However, Lyon would not abandon the mission. That night, Lyon and six others made their way to Singapore Harbour reaching it in the early hours of 11 October and planted the limpet mines. The mines exploded, destroying three enemy ships. Lyon and his men dispersed but the Japanese were on their trail.

In the ensuing battles with the Japanese, Lyon, aged 29, along with 13 of his men, were killed. Ten were eventually captured after pitched battles on several islands off the Indonesian archipelago. They were brought to Singapore and imprisoned at Outram Road Gaol. On 3 July 1945, they were put on trial for espionage, found guilty and sentenced to death. The ten were beheaded on 7 July 1945, barely a month before the end of the war in the Pacific.

However, no one would have known of the fate of Lyon and the ten men had it not been for Colonel Cyril Hew Darymple Wild. Translating for Percival at the British Surrender at the Ford Motor Factory on 15 February 1942, Wild survived internment and the Siam-Burma Death Railway and was appointed head of the British War Crimes Unit barely days after he was liberated[6]:

> Our first task was to discover the fate of certain missing pilots. A well-meant tip from a Malay driver took us on the day after the landing (of the 5th Indian Division which liberated Singapore on 5 September 1945) to Outram Road Gaol to interrogate Mikizawa, our first prisoner. Mikizawa, as commandant of the civil side of the prison, had a good deal on his conscience, having lost 1,200 Asiatic prisoners from starvation during the last fourteen months of the war. It was not long, therefore, before he led us to a lonely stretch of country near Reformatory Road (now Clementi Road), where his driver had taken him to an execution in July. He prodded about among the scrub until he found three newly made mounds with wooden crosses on them. This, he thought, was the place. The heath around was pitted with half-filled depressions and open graves, among stunted bushes and

> the insect-eating plant called Dutchman's Pipe. Evidently it was a favourite execution ground of the Japanese. Why, then, were these the only graves marked with crosses? Mikizawa did not know: they were Chinese whom he had seen executed. Unfortunately the authorities did not permit us to exhume, and the matter remained a mystery.

However, a village chief who had escaped from the island of Singkep turned up a few days later and told a story of how ten British and Australians, members of a raiding party, had been captured in the Lingga Archipelago and had been kept as prisoners on Singkep before they were taken to Singapore. However, it was the middle of October 1945 before Wild and his team was given the necessary transport to go to Singkep and look into the matter:

> Among our trophies was the admission book of the local police station and a scrap of paper bearing the names of a British officer, a warrant officer, and an able seaman, each penciled in block letters in a different hand. The admission book, kept in Malay, showed that on 18 and 19 December six 'white men' had been admitted, and all had been transferred to Singapore on 23 December. A later entry showed that three more 'white men' had been admitted on 28-29 December and had left for Singapore on 8 January 1945. The charge against each was the same, 'enemy of the State'. Attempts had been made to write the names of some of them, but, apart from those on the scrap of paper, only one was clear – 'R.M. Ingleton, Major, Royal Marines. British'. Two others were marked 'Australian', and one 'Australian (British)'. These were the only clues when we took up the hunt for the nine 'white men' in Singapore. There was no trace of such people having ever been in a prisoner-of-war camp, and the Japanese were in a conspiracy to tell us nothing. No single survivor, as it turned out, remained to tell the tale, and no written record of theirs remained beyond that found on Singkep. Yet within a month we knew their story in full, and how and where each one of them (not only these nine, but fourteen of their comrades) had met his end…

> …Of their life in captivity we have a remarkably full record. It is clear that from the first they were regarded with respect, verging on awe, by the Japanese, and in consequence were exceptionally well treated. A well-disposed Japanese interpreter supplied them regularly with books, chocolates, and cigarettes. The officers had little doubt what their fate was likely to be, but the whole party remained in excellent spirits and good health until the end. They were sentenced to death

Colonel Cyril Wild (third from left), with Colonel Koshiro Mikizawa, Commandant of the civilian wing of the Outram Road Prison, and an Australian officer, at the spot where the RIMAU men were executed and buried along Reformatory Road (now Clementi Road).

> by a military court on 5 July 1945, and on the 7th they were beheaded in the execution-ground off Reformatory Road. Their graves were those which we discovered by chance just two months after. In an unmarked grave close by were buried the Chinese victims of the later execution witnessed by Mikizawa[7].

Wild, in an article on the discovery of the bodies, noted that the Japanese held the men in very high regard and as such were responsible for marking the graves. He then quoted notes from the translated records of the Judiciary Department of the Japanese 7th Area Army:

> Let the Japanese themselves tell the last chapter. The first paragraph is from the closing address of the prosecuting officer.
>
> 'With such fine determination they infiltrated into the Japanese area. We do not hesitate to call them the real heroes of a forlorn hope. It has been fortunate for us that their intention was frustrated half-way, but when we fathom their intention and share their feelings we cannot but spare a tear for them. The valorous spirit of these men reminds us of the daring enterprise of our heroes of the Naval Special Attack Corps who died in May 1942 in their attack on Sydney Harbour. The same admiration and respect that the Australian Government, headed by the Premier and all the Australian people showed to those

heroes of ours we must return to these heroes in our presence. When the deed is so heroic, its sublime spirit must be respected, and its success or failure becomes a secondary matter. These heroes must have left Australia with sublime patriotism flaming in their breasts, and with the confident expectation of all the Australian people on their shoulders. The last moment of a hero must be historic and it must be dramatic. Heroes have more regard for their reputation than for anything else. As we respect them, so we feel our duty of glorifying their last moments as they deserve: and by our doing so the names of these heroes will remain in the heart of the British and Australian people for evermore. In these circumstances, I consider that a death sentence should be given to each of the accused. Major Ingleton thanked the court for referring to them as 'patriotic heroes'[8]...

... After the trial all the members of the party were given extra rations, and, in accordance with their request, were kept together in one room so that they could freely converse with one another. The attitude was really admirable. They were always clear and bright, and not a single shadow of dismal or melancholy mood did they show. All who saw them were profoundly impressed[9]...

... They all knew they were going to be executed. When they left their prison to enter the two trucks in which their executioners were waiting, they were in high spirits, laughing and talking and shaking hands with one another. All of us prisoners were amazed[10]...

...On arrival at the execution-ground at 10 a.m. on 7 July, 'they were all given cigarettes and rested. Then, in accordance with their request, they were allowed to shake hands with one another. They all stood up, shook hands merrily and even laughingly in a very harmonious manner, and bade each other farewell. The sky was clear and the scenery was beautiful[11]...

...Major Ingleton, on behalf of the whole party, requested the commandant of the prison and the prosecuting officer to tell the Japanese interpreter (Hiroyuki Furuta) that they were all most grateful for the courtesy and kindness which he had shown them for a long time past. He said again that they must not forget to give the interpreter this message. All who heard him were deeply moved[12]...

...The execution started and it was over by noon. Every member of the party went to his death calmly and composedly, and there was not

> a single person there who was not inspired by their fine attitude[13]...
> ...At a Staff Conference of the 7th Area Army[14], Major-General Ohtsuka (Chief Judge at the trial and witness to the executions) reported on the patriotism, fearless enterprise, heroic behaviour, and sublime end of all members of this party, praising them as the flower of chivalry, which should be taken as a model by the Japanese. He concluded by saying that all Japanese soldiers should be inspired by their fine attitude, and on reflection must feel the necessity of bracing up to their own spirits in emulation, if they hoped to win the war[15]...

Since Wild's article and the passage of more than 67 years since the executions took place, much has been written about the veracity of Wild's account and whether the Japanese officers involved had told the truth about what happened, or was it more a cover-up in order to protect themselves from the truth of the brutality and torture faced by the members of RIMAU.

Researchers and writers like Ronald McKie, Brian Connell, Lynette Silver and Tom Hall have shown how much of the testimony given by the Japanese officers upon interrogation after the war, including that of the interpreter Furuta, had been a jumble of fact and fiction, with Peter Thompson going so far as to accuse Furuta of "ingratiating himself with his interrogators, of suggesting that he shared not just the goodwill but the confidence of men in their most intimate and terrible moments.[16]"

However, it is Silver who in all likelihood has proposed the most probable explanation:

> It is evident that if Furuta witnessed any violence during Rimau's incarceration, he erased it from his mind. As was pointed out in later war crimes trials, the Japanese appeared to be extremely adept at structuring their thinking in such a way that unpleasant thoughts could be either pushed back into the background or disappear completely, as if the unpleasantness had never occurred. By the same token, small gestures of kindness could be blown out of all proportion, allowing one or two incidents to become the rule, rather than the exception. As a middle aged, well educated, fairly cultured and much travelled man, it is doubtful that without employing this device, Furuta would have been able to come to terms with violence of the type usually doled out to prisoners by the Kempei Tai, and with which he was familiar[17].

Although Wild had located the fate of most of the members of RIMAU, the location of the remains of eight were still unknown. Before he could make any further enquiries, Wild died in a plane crash on 25 September

1946. The ten men, Lyon and four others were buried at Kranji. Lyon is located separately at 27. A. 14, while the ten are buried in a collective grave at 28. A. 1-10.

However, it was not until 1994, after a long search, that the remains of two more members of RIMAU, who had been killed on Merapas Island, were found. They were 21-year old Sergeant Colin Barclay Cameron of the Australian Imperial Force and 21-year-old Sub-Lieutenant James Gregor Mackintosh Riggs of the Royal Navy Volunteer Reserve. These two young men bravely held off a small Japanese force that had landed on Merapas Island on 4 November 1944, dying in the early hours the following day. Their bravery allowed the other RIMAU commandos to escape by boat. Almost 50 years after the incident, their remains were finally brought to Singapore. They were buried with full military honours at the Kranji War Cemetery on 27 August 1994. Cameron is buried at 32. E. 2., with Riggs next to him at 32. E. 4.

The burials of Cameron and Riggs bring to 17 the number of RIMAU commandos laid to rest at Kranji. The remains of the other six lie in unmarked graves in Indonesia, known only unto God.

Victoria Cross awards at Kranji

There are two Victoria Cross recipients listed in the Kranji War Cemetery but neither are buried there and both VCs were not won in the theatre. The first was Sergeant Walter Ernest Brown, whose exploits were described in Chapter 1 and whose name is inscribed on Column 115 of the Singapore Memorial. The other VC recipient was Wing Commander James Brindley Nicolson.

Wing Commander James Brindley Nicolson VC

Born on 29 April 1917 at Hampstead, Nicolson was educated at Yardley Court Prepatory School, Tonbridge and at Tonbridge School. During the First World War, his father served in the Royal Naval Air Force and his mother was with the Voluntary Aid Detachment (VAD) in Alexandria.

In October 1936, Nicolson became a pupil pilot in the RAF and two months later was granted a short-service commission for four years in the rank of acting pilot officer. Trained at Tern Hill, Shropshire, he joined No. 72 (Fighter) Squadron, then at Church Fenton, Yorkshire, in August 1937, being confirmed as pilot officer in October 1937 and promoted to Flying Officer in May 1939. Nicolson married his wife Muriel in 1938 and they made their home at Kirkby Wharfe near Tadcaster, where Muriel lived until her death in the 1990s. Nicolson was 23 years old when he won the Victoria Cross for, "most conspicuous bravery"[18].

He was on patrol over the Southampton area with the RAF's 249 Squadron in the early afternoon on 16 August 1940 when he saw three Junkers 88 bombers crossing the bows of the squadron about four miles away and he was detailed to chase the Junkers with his section.

A wartime photograph of Wing Commander James Brindley Nicolson VC

He got within a mile of them and saw a squadron of Spitfires attack and shoot them down, so he turned back to rejoin his squadron, climbing from 15,000 to 18,000 feet. Suddenly, as he himself said, there were four big bangs inside his aircraft. They were cannon shells from a Messerschmitt 110. One tore through the hood and sent splinters into his left eye and the second struck his forward petrol tank which exploded and set the machine on fire. The third shell crashed into the cockpit and tore away his left trouser leg. The fourth hit his left foot and wounded his heel.

As Nicolson turned to avoid further shots into the burning plane, he found that a Messerschmitt 110 had overtaken him and was right on his gunsight. His dashboard was shattered and was "dripping like treacle" in the heat. The Messerschmitt was 300 yards in front, and both were diving at about 400 mph.

As Nicolson pressed the gun button he could see his right thumb blistering in the heat. He could also see his left hand holding the throttle open, blistering in the flames. The Messerschmitt zig-zagged this way and that, trying to avoid the hail of fire from the blazing Hurricane. By this time the heat was so great that Nicolson had to put his feet on the seat beneath his parachute. He continued the fight for several minutes, until the Messerschmitt disappeared in a steep dive. Eyewitnesses later reported that they had seen it crash a few miles out to sea.

On losing sight of the enemy Nicolson tried to jump out, but struck his head on the hood above him. He threw back the hood and tried to jump again. Then he realised he had not undone the straps holding him in the cockpit. One of these straps broke. He undid the other and dived out head first. After several somersaults in the air he pulled the ripcord of his parachute with considerable difficulty. It took him about 20 minutes to reach the ground.

A Messerschmitt came screaming past, but as he floated down he pretended that he was dead. But just before landing, he was spotted by a Home Guard Sergeant who mistook Nicolson for a German and shot at him. On discovering the mistake, an angry mob attacked the Sergeant and an ambulance called for Nicolson was used to take the Sergeant to hospital. As he floated down, Nicolson realised that blood was coming out of the lace holes of his boots as a result of the Sergeant shooting him in the left heel. He tried to see what other injuries he had received and found that he could move all his limbs. On landing, he found that his watch was still ticking though the glass had melted and the strap burnt to a thread.

"When I saw the Messerschmitt in front of me," he said later, "I remember shouting out, 'I will teach you some manners, you Hun!' I am glad I got him though perhaps pilots who have had more experience would have done the wise thing and baled out immediately the aircraft caught fire. I did not think of anything at that time but to shoot him down. Curiously enough, although the heat inside must have been intense, in the excitement I did not feel much pain. In fact, I remember watching the skin being burnt off my left hand. All I was concerned about was keeping the throttle open to get my first Hun[19]."

Nicolson was picked up by a passing RAF lorry. He hovered between life and death for 48 hours after doctors removed 70 pieces of metal from his body. He was in hospital for several weeks but was able to receive his VC from King George VI at Buckingham Palace on 25 November 1940. In spite of two spells of sickness caused by the severe burns he had sustained, Nicolson was eager to get back to operational flying. After some time on instructional duties his wish was granted. In August 1944, he was awarded the Distinguished Flying Cross for his service in command of No 27 Squadron, with which he had, "consistently shown himself to be a courageous and enterprising leader".

On relinquishing command of No 27 Squadron, Nicolson proceeded to Headquarters, 3rd Tactical Air Force, Allied Command South East Asia, as supernumerary – Training and Tactics. On 4 December 1944, he was again posted to Headquarters, RAF, Bengal/Burma with similar duties. His duties were mainly concerned with moving squadrons forward after each monsoon. It was dreary and mind-numbing work. By this time, Nicolson had become a near-alcoholic and was said to be suffering from a "breakdown"[20]. As a colleague noted later,

> The last time that I had seen Nick was at Boscombe Down in 1940. My next meeting with him was in India in March 1945 when I was en route to Burma – Nick was then a Wing Commander staff officer at eastern Air Command, mixed British and American formation located near Calcutta. On that occasion he greeted me rapturously

> as a long-lost brother, telling everyone the most enormous fibs about my prowess as a fighter pilot, so convincingly, in fact, that I really began to think that he was believing his own stories – Nick always had a lively imagination. After several days and nights of hard partying together, during which his good spirits, anecdotes and mimicry particularly relating to his American colleagues were quite memorable, I moved to Burma, only to learn later that he had been killed taking an unauthorized flight in a Liberator[21].

However, Nicolson's official biography written 46 years after his death notes that he had been given authorisation on 30 April 1945 to fly with 355 Squadron for a night mission. The purpose of Nicolson's assignment with 355 was supposedly to study monsoon weather conditions, identify the hazards and to develop ideas to increase safety when flying in monsoon conditions[22]. However, this contrasted significantly with his role as a trainer and in not having any meteorological experience in studying monsoon weather conditions.

It thus came as a surprise to Wing Commander Gerald de Souza, captain of the Liberator, *R for Robert* when Nicolson turned up for the night mission. The Liberator had already completed a round trip bombing mission to Rangoon when Nicolson boarded it for its second run of the day.

At 0500 hours they again took off accompanied by seven other Liberators and set course for Rangoon, some 2000 miles away. At approximately 0250 hours came the first indication of trouble when the starboard outer engine burst into flames, followed shortly after by the starboard inner engine. Efforts were made to extinguish the fires but to no avail. Recognising the hopeless situation, de Souza jettisoned the bomb load and instructed the crew to prepare to ditch. At 0250 hours the Liberator struck the sea and sunk within 15 seconds of impact. The second pilot Michael Pullen and Gunner Eric Kightley, were catapulted through the Perspex nose of the aircraft and landed in the water.

Kightley said Nicolson had been a model of calmness and had asked to do whatever was necessary to avert the crash. Kightley said he gave Nicolson the thumbs up sign before ditching and that was the last that he saw of him. Kightley, along with four others survived the crash. By a great stroke of luck, he saw a nose wheel floating nearby and managed to tie himself to it. After 16 hours clinging to the nose wheel, he was rescued along with Pullen. The other two survivors succumbed to their wounds and were lost at sea while there was no trace of Nicolson or de Souza. Liberator *R for Robert* had ditched about 300 miles from base, in an area known as the Sunderabans, approaching the mouths of the Ganges.

Nicolson was missing presumed dead on 2 May 1945, the last day of the

War in Europe[23]. His wife Muriel survived the war and in 1983, unable to survive on a war widow's pension, sold Nicolson's VC at auction to the RAF Museum in Hendon for £110,000[24]. Nicolson's son James, who had become a successful wine merchant in Leeds, was present at the auction. James, however, died tragically in a car crash on 29 April 1985, on what would have been Nicolson's 68th birthday[25]. He was divorced and did not have any children so Muriel was now left on her own having lost her husband and only son. Nicolson is commemorated on Column 445 of the Singapore Memorial at Kranji.

Captain Patrick Stanley Vaughan Heenan, "The Singapore Traitor"

One of the most controversial names listed on the Singapore Memorial is that of Captain Patrick Stanley Vaughan Heenan of the 16th Punjab Regiment. His name is located on Column 263 of the Singapore Memorial.

Born in New Zealand as a bastard son of a New Zealand governess, he spent his early childhood in Burma before heading to the UK and into the public school system. Unpopular with fellow students and not academically suited, Heenan in 1935, at the late age of 25, was commissioned into the British Army and placed on the unattached list of the Indian Army. With a group of about fifty other newly commissioned subalterns, most of whom had passed through either Sandhurst or Woolwich and were only nineteen, he travelled out to India on a troopship[26].

After the obligatory six months' training with a British regiment stationed in India Heenan failed to get an Indian Army regiment to accept him. This was almost certainly due to his bad attitude towards authority. He had to do an additional six months with another British Regiment before being accepted by the 16th Punjab Regiment, something that regiment eventually came to regret. Although he did well during a skirmish on the Northwest Frontier, he was later posted to the Indian Army Service Corps, a catch-all used to contain unsatisfactory officers away from the regular regiments. He was disliked there too, and was posted back to a different battalion of the 16th Punjab.

At this time, he took his long leave in Japan, and it was probably there that he was recruited by Japanese Intelligence. Early in 1941, his battalion was ordered to Malaya. He was very unpopular with his men and this was followed by his commanding officer, Lieutenant-Colonel Frank Moore asking for him to be posted elsewhere. Thus, he was sent to Singapore to train in Air Liaison Duties.

That training completed, his liaison unit was attached in June 1941 to airfields in Kedah. So, for a few months before the Japanese attacked

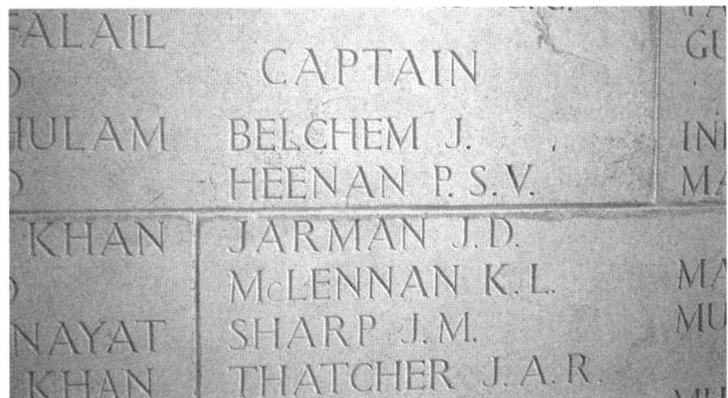

The name of the "Singapore Traitor", Captain PSV Heenan, which still remains etched on the walls of the Singapore Memorial.

Malaya, they had a well-placed spy at the heart of Malaya's northern defences. The Japanese attacked on 8th December 1941 and by the third day had destroyed almost every British aircraft in the north, Japanese air attacks being guided in by radio signals transmitted by Heenan. However, the air force in Malaya was so unprepared and ill-equipped for the Japanese fighters that even without Heenan's betrayal, "... after the first day (of the Japanese attack) the RAF virtually ceased to exist as a means of defence"[27].

Moore noted that, "(The Japanese) were performing very successful and mysterious bombing of our Air Force on the ground. Our Intelligence somehow got on to Heenan and searched his quarters thoroughly and found incriminating papers and evidence (hidden in picture frames etc)'[28].

The records of Heenan's senior officer Major James France showed he suspected Heenan of being a spy before Malaya was invaded. Caught in the act of sending information by radio on 9 December 1941, he had two radio transmitters in his possession, one looking like a typewriter and the other fitted into the case of a field communion set, with a code book.

After the war, in his anonymous book, *Great Was the Fall* (which had a very limited run and publicly available copies of which now only exist in the national libraries of Singapore and Australia), Flight-Lieutenant Alfred Elson-Smith, who had been based at Sungei Patani air base, was the first to name Heenan as the spy[29]. The book, a compilation of Elson-Smith's letters to his wife during the Malayan Campaign, shows his disgust at discovering Heenan's treachery in a letter dated a day after the Japanese invasion of Malaya began:

> When I reported at 7 o'clock tonight a further shock awaited me. I have told you in past letters of a Captain Heenan who has been liaison officer for the 11th Division to the R.A.F. Stations of Alor Star, Sungei Patani and Butterworth. Well, my dear, here's the key to

> the cause of the walloping that we have had in the north up to date. He was arrested this afternoon at 2 o'clock p.m. by Major Francis of Military Intelligence as a spy. There is no question of the authenticity of this arrest; since they have got the dope which proves his guilt beyond doubt. Just realise this b------ has been living with us in our mess for four months, drinking and playing cards and joining in our general living conditions. He has had access to our operational rooms together with a full and concise knowledge of our administration, in every form pertaining to our strength, possible strength and in short the guts of everything. This simplifies the whys and wherefores of this dreadful debacle and to what extent his activities have sold us out southwards we have yet to experience. No words of mine, or of anyone else for that matter, can express the feelings we have towards this man who though clever has sold us out so uniquely. Of course his fate is sealed, yet the damage he has done cannot be estimated since according to his own statements when he joined us, he had completed 15 years in the Army, serving in all parts of India...This man evidently controlled all the subversive elements in the northern area from the Pri River to Penang and the Thailand border and incidentally recalls to my mind the type of women he kept company with in Penang. Well, my dear, whatever I might have suspected of the natives I never gave thought to such a climax as this. No doubt the authentic information leading to his arrest will be made public one day, but you can take it from me, it was by the little things and careless indifference to our apparent stupidity that he was finally caught, and thanks to Major Francis who is certainly a credit to our military intelligence service[30].

An inquiry into Heenan's traitorous activities was held at Taiping around 15 December following which he was escorted under shackles to Singapore, according to official records that survived the war. However, no records exist as to what happened after that. Witnesses say that Heenan was court-martialled in Singapore in January 1942 and sentenced to death. As the Japanese continued unchecked down the Malayan peninsula, Heenan's fate was clear. In a bid to make sure that Heenan was no longer a threat, on Friday 13 February, two days before Singapore surrendered, he was taken down to the quayside by military policemen. He was told to look at the setting sun as that would be his last sight of it. A single bullet was fired by an MP into the back of his head and the body was pushed into the sea[31].

For close to 50 years, the story of the Singapore traitor was hushed up although General Sir Archibald Wavell reported the existence of a traitor in a report in June 1942 but did not name Heenan specifically. His despatch reported on "information sent from the vicinity of the northern aerodromes. At least one European was detected using a secret transmitter for this purpose"[32].

It was only through research by historian Peter Elphick and journalist Michael Smith in the early 1990s that Heenan's role came to light. His name remains on the Singapore Memorial as there is no official document to prove that Heenan was court-martialled nor that a guilty verdict was given. Until such time that a surviving official record of the Court Martial's verdict appears, it is unlikely that Heenan's name will be removed from the memorial.

Lieutenant Thomas Wilkinson VC

Although Wilkinson is commemorated at the Liverpool Naval Memorial for merchant seamen and not at Kranji, his contributions in this theatre of operations should be remembered at Kranji. Wilkinson was 43 years old, and a temporary Lieutenant in the Royal Naval Reserve as well as Captain of the HMS *Li Wo* during the Second World War when he was awarded the Victoria Cross[33].

Born on 1 August 1898 and from seafaring stock, Wilkinson, at the age of 14 had already joined his father's sailing sloop. In the First World War, he had served on the Blue Funnel Line, S.S. *Alicinious*, which had been converted to a troopship. Four years after the Peace Treaty had been signed, he joined the Indo-China Steam Navigation Company and by 1936, had worked up to become one of their masters[34].

Wilkinson's boat of only 1,000 tonnes was built in Hong Kong in 1938 for Jardine Matheson & Co. Designed with tall sides and a flat bottom, the *Li Wo* had been destined for the upper reaches of the Yangtse River, but because of the war, the *Li Wo* remained confined to the Yangtse delta, working out of Shanghai. The *Li Wo* was requisitioned by the Royal Navy in June 1940 and commissioned as an auxiliary patrol vessel.

It became a warship with the addition of a 4-inch gun in her bow, two machine guns high up on her sun deck and a depth charge dispenser fitted on the stern. Wilkinson then sailed his small craft all the way to Singapore. By February 1942, it was clear that the British were in full retreat and that Singapore would fall in a matter of days. As the boat pulled in to Singapore on 12 February 1942, the city was repeatedly attacked by Japanese aircraft, but the *Li Wo* managed to escape with only a few shrapnel scars on the decks.

The next day, Wilkinson was ordered to sail for Batavia (Jakarta) in order to escape the tightening noose. He, along with Sub-Lieutenant Ronald George Gladstone Stanton RNR, Chief Petty Officer Charles Halme

Rogers RN (a survivor from the HMS *Repulse* which, along with the HMS *Prince of Wales*, had been sunk off Kuantan in the opening days of the campaign) and a miscellaneous crew of 84, sailed the *Li Wo* with another converted river boat, the *Fuk Wo*, commanded by Lieutenant N. Cooke, RNR. Both vessels anchored near Raffles Lighthouse at 0500 hours on 13 February 1942. As dawn was breaking, they inched through the minefields in the Durian Straits and set a course for their target of Batavia.

Lieutenant Thomas Wilkinson VC, and a painting of the last minutes of the HMS Li Wo.

In the afternoon, however, both ships were subjected to repeated strafing from Japanese aircraft, with much damage to the boats. Wilkinson and Cooke anchored near a small island and decided that their best chance of escape lay in steaming full speed ahead at night, while laying up during the day off Singkep Island.

But as luck would have it, two Japanese bombers found the boats on 14 February. Although the ships fought back, they could no longer hide. The *Li Wo* would continue on its journey while the *Fuk Wo* decided to return to Singapore, where the ship was destroyed for fear of falling into enemy hands.

At about 1100 hours an enemy seaplane sighted the *Li Wo*, and she remained a target for the next three hours as near misses damaged both the hull and decks. Seeking the comparative safety of the Java Sea, they passed a Japanese convoy of ten ships at about 1600 hours. Then to the horror of Wilkinson and all aboard the *Li Wo*, they encountered a convoy of fifteen Japanese troopships supported by two destroyers and a cruiser (which were actually heading for Sumatra for the assault of Palembang). Wilkinson, however, mistakenly thought something had to be done to destroy these troopships before they overwhelmed the defenders on Singapore Island. Regardless of his intentions, the aim was to stop the enemy at all cost.

Wilkinson called his ship's company together and told them that instead of avoiding the convoy and fleeing, he had decided to engage the enemy head-on in a bid to inflict as much damage as possible on the enemy. Wilkinson had committed his boat and men to a final suicide mission so as to stop the enemy. There were only 13 shells left for the 4-inch gun as most of the ammunition had been expended fighting off previous air attacks.

Nonetheless, the *Li Wo* turned towards the enemy, her Battle Ensign flying. Stanton volunteered to man the totally exposed 4-inch gun on the fore deck. The convoy was 4.5 miles away and the nearest Destroyer about 7 miles distant. A scratch gun's crew joined Stanton, Acting Petty Officer Arthur Thompson took up the gun layer's position, two other Officers, an Australian Stoker, and two Able Seamen completed this gun crew.

When within range *Li Wo* opened fire with her 4-inch gun (ironically marked Made in Japan). The Japanese troop carrier was hit several times and caught fire. The third shell fired from *Li Wo* scored a direct hit on the Japanese transport. Wilkinson pressed on, his bridge machine guns blazing away, and the transport continued to burn fiercely.

Although the *Li Wo* was in its death throes, Wilkinson told his Coxswain, "I am going to ram that transport". The two ships met with a crunching of metal on metal as the Japanese crew abandoned their vessel. By 1800 hours, a Japanese cruiser had closed on the *Li Wo*, who was now without any means to defend herself. A short burst from the cruiser spelt the end of the boat.

Wilkinson ordered his men to abandon ship as rafts and wreckage supported those who had survived. However, the Japanese machine-gunned the survivors in the water. As the *Li Wo* finally perished under the waves at eight minutes past six in the evening, Wilkinson was still on his bridge while the waters of the Java Sea engulfed him.

Eventually Stanton who was wounded and several others reached the shore of a neighbouring island and met up with a group of RAF escapees and attempted to seek refuge with frightened villagers. After three weeks of rugged survival they were attacked by Chinese refugees who killed and injured members of the *Li Wo* group. Stanton decided to surrender to the Japanese so that the wounded would receive medical treatment. At Mundok, they met Rogers who had supervised the remaining *Li Wo* group and brought them ashore. Of the original *Li Wo* complement of 84 only nine men remained alive. Stanton and his gallant *Li Wo* survivors were taken into captivity where they remained for four years.

After the war, nine awards were presented to the crew of the *Li Wo*, including a Victoria Cross for the dead Wilkinson. The peacetime riverboat turned warship *Li Wo* now rests at the bottom of the Java Sea but a scale model of this proud little ship stands for all to see at the Imperial War Museum in London, as a reminder to the tremendous sacrifices made for a better tomorrow[35].

There are many more who deserve mention in these pages and it is impossible to cover all such individuals and groups. Nonetheless, the few mentioned here attest to the great courage of these men and women who were part of the "hinge of fate".

Endnotes

1 Connell, Brian. *Return of the Tiger.* London: Brown & Watson, 1965.

2 Ibid.

3 Ibid.

4 Silver, Lynette Ramsay. *The heroes of Rimau : unravelling the mystery of one of World War II's most daring raids.* London: Leo Cooper, 1991.

5 Ibid.

6 Bradley, James. *Cyril Wild: The Tall Man who never Slept.* Sussex: Woodfield Publishing, 1997, p. 101.

7 Ibid.

8 Translation of Proceedings of Military Court, 7th Area Army as cited by Wild, Cyril. Expedition to Singkep, Blackwood's Magazine,No 1572, Vol 260, October 1946.

9 Translation of Records of Judiciary Department, 7th Area Army as cited by Wild, Cyril. Expedition to Singkep, Blackwood's Magazine,No 1572, Vol 260, October 1946.

10 Interrogation of Korean Witness as cited by Wild, Cyril. Expedition to Singkep, Blackwood's Magazine,No 1572, Vol 260, October 1946.

11 Translation of Records of Judiciary Department, 7th Area Army as cited by Wild, Cyril. Expeditio to Singkep, Blackwood's Magazine, No 1572, Vol 260, October 1946.

12 Interrogation of Japanese Witness as cited by Wild, Cyril. Expedition to Singkep, Blackwood's Magazine,No 1572, Vol 260, October 1946.

13 Translation of Records of Judiciary Department, 7th Area Army as cited by Wild, Cyril. Expedition to Singkep, Blackwood's Magazine,No 1572, Vol 260, October 1946.

14 Shinozaki, Mamoru. *Syonan – My Story: The Japanese Occupation of Singapore.* Singapore: Marshall Cavendish Editions, 2005, p.76.

15 Translation of Records of Judiciary Department, 7th Area Army as cited by Wild, Cyril. Expedition to Singkep, Blackwood's Magazine,No 1572, Vol 260, October 1946.

16 Thompson, Peter & Macklin, Robert. *Kill the Tiger: Operation Rimau and the battle for Southeast Asia.* Meath: Maverick House, 2007, p. 255.

17 Silver, Lynette Ramsay. *The heroes of Rimau: unraveling the mystery of one of World War II's most daring raids.* Singapore: Cultured Lotus, 2001, p. 221.

18 "Pilot's VC for Fight in Blazing Hurricane", Daily Telegraph, 15 November 1940.

19 Ibid.

20 Letter from Chaz Bowyer to Cannon Lummis, 16 April 1983, VC Box 35, London: Imperial War Museum.

21 "Recollections of Wing Commander Tom Neil DFC AFC" in Mason, Peter D. NICOLSON VC: The full and authorised biography of James Brindley Nicolson. Ashford: Geerings of Ashford, 1991, p. 127.

22 Mason, Peter D. NICOLSON VC: The full and authorised biography of James Brindley Nicolson. Ashford: Geerings of Ashford, 1991, p. 118.

23 "Wing Commander J. B. Nicolson VC", Times of London, 9 May 1945.

24 "Fighter Ace's VC will be sold to help his widow", Daily Telegraph, 9 February 1983.

25 Mason, Peter D. *NICOLSON VC: The full and authorised biography of James Brindley Nicolson.* Ashford: Geerings of Ashford, 1991, p. 137.

26 Elphick, Peter and Smith, Michael. *Odd Man Out: The Story of the Singapore Traitor.* London: Hodder and Stoughton, 1993.

27 Probert, Henry. *The forgotten air force : The Royal Air Force in the war against Japan 1941-1945.* London, Washington : Brassey's, 1995.

28 Elphick, Peter and Smith, Michael. *Odd Man Out: The Story of the Singapore Traitor.* London: Hodder and Stoughton, 1993.

29 RAAF Officer. *Great was the Fall!: A Story of the Malayan Tragedy.* Perth: W.A. Patersons, 1945.

30 Ibid, p. 71-72.

31 Elphick, Peter, "Cover-ups and the Singapore Traitor Affair" paper presented at "60 Years On: The Fall of Singapore Revisited" Conference, February 2002.

32 Despatch 15 Dec 1941-20 May 1942, by Gen Sir Archibald Percival Wavell, Commander-in-Chief, India, CAB106/38, London: The National Archives.

33 Wikipedia. "Thomas Wilkinson, Royal Naval reserve". Wikipedia: The Free Encyclopedia. [Internet]. Accessed 11 October 2005. Available from: <http://en.wikipedia.org/wiki/Thomas_Wilkinson,_Royal_Naval_Reserve>

34 Gregrory, Mackenzie. "The Victoria Cross at Sea" THE NAVAL HISTORICAL SOCIETY OF AUSTRALIA, INC. [Internet]. Accessed 11 October 2005. Available from: < http://ahoy.tk-jk.net/macslog/TheVictoriaCrossatSea.html>

35 Wildy, Mervyn. "H.M.S. Li Wo" Allied Chinese Ships WWII. [Internet]. Accessed 11 October 2005. Available from: <http://members.dodo.net.au/~mervynw/li%20wo.htm>

Chapter 8

The Kranji Military Cemetery

To the west of the main War Cemetery lie the remains of 1,378 Commonwealth troops and their dependants who were buried in the Ulu Pandan and Pasir Panjang Military Cemeteries. Prior to the creation of Kranji, military cemeteries in Singapore were decentralised.

The two main military cemeteries were located at Pasir Panjang and Ulu Pandan. The Pasir Panjang Military Cemetery (PPMC) was rectangular and located on Dover Road. It contained about 900 graves and was opened in 1948. It also included 185 graves (from the 1907–1947 period) that were transferred from Bidadari Christian Cemetery. The PPMC was located within the huge Pasir Panjang military complex which the Singapore Armed Forces (SAF) took over by late 1971.

The plots were arranged denominationally, servicemen and dependants being mixed together. However, the Bidadari concentrations were only marked with temporary crosses and metal plates bearing minimal inscriptions. The concentrations were located on two sides of the central axis at the front of the cemetery. The Bidadari remains had not been marked with block markers as suggested by the CWGC in 1966 when the remains were transferred there. To the right of the central axis were the Gurkha graves with nearly all dependant's graves marked with special shaped wooden pegs.

The somewhat larger part to the left of the central axis contained burials of various Christian denominations. Headstones were the normal non-war type in granite and the RAF type in synthetic Portland stone, the surfaces of which were rough, being part brownish as if they were whitewashed at one time. There were numerous private crosses and about 20 private memorials scattered around the cemetery with one or two graves with kerb surrounds. There was also one Australian serviceman's grave marked with the Australian type pedestal and bronze plaque.

In the part to the left of the central axis stood a Celtic Cross about nine feet high on a square podium. Most probably made of granite, the cross was eventually moved to Kranji and is an iconic symbol in the Military Cemetery.

The Celtic Cross from the Pasir Panjang Military Cemetery, which was shifted to the Kranji Military Cemetery.

The Ulu Pandan Military Cemetery (UPMC) was on the outskirts of the Pasir Panjang complex and was held on a long lease by the ANZUK (Australian, New Zealand, UK) Forces. Although much larger than the PPMC, there were relatively fewer spaces for new burials (a maximum of 200 burials more). This was because the existing rows of graves were spaced widely apart. All grass cover was without borders with tarmac paths and, as the site is on a slope, drainage ditches and trenches. There was also a chapel and sexton's bungalow.

Although the UPMC came under the Department of the Environment's responsibility, the grass was cut by contractors arranged by the ANZUK forces. The plots were mainly denominational and with a number of markers and temporary markers. The cemetery held about 1,500 graves along with a few trees with the whole area surrounded by a fence. The chapel held two bronze plaques commemorating burials from the 19th Century in Malaya with memorial books below them recording names. Most of these burials had presumably been lost or abandoned with the plaque and register the only commemoration of these individuals.

However, by the early 1970s, with the British Army's withdrawal imminent, the British High Commission along with the Commonwealth War Graves Commission felt the need to consolidate the remains of the service dead. As the CWGC noted in a minute to the Foreign Office:

> I understood from what was said that the whole area of Pasir Panjang, including the Military Cemetery, was amongst land handed over to Singapore. The Singapore Government subsequently said that the

> cemetery land would be required for development purposes, but they offered the UK a TOL (temporary occupation license) for a maximum period of five years. The British HC's (High Commissioner's) view appears to be that eventual removal is inevitable and, that being so, the sooner arrangements are made the better from the points of view of both local winding-up arrangements and local goodwill...
>
> ...Some Chinese cemeteries in Singapore have already been moved and it is reported that one in Pasir Panjang will soon be moved – this, in the British HC's view, tips the balance in favour of their not resisting the pressure to move the Military Cemetery, the more particularly because the Chinese do not like the disturbance of remains and the Chinese Cemetery in Pasir Panjang is actually of the Hakka Sect, which is that of Prime Minister Lee[1].

The CWGC agreed to make a suitable piece of land available to the west of Kranji War Cemetery:

> The spare ground at Kranji on the west side above the Caretaker's Quarters slopes away to the west and it would seem that a very satisfactory cemetery could be established here with entry from an un-made up road coming in from the south west behind the new State Cemetery. This roadway already runs over part of the Commission's land on its route to a rather ramshackle house just outside the SW corner of the Commission's boundary.
>
> Fencing and provisions of suitable gates and the siting of the Celtic Cross feature, now in Pasir Panjang, should not prove difficult and there is already a fence (with a small service gate), with a hedge inside, running along the war cemetery side[2].

Although the CWGC was amenable to the shift, it insisted on several conditions. Firstly, the Commission would prepare the layout of the new cemetery based on consultations with the Department of the Environment (DOE) and the British Defence Ministry (MOD). They wanted an explanatory plaque set up and the questions of any other features, entrance, fencing and general grass cover would have to be, "considered in the context of ease of future maintenance"[3].

In addition, as the Military Cemetery, although separate, would be in close association with the War Cemetery, all graves would have to be permanently marked. Block markers would be used for dependants' graves (previously marked with temporary wooden crosses) and provided they were inobtrusive, any existing private memorials could be used. The DOE would provide new headstones (in local granite and carved locally) and block markers with stone tablets.

The Commission also noted the large number of graves of stillborn babies, belonging mainly to those of the Gurkha troops in Singapore. These graves would be combined into a single mass grave at Kranji. This mass grave then ended up re-interred with those remains from Ulu Pandan and Pasir Panjang that could not be identified.

Finally, the Commission wanted to remain "responsible for organising the horticultural layout, which would be of their traditional pattern, with grass cover and headstone flower borders and trees and shrubs and hedges as appropriate"[4]. It was also decided that unlike the War Cemetery, there would be a very simple and quiet religious ceremony to inaugurate the cemetery after the move.

The financial arrangements in building the cemetery were taken care of by the British Defence Ministry while the British Ministry of the Environment would settle the maintenance costs.

When the British finally pulled out of Singapore in 1971, the lands on which these cemeteries were located were handed back to the Singapore Government and by 1975, the new Kranji Military Cemetery had been set up with most graves from Pasir Panjang and Ulu Pandan having been transferred over.

The Military Cemetery also holds the remains of many distinguished individuals like that of Brigadier Eric John (Tim) Denholm-Young, the first General officer from the 5th Indian Division to land on and liberate Singapore on 5 September 1945. A famous photograph shows him speaking with a Japanese interpreter on the docks of Keppel Harbour just minutes after the re-occupying forces landed. Denholm-Young died on 27 May 1966 at the age of 66 and was buried at the Ulu Pandan Military Cemetery before being moved to Kranji. The Military Cemetery is still open to a select few, which include those veterans who were involved in the liberation of Singapore. Another Singapore liberator to be buried at the Military Cemetery was Major

The headstone of Brigadier Eric Denholm-Young in the Kranji Military Cemetery.

Derrick Coupland. President of the Singapore Ex-Services Association for many years, Coupland was given the honour of a burial at Kranji because of his contribution to the welfare of veterans and his role in liberating the country. In a very rare exception, the CWGC has kept the plot next to Coupland's grave empty so that his wife can be buried next to him when she passes on[5]. The Commission also takes care of its own staff. The previous caretaker of the cemetery, Tan Chuan Seng is also buried at Kranji.

Kranji War Cemetery's long-serving caretaker Ling Cheng Lai (left) and the author, Romen Bose, at an ANZAC Day Ceremony in Kranji.

The responsibilities of maintaining the Kranji War Cemetery are onerous and have been carried out with much aplomb by the present caretaker, Ling Cheng Lai. A Malaysian Chinese, Ling worked at the Taiping War Cemetery for over 25 years before being given the responsibility of managing Kranji. Assuming his new duties on 1 July 1992, Ling's hard work over the last 13 years can be seen in the well-manicured lawns and beautiful shrubbery that makes Kranji such a peaceful resting place for those who died in the service of their King and country. Ling, who is now a grandfather, has 12 full-time gardeners under his care in order to keep the cemetery in pristine order. It is partly due to his efforts and those of his staff that Kranji still remains one of the best kept of the Commission's cemeteries worldwide.

Endnotes

1 DFE's Visit to Eastern and Pacific Regions (Delhi, Singapore, Melbourne) April 1972 – Singapore 11 April, 22 May 1972, FCO24/1291. London: The National Archives.

2 Ibid.

3 Ibid, p.2.

4 Ibid, p.3.

5 Conversation with Captain Frederick J Francis, Son of Major Derrick Coupland, Kranji War Cemetery, 13 November 2005.

Chapter 9

The State Cemetery

The Republic of Singapore's State Cemetery is located just below the Kranji War Cemetery. Upon independence, the Singapore Government realised the need for a state cemetery where leaders of the nation could be interred. A location was found at Kranji which was appropriate as it was located next to where heroes of the last war were buried.

Yusof Bin Ishak

The first to be interred at Kranji was the Republic's first Yang di-Pertuan Negara (Head of State) and Singapore's first President, Yusof Bin Ishak. Married to Puan Noor Aishah, the couple had one son and two daughters.

Born on 12 August 1910 at Padang Gajah, Trong about 18 miles from Taiping, Perak, Yusof was a Malay of Sumatran descent and traced his lineage on the paternal side to Minangkabau, and on the maternal side to Langkat. They first settled in Penang and later, Perak[1].

He was the eldest son in a family of nine and his father, Encik Ishak bin Ahmad, was the Acting Director of Fisheries in the Straits Settlements and Federated Malay States. Yusof received his early education in the Malay school in Kuala Kurau, Perak. Two years later, he was transferred to the Malay School at Taiping and in 1921 he began his English studies at King Edward VII School in Taiping. In 1923, when his father was posted to Singapore, Yusof accompanied his parents and studied at the former Victoria Bridge School until December 1923. In 1924 he was admitted to Raffles Institution where he passed the Cambridge School Certificate in 1927 with distinction, and continued his studies for two more years in the Queen's Scholarship class[2].

While at Raffles Institution he played hockey and cricket, and took part in swimming, weightlifting, water-polo and boxing. In 1933, he became the Singapore light-weight champion. As the most outstanding cadet of the School Cadet Corps, he became the first student in Singapore to have been commissioned by the then Governor as a 2nd Lieutenant in the Cadet Corps. He was a school prefect and was co-editor of *The Rafflesian*[3].

After leaving school in 1929, Encik Yusof went into partnership with two friends and embarked on the publication of the *Sportsman*, a fortnightly magazine devoted entirely to sports. In 1932, he joined the staff of *Warta Malaya*, the leading Malay newspaper of the time. He rose rapidly through the ranks to the post of Acting Editor within a short time. In 1938 he resigned from the *Warta Malaya*, and with a few close friends, established the 'Utusan Melayu Press Ltd'. In May 1939, the now well-known *Utusan Melayu* came into being with Yusof at the helm as its first Managing Director[4].

During most of the period of the Japanese Occupation (1942–1945), Encik Yusof remained in Malaya and on the capitulation of the Japanese, returned to Singapore on 3 September 1945, and immediately resumed publication of the *Utusan Melayu*.

In 1948, Yusof visited Britain as a member of the First Press Delegation. In early 1957, he went to Japan to inspect the latest machinery which the *Utusan Melayu* had ordered. In May of the same year, he moved to Kuala Lumpur to supervise the construction of the Utusan Building. While in Kuala

The Muslim grave of the late President Yusof Bin Ishak.

Lumpur, Yusof was elected President of the Press Club of Malaya. He was the guiding light behind the *Utusan Melayu* during the difficult period of Malayan independence.

Yusof also held many distinguished public appointments within the Singapore Government. From 1948 to 1950 he served on the Film Appeal Committee and was also a member of the Nature Reserves Committee as well as the Malayanisation Commission. In July 1959, he was appointed Chairman of Singapore's Public Service Commission and became the Chancellor of the University of Singapore in July 1965.

Yusof bin Ishak was appointed Yang di-Pertuan Negara of Singapore on 3 December 1959, the first locally-born person to hold the office. Yusof was conferred the First Class Order of the Darjah Kerabat (The Most Esteemed Royal Family Order of Brunei) by the Sultan of Brunei in November 1960 and the Darjah Kebesaran Sri Maharajah Mangku Negara (S.M.N.) by the Yang di-Pertuan Agong of Malaysia in November 1963.

On 9 August 1965, when Singapore separated itself from the Federation of Malaysia, Yusof bin Ishak became the first President of the Republic of Singapore. He was re-appointed for a further term of four years in December 1967, but died in office on 23 November 1970. He was given a full state funeral and was buried at Kranji.

Dr Benjamin Henry Sheares

The other individual buried at the State cemetery is the late Dr Benjamin Henry Sheares, the second President of the Republic of Singapore. Born on 12 August 1907 in Singapore, he was the son of a former Public Works Department Technical Supervisor and rose to become Professor of Obstetrics and Gynaecology at the University of Malaya in Singapore, a holder of five degrees, and one of the most highly respected men in his field[5].

Dr Sheares received his early education at the Methodist Girls' School, and later at St Andrew's School and Raffles Institution. He joined the King Edward VII College of Medicine in 1923, and qualified with the degree of L.M.S. in March 1929. After serving two years as Assistant Medical Officer at the Sepoy Lines (now Singapore) General Hospital, he began his career in obstetrics and gynaecology in April 1931[6].

In 1940, he was awarded the Queen's Fellowship in order to do a two years' postgraduate degree in Britain, but all this was suspended when war broke out. During the Japanese Occupation, he was Head of the Department of Obstetrics and Gynecology at Kandang Kerbau Hospital (KKH) and also Medical Superintendent of the Hospital for the local patients' section. After the Japanese surrender, he became the first Singapore-born doctor to be appointed acting Professor of Obstetrics and Gynaecology at the King Edward VII College of Medicine.

In May 1947, he finally went to London for postgraduate study and in January 1948, was the first Singapore obstetrician to qualify as member of the Royal College of Obstetricians and Gynaecologists of England. In March 1948, while studying for the degree of Fellow of the Royal College of Surgeons in Edinburgh, he was recalled to Singapore to act as Professor of Obstetrics and Gynaecology. He was also appointed Honorary Consultant at the British Military Hospital[8].

He held the post of Professor of Obstetrics and Gynaecology at the University of Malaya in Singapore from January 1950 until June 1960, when he retired and went into private practice. Upon his retirement he became Honorary Consultant at the Kandang Kerbau Hospital, and retained close contact with the teaching of both undergraduate and postgraduate students.

Dr Sheares lectured in the United States and Britain and wrote many articles for international and local journals. As a personal obstetrician and gynaecologist to some members of the Malaysian royal families, he was made a Dato of Kedah and of Kelantan for his services. Upon President Yusof Bin Ishak's death, Prime Minister Lee Kuan Yew asked Dr Sheares to take on the mantle of head of state and he assumed the office of the Presidency on 2 January 1971.

He and Lee had their offices at the Istana and were acquaintances previously but developed a warm and close friendship during his Presidency. Lee called upon him monthly to brief him, and "when Lee referred to sensitive developments covering Singapore's security or economy there was immediate cognisance of the dangers that could unfold, and President Sheares would have a twinkle in his eyes or give one of his quizzical looks. It was his way of sharing the concerns of Lee. Sheares had read all the official papers and did not need to be told all over again. Lee had observed President Sheares was conscientious by temperament, soft-spoken, had applied himself ably to his duties and discharged them with distinction[9]."

Lee asked the President to accept a third term of office but Sheares was reluctant, acknowledging that he had passed his 70th year and was slowing down. He was anxious that he did not have the strength to fulfill his duties to the end. Lee's persistence finally paid off when Sheares agreed. During his third term he worked conscientiously even when he fell ill in November 1980 with what appeared to be pneumonia. He also continued to go to Kandang Kerbau Hospital without ceremony or protocol. Hospital

The grave of the late President Benjamin Henry Sheares.

head Professor Ratnam, who was worried about his busy state functions, suggested Sheares relinquish some of his teaching commitments. President Sheares pleaded: "Ratnam, please do not stop me, for this is what I enjoy most"[9]. Professor Ratnam was touched by his deference to his authority, and by his obvious love of obstetrics and gynaecology. President Sheares continued his tutorials and very occasional surgery at KKH until three months before his death[10].

When the President opened Parliament on 3 February 1981, he appeared unwell. In March, his chest x-rays indicated malignant tumours in his right lung, and although he was not told this by his physicians he knew it because he had seen his x-rays. He had once said to Lee in a soft, matter-of-fact way that at his age his lung problems were likely to be malignant, then gave a gentle sigh but there was no fear nor panic either in his expression or bearing[11]. Their last meeting was on 8 May when President Sheares expressed regret and concern that after he had fainted on 3 May 1981 he had not been able to perform his duties and offered to retire immediately. Lee demurred and noted that although there was sad resignation there was no fear in the President's eyes and he showed great composure and dignity. That night, President Sheares, went into a coma, dying on 12 May 1981 having served as President for a decade[12]. Sheares was given a full state funeral and was buried at the other end of the State Cemetery.

Today, Yusof and Sheares remain the only two occupants of the State Cemetery. The remains of the late presidents Ong Teng Cheong, Wee Kim Wee and most recently C.V. Devan Nair (all of whom died out of office) were cremated, with their ashes disposed of in accordance with the wishes of their families.

Endnotes

1 Istana Archives. "Encik Yusof Bin Ishak, First President of the Republic of Singapore". President's Office, Republic of Singapore[Internet]. Accessed on 14 October 2005. Available from: <http://www.istana.gov.sg/history.html>

2 Ibid.

3 Ibid.

4 Ibid.

5 Sheares, Joseph. *Benjamin Henry Sheares: President, Republic of Singapore 1971-1981; Obstetrician and Gynaecologist 1931-1981 A Biography 12th August 1907 –12th May 1981.* Annals Academy of Medicine, Vol 34 No 6, 2005.

6 Ibid.

7 Ibid.

8 Ibid.

9 Ibid.

10 Ibid.

11 Ibid.

12 Ibid.

Chapter 10

Kranji Today

Although the Kranji War Cemetery remains the main Second World War memorial in Singapore where the sacrifices made in the last war are remembered, there are three separate memorials and commemorations when it comes to the war dead in Singapore, namely the British military, Japanese military and local civilian remembrances. This is not surprising considering the political agenda of the returning colonial powers and the vanquished Japanese at the end of the war. For the British government and its colonial governments, it was crucial to mark the contributions made by the Empire by commemorating the men and women who gave their lives for the King. As a result, Kranji was to represent the epitome of sacrifice by British and Commonwealth forces in the Far East. For the Japanese it was also important, that even in defeat, the men who gave their lives for the Emperor be remembered as heroes. It was also crucial to commemorate Japan's bid to rid the peoples of Asia from the British yoke though for many people in Singapore, it did not seem much of a liberation.

What it did was make many realise that the British Empire was not supreme and that the White man was fallible and could be conquered by other Asians. The memorials in the Japanese Cemetery to the Japanese war dead and to its militaristic ideals thus provided a commemoration for the Japanese who lived, fought and died in Singapore. As for the local population, it would take more than 21 years after the end of the war before a proper Civilian memorial was established. Even that memorial was initially planned specifically for the Chinese community and the huge losses that it had faced at the hands of the Japanese. However, with Singapore's independence in the offing and the pressing need to galvanise the

Wall plaque at the entrance to the cemetery.

population in a bid to oppose the communists and unite the country, it had made much more sense for the Civilian Memorial to mark the sacrifices made by all communities in Singapore, thus preventing the communists from hijacking the sensitive "blood debt" issue within the Chinese community in a bid to unseat the PAP government. The "chopsticks" memorial became the first multi-racial memorial on the island and the only memorial to the local population. This memorial commemorating the local civilians was the third group of remembrances.

However, one significant group had been left out – British and European civilians. Numerous British civilians had kept the economy running during the Malayan Campaign and it was because of the demand for raw materials that British plantation owners and businessmen continued to toil even though every man was needed in fighting the encroaching Japanese. So severe was the situation that even when the Japanese had begun moving down the Malayan Peninsula, senior Malayan Civil Servants and planters were aghast at the prospect of their ranks having to put aside the work of administration and supplying the war effort in Europe to serve as volunteers in the military. Nonetheless, many did so enthusiastically and a large number of civilians signed up for active service. Many others served as Air Raid Wardens and in the makeshift Red Cross field stations. As the Japanese advanced, many British and European civilians were killed, with the remainder rounded up once Singapore fell. The civilians were first housed in the main Changi prison before being sent to the Sime Road internment camp in 1944. Numerous other smaller internment camps for civilians were also set up. Thus, the sacrifices made by the British civilians were also great but there was no proper memorial to these gallant men and women.

In 1919, the colonial government in Singapore built a Cenotaph on the Esplanade, just opposite the Sarkies' Brother's Europa Hotel (the site of today's City Hall and the former Supreme Court building) to commemorate the men who had died in the Great War. This memorial was the main place of remembrance for the war dead and was re-inscribed in 1946, to also mark the sacrifices of the war dead from the most recent war. However, with the setting up of Kranji, the Cenotaph lost its main purpose in commemorating the military dead as most ceremonies and remembrances would from now on be held at Kranji. Nonetheless, the municipal authorities continued to hold Remembrance Day ceremonies on 11 November every year. The ceremony at the Cenotaph became one that was also dedicated to the memory of the British and Commonwealth civilians who lost their lives in the war.

A view of the Cenotaph in a photograph taken in the 1920s.

By 1958, with the official opening at Kranji, the ceremony at the Cenotaph had become very low-key, with municipal officials carrying out the commemoration. Moreover, the new anti-colonial mayor Ong Eng Guan was not in favour of perpetuating such memories. A heavy downpour in 1959 resulted in the municipal authorities canceling the commemoration activities on the steps of the Cenotaph[1]. Although such services continued until the late 1960s, they were very much smaller and no longer organised by the municipal government which had been dissolved by then.

With Singapore's independence and British troop pull out in the early 1970s, Kranji has become the main focus of such remembrances for the now visiting British and ANZAC forces (New Zealand based the 1st Battalion Royal New Zealand Infantry Regiment in Singapore until 1989) who are deployed in the region under the Five-Power Defence Arrangements. Ong has long since passed from the scene and his brand of anti-colonialism has died out but his decision to end ceremonies at the Cenotaph has meant that the memorial today has lost much of its significance. Although it is still maintained, it is often used as a meeting place for skateboarders, who now use the steps to practise their latest manoeuvres.

Today, Kranji continues to play a part in the national consciousness of those nations whose men and women fill the cemetery. The ceremony at Kranji to mark the 60th Anniversary of the End of the War on 12

September 2005 saw over 2,000 veterans, their children, grandchildren and great-grandchildren attend the dawn service. Organised by the National Commemoration Committee chaired by local military historian Jeyathurai Ayadurai, the event was most likely the last big commemoration where large numbers of veterans will be present. As the youngest veterans are in their mid-seventies, it is now up to a younger generation of men and women to cherish the memories of those who are remembered at Kranji.

An interesting aside has come to light in recent months on the Union Jacks that were used to drape the bodies of POWs in Changi and various other camps during the Occupation – remains that, after the war, were reinterred at Kranji. One such flag had a much greater significance as it saw the British Capitulation in 1942 and the Japanese Surrender in 1945. The flag however, was 'missing' for many years till it was again 'discovered' in late 2005.

On 15 February 1942, as General Percival reluctantly agreed to surrender negotiations, Captain Cyril Hew Dalrymple Wild, Staff officer on Major General Lewis Heath's III Indian Corps and fluent in Japanese, was tasked as Percival's interpreter for the surrender at the Ford Motor Factory. Wild, who carried a huge white flag as the group was led to the factory, was so incensed by the Japanese propaganda units that were filming that he threw down the white flag. The Union Jack, which was carried by Brigadier Torrance, was not handed over to the Japanese. After the surrender, the Japanese wanted the Union Jack as a war trophy but Wild would not give them that satisfaction:

> The emissaries received an order at the prisoner-of-war camp at Changi that I should hand over personally to the Japanese General Staff the Union Jack which had been used on that occasion. With General Percival's permission, I told the representatives of the Japanese General Staff that I had no flag to give them. I told them that I had personally burned the flag on the evening of the capitulation[2].

For two years it was used for funerals in the camp, only a handful of men knowing its history. The Japanese officer-in-charge of the camp later insisted that it should be given up but it was still borrowed from him for funerals. When Mountbatten took the formal Japanese surrender in Singapore's municipal chambers on 12 September 1945, it was this Union Jack which was flown on the ceremonial flagstaff. A year later Wild donated the flag to the City of Singapore. A few months later, Wild died in a plane crash in Hong Kong.

For the next 12 years, the flag was displayed in a place of honour in the City Hall chambers till the Union Jack and the Legislative Assembly's

Speakers Mace were forcibly removed from the chamber by mayor Ong Eng Guan in 1958. On finding out that the flag had been removed Wild's brother David wrote to Mountbatten seeking information on the flag and wondering if it was no longer wanted, whether it could be donated to Wild's alma mater, Charterhouse at Eton, where David was the Housemaster.

In response, the Commander-in-Chief of the Far East Station Vice Admiral Gerald Gladstone sent a note to Mountbatten noting that it was virtually impossible to get the flag back:

> The newspaper reports and your assumptions are roughly correct: The Mace was also removed by the new left-wing Mayor. They are now deposited in the City Hall strong room.
>
> Before making the request you suggest, on your behalf, (which I think would very likely be refused now anyway as has already a somewhat similar one for the Mace) I would like you to consider whether your proposal is really in our best interests and that of the cold war here. So long as Wild's Union Jack is here in the Council's possession it remains, with the Mace, a symbol to many of freedom and friendliness to Britain: and there are a lot of people here who are very dismayed at the Mayor's action, who have strong feelings about it, and who would be terribly disheartened if the flag left Singapore...
>
> ...For my part, I have every sympathy with the family and would like them to have it in any case. The courage of the prisoners-of-war is a part of history which no Mayor will shake: but the flag was a personal relic of a single man. However, at this moment the flag is more a piece of politics than of history: it is quite safe, but if the Wild family want it back it will take some time for the climate to be suitable for the return you request[3].

Mountbatten left it at that but David Wild was not willing to end his bid to get the flag back. Three years later, he had the son of Field Marshal Sir Gerald Templer in his house at Eton. Appointed in 1951 by Winston Churchill as High Commissioner to Malaya after the assassination of Sir Henry Gurney, Templer was able to tackle the communist Emergency in Malaya and had dramatically improved the situation before he left in 1954. Appointed as Chief of the Imperial General Staff, Templer was in retirement when David approached him in 1961. Templer asked the UK's Commissioner General for Southeast Asia Lord Selkirk to intervene in the matter but Selkirk reported that the Union Jack was nowhere to be found:

> I had a word with Lee Kuan Yew a couple of days ago with regard to the Union Jack which was in Changi Prison Camp during the war. He affirmed resolutely that it was in the Singapore Museum... In fact, it is impossible to know what is in the museum at all. When I made my request Lee said that he had no objection to my making a thorough search, which I will endeavour to do.
>
> I think there is probably at least something in what the Prime Minister is saying, but if the Museum is in such a mess, I find it a little difficult to know why he is so sure that the Union Jack is there[4].

Two and a half years would go by before the Union Jack was finally found. The Assistant High Commissioner located the flag in a box in City Hall:

> There was also in the box a second Union Jack brought in by the liberating forces in 1945. These were the two flags which hung in the City Hall until they were taken down by Ong Eng Guan when he became Mayor at the end of 1957. I subsequently spoke to Lee Kuan Yew about the flags, and he agreed that we might have them. They now rest in my office.
>
> I have written to Tony Golds, head of the Far-East and Pacific Department in the Commonwealth Relations Office, suggesting that the flags should be handed over to the Imperial War Museum, on the understanding that if at any time in the future the Singapore or Malaysian Government of the day expressed the desire to have the flag back, they would be returned to Singapore[5].

The flag was entrusted to the Royal Navy and was handed over to the Imperial War Museum, which then loaned the flag to Charterhouse in 1967. There it rested for the last 38 years in relative obscurity. To many, the flag had gone 'missing' as very few knew of the secret return of the flag and its eventual home at Eton. In early 2005, the Singapore History Museum began plans for a new 60th Anniversary of the end of the Second World War exhibit with which to launch the opening of a new state-of-the-art Museum in 2006. It began looking for exhibits but was unaware that the Wild Union Jack was still in existence. On being told, the museum contacted Charterhouse, which told them that the flag had been returned to the IWM for restoration. The Singapore History Museum is now in the midst of negotiations with the IWM for the loan of the flag. Sixty years on, the flag, like the cemetery at Kranji, remains a tangible reminder of a not-so-distant past, when the fate of this little island lay upon the shoulders of so many who fought, perished and who now remain an eternal part of this land.

Endnotes

1 *The Straits Times*, 9 November 1959.

2 Bradley, James. *Cyril Wild: The Tall Man who never Slept.* Sussex: Woodfield Publishing, 1997, p. 90.

3 Ibid, p. 178.

4 Ibid, p. 179.

5 Ibid, p. 181.

Appendix A: Map and Layout of the Kranji War and Military Cemetery

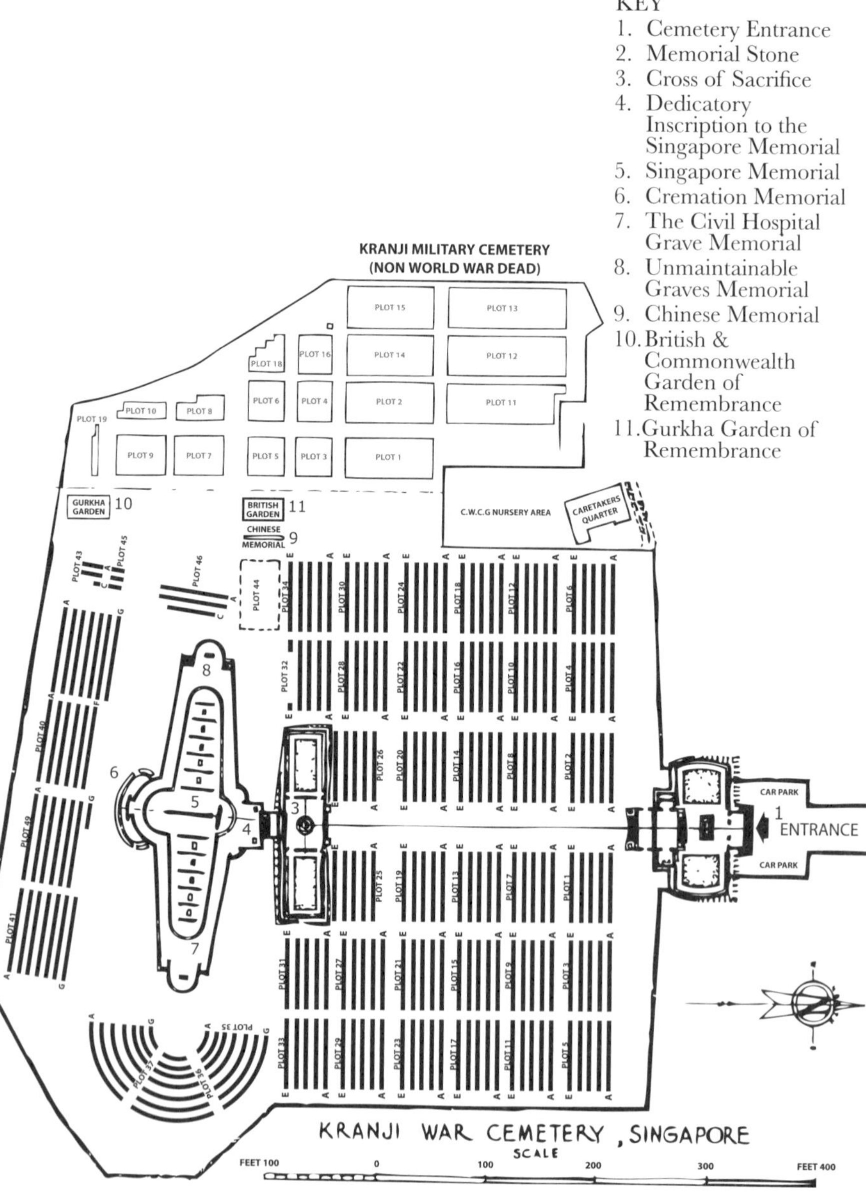

Appendix B: Layout of the Japanese Cemetery

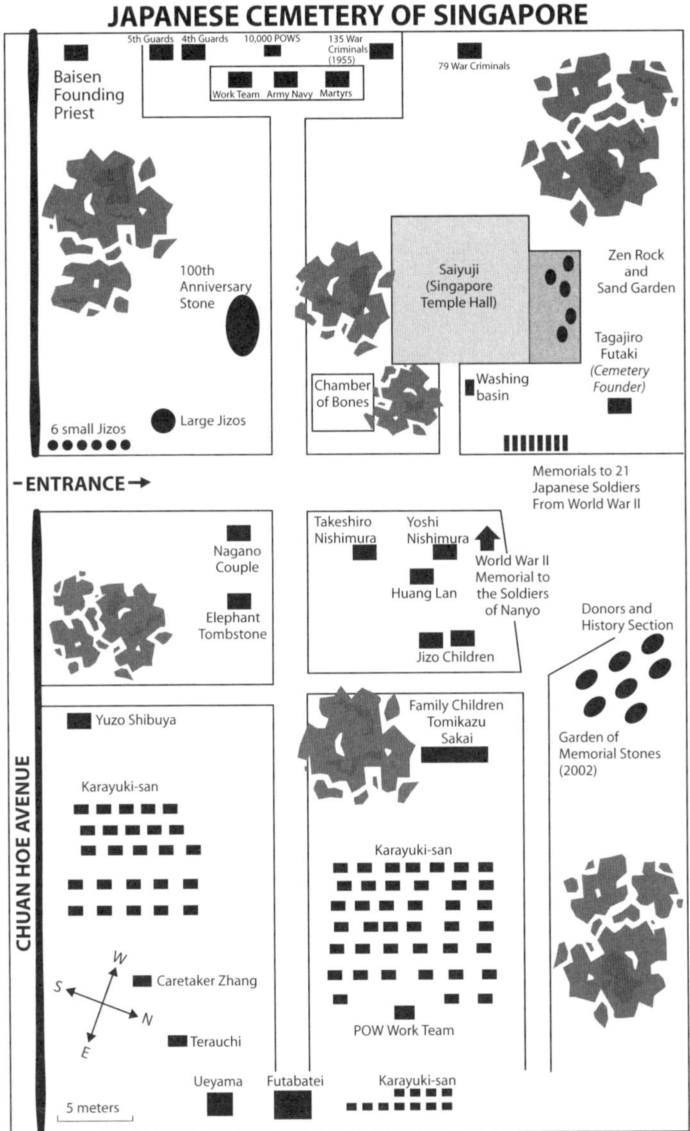

Source: Kevin Blackburn and Edmund Lim. "Singapore's Little Japan and Its Japanese Cemetery" in Kevin Y.L. Tan (ed.), Spaces of the Dead: A Case from the Living. *Singapore: Heritage Society, 2006.*

Appendix C: Original documents from the National Archives, London, showing Japanese graves and cemeteries in British-controlled territories

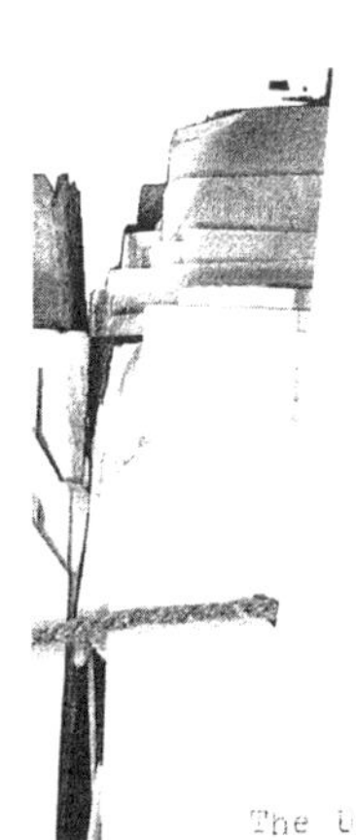

BY FAST AIR MAIL

Graves Registration & Enquiries,
General Headquarters,
FAR EAST Land Forces,
C/o G.P.O. SINGAPORE.

47

FEGRE/W/8
30 Apr 53.

The Under Secretary of State,
The War Office AG4 (PW & Graves),
Lansdowne House,
Berkeley Square,
LONDON, W.1.

Subject:- JAPANESE WAR GRAVES

Ref:- Your signal 75006(AG4B) dated 27 Apr 53. 'A'
Our signal GVS/2690 dated 28 Apr 53. 'B'

1. A list of Japanese Cemeteries in JAVA, SUMATRA, MALAYA, BURMA, REMPANG AND GALANG ISLANDS AND BORNEO is forwarded herewith.

2. The Burial Returns and Cremation Reports in respect of Japanese Casualties in BURMA have been handed over to the Japanese Consul, SINGAPORE.

3. No further records are held in this GHQ.

(Sgd) ?
for General,
Commander in Chief.
FAR EAST Land Forces.
FE/AC

COPY

File BM/GR/10010

48

JAPANESE CEMETERIES

JAVA

Tanjong Priok, Batavia	45	graves
Kampoeng Makassar Hospital Cem. Batavia	9	"
Manggarai Cemetery (Tombstones destroyed)	500	"

SUMATRA

Nil.

MALAYA

Kuala Lumpur Bellamy Road Jap Cemetery	364	graves
Batu Arang Public Cemetery	53	"
Kampong Tampong in Kelantan	1	"
Klang Public Cemetery	1	"

BURMA

Rangoon. Tamwe Cemetery	10	graves
Payagyi (961203)	102	"
Ahlone. Tamwe Cemetery	14	"
Toungoo. Centre of Le-Aingzu Village	70	"
Tenasserim District. Papun on Balin River	27	"
" Naikyi on Belin River	12	"
" Duyinzeik	55	"
" Thaton	34	"
" Zemathwe	33	"
" Moulmein	49	"
" Mudon Rly Line	16	"
Tawku Rly Line to Mergui	454	"
Wegale on Rly to Bangkok	19	"
33 other places with numbers varying from 1 to 8.	78	"
Burma Total	973	

REMPANG AND GALANG ISLANDS, not marked in any way — 157 graves

BORNEO

Jesselton	696	graves
Papar. Isolated graves	8	"
Mempakul. Isolated graves	31	"
Sandakan	156	"
Lahad Datu	13	"
Tawau	613	"
Keningau. Isolated graves	65	"
Tambunan. " "	63	"
" Kampong Tandulu	44	"
Tenom	56	"

Appendix D: Original blueprints from the National Archives, London, showing selected plans, elevations and sections of the cemetery at Kranji

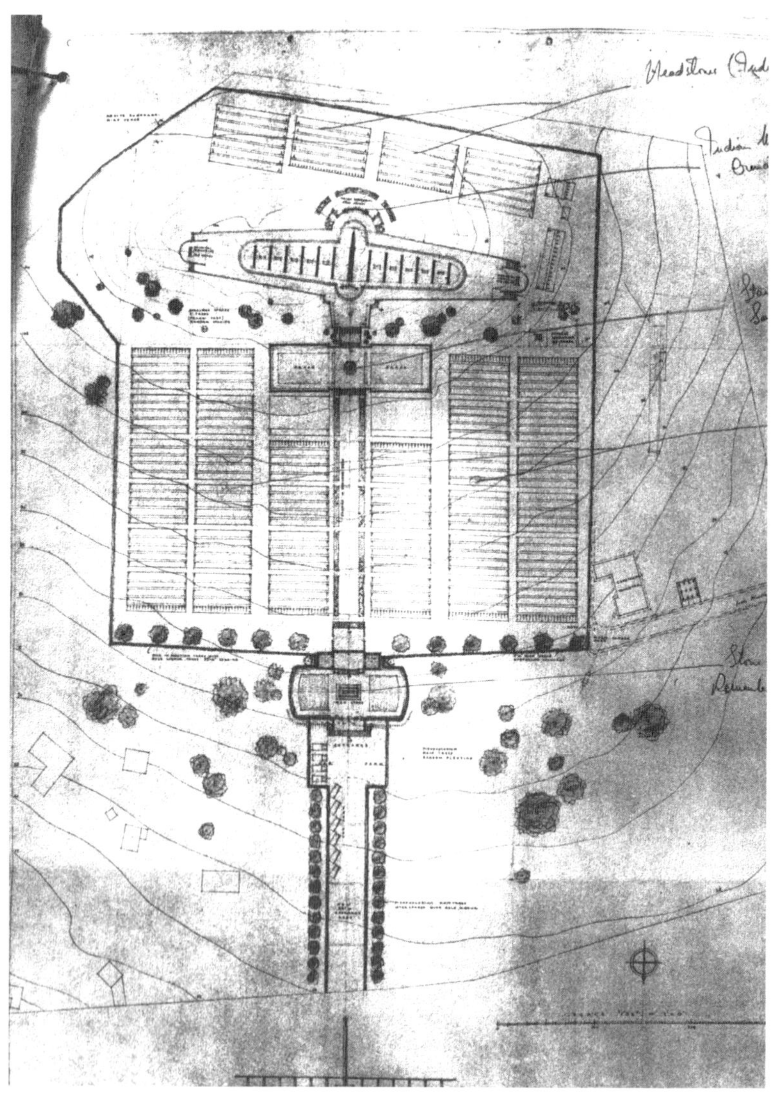

SOUTH ELEVATION
INGAPORE KRANJI MILITARY CEMETERY INDIAN

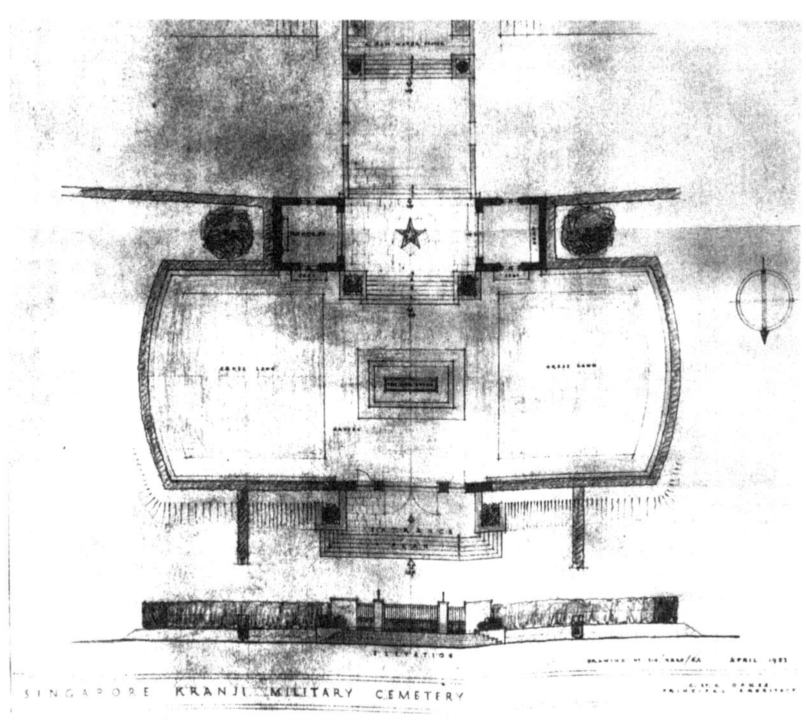
ELEVATION
SINGAPORE KRANJI MILITARY CEMETERY

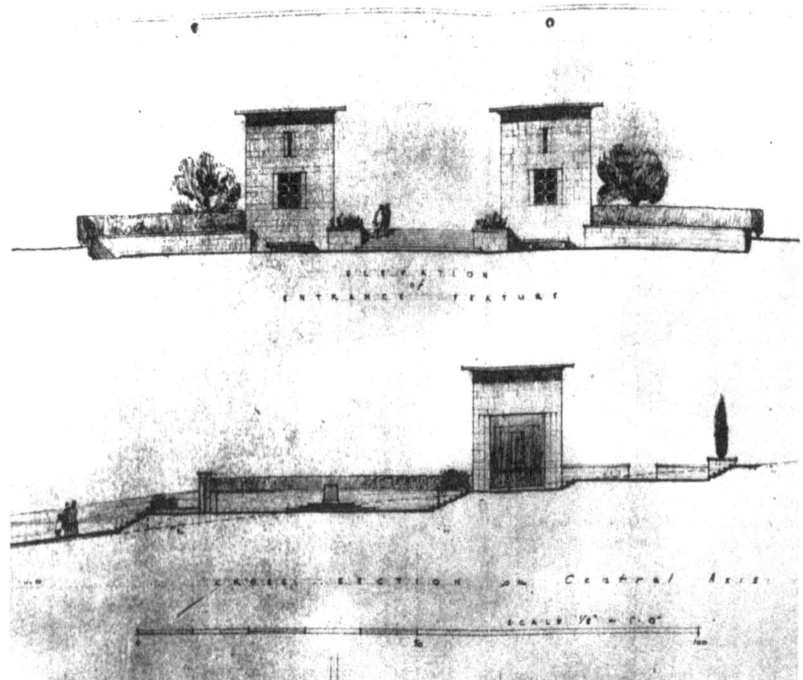
ELEVATION
of
ENTRANCE FEATURE
CROSS SECTION on Central Axis
0
50
100

Selected Bibliography

Primary Sources:

Great Britain, The National Archives (Public Records Office), London

AIR2 Air Ministry and Ministry of Defence: Registered Files 1887–1985.

CAB106 War Cabinet and Cabinet Office: Historical Section: Archivist and Librarian Files: (AL Series) 1939–1967.

CO323 Colonies, General: Original Correspondence 1689–1952.

CO1022 Colonial Office: South East Asia Department: Original Correspondence 1950–1956.

CO1030 Colonial Office and Commonwealth Office: Far Eastern Department and successors: Registered Files (FED Series) 1941–1967.

CO1032 Colonial Office and Commonwealth Office: Defence and General Department and successors: Registered Files, General Colonial Policy (GEN Series) 1950–1968.

FCO24 Commonwealth Office, Far East and Pacific Department and Foreign and Commonwealth Office, South West Pacific Department: Registered Files (H and FW Series) 1967–1974.

FO371 Foreign Office: Political Departments: General Correspondence from 1906–1966.

PREM11 Prime Minister's Office: Correspondence and Papers, 1951–1964, 1944–1964.

WO203 War Office: South East Asia Command: Military Headquarters Papers, Second World War 1932–1949.

WO222 War Office: Medical Historians' Papers: First and Second World Wars 1914–1949.

Great Britain, Imperial War Museum, London:

Brown, W.E. VC Papers, VC Box 6

Chambers, Rev G.J. Papers, 91/35/1

Nicolson, James Brindley VC Box 35

Secondary Sources:

Official Histories:

Crewe, Francis Albert Eley. *History of the Second World War. United Kingdom medical series, Part I to VI.* London: HMSO, 1953–1966.

Kirby, S. Woodburn. *The War against Japan, Vol I to V.* London: HMSO, 1954–1969

Books:

Bose, Romen. *The End of the War: Singapore's liberation and the aftermath of the Second World War.* Singapore: Marshall Cavendish Editions, 2005.

Bradley, James. *The Tall Man Who Never Slept: A tribute to Cyril Wild.* Bognor Regis: Woodfield Publishing, 1997.

Connell, Brian. *Return of the Tiger.* London: Brown & Watson, 1965.

Lau, Albert. *A Moment of Anguish: Singapore in Malaysia and the Politics of Disengagement.* Singapore: Times Academic Press, 1998.

Elphick, Peter and Smith, Michael. *Odd Man Out: The Story of the Singapore Traitor.* London: Hodder and Stoughton, 1993.

Farrell, Brian P. *The defence and fall of Singapore 1940-1942.* Stroud: Tempus, 2005.

Longworth, Philip. *The Unending Vigil: A history of the Commonwealth War Graves Commission.* London: Constable, 1967.

Mason, Peter D. *NICOLSON VC: The full and authorised biography of James Brindley Nicolson.* Ashford: Geerings of Ashford, 1991.

Probert, Henry. *The forgotten air force : The Royal Air Force in the war against Japan 1941–1945.* London, Washington : Brassey's, 1995.

RAAF Officer. *Great was the Fall!: A Story of the Malayan Tragedy.* Perth: W.A. Patersons, 1945.

Shinozaki, Mamoru. *Syonan – My Story: The Japanese Occupation of Singapore.* Singapore: Marshall Cavendish Editions, 2005.

Silver, Lynette Ramsay. *The heroes of Rimau : unravelling the mystery of one of World War II's most daring raids.* London: Leo Cooper, 1991.

Ward, G. Kingsley. & Gibson, Major Edwin. *Courage Remembered: The story behind the construction and maintenance of the Commonwealth's Military Cemeteries and Memorials of the Wars of 1914–1918 and 1939–1945.* London: HMSO, 1995.

Whitelocke, Cliff. *Gunners in the Jungle: A story of the 2/15 Field Regiment, Royal Australian Artillery, 8 Division, Australian Imperial Force.* Eastwood, New South Wales: The 2/15 Field Regiment Association, 1983.

Articles:

"A Singapore Memorial", *Times of London*, 18 March 1952.

Blackburn, Kevin and Lim, Edmund. "Singapore's Little Japan and Its Japanese Cemetery" in *Spaces of the Dead: A Case from the Living.* Ed. Kevin YL Tan, Singapore: Singapore Heritage Society, 2006.

"Fighter Ace's VC will be sold to help his widow", *Daily Telegraph*, 9 February 1983.

Lam, Pin Foo. "Japanese Settlers were here before the War". *The Straits Times: Life*, 25 February 1998.

"Pilot's VC for Fight in Blazing Hurricane", *Daily Telegraph*, 15 November 1940.

Sheares, Joseph. "Benjamin Henry Sheares: President, Republic of Singapore 1971-1981; Obstetrician and Gynaecologist 1931–1981 A Biography 12th August 1907–12th May 1981." *Annals Academy of Medicine*, Vol 34 No 6, 2005.

"Singapore Memorial Unveiled", *Times of London*, 4 March 1957.

"Singapore Victims of Japanese", *Times of London*, 14 September 1945.

"Tribute to 24,000 Service Men", *Times of London*, 2 March 1957.

"24,000 Honoured in Singapore", *The Telegraph*, 4 March 1957.

"War Hero Married", *Sydney Morning Herald*, 6 June 1932.

Wild, Cyril. "Expedition to Singkep", *Blackwood's Magazine*, No 1572, Vol 260, October 1946.

"Wing Commander J. B. Nicolson VC", *Times of London*, 9 May 1945.

Newspapers:

Syonan Shimbun, 1944–1945.

The Straits Times, 1945–1975.

The Malayan Tribune, 1945–1948.

The Times of London, 1945–1946.

Websites:

ANZAC Day Commemoration Committee, "List of Australian Winners of the Victoria Cross". ANZAC Day Commemoration Committee 2005. [Internet]. Accessed 27 September 2005. Available from: <http://www.anzacday.org.au/education/medals/vc/austlist.html>

Commonwealth War Graves Commission. "Kranji War Cemetery and the Singapore Memorials". Commonwealth War Graves Commission. [Internet]. Accessed 26 September 2005. Available from: <http://www.cwgc.org/cwgcinternet/publications.htm>

Government of Malaysia. "History of the Constitution" Centre of Government Information and Service [Internet]. Accessed 29 September 2005. Available from: <http://mawar.www.gov.my/MYGOV/BI/Directory/Government/AboutMsianGov/GovConstitution/HistoryConstitution/>

Gregrory, Mackenzie. "The Victoria Cross at Sea" THE NAVAL HISTORICAL SOCIETY OF AUSTRALIA, INC. [Internet]. Accessed 11 October 2005. Available from: < http://ahoy.tk-jk.net/macslog/TheVictoriaCrossatSea.html>

Istana Archives. "Encik Yusof Bin Ishak, First President of the Republic of Singapore". President's Office, Republic of Singapore[Internet]. Accessed on 14 October 2005. Available from: <http://www.istana.gov.sg/history.html>

Pan, Shou. 1976. "Memorial Epitaph to the Civilian Victims of the Japanese Occupation", translated by C.M. Wong. *Journal of the South Seas Society*. [Internet]. Accessed 26 August 2004. Available from: <http://www.knowledgenet.com.sg/singapore/shf/e_journal/articles/EJV1ART005.htm>

Stubbs, Peter W. "Singapore Cremation Memorial" *KRANJI,SINGAPORE War & Military Cemeteries* [Internet]. Accessed 26 September 2005. Available from: <http://www.petrowilliamus.co.uk/kranji/kranji.htm>

U.S. Library of Congress. "Road to Independence" Library of Congress website [Internet]. Accessed 29 September 2005. Available from: < http://countrystudies.us/singapore/10.htm>

Wikipedia. "Thomas Wilkinson, Royal Naval reserve". Wikipedia: The Free Encyclopedia. [Internet]. Accessed 11 October 2005. Available from: <http://en.wikipedia.org/wiki/Thomas_Wilkinson,_Royal_Naval_Reserve>

Wildy, Mervyn. "H.M.S. Li Wo" Allied Chinese Ships WWII. [Internet]. Accessed 11 October 2005. Available from: <http://members.dodo.net.au/~mervynw/li%20wo.htm>

Picture credits

Australian War Memorial: Page 428 (both). Brian Houldershaw: Page 357 (both). Imperial War Museum: Page 345, 421. Ministry of Defence, Singapore: Page 417. Ministry of Information, Communications and the Arts, Singapore: Page 437, 439. All other pictures provided by Romen Bose unless otherwise indicated. Every effort has been made to trace and credit the sources of photographs and illustrations used. Please contact us if there have been any inadvertent errors or omissions.

Index

1/17th Dogras 210
148 Field Regiment RA 360
15th Indian Corps 203
16th Punjab Regiment 424
18th Japanese Division 72, 79, 80, 82, 88, 89
1st and 2nd Battalion, The Malay Regiment 89
1st Battalion Royal New Zealand Infantry Regiment 445
2/15th Field Regiment 344
2/1st Punjab 210, 211, 212
2nd Singapore Infantry Regiment 104
35th Light Anti-Aircraft Regiment 361
44th Indian Brigade 80, 82, 83
4th Federal Infantry Brigade 104–6, 116
5th Indian Division 203, 204, 207, 209, 211, 212, 219, 228, 238, 239, 247, 276, 281
5th Japanese Division 73, 79, 80, 82
7th Coast Artillery Regiment 51
8th Division 360
III Indian Corps 14, 15, 36, 52, 61, 74, 93, 96
XXXIV Indian Corps 236

Abdul Rahman Putra Al Haj, Tunku 268, 309, 376, 401
Air Filtration Plant 24
Air Filtration Plant No. 3 35
Air Headquarters 48, 84
Air House 66–7, 108
Alicinious, SS 427
Allied Land Forces South East Asia (ALFSEA) 371
Amaterasu, Sun Goddess 384
AMDGW (Air Ministry's Department of General Works) 65
Anstey, Brigadier John 192–3, 304
ANZAC 445
ANZUK 433
Armstrong, Lieutenant Colonel Guy 252, 256, 298
Army Medical Corps 354, 356, 366

Baker, Catherine M.S. 216
Barber, Noel 21
Barisan Sosialis Party 397
Barth, Ronnie 91, 99
Batavia (Jakarta) 427–8
Bennett, Major General Gordon 14–15, 80–1, 83, 89, 93–5, 343, 380
Betty, Captain P.K. 360
Bidadari Christian Cemetery 356–7, 363, 371, 432
Black, Governor Sir Robert Brown 378–81
"Black Thursday" 378
Blackwell, A.G. 91
Blomfield, Sir Reginald 350
"Blood Debt" issue 268, 341, 396–7, 401–2, 444
Bose, Rash Behari 275, 308
Bose, Subhas Chandra 258, 275, 276, 277, 308
Bradshaw, Major F.W. 360, 362
British East India Company 29
British Military Administration (BMA) 104, 223, 226, 227, 276, 284, 290
Broadhurst, Lieutenant Colonel Douglas Keith 232, 304
Brooke-Popham, Air Chief Marshal Robert 60, 63, 70–2, 86, 114
Broome, Major Richard 285
Brown, Gunner Walter Ernest 343–6, 420
Brownie, Captain G.P. 233
Browning, Lieutenant General Sir Frederick Arthur Montague 230, 298, 386–7, 392
Bukit Larangan 29–30
Bukit Timah 14, 16, 75, 80, 82–3, 88, 94–6, 103
Buona Vista prisoner-of-war Camp 363, 371
Burgess, Captain J.B. 360
Burma 203, 216, 253, 259, 263, 275, 276, 281, 346, 359, 391, 422, 423, 424
Burns, Robert 223
BUTTON, Operation 234, 235, 292

Cable and Wireless Office 90–2, 99
Cameron, Sergeant Colin Barclay 260, 420
CARPENTER, Operation 177, 292
Cathay Building 275, 277
Cavenagh, Governor Colonel Orfeur 30
Celtic Cross 357, 433–4
Cenotaph 352, 444–5
Chambers, Reverend Gilbert John Marion 361–2
Changi Fire Command 49

Changi Prison 262–263
Chapman, Lieutenant Colonel Frederick Spencer 285, 304
Charlwood, E.C.H. 247
Chiefs of Staff, British 230
Chin Peng @ Chen Ping @ CTP 231, 284, 285, 286, 287, 289
Chinese Memorial 355–6
Chinese Middle School Riots 397
Choy, Elizabeth 374
Christison, Lieutenant General Sir Alexander Frank Philip 203, 204, 205, 206, 238, 240, 283, 285, 291, 298
Chua Koon Eng @ Choy/Bill 159–60, 162, 166–71, 305
Chungkai 347
Chungking 251
Churchill, Winston Spencer 230, 298
Cipher Room 39
Civil Hospital Grave Memorial 354–5, 374
Civilian Memorial 395–408, 444
Civilian Monument, the "Chopsticks" 267–274
Coles, Second Lieutenant F.J.P. 360
Colonial Office 374–5, 378, 380, 391
Combined Operations Headquarters 46, 58–67, 69–71, 74–9, 84
Command House 66–7, 108
Commander, Anti-Aircraft Defence (CAAD) Room 52–6
Commonwealth War Cemetery in Yokohama 391–2
Commonwealth War Graves Commission 363, 346, 347, 365–9, 372, 380–1, 392, 432–6
Cooke, Lieutenant N. 428
Cooper, Captain E.T. 253
Copley, Lieutenant Commander David 40, 88
CORONET, Operation 280, 292
Coupland, Major Derrick 436
Cox Terrace 22, 23, 26, 32, 34
Crawford, John 30
Cremation Memorial 353–4
Cross of Sacrifice 350, 381
CULVERIN, Operation 292
Curtis, Brigadier A.D. 40, 44, 49–50

Daijingu Shrine 384
Daniels, Padre 361, 362
Davies, Derek Gill 172
Davis, Major John 190, 285, 305
De Souza, Wing Commander Gerald 423
Dedicatory Inscription to the Singapore Memorial 351–2
Denholm-Young, Brigadier Eric John (Tim) 435
Denning, Esler 386, 392
Dobbie Rise 11, 22, 23, 32, 110
Donough, Cuthbert Oswald 90–2, 99, 113
DRACULA, Operation 203, 292
Draycott House 66

East Coast Road 396, 398
Edinburgh, Duke of 378, 379
Edmett, Sapper Leslie Reginald 411–12
Elphick, Peter 427
Elson-Smith, Flight Lieutenant Alfred 425
Eton, Charterhouse 400, 447–8
Exmouth Harbour 413–14

Faber Fire Command 49, 50
Far East Combined Bureau (FECB) 60, 70–4, 77–8, 114
Federal Government 404–5
Federated Malay States Police Force 352, 354
Federation of Malaysia 375–6, 379, 401, 405, 406, 439
Fighter Operations Rooms 46, 48, 53
Firbank, Colonel L.T. 29
Flagstaff House 59, 63, 65–7, 84, 108
Fletcher, Lieutenant R.G. 360
Force 136 176, 217, 218, 227, 231, 235, 236, 254, 260, 281, 282, 285, 286, 304–6, 394
Ford Motor Factory 16, 88, 95, 96, 383, 415, 446
Fort Canning Country Club Investment Ltd 109
Fort Canning Hill 10, 11, 12, 17, 23, 30
Fortress Plotting Room 25, 26, 35, 46, 55, 84
Fortress Signals 38, 70, 75, 90
France, Major James 425
Free India Provisional Government (FIPG) 275, 277
Fuk Wo, HMS 428
Fukudome, Vice Admiral Shigeru 206, 208, 244, 285, 291, 307
FUNNEL, Operation 177, 292

"G" Clerks Fortress Operations Room 24, 44–5

Garden Island Naval Base 414
Gardner, Air Vice Marshall Sir Percy Ronald, the Earl of Bandon 229, 253, 298
George V, King 344, 367
George VI, King 213, 422
Gill, MacDonald 347
Gimson, Governor Sir Franklin Charles 373–5
Gladstone, Vice Admiral Gerald 447
Gloucester, Duke of 379
Goh Keng Swee 271, 377, 405
Goodman, Brigadier E.W. 14, 93
Government House 30, 61, 67
Gun Operations Room 13, 14, 35, 39, 46–9, 53, 55, 69, 75, 84
Gurkha Garden of Remembrance 357
Gurney, Governor Sir Henry 447
GUSTAVUS, Operation 157, 158–61, 171

Hawthorn, Major General Douglas Cyril 231, 236
Headquarters Malaya Command 10–12, 21, 32, 62–3, 70, 74, 84, 97, 109, 110, 114
Heath, Lieutenant General Sir Lewis 14–15, 36, 63, 70, 75, 80, 89, 93–5
Heath, Major General Lewis 446
Heenan, Captain Patrick Stanley Vaughan 77, 78, 424–7
Higashitsuji, Kunio 390
Hill, Captain Sir Arthur 368
Hirohito, Emperor of Japan 281
Holland, Rear Admiral Cedric Swinton 203, 204, 205, 206, 208, 209, 214, 238, 239, 242, 247, 252, 253, 255, 283, 285, 300
Holmes, Sir Charles 347
Hone, Major General Sir Herbert Ralph 207, 290, 300
Hong Lim constituency 400
HORNBILL, Operation 414
Howard, Jim 40, 103
HQ Far East Air Force 65

Imperial Guards Division 79–88
Imperial War Conference 367–8
Imperial War Museum 11, 21, 27, 42, 49, 52, 97, 99, 400, 429, 448
In Cipher Wireless 38
INA Monument 274–276
India Mission 231
Indian Army Service Corps 353–4, 424
Indian Independence League 275
Indian National Army 258, 359
Ingleton, Major Reginald Middleton 416–18
Institution Hill 59
Ipoh 287
Ishiguro, Lieutenant General Teizo 253, 254, 291, 307
Iskandar Shah, Sultan 29
Itagaki, General Seishiro 206, 208, 209, 211, 213, 226, 240, 244, 245, 247, 248, 249, 250, 254, 278, 283, 284, 285, 290, 307

Jackson, Captain V.R. 360
Japanese "surrendered personnel" 207, 243, 264, 284, 387–93
Japanese 25th Army 79
Japanese Association, the 390, 393
Japanese Cemetery 263, 263–265, 388–93, 443, 451
Jardine Matheson & Co 427
JAYWICK, Operation 260, 292, 412–14
Johor State 209, 213, 214, 242, 259, 262, 266
Joint Appeal Committee of Japanese-massacred Chinese 395–6
Joint Intelligence Committee (JIC) 280
Jones, Hugh 361
JURIST, Operation 214, 230, 231, 292

Kanchanaburi War Cemetery 347
Kandang Kerbau Hospital 440–1
Karayuki-san 388
Kawahara, Major General Naoichi 253
Keppel Harbour 206, 208, 211, 212, 281, 291
Kheam Hock Road 66
Kightley, Gunner Eric 423
Kimura, General Hyotaro 244, 284, 290, 307
Kipling, Rudyard 349, 351
"Known Unto God" phrase 349, 420
Ko, Teck Kin 399
Krait 412–14
Kranji Military Cemetery 346, 356–7, 432–6, 450, 454–6
Kranji War Cemetery 346–9, 351, 355, 363, 371, 374–5, 379, 396, 420, 434–6, 443, 450, 454–6
Kranji War Memorial 259–263
Kranji-Jurong Line 82–3, 87, 116

Kuala Lumpur 236, 253, 254, 257, 270, 271, 390, 404, 405
Kwa, Chong Guan 19–20

La Cambe Cemetery 387
Labour Front Party 377–8
Lai Teck @ Lai Te @ Chang Hong 285, 286, 287
Latrines 41–2
Layton, Vice Admiral Sir Geoffrey 70, 78
Lee, Kuan Yew 258, 268, 272, 285, 309, 377–8, 397, 399–406, 434, 440–1, 448
Leonie Hill House 30
Li Han Kwang/Lee Han Kwong @ Lee Ah Cheng/Lee Tsing 159, 163, 165, 167, 305
Li Wo, HMS 427–9
Liang Yuan Ming @ Lee Chuen/Lee Choon 159, 305
Liberator *R for Robert* 423
Lim Bo Seng @ Tan Choon Lim @ Tang @ Ah Lim (B.B. 192) 80, 276, 282, 285, 306, 395
Lim Chin Siong 378, 397
Lim Han Hoe, Dr 249
Lim Yew Hock 377, 378–9
Ling Cheng Lai 436
Lomax, Signaller Eric 85, 102
Longmore, Air Chief Marshal Arthur 380
Lucas, Brigadier Hubert Francis 12, 15, 93, 97
Lung Chiu Ying @ Ah Long/Ah Loong 158–9, 162–8
Lutyens, Sir Edwin 350–1
Lyon, Lieutenant Colonel Ivan 260, 412–20

MacArthur, General Douglas 131, 143, 150, 180, 194, 196, 197, 290, 302
MacColl, D.S. 347
MacGillivray, Sir Donald Charles 379
MacKenzie, Colin Hercules 154, 158, 180, 183–4, 306
Mackie, Douglas James 220, 221, 222, 228
Macleod-Carey, Lieutenant Colonel C.C.M. 50
Macready, General Sir Neville 366
Maeda, Japanese Consul General 399, 401
MAILFIST, Operation 229, 230, 293
Makepeace, Second Lieutenant A.G.R. 360
Malacca, Straits of 202, 221
Malaya Command 343, 360, 383
Malayan Broadcasting Corporation (MBC) 277
Malayan Campaign 259, 264, 274, 277
Malayan Civil Service 36
Malayan Communist Party (MCP) 237, 268, 282, 289, 401
Malayan Emergency (Communist Emergency of 1948) 287, 288
Malayan People's Anti-Japanese Army (MPAJA) 254, 282
Malayan Union 255, 285, 287
Malaysia Day 268, 271, 272, 401, 405–6
Malaysian Chinese Association (MCA) 377, 405
Malaysian Indian Congress (MIC) 405
Malaysian Navy Base 107
Mansergh, Major General Eric Carden Robert 203, 204, 205, 206, 207, 208, 210, 242, 291, 300
MARKET GARDEN, Operation 144, 293
Marshall, David Saul 377–8
MATADOR, Operation 63, 74, 114
Memorial for Army & Navy Personnel 390
Memorial for the work team members who died at their post 390
Memorial Stone 350–1
Memorial to the Martyrdom of Patriots 390
Merapas Island 414–15, 420
Merdeka Talks 378
Messerschmitt 421–2
Messervy, Lieutenant General Sir Frank Walter 254, 301
Mikizawa, Koshiro 415–17
Miksic, John 19–20
Military Hospital, Singapore (Alexandra) 207
Miller, Harry 222, 223, 228, 243, 244, 249
Mizuya, Tomokatsu 390
MODIFIED DRACULA, Operation 203, 293
Moh Wing Pun @ Muk Ching/Mok Kee/Lee 160, 162, 167–70, 306
Moonshi, Dr. 247
Moore, Lieutenant Colonel Frank 423–4
Morib 231, 236, 257
Mountbatten, Lady Edwina 224
Mountbatten, Vice Admiral Lord Louis Francis Albert Victor Nicholas 103, 203, 207, 209, 223, 224, 229, 230, 236, 237, 239, 240, 244, 245, 246, 247, 248, 249, 252, 254, 257, 265, 281, 282, 283, 290, 291, 301, 385–6, 389, 446–7
MPBW HQ (Ministry of Public Buildings and Works) 65, 67

Munby, Sergeant Richard 225, 228, 239, 240, 251, 255, 256
Municipal Building (City Hall), Singapore 225, 238, 243, 245, 251, 252, 254, 257, 283

National Army Museum 27
National Committee for the Care of Soldiers' Graves 366–7
National Heritage Board 63
National Parks Department 18, 19, 21, 22, 26, 27, 32, 109–110,
Navy, Royal 243, 248, 253
Nelson, HMS 201, 205, 243, 295
Netherlands East Indies (Indonesia) 352, 413–14
Newbigging, Brigadier T.K. 14, 93, 95, 96
Nicholson, Brigadier John Gerald 386
Nicoll, Governor Sir John Fearns 391–2
Nicolson, Wing Commander James Brindley VC 420–4
Ninomiya, Ken 391–3
Numata, Lieutenant General Tokazo 202, 214, 244, 248, 291, 307

O'Shanohun, Captain Frank 192–4, 290
Official Peace Treaty 387–8, 390, 396–7, 399
Oguri, Colonel G. 253
Ohtsuka, Major General 419
Oil Store 42
Oishi, Lieutenant Colonel 398
OLYMPIC, Operation 280, 293
Ong, Chit Chung 109
Ong, Eng Guan 400, 445, 447, 448
Onishi, Major 398
Ord, Governor Harry St George 30
Orderlies Room 35, 40, 103
Outram Road Gaol 415, 417
Oxley Hill 30

Padang, the (Singapore) 238, 240, 242, 243, 244, 254, 258, 262, 284
Paine, Padre 361–2
Pan Shou 272, 406
PAP government 397, 400–1, 405, 444
Papayya, Lance Naik 411–12
Pasir Panjang Military Cemetery 356–7, 432–5
Pearl Harbor 72, 79
Peet, George 243
Penang 44, 76, 115, 201, 202, 203, 205, 206, 208, 209, 221, 230, 287, 290, 291, 292, 293, 390
Penney, Major General Sir William Ronald Campbell 249, 302
Percival, Lieutenant General Arthur Ernest 9–17, 20–1, 31, 36, 39, 40–2, 44–5, 52, 54–6, 58–60, 63, 65, 70, 72, 75, 79–99, 110, 114, 197, 254, 302, 383, 415, 446
Pike, Canon V.J. 381
Porpoise, HMS 414–5
Port Dickson 230, 231, 233, 236, 257
Power House 42, 43
Power, Admiral Arthur 206, 240, 252, 302
Prince of Wales, HMS 46, 73, 77–9, 114, 428
prisoners of war (POWs) 207, 216, 217, 218, 219, 220, 223, 224, 226, 242, 243, 252, 262, 263, 264, 266, 345, 359, 371–2, 377, 383–5, 388, 446
Public Records Office (National Archives UK) 27
Public Works Department 27
Pulford, Air Vice-Marshal C.W.H. 58–9, 64, 411–12
Pullen, Pilot Officer Michael 423

Radar Detection Finding (RDF) Units 48
RAF Filter Room 48
RAF Headquarters Sime Road 47, 59, 61, 64–5, 114
Raffles College 208
Raffles Hotel 226
Raffles Institution 438, 439
Raffles, Sir Thomas Stamford 29–30
Rajaratnam, S. 377
Rangoon 134, 138, 139, 143–7, 150–1, 195, 197, 199, 201, 203, 204, 205, 209, 216, 219, 221, 230, 281, 291, 423
Rayman, L. 247
Red Cross Society 359, 362, 365, 366, 444
Rendel Constitution 377
Rendel, Sir George 376
Repulse, HMS 46, 73, 77–9, 114, 428
Richelieu, HMS 243, 295
Riggs, Sub Lieutenant James Gregor Mackintosh 260, 420
RIMAU, Operation 260, 293, 414–15, 417, 419, 420
Roberts, Lieutenant General Ouvry Lindfield 229, 236, 253, 254, 291, 302
ROGER, Operation 230, 293
Rogers, Petty Officer Charles Halme 428–9
Ross, Harold Robert 347–8

Royal Artillery 344, 352
Royal Botanical Gardens at Kew 368

Saigon 209, 290
Saigon (Ho Chi Minh City) 386, 389, 414
Saigon Military Cemetery 363, 371
Samuel, Doraisingam 18, 109
Secretary of State for War 367, 372
Sek Fu *see* Yi Tian Song
Selkirk, Sir George Nigel Douglas-Hamilton, Lord 269, 270, 271, 278, 309, 403–5, 447
Shakkyozan Nihonji 388
Shaw Road (Jalan Hang Tuah) 254
Sheares, President Benjamin Henry 261, 439–41
Sheppard, Mervyn Cecil Ffrank (Tan Sri Mubin Sheppard) 252
Shibata, Vice Admiral Yaichiro 244, 255
Shinozaki, Mamoru 384
Siam (Thailand) 219, 244, 259, 263
Siam-Burma Death Railway 259, 263, 352, 359, 415
Signal Room 38–9
Signals Control Room 13, 15, 37, 39
Sime Road Internment Camp 359, 444
Simmons, Major General Keith 42, 44–5, 61, 69, 80, 93, 95, 97
Simson, Brigadier Ivan 11–12, 14, 79, 93
Singapore Base District 66, 103–4, 107, 116
Singapore Chinese Chamber of Commerce 397, 400–1, 404, 406–7
Singapore Chinese Middle School Student's Union 378
Singapore Civil Defence Force 20, 27
Singapore Club 12
Singapore Command and Staff College 107, 109
Singapore Golf Club 59
Singapore Memorial 346, 350–4, 381, 420, 424, 425, 427
Singapore Special Branch 397, 400
Singapore town 15, 29, 30, 86, 102
Singapore, reoccupation of 203, 209, 214, 216, 227, 231, 277, 282
Singh, Captain Mohan 274, 308
Singkep Island 416, 428
"Sleeping Beauties" 414
SLIDEX cards 38
Slim, Field Marshal William Joseph 205, 302
Smith, Michael 427
Soh, Felix 18–21, 26–7
"Sook Ching" Massacre 267, 273, 355, 395, 407
Southeast Asia Command (SEAC) 203, 204, 208, 213, 217, 218, 221, 227, 229, 230, 231, 238, 239, 248, 253, 280, 281, 282, 283, 284, 285, 286, 290, 386–8
Southern Army, Japanese 202, 209, 284
Special Operations Executive (SOE) 231, 260, 304–6
Spooner, Vice-Admiral Ernest John 411–12
St Andrew's Cathedral 374
St Desir De Lisieux Cemetery 387
Stanton, Sub Lieutenant Ronald George Gladstone 427–9
Stopford, Lieutenant General Sir Montague George North 240, 303
Straits Settlements Volunteer Force 44, 70, 80, 356, 363
Straits Times 18–19, 27–8, 109, 209, 222, 223, 226, 228, 243, 255, 256, 278
Strawbridge, Captain 252
Stubbs, Ray 34
Supreme Allied Commander, Southeast Asia Command (SACSEA) 152, 204, 205, 228, 239, 243, 248, 249, 252, 253, 255, 256, 277
Surrender, Instrument of, signed on HMS *Sussex* for Singapore 203, 205, 254, 310–21
Sussex, HMS 206, 243, 283, 295
Swords, Japanese surrender of 254
Syonan Chureito 341, 383–4, 389
Syonan Jinjya 384

Tan Chong Tee 157, 160, 162, 169–71, 306
Tan Eng Wah Construction company 60
Tan Kong Cheng 158–60, 306
Tan, Cheng Lock 377
Tan, Chuan Seng 436
Tan, Kah Kee 80, 394
Tan, Teng Teng 109
Tanaka, Hiroto 399, 401–6
Tanaka, Japanese Consul-General in Singapore 267, 270, 272
Taylor, Brigadier H.B. 82–3
Telephone Exchange 36–7
Telok Datok 231, 236
Templer, Field Marshal Sir Gerald 447
Terauchi, Field Marshal Count Hsiaichi 202, 203, 209, 210, 248, 251, 265, 266, 281, 284, 290, 307, 385–6, 389–90

Tetsuka, Tokiyaki 390
Thomas, Francis 377
Thomas, Governor Sir Shenton Whitlegge 11, 73, 80
Thompson, Acting Petty Officer Arthur 429
TIDERACE, Operation 152, 203, 204, 206, 210, 214, 215, 220, 223, 231, 255, 283, 290, 293
Toh, Chin Chye 377, 399
Tojo, General Hideki 258, 308
Torrance, Brigadier K.S. 14, 45, 86, 93, 95–7, 446
TROPIC, Operation 192, 293
Truman, President Harry S. 230, 303
Tunku Abdul Rahman *see* Abdul Rahman

Ulu Pandan Military Cemetery 356–7, 432, 433, 435
Uma Devi, G. 20
UMNO 375, 377, 405
Union Jack 400, 446–9
Unmaintainable Graves Memorial 353
Uozumi, Rear Admiral Jisaku 202, 203, 308

Victoria Cross (VC) 344, 345, 420–4, 427–8
Victoria Institution, Kuala Lumpur 202, 203
Villers Bretonneux 344

Walker, Vice Admiral Harold Thomas Coulthard 201, 202, 205, 206, 291, 303
War Memorial Hall (North Transept) 374
War Office 53, 60–3, 145, 184, 264, 366, 371, 372, 387, 392–3
Ward, Jim 361
Ware, Fabian Arthur Goulstone 347, 365–8, 373
Wavell, General Sir Archibald 13, 15, 38, 85–90, 94–5, 116, 426
Wearne, Padre 361–2
Wheeler, Lieutenant General Raymond Albert 201, 202, 205, 206, 290, 304
Wheeler, Padre 361
Wild, Colonel Cyril Hew Dalrymple 14, 93, 95, 96, 415–19, 446–8
Wildey, Brigadier A.W.G. 14, 44, 52–5, 93, 98
Wilkinson, Lieutenant Thomas VC 427–9
Williamson, Major Edward 384
Wilson, Rev. John L. 201, 202, 205, 206
Woods, Archdeacon 374–5
Wu Chye Sin (Goh Meng Chye/Ah Ng) 158–170, 306

XDO and Signals Room 35, 40–1, 46
XDO, OOW and Telephones Room 35, 40–1, 46

"Y" SIGINT Unit 70
Yamashita, Lieutenant General Tomoyuki 16, 40, 80–3, 88, 95, 96, 103, 384
Yangtse River 427
Yi Tian Song @ Tan Sek Fu/Tan Shi Fu/ Chan Siak Foo 160, 162, 167–71, 306
YMCA (Young Men's Christian Association) 103, 226
Yusof Ishak, President 261, 437–9

"Z" Special Unit 348, 412–14
Zhang, Ya Gong 390
ZIPPER, Operation 144–50, 177, 180, 183, 186, 209, 227, 229–37, 255, 281, 283, 291, 293, 294